WWII Diary of a German Soldier

by
Helga Herzog Godfrey

authorHOUSE™

1663 LIBERTY DRIVE, SUITE 200
BLOOMINGTON, INDIANA 47403
(800) 839-8640
WWW.AUTHORHOUSE.COM

First published by AuthorHouse 6/15/2006

ISBN: 1-4208-4963-8 (sc)
ISBN: 1-4208-9285-1 (dj)

Printed in the United States of America
Bloomington, Indiana

This book is printed on acid-free paper.

<u>Dedication</u>

As Eugen Herzog's daughter Helga, I am proud to present and dedicate this book to my beloved father and my mother, who translated these diaries from his shorthand.

In addition, I wish to express my gratitude and appreciation to my husband for the many hours of his assistance in publishing my father's war diary.

Table of Contents

Father near death. Miserable, insensitive pigheaded commanding officer denied furlough request. Frenzied construction of defensive emplacements.

Assassination attempted on Hitler. Oh, if only it had been successful! The beginning of the end – Retreat!

Orders of the "Führer", every German should die for his Fatherland! Captured by the Americans, underhandedly turned over to the French for slave labor.

Will this New Year bring my freedom from this suffering and malnutrition? I finally received my "R"! I want to be a human being again!

Daily struggle for food and normalcy of life. Brother Richard died as a Russian POW in Siberia.

Eugen J. Herzog

<u>Preface</u>

"I hope and wish, that I will be able to bring back home with me these diaries. I had always hoped, that my superiors and later on my captors would not find them and confiscate them."

"They should be for later on, a true and honest mirror image of my years, months, days and hours in this miserable war, my subsequent imprisonment and all its consequences. It should be a memory for me and in my old days, God willing, reflect the state of my mind, and for my children and grandchildren as well be a lasting legacy of a very sad time!"

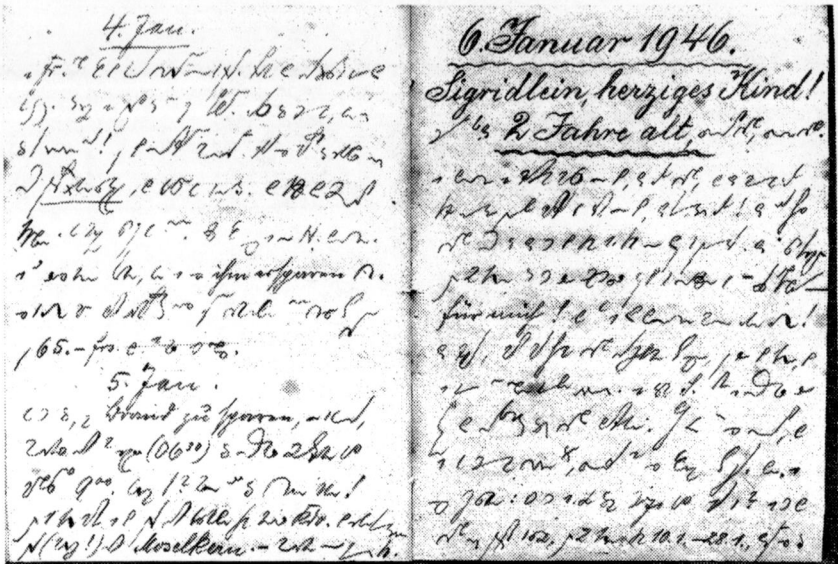

Two Pages of Papa's Diary using the Gabelsberger Shorthand

❧

No attempt has been made to create a story using his diary entries. This book reflects his innermost feelings, thoughts and experiences as he entered them into his diary starting when he was drafted, through the war years, and subsequently interned as a POW in a French labor camp. Followed by an epilog of his readjustment to being home again, with his family and resuming his love of teaching children.

It should be noted that his home was located in the then French Occupied Zone of Germany.

Introduction

His personal life

My father was born in 1903 in the small farming village of Sembach, Germany. He excelled in school and his teacher encouraged his parents to let him go to a university. He became a teacher and was assigned to the school in Hochstätten, where he subsequently met his future bride, my mother Therese (Rösel) Wagner. They later moved to his hometown of Sembach, where he would teach the upper grades, 5th through 8th, in a two room schoolhouse.

Prior to being drafted in 1939, an incident at the time of the Jewish persecution ("Kristallnacht") nearly caused him to be sent to a concentration camp. A well liked Jewish family was humiliated by an SS troop. Their possessions were destroyed, while the towns people stood by and watched horrified, too frightened to act. My father uttered overheard comments as to the "unworthiness of such behavior", which was promptly reported by someone standing next to him. He was summoned to a local Nazi Tribunal and labeled as "one against the regime". Only because of an old time teacher friend and classmate, who was influential and put in a good word for him, was my father spared severe punishment.

However, this incident was unknowingly recorded in his personal records and followed him throughout his military service, preventing him from becoming an officer, although he was never told the reason why.

He had three children, a son and two daughters, was a loving husband and father, taught school for 30 years in his hometown, was transferred shortly before his retirement as superintendent to a larger school and continued to direct choirs and play the church organ.

Celebration of their 50th Wedding Anniversary August 24, 1979

This diary is also a touching expression of love to his wife, who honored the memory of this man, to whom she looked up to for sixty years. His hope for her well being in his far away homeland gave him with his faith in God, the strength to survive.

Mama at the age of 87, with her perseverance of mind and self-discipline, which was so typical of her, realized, the importance of passing on his writings to future generations. It was a last service of love to him beyond his and her death. He lived through her strength and through a god given grace was able to end his life in her arms.

He contracted Parkinson's Disease and died in 1989 at the age of 86 with his wife of 60 years at his side.

Therese (Rösel) died at the age of 93 in 2002.

Papa's War Diary

1939

26, August 1939

I am using a short break, to write a few lines. There is no mobilization yet; at least we don't hear anything. We are housed in a large schoolhouse and daily new transports of men arrive. A tremendous number of reserves must have been called and all the trains are overcrowded. 400 additional men arrived today. They are mostly new faces, a few familiar ones. Rubel came around 11 o'clock. I was here at 9 o'clock and did not need to rush. We just hang around and have not even received our uniforms.

The mood is depressed. We stand for hours in the heat and are very, very tired. All school benches were taken to the yard and we sit or lay on them, until we have to line up again.

We slept on straw in the schoolrooms.

27, August 1939

"Kerwe Sonntag!" (Town Festival Day!)

While the people at home are enjoying the parade, we sit in the schoolyard on benches and write home. Some young boys pick up post cards or snacks for us from town.

Papa in center with hands behind his back

We finally get our uniforms including gas masks, etc., and are loaded onto trucks and taken to Wiesbaden.

I lead the troop transport and report to the lieutenant there. We are divided up and are to hike to Dietenmühle, ½ hour from here. We find accommodations in an old, roomy house and fall asleep dead tired on straw in several rooms. Tomorrow we will go by bus to the new post.

At home they will be at the dance, having fun and here we are hungry. We are still lacking provisions and supplies. The facial expressions are serious, but composed.

28, August 1939

A very boring day, nothing is going on. At night we listen to the radio and still hope for a peaceful solution.

29, August 1939

The accommodations and provisions are improved. I have been assigned to the active troops. Most of them are from Southern Germany. Breunling and I are sitting together, read newspapers and listen to the radio.

30, August 1939

Today was supposedly the last negotiation effort of Germany and England. Everywhere there is silence.

31, August 1939

Today there is an oppressive heat, both in the weather and in politics. Everyone feels something is about to happen. In the evening the German recommendations are publicized. Everyone is hopeful, because the demands are so moderate and to the point.

1, September 1939

WAR!

This morning at 04:45 the German attack started on all fronts. Now it has arrived, the dark hour, which we have feared. O God, what will be happening?

If only our families will be safe. I am calm and hopeful. At 10 o'clock there will be an assembly of the Reichstag's legislature and a speech by our leader. Hitler has put on his military uniform and has vowed not to take it off, until victory is ours. He has even designated successors in case of his death. In the meantime the fighting is beginning.

Papa in required off base uniform

As of today we are wearing our helmets and gas masks every time we leave the base. Food rationing has started. The people of Wiesbaden are calm. How many poor guys already have lost their lives today for this insanity?

Today I am thinking a lot of Norbert. He is supposed to go back to school after his summer vacation. I heard however, that schools are closing? The news from the front differs greatly, the Germans claim, they have destroyed all Polish airbases, the Poles say, they have shot down 7 German bombers.

2, September 1939

Today the shift changed. I will be working from 8 pm until 4 am for one week. The night is terribly long. We try to sleep on a table in the cellar. It is forbidden under severe punishment to listen to foreign broadcasts. The operations in Poland seem to move well. The success in the east is amazing and our troops advance with lightning speed. The corridor has been already secured.

6, September 1939

The reports from the front continue to be good. Krakow and Bromberg were taken. The Polish government has fled Warsaw. We are 60 km from Warsaw.

9, September 1939

Today I went to Dotzheim. My mail cannot be found. Some of my buddies have left and others have arrived. I am glad I am in Wiesbaden. At night I walked around a little. The city has a total blackout. There are no more flashlights available. The German troops are close to Warsaw, a glowing success. The Poles are retreating. But what is going on in the west? Saarbrücken and other towns in the west have been evacuated and the refugees are brought inland.

10, September 1939

This is another boring Sunday. I slept from 4 to 6 on the floor. I had a dream of Norbert, I hugged and kissed him and then woke up. If only this crazy war was over! This afternoon I want to visit my hometown friends from Sembach. They all have hard duty and are homesick. I don't want to complain. Now my shift is from 4 am until 12 noon.

14, September 1939

22 years ago today I went to the teachers college for my entrance exam and today I am a soldier.

Further successes in Poland are reported. Our troops are excelling including the Air Force, motorcycle units, and tanks. Tomorrow, Rösel is supposed to come. How I am looking forward to her visit.

16, September 1939

The birthday of my dear wife! Unfortunately, today is the day of the vaccination for typhus. That will mean a very sore chest. I am running a fever. Waited that afternoon at the railroad station from 3 to 6. She did not come. I am a little worried and go to Hauser's, but she is not there either. She had written, that Helga has a sore on her eye. I hope it is nothing serious. I try to place a call to Kron's, our neighbor, and wait from 7 to 9:30. Finally I receive the news that Rösel has already left with Norbert. I am so relieved and go right back to Hauser's, where I meet them. What a joyful, happy reunion. And Norbert, my big boy. What a wonderful birthday!

Mama (Rösel) and "Murschel" (Helga)
(Last summer of peace)

17, September 1939

In the morning we go downtown to a cafe. For Norbert, the trip is an experience. I take him to my quarters and show him my rifle. I am very tired, almost exhausted because of lack of sleep.

18, September 1939

Today they have to leave. It is now 14:00 hours and I am waiting for them. Norbert, he is so trusting and open-minded. He is asking a lot of questions, likes to stop in front of toy stores. This morning I had coffee at Hauser's and still some of the good birthday cake. In the afternoon it starts to rain. Then comes the good-bye. Norbert laughs and does not take it too hard. But I will be homesick.

20, September 1939

The days are dragging on. Yesterday, Hitler had a speech in Danzig, which was not very convincing! When is this war going to end? Hopefully soon!

21, September 1939

Again I have no mail from home! I am so homesick and I want to know how my sweet little daughter, "Murschel", is doing. Always the terrible fear that something has happened to them.

In addition to my bad mood, we were chased out of bed for the 2nd vaccination. The reaction is worse than from the first shot, pain, fever no appetite, tired and listless.

27, September 1939

Lt. Becke, what a creep! He is exercising and working us like dogs, worse than the worst of basic training! We are dead tired and I am sick of it.

I have a furlough coming up next week and I am looking forward so much. I had a letter from Rösel and drawings also from my sweet little "Murschel".

29, September 1939

The Day When Warsaw Fell!

I am so exhausted, because we have so little sleep. Not too much fighting going on in the west, but still there were great losses of life.

6, October 1939

Will I get my leave? I sure hope so. Maybe I can catch the 17:44 train. My baggage is heavy, the joy of the reunion with my loved ones even bigger. Got the train to Bad Muenster and from there, a ride and was home in 10 minutes.

The children are sound asleep. The in-laws almost did not recognize me as I stormed up the stairs. How peaceful they are both sleeping. Norbert so trusting and such a good kid, and little Helga, my sweet little "Murschel", with her bandage over her eye. I kiss her and whisper in her ear: "Sweetheart", "Kätzchen (Kitty)" "Hamuchen (little calf)". Then she blinks her eyes open, recognizes me, laughs, and happily wraps her little arms around my neck. Oh, what unspeakable happiness!

Norbert sleeps in the bathroom. We talk in the kitchen, eat something, and then go to bed. The next morning I take the 6 o'clock train to Neuhemsbach. I let the kids sleep.

Arriving in Neuhemsbach, I was able to get a ride with the milk truck. A lot of people recognized me and greeted me. What a happy reunion in Sembach with Rösel. She had a cold, poor thing. We quickly built a fire in the kitchen and she baked a cake.

Later, my good old father came walking up with his limp with my never tiring, wonderful, mother. Oh, dear God, keep these two wonderful parents safe for me for a long time.

The garden is a wilderness and no one cares, but I am so happy.

8, October 1939

Father is back again. He drinks coffee with us, talks about his military time, and is happy. I will never forget how he clumsily showed me the "presentation of arms".

The next day I have to say good-bye after going through all the mail. Father shakes my hand and says: "I hope I will see you again!" For a long time he stood there by the schoolhouse and watched me walk away. Mother already went ahead with Karl and the little wagon with my luggage. At the station she is trying to be brave and not cry. But the tears come and she quickly walks away, turns one more time, and calls: "Write to me, won't you?" I know she will cry all the way home.

We have a lot to carry, but soon are in Hochstätten. Helga is hiding behind the door trying to play "peek-a-boo". With great sadness I think of leaving tomorrow.

9, October 1939

How quickly the hours fly by. Rösel fixes all my favorite foods. We sit quietly together and talk like we used to when we were young and in love.

Papa in dress uniform with Mama and Helga

In the afternoon we go for a walk. Helga is holding my hand, and I ask her: "What does Papa call you?" She answers: "Hamuchen", "Vögelchen", "Murschel"(terms of endearment). The time to say good-bye comes closer and closer. One more kiss and an acquaintance from Pirmasens drove me to Bad Muenster in the pouring rain. Oh, what wonderful happy days these were.

10, October 1939

Rösel wrote to me, that Helga was asking the question: "Who is going to bomb our house? The French or the English?" Also that she cried desperately, when someone told her that her bed could catch on fire. Also when they talked about me, she said: "Maybe if we hide behind the door in the kitchen, turn the light off and are real quiet, then Papa will come back?" Poor little innocent child!

20, October 1939

I have not written for quite a few days. What is there to write? One day is like the other. Within me still are the memories of my beautiful furlough at home, worth more to me than this whole nonsense. Chamberlain has stubbornly refused any peace suggestions. What will happen now? I was right; this is going to be a bad turn of events.

21, October 1939

I have guard duty. I am sitting sleepily at the table and take care of the paperwork. It is pitch dark outside and pouring rain, as it has been for days now, very depressing.

Just got some hot coffee, terrible stuff, I eat the good cake from home and write a letter to my sweetheart.

28, October 1939

On Nov. 1st, I am supposed to get my NCO rank. I had some mail and read, that Helga has tonsillitis again. All of a sudden I got the idea to try for a furlough. Immediately went to Lt. Doll for permission. Finally I get the OK. At 16:00 hours, I am sitting in the train and arrive in Hochstätten at 20:00. The great joy in seeing them all.

My little sweet girl is already in her pajamas and hugs and kisses me. I am so glad, she is well again, no more fever, just a little coating on her tonsils. The next morning she wants to come to bed with us to smooch.

29, October 1939

A beautiful day! In the afternoon we go for a walk with the children. We later listen to the radio and are happy just to be together. Later before going to sleep, Helga says her little prayer "Müde bin ich geh zur Ruh" just perfectly. She speaks as well as a 5 year old. Then we turn off the light.

30, October 1939

I slept so very well and did not wake up until 8 o'clock. The little one wants to come to my bed and smooch again, but Mama says to her: "Let Papa sleep a little longer, he is very tired". She very quietly lies next to me and waits until I wake up. Then she continually gives me kisses and wants me to call her by the special nicknames I have for her: "Hamuchen", "Vögelchen", "Murschel", and now we have a new one, "Eichkätzchen" (little squirrel). I have to tell her, how the squirrel collects "Nuss Nuss" (nuts) for the winter and how it holds it in its little paws and eats it and she just laughs and laughs.

Later, I take the battery out of the car with Norbert and practice some math with him; he does quite well. He is interested in everything military. Then it is time to say good-bye again. The children go to the station with us. All afternoon the little one does not leave my side. Hangs onto the button on my coat and asks me to hold her hand. As I get on the train she laughs and waves and that is the "picture" I take with me, the three of them.

Helga (Murschel), Mama, and Norbert

4, November 1939

What a great big disappointment. I did not make NCO. Why? I do not know.

6, November 1939

Norbert's Birthday! All day long in my thoughts I am at home with my loved ones. In the morning it was foggy, but then turned into a beautiful sunny fall day. At 14:30 I am to report to the CO and maybe transferred to Dotzheim for a week. Maybe I will be qualified. I hope so. I had some disturbing news in the last letter. Oma is sick? I hope it is not anything serious! In my evening prayer I wish my loved ones the best.

8, November 1939

No mail again today. The Lt. called me up front and I had to do CQ. Had the troops step out and report; it went pretty well. Now I sit in my office and do the reports.

Tonight we listen to our leader's speech. Later on there was the terrible assassination attempt on the life of the Fuehrer. What a shame, this did not succeed. What is going to happen now? We heard all furloughs are discontinued. Everyone is disappointed.

15, November 1939

Still the days are beautiful with Rösel visiting me here in Wiesbaden. During the day I am the barracks administrator and at night we go downtown to do a little shopping, some gloves and a purse for Rösel. We have a little more money now, so I want to please my sweet, loving wife. We are making plans for Christmas and are thinking about what to give to the children. In the evening we plan see a movie or go to the theatre.

16, November 1939

Last night we saw the Operetta "Clivia". Not too good, but I got a chance to show Rösel the lovely theatre. Today we saw a beautiful film "The Trip to Tilsit".

17, November 1939

Today the Lt. came and brought me the furlough permission slip. We can leave immediately. 5 days! Wonderful! Stopped by Hauser's to thank them for their great hospitality. I am looking forward to the reunion with the children.

Helga talking to Papa

18, November 1939

We took the 12 o'clock train home. The children were waiting. Interestingly, Norbert rushed up to Mama and the little "Murschel" ran up to me with her embraces and kisses. At first she is always shy and does not say anything, then she will warm up and talk like a book. She looks so cute in her brown coat and little blue hat. I am so happy to be home again and that night we sleep well.

20, November 1939

With the 8:20 am train we go to Sembach. Only a few people see us in town. The schoolhouse is in bad shape. In both schoolrooms the furniture has been moved out, the shelves are sitting in the hallways. Bottles and glasses broken, the desks and chairs moved to the attic. My "show and tell" material disappeared. I am upset! What a good idea that I had moved the books of the library to the attic last summer. A carpenter had to build a wall in the middle of one of the schoolrooms, so that two corpsmen could live there. They leave the lights burning in the cellar during the day and act unworthy of German soldiers. What is going on with my school? The young people have gone to the dogs. I am not happy about that. I have a lot of work and just going through the mail is a chore.

Soon my parents come and they are so happy, to see me. Both of them have a habit not to show their joy openly. My mother is busy and wants to help everywhere. She has worked so hard in the garden and weeded the whole thing. I say hello to all the neighbors and enjoy the good bed.

23, November 1939

Today, the beautiful leave time is over. In the afternoon we go to Bad Kreuznach. We have an appointment for Helga at the pediatrician and she is well and healthy.

Then we do a little shopping and go to Café Lehmkühler. I had said good-bye to Norbert this morning already, because he had to go to school. He almost got a little teary eyed. My little "Mouse" is so sweet and at the railroad station she did not cry. I get on the train with them until it is supposed to leave. Rösel lifts the child up to the window and I squeeze her little hands. Then the train disappeared into the dark of the night and I am alone again. Oh, this miserable existence. When will this war come to an end? I take the 21:03 train, which was very crowded, to Wiesbaden.

Papa and Mama strolling with Helga

27, November 1939

Oh, how hard it is, to get up early in the morning, when it's still dark and do the exercising. I am thinking how long do I still have to do this?

30, November 1939

In the evening I hear the NCOs in the room next to me talk about who is going to be promoted. I hear my name mentioned and I am hopeful again.

1, December 1939

Unteroffizier! (NCO)

Today is supposed to be the big day. I am doing my duty in expectation that I will be informed of my promotion. The morning passes, Capt. Hornung comes, has a punishment read, but nothing about my promotion. A big disappointment! After lunch, I take Sergeant Schmitz aside and ask him if he knows anything. I hope I will hear something in the afternoon. During class around 3 pm the sergeant looks for me, shakes my hand and says: "Herzog, I congratulate you on becoming NCO!" There it was. The other NCOs and also my buddies, congratulate me. My joy was complete. I go to the quartermaster and get the "tinsel" for my uniform. I guess tonight, I have to get a case of beer for the NCOs and my buddies to celebrate.

3, December 1939

It is nice to be NCO. I slowly learn everything. This morning I had to give a talk on the political situation. I am always happy to receive mail from home. I get letters from the children in Hochstätten and at least 3 letters from mother in Sembach. The exercising is boring but still interesting, because I learn a lot.

6, December 1939

Wedding anniversary of my parents! At home there is "St. Nicholas Day". Unforgettable, how the two sweet children always sing the St.

Nicholas song with Rösel. Especially Norbert. We all hope, there will be some leave time for Christmas. This war is so boring. We expect there will be an offensive in spring.

10, December 1939

Two years ago today, good old "Uncle" Seebode died.

All details are again presented to me. In the afternoon I went with Aunt Gretchen to buy a piece of jewelry for Rösel. I hope she will like it. I would like to have a fountain pen. Will she give it to me for Christmas?

12, December 1939

I wrote a letter to Mrs. Seebode. From Jakob Herzog and Bolander I have no answer yet.

14, December 1939

Today is another anniversary; 15 years ago I arrived in Hochstätten for the first time. I praise this day and my fate, which let me find my happiness. I will write her a letter expressing my love.

With my comrades, I am highly regarded, since I present my lectures clearly and distinctly. Also, the other NCOs approve of me.

15, December 1939

I have not written in a few days. Today we did a very good open field exercise. We marched in light snow to Georgenbonn, where a machine gun nest was to be overtaken. I shoot along with everyone else and take over the machine gun from my opponent. Then I am in the defense position of our group. Lastly, I shoot according to the exercise, a magazine containing 25 blank cartridges in short succession. Now I know the lightweight type #13 machine gun. Then there is a quick march back. I have no problem with the saluting. We are very tired, no rest all day. Christmas is just around the corner.

17, December 1939

There is talk that leave time is beginning tomorrow. I went downtown one more time to do last minute shopping. The fragrance of the Advent Wreath fills our room.

18, December 1939

Hurrah! Furlough! What a mood. As always, things are hectic. My little Helga will love the decorations on my uniform. I put all the gifts in my suitcase and catch the late evening train. It is dark when I arrive. In the living room I hear the children's voices. In the kitchen I say hello to my sweetheart and the in-laws, then the children. They are all so happy. Norbert heard me and says to Helga: "St. Nick" is coming. That's why they were so quiet; but then, Papa came instead of St. Nick. The little one, now 4½ years old, asks: "Who gets to carry the child upstairs? Babba (Papa)?" She knows how to pray a lot of different little prayers, "Müde bin ich geh zur Ruh", which I also had prayed as a little boy. And even the Lord's Prayer, which she learned from Oma. Then they crawled under the covers and when I looked in on them ½ hour later they are fast asleep.

19, December 1939

What a wonderful feeling to sleep in a bed again as long as you want. In the afternoon I go with Opa in the vineyard to help him turn the frozen clumps of dirt away from the vines. It is strenuous work but healthy. The air is crisp and clear, the ground covered with light snow. Oh, beautiful homeland! In the evening, a quiet hour by the warm stove. I help Norbert with his homework. His script could be a little better.

20, December 1939

Today we go to Sembach. Norbert can come along. Up there, things are in a mess. The house is cold and unfriendly, the doorknobs and mailbox are rusted. Everything is covered with dust. There is still no school and no one seems to care. We build a fire and wait for hours until the kitchen warms up. Soon my father comes. When he sees me, a sunny smile lights up his wrinkled face and he says: "Alright!" Then he slowly walks up the stairs in back and stays for hours to visit. A little later mother comes and how happy the two of them are. They are poor but want to give the children a Christmas gift, even if it's only something small.

21, December1939

We are still in Sembach. I cannot enjoy my furlough here because I have so much writing to do. The minister visited me also. How glad I am that I had moved things out of my schoolroom! My zeppelin and the model airplanes, those "punks" had thrown out the window.

23, December 1939

Today the children are in great expectation of Christmas. They talk about "Christkind", but what a surprise, Norbert does not believe in it anymore. He confesses that he did not believe in it last year, but did not show it. When I asked him, where the zither came from, he said, you bought it in Kaiserslautern. Too bad! But he must not tell Helga. The sweet child is still so trusting and I want to preserve this faith of her beautiful young years as long as possible. Today the cakes are baked and a wonderful festive fragrance fills the whole house. We want to celebrate Holy Night tonight, one day early, so I can enjoy the excitement of the children an extra day.

"Christmas Eve"

At about 5 o'clock, Opa keeps the children busy in the kitchen, while Rösel and I decorate the Christmas tree. I brought some new colorful bobbles and red candles, in addition, some old decorations from Rösel's parents. The tree turns out real nice. Now we put the presents on the table, the candles are lit and "Christkind's" silver bell is rung. I go to the kitchen, pick up Helga and we all enter the beautiful, festive room.

Norbert is modest in his exuberance, but his eyes are shining. Helga's eyes are always an experience. The light of the candles is reflecting in her dark eyes. We sing, according to tradition, all the beautiful old Christmas songs, myself at the piano, Rösel with Helga on her lap and tears of joy in her eyes. Helga sings the loudest and the clearest and knows all the verses to all the songs. The presents were wonderful, for my sweet wife a purse, gloves and other small things. For Norbert an erector set by Märklin and a sweat suit, a book to read: "Heini, The Big City Boy". For Helga a teddy bear, the little "grocery store" with new additions, for myself a new fountain pen, which I really was hoping for. For father a box of cigars, for mother a bottle of "Enzian" liqueur. For the in-laws there are several small things for practical use.

We then eat "Christmas Eve Supper" and the children go to bed with happy dreams. The new teddy of course had to go to sleep with Helga. We sat up for a long time and I am thankful for all the joy in my life.

Snowy Christmas with Helga

22

24, December 1939

For us it is the first Christmas Day. We play with the children. Helga keeps putting her dolls into the doll carriage, covers them so they can sleep, takes her new teddy for a walk, and sings all day long. Norbert starts building with his erector set and I help him with it. We spend a beautiful day and enjoy a quiet hour at night by the warm stove. Then we go to sleep. That night I got sick. It started with a sore throat. During the night I woke up with fever. The next morning I could not get up.

25, December 1939

Christmas in bed! In the afternoon my mother comes, she wanted to see the children. She is shocked to find me sick in bed. Rösel makes cold compresses to get the fever down. Tomorrow we want to call the doctor. I am certainly getting the best of care here with my loving family.

30, December 1939

The children look in on me. The sore throat and the pain in my back continues. But I think I am slowly improving.

31, December 1939

The last day of this fateful year of 1939. I try to get up, I am terribly weak and dizzy, but happy to be able to sit by the warm stove. My fever is gone, the children are in bed, Rösel makes glühwein (hot wine), and we listen to the radio, eat cookies, and sit happily and quietly together.

1940

<u>Midnight of 1940</u>

The bells start to ring at midnight according to tradition, but no fireworks. We wish each other a "Happy New Year" and go up to the children. Helga is sleeping so sweetly, what all do I wish for this precious child? Norbert was allowed to stay up for the first time.

My fervent wishes rise to Heaven for my loved one's health and most of all peace, which we hope the New Year will bring.

<u>1, January 1940</u>

A crystal clear cold New Years Day. I get up a little in the afternoon. The doctor says I am improving but cannot get back to my military duty yet.

<u>3, January 1940</u>

Everyday I feel a little better. I am not in a big hurry to get back to Wiesbaden. Lt. Doll advised me to report to sickbay when I get back.

<u>8, January 1940</u>

It is time to say good-bye again. I pack my bags and enjoy every minute with them. Unforgettable for me, how Norbert stands there when I embrace him, kiss him on his forehead and tell him: "Be well, my dear boy!" and he suddenly starts crying with his head down wiping his eyes.

We then go to the railroad station and I kiss them good-bye. Helga says: "One more kiss, Papa!" but she does not cry. Then the two of them run along side of the train, holding hands and wave until the train turns the curve, then they are gone! Oh, home, sweet home!

<u>9, January 1940</u>

Nothing of importance has occurred. I am happy that I could be home with my loved ones. I check in with sickbay and my urinalysis showed nothing suspicious. The pain in my back is getting better and I can report for duty again.

10, January 1940

We move back into the museum. Everything is better there, 2 men to a room, mine has the cold tiles, but I do have a closet.

Duty has started again. It is awful to have to get up at 2 am and then sit in the cold damp cellar for 6 hours. It is worse when you try to sleep and can't because it is too noisy. You toss and turn and can't relax because someone is constantly coming or going.

16, January 1940

We have freezing cold weather and temperatures of –27 C degrees. I hope I won't catch a cold! We all moved again and I was lucky and got the nicest room with a stove.

23, January 1940

Rösel writes that they could not come because of the terrible cold and she was right. I am surprised and happy, that the children are well. Norbert is a strong boy and goes ice skating every day. Helga walks with Opa also daily.

29, January 1940

The terrible cold weather has not let up yet. No one can remember such a bitter winter, worse are the icy streets. Snowplows are on all the Wiesbaden roads and snow is piled up several meters high. Walking is treacherous. Today I am sending 50 cigars to my father for his birthday.

31, January 1940

Today my father is 63 years old! I wish him well!

1, February 1940

Today at 10 o'clock Rösel arrives. I found a room for her in the "Hotel Margarete". The food is good and she has a nice room. They give me a couple of days off to stay with her. At night we go to the theatre and the next day I buy her the ring with the beautiful aquamarine stone. Later on we see the movie "Opernball". Everything in Wiesbaden is expensive!

<u>7, February 1940</u>

I have leave time from 7-12 Feb. and we go home together. Rösel went into the house first by herself. The children did not know I was coming.

Rösel said to Helga: "Go outside, I have brought you a big life doll!" She went to the front door and did not see me behind the door. I called to her softly, she turned around and without hurrying walked up to me, put her little thin arms around my neck and kept on kissing me. What a wonderful feeling, to have my good bed again!

<u>9, February 1940</u>

With the 8:50 train we go to Sembach. It is good to walk through the clear fresh winter air from the station. In town I go to say "hi" to my school kids. They are in Zapp's and wait for me. Was there just a little bit of vanity involved? I salute and they all are amazed to see me in uniform. Am I still their teacher? How strange has everything become! Still I am grateful to my parents, who let me become a teacher, this profession I have come to love.

Then mother arrives first. She is always happily excited, when she sees me. She has given birth to us in great pain, but she loves us as well as the grandchildren with an everlasting love. Later father comes too. As always he opens the door hesitantly, then he greets us quietly, but with an inner joy. Then I get to work.

<u>12, February 1940</u>

We return today with the suitcase heavy with apples.

<u>13, February 1940</u>

Today I have to leave. This morning my "Murschel" came to bed with me to smooch. She told me the fairytale of the "Bremer Stadtmusikanten (The Bremen City Musicians)" freely and perfectly, better than a 2nd grader. Afterwards I had to tell her the tale of "Frau Holle" and she listens attentively. In the evening I take the 7:35 train to Wiesbaden. The child gives me many kisses and Rösel carries her to the door, from where she waves as long as she can see me. Norbert goes to the station with me but he is too big now to cry.

As soon as I get there I receive the news that I'm transferred to Gensingen. First I have mixed feelings. The next morning there are a lot of things to take care of. Formalities such as to notify all departments, take the suitcase to Hauser's, pick up my transfer papers, pack, etc. My cooking utensils have disappeared, I wonder who is the thief. The train is 1 hour late. I arrive in Gensingen in the dark with my heavy bags. I start on my way and I think of the infantry who has to march with heavy bags all the time. It takes me ½ hour to the village. I ask where the camp is. It is cold and clear with a starry sky. By the bridge I slide down the icy dam. Finally I see the lights of the camp and report to the guard.

Oh, what a first sad impression! I am wringing wet from sweating! I get my bed sheets, my cup, plate, silverware, etc. and after reporting to Captain Dr. Scheuerpflug, I look for my room. There are 5 other men in my room.

14, February 1940

Everything is very primitive. It's a former work camp, the duty is pleasant, there are a lot of familiar faces, the food is not bad, the boss OK. No room to exercise, because the field is all iced up.

Papa at the Gensingen barracks

16, February 1940

I am assigned to the 11th Corporal Unit and they are all young people. It is terribly cold; especially our ears suffer from the bitter cold. We fire up the stoves in our room but at night we still are cold. We share breakfast with the officers.

17, February 1940

I take a Sunday furlough. On the trip I have a sudden worry or feeling, that something is wrong at home. Indeed, something was wrong. Rösel had a very bad sore on her arm. Hopefully not blood poisoning! I am very disturbed; on top of this a soldier is quartered in our Hochstätten house, which bothers me just by his presence. I will call the doctor this evening. With the fever, she has to be in bed. It seems to be some kind of a boil that may have to get lanced. We changed the dressing during the night.

18, February 1940

Went by train to the drugstore in Alsenz to buy gauze and salve. Walked back home in a wonderful frosty clear winter day. The sun was glittering in the snow and the whole world was a blinding white. On the way home my only prayer was for my loved one's well being with great faith in my God. She is in good spirits and hopefully the infection will subside. In the evening I have to leave again. For you, my sweet lovely wife I would walk to the end of the earth. I put both children to bed then I have to say my good-byes again in hopes that the next few days will bring her improvement.

19, February 1940

Called home that evening. My thoughts all day were with her. She has to stay in bed a few more days and the doctor gives me the assurance, that there is no blood poisoning.

21, February 1940

I have a new job. "Unit Leader" of the 9th Company. All untrained people, but they are nice and I get along well with them.

22, February 1940

I have news from home. Norbert wrote a long letter to me. I have not yet visited our relatives in Gensingen.

One just doesn't get out of this camp. I am very tired.

23, February 1940

News from home again, tomorrow she can get up.

No one knows, when we can get out of here.

24-25, February 1940

Another Sunday furlough in Hochstätten. Rösel is well again, but her arm still looks bad. A large wound with lots of puss. Thank God, it is better. Norbert picked me up at the train station.

In the afternoon he plays with his erector set. He is technically very talented. Helga plays with a race car, rather than her dolls. Is there race car blood in her veins? The in-laws have soldiers quartered in their house again.

We had two beautiful days. In the afternoon we go for a walk and there are finally some signs of spring. There is sunshine covering the countryside, but snow is still on the ground. In the afternoon we sit comfortably together and I am always spoiled with food and drink.

At 10 pm, I leave again for Langenlonsheim, which is across the river from Gensingen. It's just hard to sleep, because it's too hot in the room since the stove has been fired too high.

26, February 1940

We still do not know if we are going to leave.

28, February 1940

The captain likes me. I moved in with NCO Bergmann.

29, February 1940

The last day in February! Tomorrow the captain is supposed to leave. I have now gotten so used to the place that I really do not want to leave.

1, March 1940

Capt. Scheuerpflug is saying good-bye. Smiling as always, he steps in front of the company. I know his heart is sad, but he does not show it. A fine and decent human being. He will go to Dotzheim. Two NCOs are already gone. I don't really want to go to Dotzheim.

2, March 1940

The new ones arrive, among them is Adolf Zapp. He has a helpless expression on his face.

The new captain drinks 12 glasses of beer every night. We have to walk 16 km for sharp shooting practice today. I enjoyed it very much.

Afterwards, I go to Hochstätten. My family is happy even for the few short hours we are together. I leave at 10 pm for Langenlonsheim and walk across the bridge to Gensingen.

At the sight of the starry sky, I think I will die being homesick.

3, March 1940

A beautiful spring Sunday! In the afternoon I go for a walk on Binger Strasse, I then get the idea of calling home. From a private home I talk to my sweetheart. I ask her to come and see me the next morning with the children. I will be waiting for them in the small cafe in town.

4, March 1940

My loved ones are here! In the morning at 10:30 I see them standing on the bridge, Rösel, Norbert, Helga and Oma. What a Joy!

We march singing into town, with the dog "Michel" in front. When we return, little Helga and Oma are standing on the bridge and wave at me smiling. My little sweetheart! I rush back to them and we greet each other and enjoy the dog "Michel". He can shake his paw and sits up "pretty" and then I can take my family to my quarters and introduce them to my buddies.

Suddenly we get orders to leave for Dotzheim. We have to rush and pack very quickly and Rösel helps me. In the meantime Helga got very tired also the room is overheated. We take her coat off and put her on my stripped bed. Then the orders come to leave. Outside the others are ready in full gear. A quick good-bye with the children who are standing by the window, then we cross over the bridge. For a long time I wave to them with my handkerchief until I can see them no more. After arriving in Dotzheim, we greet Capt. Dr. Scheuerpflug and are divided into separate rooms. A dreary first impression!

5, March 1940

Today the recruits are coming, more than 200 men. They are all people about my age. They will not be too happy, that there will be 12 men to one room. I am in charge of the 1st Platoon of the 2nd Corps. Getting uniforms, medical exams, etc.

6, March 1940

Today the new recruits were issued their uniforms and have the usual medical exams.

7, March 1940

Slowly the training is beginning. How clumsy some people are. Once again in Gensingen, I am homesick.

10, March 1940

Memorial Day! There is a big celebration on the large exercise grounds. It is cloudy and cold. When will it be spring?

Today is my brother Richard's birthday.

11, March 1940

Last night we had frost and everything is white. Yesterday and today I have "Officer of the Day" duty. In addition, I have "barracks duty" all this week. I have to scream so much that my throat has become sore. That is the last thing I need!

My sweetheart sent goodies to me by mail, because the food here is so bad. There are to be no approvals for Easter furloughs.

17, March 1940

Palm Sunday

I wish I could be home! I congratulated the future confirmation class by phone via Mr. Metz. It has been raining all day!

Here I am sitting in the Café Gude. Later I will go to the army base in Frauenstein. At 2 o'clock I go to Freudenberg, to tour the Armed Forces News Center and then leisurely walk to Schierstein. It is drizzling. From there I took a bus to Wiesbaden to see the movie "Fürst Woronzeff".

18, March 1940

Now Palm Sunday is over. I wonder how the children were doing yesterday? Have they been thinking of me? I am certain of that. A dreary steady rain is falling. Through the night it poured.

19, March 1940

Today I have presented another request to Capt. Scheuerpflug, pertaining to my promotion. If it does not work out this time, I will not pursue it any further at this time. I wonder if there will be furloughs?

20, March 1940

Easter Furlough

Oh, the joy, when the Sgt. ordered me to his office! It all went very quickly, my train left at 11:50 and I have 6 days with my family.

I had an unfortunate confrontation with a physician, Dr. Baron, because of my photographing the Rhine Bridge, which almost had unfortunate consequences because of this fool. I was angry and afraid to be arrested, but after hours of delay I only had to turn over my film, the camera I could keep. I tried to hitchhike and still made it home at 7 pm.

In Bad Kreuznach, I meet Rösel, who coincidentally was visiting the Hembds. How happy she was! When we arrived at home, Helga was sent to open the door where I was hiding. They told her to go and see what kind of package Mama brought. They are all surprised and the children greet me with great joy, especially Helga who silently hugged and kissed me several times.

My family is my whole life! These are beautiful days, which I look forward to so much. I do not want to think of farewell. Tomorrow morning we want to go to Sembach.

21, March 1940

Maundy Thursday

We take the 8 o'clock train to Sembach. Norbert comes, too. My parents were happy to see me and father was standing in the street waiting for me. In the schoolhouse soldiers are again being quartered. This time I do not want to write very much.

We send Norbert on an errand to the Stang's in Rohrbach with his bike. He rides it quite well, and with care on the wet street. A half hour later he happily returns and has successfully accomplished his task.

22, March 1940

Good Friday

I go to the church service with Rösel and Norbert. My former students, who are to be confirmed, look at me curiously. Taubenreuther, a classmate from the "Fichtelgebirge", plays the organ.

In the afternoon we go for a walk in beautiful weather on the Kaiserstrasse and afterwards visit Alice.

23, March 1940

We filled two sacks with apples and one with potatoes. We were able with the help of a farmer, and his cow drawn wagon took the sacks to the train station. The children love to eat apples so much. We stop in to see Alexander's in Alsenz on the way home. In the evening we color eggs.

24, March 1940

Easter

It will be a beautiful day! Early in the morning we get up. Yesterday, down in the little garden we had placed the nests. Norbert and I, without Helga knowing, quickly hide the eggs. Then we go back with her, to search for the eggs. The joy is not so overwhelming anymore, as the child is much too mature to believe in the "Easter Bunny". Then we go to the cobbler May, to pick up my resoled boots.

In the afternoon the weather is beautiful and we walk up to the Altenbaumburg Castle. The child playfully walks along. In the morning Norbert finally gets to ride his new bike for the first time. Rösel's parents did not come up to the castle with us, but waited for us in a garden café in town. On the way up we often stopped and rested. Up there, it is nice and warm and very crowded with soldiers. Among them are a couple of guys from my earlier company assignments in Muenster, Westphalia.

Papa takes Helga and Norbert on their Easter walk

As always the lilac trees are in full bloom and their fragrance is intoxicating. We wander around and take beautiful pictures, and then walk back to town and meet the grandparents. We had a beer, then went to the station and caught the train home. Along the way we meet Keiper from Obermoschel, from whom I bought my car 10 years ago.

How beautiful are these evenings, when the children are asleep. Norbert is so uninhibited when he says good night to me. Thank goodness he is not shy, wraps his arms around my neck and kisses me. Then he cuddles under the blanket.

Helga can give such sweet little smacks, while saying repeatedly, and also to Mama, I love you so much! Then we turn out the light and a short while later they are sound asleep.

25, March 1940

2nd Easter Day

Today the weather is not so nice. In the morning the kids come to our bed to cuddle and play. In the afternoon we drive to Bad Kreuznach to see a movie, which unfortunately was sold out. Instead we go to the café, to have coffee and cake, plus hot chocolate for the kids. Tomorrow I have to leave again!

26, March 1940

It is the Tuesday after Easter. One more time the children come in the morning to bed to cuddle. These are such happy hours. One is to my right, one to my left. We kiss one another and they talk up a storm. Helga is then asking: Tell me about "Michel" the doggie, the tale of "Hänsel and Gretel", "Frau Holle" and the "Bremer Stadtmusikanten!"

In the evening I have to leave again and there is always the farewell pain. Rösel and the children go to the station with me. Norbert is being brave and he says: "Come again soon!" Helga sits on the railing and wants me to kiss her again, she says and again. Then they run along the train and wave as long as they can see me. I sit down by the window and my thoughts take over.

27, March 1940

On the first day back I am "Officer of the Day", that's a pretty nice position and one forgets being homesick. On Mondays we get to see a movie.

2, April 1940

I want to create a choir for the "Mountain Festival". The captain gives me leave time to pick up some sheet music. He generously lets me leave Friday. How happy they will be!

Furlough! How surprised are they, when I walk in the door. Norbert caught up with me on the way. By the door I wait and he says to Mama: "There is a strange man at the door!" When she sees me she flies into my arms.

7, April 1940

This morning I go to Mr. May to pick up the sheet music. Helga comes with me holding my hand. In the afternoon, after a nice walk, we drink the last of the real bean coffee, what a treat!

On the train I meet Elsbeth Hauser, she is very nice and insists, that Rösel come soon with the children.

8, April 1940

It is Monday again and I begin the day with the choir rehearsal.

9, April 1940

The weather is horrible and spring does not seem to come. My mother has sent another package with butter and eggs to me. The food here is lousy, so I really appreciate these special gifts. She writes: "that it makes her so happy if she can do something good for me". I know her heart is bleeding. May you spend many years in good health and enjoy your children and grandchildren!

The food is still bad and that is why I certainly can use these gifts of love.

We Have Invaded Norway

14, April 1940

I go to the movies again, what else is there to do? During the morning, I had the choir practice and they did very well.

15, April 1940

Mountain Festival

The evening is a full success for me. The 3 choir selections we performed resulted in standing ovations. The captain and the other officers were pleased. What good does that do for me? Where is the ROA?

18-19, April 1940

This was my first guard duty. Everything went well, but I am very tired the next morning with no sleep. There is shooting practice in the afternoon and I take my unit to the area.

20, April 1940

Yesterday I receive the news that Helga is sick. She is coughing and has a fever. I am concerned. Rösel puts cold compresses on her at night and in the morning she feels better. I am a little worried and ask for a furlough under the pretense to take back the sheet music.

When I arrive at 4 pm, I see Norbert standing by the bridge. He blushes, acts embarrassed, and seems somewhat nervous. He slowly walks up to me, shakes my hand, and greets me in a touching manner. I ask him how Helga is doing and everything is OK, which makes me happy.

Helga greets me by the front door affectionately and loving as always. They are getting a bath and we stay up for a little while. She always wants to come in our bed, and then she is so tired, that she falls asleep very quickly.

21, April 1940

Sunday Furlough In Hochstätten

Norbert and I go to the shoemaker with my boots. Helga plays with her ball. In the afternoon we go for a walk.

At 7:30 pm I have to leave. As always, Rösel and the children go to the train station with me. They run alongside the train and wave, until I can't see them anymore. Oh, precious home.

22, April 1940

The days are all the same. The work is OK, but my ROA is just not happening.

28, April 1940

I am planning to have Rösel come to Rüdesheim on May 1st and 2nd. I go by train for 1.30 Marks and then look for a room. I find one in the Café Reichsadler. At night I go back by steamship with a group of other soldiers. They end up in a party mood in the genuine fun and happy ambiance that is typical for this region of the Rhine.

1, May 1940

No May Day celebration.

I take the train to Rüdesheim and there indeed, my sweetheart is sitting in the Café Reichsadler. We stay a while, decide that we want to spend the 2 days together, and order dinner. This is difficult even though we have ration coupons.

In the afternoon we climb up to the Niederwald Denkmal (Memorial). It's a beautiful sunny day, almost like summer. We exchange old memories and drink a good Rhine wine.

Then we slowly walk back through the vineyards. But the night belongs to us!

2, May 1940

Christi Himmelfahrt (Christ's Ascension Day)

A holiday today.

We get up early and plan a Rhine River Cruise to Bacharach. We are not able to get any lunch but that's OK. We leave at 12:48 pm, find a nice seat, and get to Bacharach at 2:30 pm. We walk through the town past St. Werner's Chapel to the Stahleck Castle. The view from there was magnificent. We remember the beautiful "Pfingst Ausflug (Whitsuntide/Pentecost outing)" years back, when Norbert, just a toddler, took his afternoon nap in the woods near Bacharach.

We then walk back down to the Rhine River, but the boat is late. The weather is absolutely gorgeous and we sit in the stern of the ship and roast in the late afternoon sun.

We get a little impatient, because the ship will arrive back much too late. Finally at 7 pm we arrive, and Rösel's train is supposed to leave at 7:10 pm. I see how she is running; poor thing, and I hope she will not stress her heart. I'll worry until I get the next letter from her. I have to hurry, to catch my train.

These were two wonderful days!

3, May 1940

The work continues as always. We follow the news reports of our troops in Norway and wish; we could have been part of this operation.

5, May 1940

Another Sunday. It is cold and pouring rain. I am bored and don't know what to do with myself. I decide to go to Rüdesheim and catch a steamship in Biebrich, on which I am the only passenger. It is too cold and windy to be up on deck, so I sit indoors by the fire to get warm. In Rüdesheim I get off, go to Café Reichsadler, have a bad cup of coffee and write a birthday letter to my mother. Later I take the steamship back.

8, May 1940

Mother's Birthday! In my thoughts and mind I wish her the very best, most of all good health. May be there is a happier life ahead for her, as she has had so far.

Today a notice was posted, that a troop attachment was being formed. Everyone is in joyous expectation to get away from here and there is talk about Norway. I would not mind it.

10, May 1940

German troops marched into Holland, Belgium, and Luxembourg. This war is full of surprises! Even though there were rumors it still came unexpected. Our armed forces are incomparable! The newspapers, both foreign and domestic, are full of praise and surprise. We are all upset, that we are not part of it, but can't seem to get away from this replacement troop.

11, May 1940

All furloughs are discontinued. Also visits from families. I telephone Rösel and find out, that Helga still is not well. What is wrong with the child? She runs a fever almost every night. In the daytime she seems fine. This is very strange. Now they will not be able to come and see me over "Pfingsten" (Whitsuntide/Pentecost).

13, May 1940

I was just going to lunch when the guard told me that a man and a young boy are looking for me. Joyful expectation! Could it be Christian and Norbert? I go back and indeed, there comes my dear big boy his eyes searching for me. We greet one another enthusiastically. They all came. Christian and Norbert are going back to Hauser's and I follow after lunch. There is my sweet little "Murschel" in her pink wool dress and I can see right away, that she is feeling better. Rösel, my sweetheart! After coffee in the afternoon we take a walk to the Chausseehaus, have a glass of wine and apple juice. "Murschel" walked along bravely, for a little while I carry her, because she got tired. In the evening we go back on a crowded train. Norbert says he feels chilly and looks very pale. I hope he won't get sick. He sleeps on the sofa and Rösel, Elsbeth, and I go to a movie, but I feel restless and worried. We come back at 11 pm and find Norbert with a high fever. What is wrong with him? What bad luck! One cannot enjoy anything! I leave with great worries and cannot wait until morning.

14, May 1940

Today it's back to work, but I feel very uneasy. By coincidence I am off for 2 hours in the morning. I go downtown and can hardly open the door with the tension in me. Norbert is still in bed and still has a fever, but seems cheerful. They have moved him from the sofa to a bed. He is asking for something to read. Uncle Christian gives him "Robinson" and he reads moving his lips (just like Opa). I am asking for the afternoon off and stay with my loved ones all afternoon.

15, May 1940

When I see them at noon, Norbert is up, looks a little pale, but otherwise seems to feel OK. We all go downtown and he insists on coming along. I wanted to show him different things. We go into some stores together and he is so sensible and interested in everything. Then we go up on top of the Neroberg with the cogwheel train. There is a lot to see. He is very interested in the cogwheel train. We look at the war memorial, look at the city through binoculars, go to the look out point, the souvenir stand, take pictures and have a glass of lemonade. In the city we buy a hat for Mama and a couple other things, go to a café and have ice cream, coffee and cake. "Murschel" is so full of enthusiasm that she runs everywhere and falls down a couple of times, but does not cry, but laughs. When she gets tired I have to pick her up and carry her. She wraps her little arm around me and strokes my face. How happy I am within the circle of my family. It gets late when we come home. Helga gets to sleep on the sofa, which she really enjoys. Tomorrow they want to go back.

18, May 1940

Yesterday I was still "Officer of the Day", but today we have to go to Halle. Now we pack in a hurry and are taken by truck to the station. We go to Frankfurt by public train. Here we find out that all public trains are off limits for military. We have to wait until evening. The buddies go to the zoo and I look around town. At 18:50 we leave from Frankfurt East and can even sleep a little. When I wake up we arrive in Merseburg. In the dawn I can see the giant chimneys of the Leuna Factory. Now we are almost there. We are well taken care of by the Red Cross with coffee and hot soup. We go to the tram and take it out to the school, a long ways out of town. Through the gate and many buildings we finally find the "Officer of the Day" and barracks No 3. I am amazed about the beautiful buildings and the huge complex. This must have cost a pretty penny!

23, May 1940

The food is horrible and I have no mail from home yet, even though I have given Rösel my new address, but I am not worried. It is hot and we are tired. I am assigned to teach and grade some tests.

30, May 1940

Tomorrow we are supposed to have an exam. Finally I received some mail from home. Later I will remember maybe, what terrible days I lived through, waiting for mail.

1, June 1940

Today is our travel day, the exam in the morning. Present were Lt. Deunling, Major Ewald and others. I was requested to give a summarization. Then the mad rush until our leaving. With our marching orders we quickly say our good-byes and hurry to the station. We are sick and tired of this place. In Frankfurt we have an hour layover. We eat something and then continue through the "Goldene Aue", a rich beautiful land!

The last light of the evening sun reaches into the Lahn Valley and soon it will be dark. We arrive around midnight in Wiesbaden and stay overnight in the museum.

2, June 1940

We hear that the recruits we had trained are still here. Maybe I can request a transfer with them.

3, June 1940

This morning the captain returns from his furlough. I report back to him. He is in a good mood. I immediately put in my request, but encounter his worst kind of resistance. He screams at me and threatens to put me in prison if I ask for one more transfer. I am very depressed. In my anger I put in for 6 to 7 days leave time. Of course he allows me only 2 in the mood he is in. Well, OK. I leave immediately and at home they are all happy to see me.

4, June 1940

Furlough

We go to Sembach, as I have several things to do there. There are soldiers in the schoolhouse again. Everything is so beautiful at home! How sweetly my love takes care of me! Here I want to forget, and if it is only for a few hours, the sad military life. Tomorrow we will go to Hochstätten and I am looking forward to a few hours with my children.

5, June 1940

Helga does not eat well and is very skinny. Norbert is a strong boy and rides his bike everywhere. With the 7:30 pm train I have to leave again and all three of them see me off. They wave until they cannot see me anymore; the sadness and homesick feelings take over again.

6, June 1940

The new recruits still are not here. What will I do? I am so angry, that I cannot even look at the captain. In his class I sit there bored staring straight ahead and the exercise class I do with disgust.

7, June 1940

I am to report to the captain. What is going on? He might feel like making up for something, because he offered that I accompany Private Kniest to Charleville. I am elated! Quickly we do our preparations and load up the equipment from the museum in the afternoon. Of course we go over Hochstätten. They all come running out of the house in amazemenlt, that I am here again. We are treated royally and stay overnight.

Helga does not seem to feel well. She is sweet and plays but there is something in her eyes I do not like. Rösel wakes Kniest and I in the middle of the night from a deep sleep. It is 2 am and we have to get ready. Oma says Helga slept restless and seems to have a fever. I go into the room and her forehead feels hot. How often have we gone through this! She awakes; wraps her little arms around my neck and won't let me go. Starts crying and says: "Stay here, stay here"! I feel as if my heart is going to break. I ask if something is hurting but she shakes her head. I have to tear myself away saying, I will bring something nice for you the next time I see you.

We then get in the truck accompanied with all the good wishes and drive into the night over the new highway. How great is this trip in the cool morning breeze. The following experiences will be very extensive.

8, June 1940

Our Mercedes diesel truck runs like a charm. We drive through the charming countryside of the Hunsrück and arrive in Trier at 7 am. Here we pick up equipment, which was ordered ahead of time by telegram. Everything was very well organized. We then have breakfast and look at the Porta Nigra, the ancient gate from the Roman times. Trier is still a picture of peace. We continue on over the Luxembourg border and enjoy the beautiful hilly country. Around noon we are in Luxembourg.

The people are cool but not unfriendly. In a pub we get some cheap beer for 15 Pfennigs, and they accept German money. What a dirty place with men hanging around drinking beer and talking loudly. We eat a bratwurst, I take a few pictures, and we continue on.

We have good roads over Mersch to the picturesque Schönfels, where we unload some of the equipment. We cross into Belgium by

Arlon. Here we see the first signs of war. Bombed out houses, a lot of military. The stores to which the civilians have returned are busy though. I write a few postcards home and we get back on the road again. We are beginning to see destroyed towns, the roads are in terrible condition and every few hundred yards there are holes made by dive bombers. A few graves along the roadside, dead horses, abandoned cows, cats, and dogs. For hours we see destroyed towns, a tremendous amount of soldiers, convoys of thousands of trucks. From where does Germany take all these men and equipment?

The further we drive the worse it gets. We do not see the enemy though but we are constantly detoured. We cross the river Maas and see a lot of detonated bridges rebuilt by our engineers. Way below in the valley, Chassepierre has been destroyed. The leaves on the trees are thickly covered with dust and the roads are in terrible condition. It is becoming a strenuous trip. Towards evening we come to the valley of the Maas, to the left, the city of Sedan. French artillery is shooting across the valley. The streets are a complete crater field and driving is becoming a challenge. We arrive at 8 pm in Messieres, which was badly destroyed, mostly the bridges.

We try to find our unit headquarters and it takes us almost 2 hours to find it. Finally through the directions of a helpful Lt., we find the Rue de la Perpinon and report to the respective office. The major is arrogant, but 1st Lt. Ott friendly. We take care of our orders and then relax on the grass. Inside the house there is senseless destruction. We are dead tired, but cannot go to sleep yet, because the material we have loaded is supposed to get picked up in the night. Indeed at 11 pm an NCO from the German artillery unit shows up and in the light of a flashlight we throw the equipment into his truck without checking it. Then he drives off into the dark night.

We ask if the planes come at night and get the answer: Yes, they come every night. We look for a bed in the house, find mattresses and blankets and I fall asleep immediately. A half-hour later we are awakened by artillery fire, we drowsily get up and look out the window. There are flares everywhere and we hear the droning of the French planes. Strangely I am not afraid, even though for the first time I am in real danger of my life. It was a titillating feeling not without a thrill.

9, June 1940

It is Sunday. Oh, if I had only known, that at this precise hour, at 7 am, not even 50 km from here in the forest of Sommeauthe, my poor cousin Friedrich was killed in action.

We get some coffee and receive our orders for the return trip. We first walk through town and are abhorred to see the destruction and evidence of looting. There is hardly anything left. Who has done this? In spite of the signs everywhere "Looters will be shot on sight" people just don't care. I meet an older lady with her prayer book, obviously wanting to go to church. I try talking her out of it.

By noon we reach Sedan. Not much is left of this beautiful town. We find a cat with newborn kittens in a closet, no sign of people. Where are all the civilians? We continue on to Douchery, where Napoleon handed over his sword to Bismarck in 1870. We pass a bunker and a little further, storage of captured equipment, a yard full of cannons and a barn full of uniforms and steel helmets.

By late afternoon we come to a severely shot up village, where we finally find a field kitchen. Our infantry comrades shared everything they had with us, cold potatoes, a large piece of roasted meat with sauce and French white bread. We ate until we were full and drank milk with it. They milk the cows, which walk around abandoned, mooing because of thirst and the heat. I ask if I could have one of the kittens and an infantry buddy from Hanover went to the stable and found a cute one, with gray and white markings. Quickly we find a small basket, padded it with hay, and tied the lid. I take a plate and a beer bottle filled with milk. As a sign of our gratitude we take a package for one of the guys to mail. Our drive continues through dusty woods and over horrible roads. Sometimes I bounced so hard that I hit the ceiling of the truck with my head. It's a miracle this vehicle does not fall apart.

The kitten cries miserably and tries to get out of its prison. An hour later it gives up the fight and exhaustedly falls asleep. But as soon as the truck stops, or the motor starts up, it is crying again fighting for its freedom. But you have to get through this, I think, because I want to bring you home to my children. I often think of Helga and I hope the child did not get sick. We tank up in Arlon, Belgium and drive through Luxembourg.

In a small pub we eat some sausage and drink cheap beer. Then cross over the border with no checkpoint. In Trier we cannot find a place to stay overnight and have to continue on to Ruwer, stop there because we are totally exhausted and the poor little kitten as well. It cries and probably is very hungry. A nice family puts us up overnight, but first we take care of the kitten and the truck. Across the street some friendly people offer to put the kitten overnight in their barn, so it does not run away. We put some milk in the plate for it and then go to bed, as we are dead tired.

10, June 1940

On the way we are going to make a stop at home! We thank the old lady who is washing and dressing her kids. These people have very little themselves, but gladly share, this is heart warming. We drive over good roads through the Mosel valley over the Hunsrück high road to Stromberg. A soldier there with the artillery would have given us a fortune for a single French helmet. By two in the afternoon we make it to Hochstätten and are welcomed with great exuberance. The child is healthy and I am happy. Our big military truck is the talk of the town and admired by everyone.

Papa holding the kitten (Note French helmet on the bumper)

We enjoy a meal, turn over the little cat, which my children are crazy about and leave late for Wiesbaden.

49

The new recruits have arrived. While we are still telling about our experiences, the captain comes and wants to hear our stories too. Everyone envies us. We learn that a new course will start. The new recruits are a mottled lot of all ages. They get their uniforms, physical exams, etc. This time I am in the 3rd unit with Lt. Kampman. I have 2 corporals, one a teacher, the other a minister. Unfortunately there are so many ignorant young punks and it is torture to have to get along with people with whom you don't have anything in common.

19, June 1940

My Birthday

I can't believe I am 37 years old! My father was this old when he went to war (WW I). Rösel and my sweet mother sent a package with goodies, food, cake, and cookies. I am happy and know they are thinking of me.

24, June 1940

Furlough

It's a Sunday furlough, for which I am so happy. Rösel is with Helga in Sembach, but I take the train to Hochstätten. Norbert gets on the train to join me. He is so happy, when he sees me. When I ask him if he remembered my birthday he shyly reaches for my hand and says: "Happy Birthday, Papa!" Rösel meets us half way. How young and beautiful she looks, just like she did 15 years ago, when we first met. "O God, keep her well and safe for me!" She came by bike and the first thing she says is that Friedrich was killed in France. It affects me deeply, my cousin, the pride and joy of his parents. Mother has heard it too. This is her only nephew. We go to the garden and eat strawberries and gooseberries. Wonderful! Helga is happy that I am home again. At night I have to carry her to her bed and kiss her many times.

The schoolhouse is filled with soldiers.

25, June 1940

The next day I go by bike to Mehlingen and I cannot describe my feelings and emotions when I see my uncle standing on the steps, crying like a baby. If only it was not true, but it is. I go into the familiar house, embrace my aunt, who is sobbing uncontrollably. Is it really true? She can only nod. Then the two sisters come.

There was the official notification accompanied by a package, which contained his belongings that were delivered by the postman. On the package someone had written: "He fell for greater Germany and his country!" That is a terrible fact! They are still in a state of denial and my aunt asks: "Is it really official?" They would cling to a piece of straw. We don't know any details. Of course they don't feel like doing their work. My aunt tells us he was always so enthused to be a soldier, but did not like the infantry and had made several unsuccessful attempts, to be transferred. He was an Eichert, the last Eichert to carry on the name. Mother says how it hurts to think that the family has died out. On his picture he looks so much like our grandfather and also resembles my brother Richard. They both had that certain restlessness and the love and passion for motors and engines. Their pain is unimaginable. I believe the poor people do not realize in the beginning, what they have lost. The sympathy of the whole village is touching. He is the first and only one of all the surrounding towns, who has fallen. I went home very sadly and depressed.

That evening I go back to Wiesbaden and for days I'm not myself.

28, June 1940

Rösel writes that the very talented colleague Fritz Kron has been killed. What a waste, this senseless murdering of people! My loved ones are fine. Rösel has a lot of work with the strawberries in the garden.

1, July 1940

The War With France Is Over

I would have wanted to be part of it! Instead I sit here in Wiesbaden, and I am sick of it!

15, July 1940

Another Sunday furlough in Sembach! I want to pick up sheet music for the "Mountain Festival". That was a good excuse for the leave time.

Father is awaiting me in the hallway to say "hello". Mother is working hard as always. Rösel and the children had come up a couple of days before to work in the garden. There are still plenty of strawberries and gooseberries and Rösel cooks my favorite meals and does everything to show me her love. It makes me sick to go up to the attic in the schoolhouse and see the mess and clutter there. I don't leave until 7 in the morning. Father wanted to come and say good-bye, but he must have overslept. Rösel came along with her bike, because of a basket with fruit, which I am to deliver to the in-laws in Hochstätten. She is so sweet and caring! When we say our good-byes at the last curve she says to me: "You look more and more like your dad". For a long time we wave to each other, then she returns.

I get off in Hochstätten, give the fruit basket to the in-laws, eat something and then wait for a car that is supposed to take me to Bad Muenster, where I was supposed to catch the E-train to Wiesbaden. Of course no car! Then good old Opa rode with his bike and I with the other one the almost 10 miles to Bad Muenster. I feel sorry for him, after all he is not the youngest anymore, and his health is not that good. He is lagging behind but I have to push on, as I have to be in Wiesbaden by 2 o'clock. What bad luck! When I get to the station I leave the bike by the gate and just barely make the train. In this moment Opa arrives, we could only wave to each other and he then went home with both bikes.

Exhaustedly I fell into the seat. At 2 o'clock I stood in my wringing wet uniform in front of my class. The rest of the afternoon and tomorrow I have to rehearse with the choir, so the "Mountain Festival" will be a success.

21, July 1940

Another Sunday filled with being homesick! I don't know what else to do, so I go to Rüdesheim, where I have so many happy memories with my love. I take a trip to Bingen, climb up to the Burg Klopp Castle, and feel the incredible loneliness.

Suddenly I meet "Aunt" Hedwig, the kindergarten teacher from Hochstätten. She just happens to have a photograph of my "Murschel", as she is lying on her cot at rest time with her arms under her head. How sweet and precious, my little girl! She lets me keep the picture and I happily look at it again and again.

In the evening I take the Rhine steamer back. That is always such a beautiful trip. One can always abandon oneself to one's yearnings.

28, July 1940

Furlough in Hochstätten! The reason is to bring back the sheet music. The captain is pretty good about this. How thrilled the kids are. "Murschel" wraps her little arms around my neck and Norbert wants to know when I will become an officer. Rösel unfortunately has a painful sore on her leg and it is hard for her to walk. I insist the doctor be called. My brave big boy walks with me to the station. Before, I have to carry "Murschel" into her bed and lie down next to her. She holds me tight as she falls asleep. I gently ease myself away. Norbert sits on the barrier at the station and has tears in his eyes. My dear good boy! My complete happiness is my family!

30, July 1940

I have requested a voluntary training course for officer's training. No luck! A sergeant was admitted. S/Sgt. Holland becomes my best friend. Quite a few buddies were transferred to detach pipelines and cables. I wish I could have gotten out of here with that group. They will see and hear things, while I sit here and rot. Why, I don't know. Why could I not get to Paris or Belgium or Holland or anywhere else to get to see these countries and its people, I am disgusted! I am sick of the daily exercising in the square.

7, August 1940

It is 26 years ago today my father went to war. I enjoyed giving a successful presentation about the aircraft recognition service. I think I did pretty well. But I am a little concerned about the so called "courage tests", such as jumping from a 4 meter high tower. We don't get around to it though, because a "big cheese", Lt. Col. Fisher is supposed to check us out. He is wearing a monocle and has the worst kind of military behavior. Well, we got through that.

11, August 1940

What a beautiful Sunday! I have asked the family to come to Bingen, where I will meet them. A friendly buddy from Berlin takes me from

Mainz to Bingen, where I wait for them in the Café Horn. Through the window I see them coming and the thrill in my heart is indescribable.

I walk out and greet them. I am so happy to see the children so healthy and chipper sitting next to me. Helga acts so grownup and sensible, what a joy to see her like this.

I take her by the hand and we walk with the others up to the top of the Klopp Castle. Opa and Norbert are waiting for us in the curve and we climb up the steep steps. Here up high by the terraced vineyards I tell them about my success. Rösel is proud and happy. The child keeps on running up and down the vineyard steps and walks along the walls, what energy, but Oma worries. I love watching her joy of life. After getting to the top of the castle I show them, where I met "Tante" Hedwig the kindergarten teacher. Then they look through the binoculars I brought, across the lovely Rhine Valley, "God's Country", and the beautiful and majestic Rhine River. Norbert is very interested in everything and I explain the countryside to him. Then we go back down to the city, "Murschel" up ahead as always. We sit down at a bench and take a few pictures.

Papa, Norbert, and Helga waiting for the steamship

Finally our steamship arrives. Norbert had done a trip by boat 2 years ago to Koblenz, so it is nothing new to him. We have our picnic and my loving wife has brought all kinds of goodies. So the eternally beautiful Rhine landscape with its lovely shorelines gently glides by. The children absorb everything. We pass the beautiful, legendary Loreley. Finally, but much too fast, we are in St. Goar. We were here once before by car with my parents. We find a lovely spot right by the river and stay there for an hour or so. The children throw rocks in the water, climb around an old boat, and have a race along the shore. Eventually we walk back through the town's main street to the pier, get on, and ride back in the evening sunshine. I sit with Helga by the railing and every time a ship passes, she yells brightly, "Yoo-Hoo"!

I study her little face and decide she looks like a Hoffman (Mama's family). That's all right; she is still my flesh and blood.

When we arrive in Bingen, we have enough time to go to a café for an ice cream. Then we have to part. My loved ones go to the railroad station and I wait for the next boat and ride back immersed in my daydreams. It is dark when I return. What a beautiful day this has been!

16, August 1940

The Captain informs me, that the three of us, who are to be transferred to Halle, can have a few days of R & R. A truck is leaving tomorrow for Paris and I could go along, if I didn't have such worries about them at home. I heard that Rösel has a sore, which had to be lanced by the doctor. I do not dare to go to France now and definitely want to take my leave time. I wrote them, that I am coming. We spend wonderful days together. Sometimes the children upset Oma and Opa but then they are sweet again. In the afternoon Helga goes with Oma and Opa into the vineyard with her little red scarf, which Rösel knows how to tie so cute around her head. We stand by the bathroom window and look across in the vineyard until we see them. Then she calls with her bright little voice: "Yoo-Hoo, Babbaaaa!" She recognizes me by the window and we wave to each other. What wonderful days these are without hurry, just relaxation.

Norbert pleases me with his piano playing. We can even do a four hand together. How quickly he comprehends. Helga plays with her dolls and her friend Lilli. The little mouth goes continuously. Norbert can ride his bike all the way to Alsenz and the pharmacy.

The children are growing up and I am missing it all. Oh, how that hurts!

20, August 1940

I have decided to go to Sembach by myself. Rösel does not need to come and mother can cook for me. She will enjoy that. In the evening they both come. I fire up the kitchen stove and I enjoy the coziness of my home. Mother is so happy to be helping me out. In the evening we go together in the garden. Father tells me what all he has done. He pointed out the apple trees, which were hurt by the frost and the new early potatoes. We dig up a few. Then he tells me that he wants to trim the trees in spring. We pick the last peaches and mother picks some beans for me to take back. Fall is coming.

21, August 1940

I am still in Sembach. Mother comes and takes care of things and cooks my favorite meals. I go upstairs into the schoolrooms and I was glad to hear that they are supposed to be used as such again. I hope so anyway. I go into the attic library and pick out some books for Norbert. His favorite is "Robinson Crusoe". Mother tells me in tears, that things are very sad in Mehlingen since they received the news, that Friedrich was killed in action. Then I get ready to leave. Mother is as always brave, but when I shake father's hand in the hallway, he bursts into tears. I know he loves me, even though he does not show it. By the last curve I turn and wave one more time. Cousin Jakob has taken the basket with beans on his bike to the station for me. Norbert picks me up in Hochstätten and I have two more beautiful days there.

23, August 1940

It is time to say good-bye again. Norbert sits on the gate and kisses me. How sad always, these farewells!

24, August 1940

Check up! I think I did well! Major Fraisse comes in my classroom and attends my lecture on aircraft identification. There was another trip to France but I was not chosen to go along.

25, August 1940

It is now decided where we will be transferred, not to Halle, but Potsdam. That's OK with me. I hope to get to see Berlin. We requisition a few more things, an air force shirt, dress pants, collar stays, a visor cap, etc.

28, August 1940

I ask for one more leave. It is granted. My loved ones do not expect me.

29-31, August 1940

Furlough

I enjoy being back in the arms of my loving family! I sleep well, rest, and relax. If only the weather would be better. Norbert reads "Robinson Crusoe". Helga tends to be quarrelsome and snippy, a typical little girl. Norbert plays the piano and builds with his erector set.

After returning to Wiesbaden I have to pack quickly. It is a problem because I cannot get all my stuff into my backpack. My suitcase is completely full too and I do not get a chance to say good-bye to the captain. With the Luftwaffen license and the orders in my pocket I drive to Frankfurt. I meet Officer Traum and we catch a troop train to and from the front directly to Berlin. We are lucky and can ride in 2nd class; we turn off the lights and lay down to catch some sleep. No one bothers us; just a few infantry buddies join us en route.

1, September 1940

We Arrive In Berlin

We rub our eyes, grab our baggage, and drag it to the baggage check. First I see the famous winter garden. We walk along Friedrichstrasse and cross Unter den Linden; I am disappointed. A wide, empty, lonely street lined with young linden trees; that's it.

There are very few people in the street. Berlin is a dead city, that's because of the air raids. These poor people have to sleep every night in a bunker, shelter, or basement. We go to a café and drink terrible coffee and eat an even worse piece of cake. Germany has gotten very poor. We walk through Wilhelmstrasse and the new Reich's Chancellery.

That afternoon I get to ride the underground for the first time. Soon I get used to the brightly lit up "U". We walk through the elegant west part of Berlin, past Kurfürstendamm, the Zoo, and Kaiser Wilhelm Gedächtniskirche (Memorial Church). In the afternoon it is time to check in and we go to Potsdam by subway. What will await us? I am impressed with the tremendous speed this electrical fast train gets us there.

I had no idea what horrible 10 weeks would lie ahead of me. We get off with our heavy luggage waiting for a bus. Well, no bus! Finally a truck takes us to the intersection of Wildpark, and leaves us off. From there we have to hike another 15 mi. What torture, with rifle and all. We finally see the sign: "General Weber Kaserne". We march under the sovereign national emblem, the German Eagle, wringing wet we make the last 100 meters, we find Block B, I throw off my backpack, receive sheets, find my room and collapse.

2, September 1940

The Kaserne complex is very nice and must have cost a lot of money. Parquet floors, impeccable wash rooms and toilets, etc., only the hard wooden beds we are not happy about.

3, September 1940

What I am writing now I can only describe briefly and as an outline. I have my first meeting with the dynamic NCO Latuske. The next day already a sharp wind is blowing and we have an exam in the manner and attitude of a soldier, practicing the marching and presentation of arms. Then the tough sport exam: The test of courage by swimming in the icy water of the lake. The food leaves something to be desired and we have air raids almost every night. The written exams are finished and we have to improvise, for example: "Come on up and speak for 10 minutes about the meaning of honor, obedience, courage, etc."

The expectations increase with the grueling marches in the fields in high wet grass. What beautiful country! A relief is the Saturday and Sunday in Berlin. Most of the time I have a room in the Hotel Anhalt, not far from the subway station. I try to see all the sights, but Berlin is poor and there is not much to eat anymore. I watch the changing of the Honor Guard at the Reichs Memorial. I would like to see Hitler, but no such luck. Captain Walkoff works like a dog, doing all the presentations in weaponry and exercising. We are all scared when he calls on us. He is definitely the sharpest and most dynamic soldier I have met. We have orientation outdoors and map reading practice. The 3,000-meter run, which I manage with enormous frenzied strain of all my strength. And make good time. Also I did very well in throwing hand grenades.

4, September 1940

Captain Walkoff surprises everyone with his personal achievements. No one surpasses him, not even the sport teacher. The air raids are a torture. During the night the English bombed three times and we spent the whole night in the cellar. I will never forget the long boring hours by the window across from the pine forest or in the cold cellar wrapped in a blanket lying on the concrete, or standing guard in the yard with the sky lit up from flares and the infernal shooting of the ack-ack. Once a bomb fell very close to our barracks, so close that I heard the hissing sound just before detonation. The next day we were so tired, that we struggled with the stress and concentration. Oh, if only these classes were over!

1, October 1940

Only 4 torturous weeks have gone by. The main stress is still to come. We continue to be amazed about the incredible endurance of this man. We actually admire him, but fear him as well.

3, October 1940

The tremendous march in combat uniform of 50 km. and combat training with blank cartridges. At noon we eat from the field kitchen. We are tired as a dog, but I have no problems. Thank God I have good feet! We see the immense wide fields of the north German farms. The return march is horrible. We hardly make any headway in the sandy soil, sometimes up to your ankles. During a short pee break I try to pull off my one boot, because my sock has bunched up. That was a mistake, because my foot is so swollen that I can hardly get my boot back on. I am limping but I clench my teeth and bravely march on. Late at night we arrive. In the light of a flashlight the "Mighty One" says the following sentence: "I was very pleased with your attitude and achievement". This made us unbelievably happy, because to receive an appreciative comment from this man meant something extraordinary.

The next morning indeed we had easier duty and could sleep in. Oh, but the feet! Most of them had blood in their boots, but I was OK, only they hurt, as well as my knees.

24, October 1940

We get to know Capt. Walkoff from a different side. He is superior, arrogant, and unsurpassed in drinking. After the partying there was an air raid until 7 am. Horrible!

But the fight goes on!

26, October 1940

The dishonesty that happened was followed by punishment. No Sunday leave time. Worse yet, the forfeiting of his good will. We are all very depressed.

30, October 1940

The 1st snowfall! The course is slowly coming to an end. I think I did well. Today the mighty one has an assignment for me. I have to give a presentation about the basis of aircraft reconnaissance.

6, November 1940

Norbert's Birthday

He is 10 years old today! And my big day! I did a very good job on my speech with a slide show and everyone appreciated it and complimented me on it. We also had a check on our wardrobe. There was a long warm eye contact from these ordinarily cold eyes. "And these are your kids? Two of them?" A new puzzle, this man! At 3:28 o'clock precisely I thought of Rösel, my sweet wife giving birth to our first-born 10 years ago.

7, November 1940

We are counting the hours and do not yet know who has passed.

8, November 1940

The farewell evening, which turned into a terrible drinking orgy at midnight. At 3 am he begins to perform Russian dances and smash all the glasses into the wall. But amazingly he stays sober! Incredible, what this man can drink without getting drunk! That same night I hear from a reliable source, that I passed the exam.

9, November 1940

What a day! He makes an appearance, somewhat pale, but in good control. We have a totally different picture of him. The general mood is high with anticipation, because we do not know the outcome. We heard that only a small minority has made it. My hopes have sunk to the 0 point. I am so nervous I am shaking. Then comes the feared list and everyone is shaking in his boots. Finally I hear my name and I take a deep breath. Hooray! I have passed! What a feeling! Indescribable! What about all the buddies and their disappointments of failure? Out of 130 men 36 did not make it. They will have to repeat the course. Now I cannot wait to take my happiness home to share with my loved ones. No one knows better than my sweet little wife, how hard I have fought for this! My joy is not overwhelming, just a quiet happiness in my heart. I pack quickly, say my good-byes, and leave Potsdam, I hope for good!

I run through the gate in full gear and I do not want to see this place anymore, where I have spent many miserable hours. I am wringing wet when I get to the subway station. I check my luggage, only take my camera and the afternoon belongs to me to do a little shopping. I get an umbrella for Rösel, a fountain pen, and a harmonica for Norbert, for "Murschel" a little raincoat. I am so happy, to get these gifts for them. I stay overnight in the Hotel Silesia, clean and cheap. At 6:44 am the train is supposed to leave for Insterburg.

10, November 1940

Impressions of this trip: The endless, wide-open flat country of the German East. For hours I see pine forests and small farms. The closer we travel east, the colder it gets. Swamps, with the heather still blooming, and Polish children along the train tracks, plus French POWs. At the stations the Polish signs have been painted over and replaced with German writing.

The reason for this trip is my visit on the way home with "Tante" Martha and her family, our good friends. Slowly it is getting dark. Oh, Martha, how far away you live! The lights have not been darkened in Königsberg yet, so far no bombings here by the English. The train keeps clattering on. I finally get to Insterburg. There is deep snow here like in Russia and the city is full of soldiers. Martha is about to faint, when she opens the door and sees me. Her husband is here and I am warmly welcomed. They still have enough to eat and Martha treats me royally. After dinner we listen to the radio, talk about the families and share memories. She shows me pictures of my loved ones, which Rösel had sent along with a gift for the new baby, a little boy. Then we admire the little guy, a darling child. Martha has a good husband and we talk for a long time in their cozy living room. I sleep so well that night, the first time in a long time in a good bed. In the morning at 5 o'clock I hear Martha getting up to take care of the baby.

At 7 am I get up, say good-bye to Martha's husband and get ready to leave. I promise to send her some pictures soon. The bus comes and we part with the assurance of happy memories of this somewhat impromptu visit. A young woman with 2 children is my travel companion and after a long trip I get back to Berlin, pick up my baggage and rifle out of the locker and get on the 10 pm troop train.

Good-Bye Berlin

I get comfortable and fall asleep in less than an hour on the bench in the train. In Frankfurt I get immediate connection to Wiesbaden. Introduction to the Captain, who wishes me "Good Luck" on my passed exam and I meet the new comrades.

12, November 1940

My first day of duty; I immediately ask the boss for furlough. He grants me 7 days. Hooray! How happy I am! I cannot wait until I am home. The train goes much too slow! Finally I arrive in Hochstätten. At 7:30, there she is, my darling wife, as fresh and beautiful as ever waiting for me. I want to know how the children are and I tell her right away, that I passed the test and she is happy for me. They all fly into my arms, my big boy with his trusting nature and my sweet little "Murschel".

My sweet little "Murschel"

Now I have to tell them everything and unpack the presents. Helga only gets the candies, the raincoat we save for Christmas. We go to bed soon, after I tell the children that they can come to my bed in the morning. Oh, my precious home!

13, November 1940

I slept so well! Finally a bed at home with people who love me and take care of me. The children are awake very early and Norbert is dressed already. He gives me a good morning kiss and tells me he is happy to have me home. Helga comes in her cute floral PJ's and snuggles under the blanket. When we hear Mama coming up the stairs, she hides and I say, "Our child is not here!" She giggles under the blanket and screams excitedly, when Mama touches around the blanket and pretends to look for her, finally lifts up the covers and sees her little head. So we have to continue to play this little game. Then we get up and drink "Koofiechen" (coffee). She still does not eat well and stays at the table. Norbert eats well but too hastily.

15, November 1940

I go with Norbert to Dr. Gralka for a checkup. He looks at the magazines in the waiting room and acts very grown up. He answers all the doctor's questions correctly and is not shy at all. His heart and lungs are healthy, his posture not that good, he is underweight. His digestion is too hasty. He gets medication and we leave.

I go with him through town and he wants to buy a weight for Mama's scale and a pickle fork. Of course his favorite place to stop is the toy stores. He does not know yet what he wants for Christmas. Then we go home and report the doctor's findings. Oh, I would so wish I had him in my class and be able to be his teacher. He does not learn that much with the sad school situation, especially in math and geography. He enjoys reading, especially my books. The evenings are so wonderful.

We go upstairs; together they cuddle into their beds and say their prayers, which are so touching. Helga covers up to under her chin, we kiss them good night, turn out the lights, and go downstairs. Oh, when will I be able to be home again for good?

16, November 1940

I walk Helga to the kindergarten, which is what she wants. I take her by her little hand and we walk through the village while she talks continually, the little chatterbox.

She takes her little jacket and red gloves off and stays without a problem.

17, November 1940

We took Norbert with us to Sembach. He is happy to see his old friends. He loves to sleep by himself in the old playroom next to the kitchen. In the afternoon Rösel and I go to Mehlingen to visit with the aunt and uncle. Both of them are sad but composed. Maybe time will heal the terrible hurt of Friedrich's loss. Poor guy! What a waste! We have coffee and cake and leave late afternoon, not before I look one more time at the small attic room, where I was born.

18, November 1940

In the afternoon the girls meet for the Hitler Youth meeting in the schoolroom. We visit our friends, the Gödtel's and spend a lovely evening with them.

21, November 1940

Today we go back to Hochstätten. We also saw Jakob and Alice, and admired their new little baby girl. Bogged down with a lot of luggage, the three of us march to the train station. We have an excited reunion with "Murschel" and immediately after lunch we go to the vineyard, where Oma is already working hard. The three of us help to spade the dirt. Working the heavy clay dirt is tiring and I stop to rest often. Rösel laughs at me. Around 6 pm when it starts getting dark, we head home. From far away I can see the two rascals coming to meet us. They wave and we go home together. On the way the child plays hide and seek and we spend another beautiful evening together.

24, November 1940

We visit in Feil. Rösel and I walk up through the lovely, well-known hillsides like a young couple in love. When we pass the vineyard we are proud of all the hard work we have done. Then we walk up the new road which the Polish prisoners have built and look back from way up high to the beautiful little village, nestled in the valley, with the smoke rising from the chimneys and the morning fog still laying over the fields.

We then continue on and stop at Willi and Gretchen to say "Hi". We are treated to coffee and cake and then continue on to the Aunt Babette, Oma's sister. All good people!

It is dark by the time we walk back and we are getting a little bit of drizzle. On the top of the hillside we stop and I kiss my sweet little wife more fervently than I have in a long time. How very grateful am I to have found this wonderful partner for life!

26, November 1940

I decided to leave at 3:30 pm, because I am assuming it will be difficult to get lodging later, since I do not have a bed or closet anymore. I take a few more pictures. "Murschel" sits on the railing of the station again and wants kisses. "Come back soon", she says. Then the two of them run around the building to wave at me on the train until the little white coat and red hat disappear.

Saying good-bye to Papa

1, December 1940

At 1 pm I start my duty as the NCO in charge. I have enough time to read and write. How else shall I pass the time? Tomorrow the first recruits arrive, I feel sorry for them! What all is going to await them?

2, December 1940

Their training is beginning with greetings and indoctrination. They have not been given uniforms yet. It is very cold and the ovens in the bathrooms have to be fired. The captain can see that I do my best.

5, December 1940

Little by little all the recruits arrive; out of 350 men, 150 are sent home as unsuitable for military service. In my new room there are 3 good buddies. NCO Otto, Herman, Klein, and I. Herman went to get a Christmas tree, glass baubles, and candles. He also made an Advent Wreath and it is now very cozy in our room. I am saddened to think of Christmas and how most likely I won't be able to get a furlough to be home with my loved ones. It's just about to break my heart!

8, December 1940

Another Sunday and the stores are open. I buy sparklers for the Christmas tree, an orange knife for Rösel, a paint box for Norbert, a knitting kit for Helga and a book for cutting out dolls. Besides I still have the little raincoat for her from Berlin. Maybe I have to mail the things home.

A few days ago we had to introduce ourselves to Comdr. Fraisse, who was just promoted as well as the future officers.

15, December 1940

I spend another Sunday in Mainz. I buy the last Christmas presents and look forward to the reunion with my family, because I just found out that I am able to have leave over New Years. I also learned, that the captain is thinking of transferring me, but not before Christmas. I talked with NCO Walters, who wrote a very good recommendation. Also my superior will write a letter of assessment.

16, December 1940

One more guard duty. Will it be the last one?

18, December 1940

Since December 1st, I am directing the camp choir. I have good people and they are pleased with my work and efforts. They want me to be back by December 30th, so I can direct them for the belated Christmas Party. I had it pretty easy and only exercised a few times. Boy, did those ears and feet get cold in the snow! I have a good bed and warm blankets. Daily when I look into my closet I see the pictures of my loved ones. We have more and more air raids.

20, December 1940

My transfer is granted. The question is where. Two more NCOs are leaving. They talk enthusiastically about the Spanish border. I myself don't care just let me get away from Wiesbaden. I am rushing to get ready for my trip home.

21, December 1940

Furlough

Quickly I pack my suitcase and two smaller packages and get going. Arriving at home I open the door with my heart pounding. Rösel flies into my arms. Then the children greet me excitedly and the in-laws are happy to see me. I eat and talk. Is there anything more rewarding, than bringing my two darling kids upstairs to bed so cute in their flowered pajamas? I am touched by how they say their simple little prayers they were taught, something so pure and divine. Then they happily go to sleep. Helga has both her hands together under her right cheek. We still sit together for a long time.

22, December 1940

Of course they have to come into my bed in the morning. I hug them and we wrestle and they compete with their loving me. Then Mama dresses them. In the afternoon Norbert has a Christmas performance in school and he wants me to be there. He has to recite a poem and is not nervous at all. His poem was:

> "Mir ist das Herz so froh erschrocken
> Das ist die liebe Weihnachtszeit
> Ich höre fernher Kirchenglocken
> Mich lieblich heimatlich verlocken
> In märchenstille Herrlichkeit."

Translation:

> "My heart was happily excited
> This is the dear old Christmas time
> I hear from afar the church bells ringing
> Which in a lovely way lure me
> To a magical glory".

He did very well and I was so proud of him. How I thank you, O God, that you let me find this family with so many valuable characteristics, which passed on all that goodness to their only child and with it onto my children.

23, December 1940

Christkind will come this evening, one day early. What joy! Rösel washes the children by the stove. We cannot bathe them, because the room is too cold. Afterwards they are sent to the kitchen and there are happy preparations and impatient expectations. Norbert knows as of last year but Helga still believes firmly in Christkind. May she still keep her sweet childlike faith for a long time!

Opa has already put the tree in its stand and we now decorate it. The gifts are wrapped in colorful paper. We then have supper and that's when I notice, that the child is not as lively and her forehead feels hot. I hope she will not get sick over Christmas! I feel a little down, but Rösel is confident it is nothing.

Now our annual Christmas celebration repeats itself. All are in the kitchen and I go into the living room to ring the silver bell, then rush outside to pretend that I just got a glimpse of Christkind leaving. Then they come in. What bliss and joy! Always fresh and new! Helga's eyes are shining and in silent wonder she looks into the shimmering lights. Then she looks at the presents on the table, but is not overjoyed. She does not feel well! Why must there always be a bitter drop "in the cup of joy"? We light the sparklers, I sit down at the piano and play, and we sing all the wonderful old Christmas songs. Then the children say a prayer and only then we open the presents.

What splendor! There is a new doll carriage for Helga, actually it's the old one fixed up by Opa, the new little raincoat from Berlin, an edible gingerbread Santa from Mainz and what heavenly joy, her own little iron. For Norbert there is a paint box, a book with children's songs, a model of a plane, and a drum with stationary. For Rösel, the face cream, the orange knife, a songbook for the piano, chocolates, etc. For Papa a new white shirt and Norbert made me a calendar to hang in my closet. So we all are happy and play games for a while. Unfortunately Helga does run a high fever and my good mood is down again. I do not sleep very well, because I listen to the fast breathing of the child. In the morning the temperature is down and she seems better.

24, December 1940

Norbert plays downstairs and we keep Helga in bed. We have a feeling from experience that her fever will go up again at night. Even though we do not expect her to get seriously sick, our mood is dampened. We dress her in her little wool sweater and I have to tell her stories. About "Michel", or "when you ran across the yard with the hot coffee pot", an episode I once told about in Potsdam. When she gets tired she turns her head to the side but keeps listening. I look into her throat she willingly opens up her mouth and says aaahhh. She seems to have a coating on her tonsils. In the evening the fever is up again. We sleep on either side of her and keep Norbert away from her. She sleeps restless and her little head is glowing hot. In the morning she still runs 39.4C.

25, December 1940

Christmas Day

If her fever is not down by tonight we will call the doctor tomorrow. In the afternoon grandmother is coming from Sembach. "Gross" (her nickname for Grossmutter) has to sit down at the side of her bed. She brought a few things, a shirt for Norbert and for Helga material for an apron.

Her fever is going up and down. Strangely she is in good spirits but is very thirsty. She drinks raspberry juice and lemon juice with aspirin for the fever. She is so cooperative and understanding. She wants to get up and see the Christmas tree. When the doctor comes in the afternoon she starts crying. I try to console her and tell her the doctor just wants to make her feel better. But when the doctor wants to look into her throat and asks for a spoon, she starts crying again. Mama has to wrap her into a blanket and sit by the window. Now she screams bloody murder and refuses to open her mouth. We have to pry her mouth open forcefully. Oh, you poor sweet child, how such torture cuts into my heart! Mama has to hold her hands and Opa and I try to open her mouth. We end up hurting her at the corner of the mouth until it bleeds. Now this has gone too far. I try talking to her and say: "If you open your mouth as wide as you can and say aaahhh, we then will not need the spoon!" Then she quiets down and opens her mouth and the doctor can see, that it is not diphtheria, but tonsillitis. We feel better and get her back in bed and she calms herself down. The doctor writes a prescription for a medication for gargling, which Opa picks up going by train to Alsenz. How nicely she is able to gargle! She learned that while brushing her teeth. At night her fever is up again and I have to lay down with her. All my love pours out to this, my precious child. I kiss her hot little hands and stroke her hair and whisper: "You sweet child!" and at the same time I pray: "Dear God, keep this child healthy and happy!" I put so much faith into my God and have never been disappointed.

26, December 1940

During the next day she is beginning to feel better and wants to look at picture books. Grandmother (Grossmutter) has to stay by her bed, but she has to leave again in the afternoon. Rösel accompanies her to the train station. I decided to leave early in the morning instead of tonight. Helga's breathing is still rapid, but I am confident, that she will get well soon.

We light the candles on the tree one more time and the sparklers. Then we sit at the table and play games or talk. Tomorrow will be a bad day, my last one always is. We eat cookies and drink liqueur, sit by the warm stove and enjoy our togetherness. Then I go and get the zither and play all the songs as I did 30 years ago, when my parents laid down the foundation for my personality and my musical talent. I hope that Norbert will continue the tradition, for he is musically inclined and plays the piano very nicely. I am surprised what wonderful work Rösel has done with him. So we sit together and I enjoy the precious minutes as if they were hours. We take Norbert to bed, he hugs me, and when I ask him, "are you glad I am here?" he answers with a big grin: "Yes!"

I am afraid I will oversleep and my train leaves at 6 am. Both children are awake and I get ready and say my good-byes, with the fervent wish for them to stay well. I tear myself away and walk into the dark night.

27, December 1940

I arrive at 9 o'clock in Wiesbaden, pick up my laundry, and go up to Dotzheim. I find out, that I am not transferring to Southern France, but to Le Havre. I don't know how to feel about this! The English Channel Coast? I did not want to go there!

I pack all afternoon. In the evening I take a few books, some magazines and a bottle of wine to Gretchen's and say good-bye. They have always been so kind to me. There were cookies, books and several presents, also some mail from the NSDAP (National Socialistic German Workers Party). I called Rösel and she tells me, that Helga is better. The doctor was there and she can get up tomorrow. Thank God!

28, December 1940

Good-bye To Wiesbaden

16 months I've spent here, with the exception of the short time in Gensingen, Halle, and Potsdam. Maybe I will regret that I requested a transfer? At 10 o'clock we are ready. I've turned in my rifle, had

dragged it around long enough! Other than my luggage I have nothing to carry. I say good-bye to some of the good buddies. We are taken in a Mercedes in a treacherous ride in spite of ice and snow to the Mainz main railroad station. The military train is filled up and several hundred men do not find room. Many are lifted up through the windows. I stay back and take a regular train to Bingerbrück. From there I try to telephone to Hochstätten, but cannot get through. I was lucky to get a seat until Saarbrücken. I leave my luggage at the station and try to put a call through to Hochstätten. Twenty minutes later I was able to talk to Rösel and Norbert. I have never felt them so close and understood them so well. I have only been away from them for one day and already I am so homesick.

I now wait for the special fast train to Paris at 10 pm. I wait at the station with several hundred soldiers of all ranks until the train finally pulls in. I am lucky. I get into a compartment of officers, doctors, etc. in 2nd class. I quickly take off my coat, as to not give me away and pretend I am sleeping. This way I get a seat anyway.

29, December 1940

At dawn I see the dirty city limits, the gray houses, the dreary looking gardens, and the poorly kept train track areas. I notice that in France the trains run on the left track. We pull into the station Gare de l'Est. I exchange some money into francs and take the Metro to Gare St. Lazare, then to the command post for my papers. I eat two fried eggs and white bread in a small coffee shop and have the opportunity to observe French toilets. Then I ride with my pass to the Place l'Opera and Montmartre. I am surprised how dirty and dilapidated a lot of the residential areas look. I take several pictures and later see the infamous Place de la Concorde, where in 1789 the guillotine stood. Here are the beautiful parts of the city. The Liaison Officer secured a room for me in the Hotel Jeanne d'Arc.

There I meet a NCO, with whom I immediately have a great rapport. He has the EK (Iron Cross) 1 and 2, speaks fluent French and I would like to be friends with him.

Papa in Paris

He shows me the Seine River and the Eiffel Tower. What a tremendous structure! The merchants, black, brown and white, all pushy characters, offer all kinds of wares. But I don't have enough money with me. From the Trocadero, I enjoy a magnificent view over Paris and the famous landmark, the Eiffel Tower. Then we go downtown and have a fabulous meal in the restaurant Café de La Paix. A 6-course menu of wonderful food, especially the mushrooms with white bread and burgundy. Everything is not very expensive. My new friend has met a lovely girl, who he invites for dinner. But I guess he did not get too far with her because later I saw him with another one. He is right, let them have a little fun, especially the flyers that don't know how long they have to live.

My French bed has a roll instead of a pillow and is very soft. I sleep until early morning and we go to the station together and take a train out of Paris.

30, December 1940

In our compartment are several elegant French people. An older couple dressed in black for mourning. Most likely they have lost a son in this pathetic war! They sigh and thank us very politely for the attention we give them. I intend to show the French people, that not all of us are barbarians and brutes. I see a lot of Stuka (type of dive bomber) destruction along the way. By noon we reach Caen, my destination. Here I have to say good-bye to my new friend.

I leave my backpack at the station and find my new Regiment 13. I finally find it in the Rue de Verdun. Not a very good first impression! I am not pleased about the introduction to the two new officers; they are as usual unfriendly and stubborn. So, I am again looking into a dim future ahead of me. I find out that I will be in Company #1, hopefully not with the notorious Commanding Officer 1st Lt. Wolf!

I look around the city and study the French life. All in all it is very dirty. In the evening I eat in a restaurant a very good meal. I meet buddies Hübenthal and Schneider from Co. #17 and they have already taken care of their pleasures for the night. My bed in the Hotel de L'Angleterre is not good, like all French beds, too soft.

In the morning it is raining. We are loaded onto a truck, I pick up my backpack on the way, and we are off to this new department.

31, December 1940

New Years Eve

Oh, what a sad day! Had I only known that at this very hour my sweet precious boy at home was very sick. I would have been desperate! It was better I did not know! But my thoughts are with my loved ones all day anyway.

First we report to the new department, and then a room is secured at the command post in the Hotel de France. Here I should spend my first New Years. Then the decision is made, we will be in Company #1 with the notorious Lt. Wolf. My first impression of him: A "by-the-book" army man.

Of the trip from Caen to Vire is to report that it was very monotonous. Up and down through hilly country on straight roads through endless grazing land. The black and white Holstein cattle stay outside day and night. Bushes, hedges, and trees are unkempt, gardens are overgrown with weeds, almost no fields that are tended or planted. Houses that are dirty and in need to be painted, the yards full of weeds, a land of cattle herds. Well, the country is famous for its fromage (cheese).

I take my luggage to the hotel where I am supposed to live and look at my room. I would like to be home! Oh, home, sweet home! How shall I spend this evening? I don't want to see anybody, but want to be alone.

In the evening I eat a very good dinner at the Hotel St. Pierre, then wander through the city a bit. At 9 o'clock I sit down in the lobby of the hotel, order hot rum toddy and write a big letter to my loved ones. All my emotions and everything that is precious to me I put into this letter. I take my time, smoke a good cigar, write, and think of my happiness at home. No one can take this hour from me. It is 10 o'clock, then 11 o'clock. In this hour I am most lovingly connected with them at home. Between 11 and 12 o'clock, the last hour of the old year, we think of one another with all our hearts and souls.

Had I only known, that Rösel was at this time sitting at Norbert's sick bed. It was better I did not know. Slowly the hour drags on. At 11:45, I interrupt my letter and go to my room. I stand by the window, turn off the lights because of the blackouts, and look east where I know 1,000 km away is my German country and home with the dearest people I know. I am heartsick and think if only I could fly there to you and embrace you.

How hard is this war! Finally the hour of midnight rings from the church steeple.

1941

<u>New Year 1941</u>

At this moment, my heart and soul are flooded with so much love. All my senses and thinking are concentrating on Hochstätten and Sembach. May all my most fervent wishes, which I send to Heaven, be fulfilled. I know that my love is thinking of me, even though we are 1,000 km. apart, yet we still are so close in our minds and thoughts. What are the children doing? Oh, I did not know that Norbert was running a high fever that night! We are so used to it, that our children tend to be sick over the holidays. A pure unspoiled joy has seldom been ours.

I stay another 5 minutes or so deep in thoughts alone in my room, then get undressed and go to sleep with my last thoughts of my loved ones.

<u>1, January 1941</u>

I wake up with my first thoughts of my family. Today I will make myself a nice day. I go to the hotel to eat dinner and move out to a better place with a nicer room that has steam heat and running water. I want to go for a walk, but it is pouring rain. I wonder if it is this mild at home? At night I eat at the Hotel St. Pierre together with a very nice French lady, who is also a teacher. We have a lot to talk about. I am always amazed about the excellent French cuisine. For example I get soup, a filet mignon with French fries, spaghetti with tomato sauce and for desert, cheese, as much as I want plus oranges and pears in a delicious sauce, and all the beer I want. The whole thing cost me 26 Francs, which is about 1.30 Marks. The evening I spend in my room reading my good book in bed. It is very cozy and comfortable, but this will change and duty will begin soon.

During the night it begins to snow and in the morning we have a winter wonderland.

<u>2, January 1941</u>

Today I found out in the BOQ (Bachelor's Officer's Quarters) through Lt. Przybilsky, that I would be in Company #1 with the feared Lt. Wolf. Oh, well! I report to the commander's quarters and find myself across from a young man, who immediately notices, that one of the buttons on my shirt was open. I also have to move to a private room. I meet the captain of the division command and his facial expression is typical and I don't expect anything positive. He immediately informs me that there is no chance of a promotion. I get this sick feeling in my stomach.

The noon meal at the unit's mess hall is excellent. They sure know how to spice up food deliciously. In addition there is a free bottle of beer every day. In the afternoon I participate in the "cable detail". It is getting colder. Tomorrow I have to move out. After checking out about 20 houses I finally found an apartment that I like. Oh, how wonderfully soft are these beds and how cozy to go to sleep at night after reading a little.

At 7 am I get up for the line-up. Then breakfast with unlimited coffee, lots of butter and jelly, then we have "cable detail". The boss is a decent guy, and the comrades seem OK too. The group from Bavaria and Swabia is dull and indifferent.

3, January 1941

Today I am moving. My landlord is Mr. Legalle. He has a stiff arm and a skinny wife. There is a maid, Renee, Madame Yvonne, etc. The room is clean with a good bed. Unfortunately no running water or heat and it is getting colder. I have some coal I brought over but these French fireplaces do not give off any heat. I am glad for the closet and have room for all my things. Inside the door I hang Norbert's calendar. Everyday when I tear off a sheet, I think of my trusting big boy and when I am homesick, I drink a little of the delicious cherry with rum liqueur which Rösel gave me. The room is cozy and if I can get it a little warmer, I will like it here.

4, January 1941

I write home daily, but know I cannot expect any mail yet for at least 10 days. I am not worried yet. Vire is a nice small city and I try to buy a few things. A box of angora wool, also for 750 Francs (37.50 Marks), a pretty silk robe for my sweetheart. Also I am looking for material for a coat for Oma, socks for Norbert and Helga.

5, January 1941

One day runs into the other. We had a heavy snowfall and it is very cold. In the morning after line up while it is still dark, we march up to the mess hall for breakfast singing waking up all the French people. We then have an hour class about nothing much.

Some of these people are at an incredibly low mental and intellectual level. All they know is how to booze it up. Last Saturday we did a march of 25 km through the snow. Very healthy! I make my observations about how many people made officer, who did not deserve it. They make it so difficult for me. If I only knew why! Some of these "pumped-up monkeys" in officer uniforms running around with their egos making big time money. How I hate them! In particular Lt. P. this arrogant high and mighty punk! After dinner they play cards and drink cognac and try to make witty conversation, but don't have the first inkling about it. 1ˢᵗ Lt. Wolf: "What, what!" He is not stupid, but a fool.

8, January 1941

Finally a little stove. It is not the greatest, but better than nothing. Now it is more pleasant to stay here at night. I have moved my stuff into the closet.

9, January 1941

I am looking for someone to do my laundry and find Madame Francois. I almost fell over backwards when I walked into this dirty place. I see ½ dozen filthy children and a bunch of lazy women and this awful smell of sordidness and poverty. I should have my washing done here? I am hesitant and later on find the very clean Yvonne le Bourge.

11, January 1941

Nothing new, only that it has turned very cold. I have orders together with NCO Kleiser to investigate a telephone cable failure. We drive with our truck a few miles into the country and look for the damaged line. By installing a bypass, the disturbance is supposed to be fixed. We have to go out one more time in the morning.

13, January 1941

In the old school we take a bath. Hopefully I did not catch a cold. This is more than primitive! The evenings are beautiful. I make conversation with Monsieur Legalle and improve my French. The hour before going to bed is my nicest most private time. I turn on the two extra light bulbs I have bought and read my book. Then I'll have a little drink of my cherry with rum, before going to sleep. In the morning my landlord wakes me. I am content here and would like to stay.

The young soldiers are sharp, but I can't get close to them. They have been on the front and seen some action, but now they booze it up.

14, January 1941

Finally, after sixteen days the first letter! I open it with my hands shaking and read it hungrily. Just as I was afraid, some one was sick again, this time it was Norbert. He had just like Helga, a serious tonsillitis. On the 30th of Dec. he was in bed with a high fever, which climbed on New Years Day to 40.7C. He always fears the nightmares and hallucinations he used to have as a small child. The high fever lasted 3 days then he could get up again.

16, January 1941

There is another variety show during the evening. A French group of artists delights a full house. I am just so amazed about all the many people we have and all the many soldiers! At night I get into my bed with great well being, my bed is warmed with a hot water bottle. In the morning I wake up and my first thoughts are directed to my loved ones. I have bought a few things for them.

Today I find out that I am leaving. The 1st Lt. has made the decision.

18, January 1941

Transfer from the "Air Force Reconnaissance", Regiment #13 to the Luftgau Command Post in Etampes. I need the morning to pack and say good-bye. Then leave Vire by train at 2 pm.

The snow is melting and the streets are a terrible mess. The boots get wet and it rains and snows continually. A French soldier is very helpful at the Montparnasse Station. I have someone take my heavy luggage to the station Austerlitz. The guy is expensive; he wants 40 Francs (2 Marks). Then I take the subway to the Rue Faubourg. I find a very nice clean hotel room with a separate bathroom and an elevator in the Hotel Liege on the Boulevard Strasbourg.

The next morning I get up not too late, have breakfast and look at this beautiful city of Paris.

By the way, 70 years ago yesterday was the "Day of Versailles" 1871 to 1941!

19, January 1941

I go to the Place de la Bastille, then by bus to the famous Arc de Triumph with the tomb of the Unknown Soldier and experience the grand spectacle of the daily changing of the guards. What a magnificent sight to see our soldiers in their impeccable gray uniforms marching in parade step around the star (Place de l'Etoile) The French people watch curiously. Then the whole troop marches along the 2 km long street, the Champs Elysees to the Naval Headquarters. I eat lunch at the Café de la Paix and look at some of the sights of Paris. I walk up close to a third of the Eiffel Tower, about 200 steps. To climb all the way up takes about 1 hour. Then I go to the Dome des Invalides to look at Napoleon's Tomb and slowly work my way back.

In less than an hour I am back in Etampes, I report to the regional headquarters and find out that I have been assigned to the 5th Unit, which means I will stay close to Paris and not be moved to southern France, as I had hoped. In the darkness I find my quarters, get my 2 blankets and sleep on the hard floor with a few other scattered soldiers. One guy is coughing all night and I cannot get to sleep. Just fall asleep close to morning for a couple of restless hours.

In this war one gets hard. I go to the office of the "NAFUE" and find out, that I am assigned to a special teaching post as an instructor, directly to Corbeil. So I pack my stuff again and go back to Paris.

20, January 1941

I go to the FLUKO (Air Watch Detachment) in Paris and meet up with old buddies and some of the young recruits. At night I take a train from the Gare de Lyon to Corbeil. I leave my backpack at the station and only take my suitcase. What will await me? I get there wringing wet and report to Lt. Kreske. I have the feeling he is a decent guy. He shakes my hand and I get my quarters. At first I am disappointed when I see the primitive wooden bed, but the central heat and running water make up for it. I will get along well with comrades Hein and Schwartz. Tomorrow I will have my backpack brought over.

The first surprise, an orgy of drinking. I am appalled! How can these officers drink like this, champagne, schnapps and beer? They literally swim in alcohol. I stay away as far as I can. This is disgusting!

21, January 1941

My duty begins and is not too bad. I am not killing myself. Immediately I write the new address to my loved ones. It is: L 06077/A. When will I hear from them?

Every Sunday there is a market with pretty good things to buy. I pack a package for my father's birthday with the cigarettes and cigars I have collected as well as six handkerchiefs.

I also meet Major Diffenhart, who takes notes during our talk. Maybe he will be influential in helping my predicament of always getting passed by at promotion time? I hope so!

27, January 1941

The food is good; it is prepared by a cook and served by French waitresses. They are constantly building and these barracks look like they would be here forever.

At 11 o'clock is "Lights out!"

30, January 1941

I am considering the purchase of a blue suit and a gray coat for Norbert. When we march over the bridge of the River Seine singing, the French people watch curiously. I must admit our old soldiers are still pretty sharp.

31, January 1941

Father's Birthday! He is 64 years old today. I think of him and wish him all the best.

Today is an inspection by Lt. General Dr. Weissman and Col. Von Wech. It does not faze me. The whole inspection was a ridiculous fuss over nothing.

2, February 1941

I still don't have any mail from home and I am getting a little worried. After making a phone call I found out that this idiot from the postal service in Etampes returned all my mail instead of forwarding it! Now I really have to wait! Hopefully no one is sick again! I will put in for a day of leave to go to Vire, as I want to purchase there a sweater, some wool, and a sweat suit.

It has snowed again and is bitterly cold.

4, February 1941

I am in Paris and try to get a train from there to Vire, but find out that the last one left 10 minutes prior. What to do now? I decide to stay. Spend an hour in the Luxor Hotel and then visit the magnificent church Sacre Coeur on the hill of Montmartre. I decide to go to dinner in the soldier's mess hall. Well, that was a mistake. The food was horrible. In the afternoon I go and see the famous Moulin Rouge with its fancy show of beautiful nude women. But I like the pureness and naturalness and have before me the picture of my lovely wife. In the evening I sleep in the hotel Chateau d'Eau, cheap and clean.

6, February 1941

After my return I immediately check for mail. Nothing! My God, now I am quite worried and don't know what to think.

7, 8, 9, February 1941

These were three days of torture! I ask every day, but nothing. I am shaking and so upset, I cannot concentrate on anything. Daily I am mailing a card with my concerns.

10, February 1941

Finally! What a relief! I get a whole stack of letters at once, among them a letter from my mother. What a burden off my shoulders! I am in a good mood again.

From now on the mail gets here daily. My little sweetheart writes me such cute little letters, almost without mistakes and that pleases me so. Why do I have to be so far away from my children?

15, February 1941

What is wrong with me? I could not get up this morning after a terrible night. I am running a fever. Maybe I have the flu? I stay in bed all day. At night my temperature went up and my back and knee joints hurt. My eyes feel hot and I think my head is splitting apart. I toss and turn in bed and the hours are just crawling by. I take an aspirin, but I have not felt this sick in a long time. Of course I cannot work and I am lying awake for hours. I am also starting a painful, dry cough. The fever stays high and I am very restless.

16, February 1941

What a horrible night! My bed is hot like an oven, probably from the fever. I was awake from 3 to 7 o'clock, in addition to that, the inconsiderate people! One is constantly playing his accordion another smokes his disgusting pipe! Oh, if I was only well again! What a boring Sunday! I try to get up a little around noon, but I have no appetite. Now also my nose is getting all stuffed up and I look sick!

17, February 1941

My buddies made me go to the doctor. I am concerned to walk in the icy cold air with a fever. He examines me, gives me a shot, and says: "This will help get you back on your feet!" He checks my lungs, prescribes some pills and I go back to bed.

The sickrooms are overcrowded, and not enough care. I take my own temperature and it is up again. During the night I am very restless and almost constantly coughing.

18, February 1941

Today I still have to stay in bed. My throat still burns and very dry. I spend a whole day in sick bay, periodically, I would get up. I was totally fever free during the night. When the Lt. saw me, his face had the look of pure displeasure, which left me cold. This morning I have to see the doctor again, he is quite a nice young man. He does a quick exam and tells me I am OK. I still feel weak, but this afternoon I will try to go back to work.

And indeed that afternoon I experience the sad humiliation by this rude young inexperienced "punk". What is going on? Is my appointment for promotion to officer in question again? I am getting to the point of just not caring anymore.

20, February 1941

My health seems to be slowly getting better. However, I was sick a day longer than anticipated. Today was my first day back at work.

21, February 1941

After the beautiful spring weather we've had, today it snowed the entire morning.

24, February 1941

Fasching (carnival)! I did not notice anything about it. Why can I not be home with my children? At this hour maybe Norbert and Helga are going from house to house all dressed up in their cute little costumes. How I would like to give them a big hug! Why do we have this idiotic war? I am utterly discouraged and disillusioned!

28, February 1941

I still have my hopes up for March 1st. Will it fulfill my long awaited hopes?

1, March 1941

Of course not! I become indifferent, dull, brooding and depressive! I am just glad the food is good and so is my bed. The duty is not too bad. One has to be very tolerant though of one's roommates and their idiosyncrasies like Höning with his stinking pipe and Ellwitz with his guitar and accordion.

6, March 1941

Travel day for all of us. I am putting in for leave time to go to Vire, but Capt. Jetter does not want to authorize it. I drive to Lieusaint to speak with him personally. I find out, that my papers seem to be correct and I am hopeful again. The captain is very nice to me and I am feeling so much better. In the evening I go back with Keller and we go to a movie. It is the only thing we have for amusement in Corbeil.

8, March 1941

In the morning at 9:50 o'clock I drive to Paris and since the weather is nice I visit some of the parts of the city I do not know yet, like The Latin Quarter, the Sorbonne University, the Pantheon and the Odeon.

Rösel wrote me on a card, that my sweet little "Murschel" waits daily for a letter from me.

Here is a little letter, which Helga dictated: "Dear Papa; guess what! Yesterday I rode on a donkey. I also got to lead him to go to the vineyard, but he was blind on one eye. I am your "Herzekind" (child of your heart) your "Hamuchen" (little moo-moo calf) your "Vögelchen" (little bird), your "Murschel", your "Hexchen" (little witch), and your "Lausemädel" (tomboy). I will go to school soon. Can I have a backpack from you? I think of you every night and send you lots of kisses. Come soon and bring us pretty things, for me a doll carriage, greetings from your "Häschen" (little rabbit) and your "Lämmchen" (little lamb) and your "Rehchen" (little deer) and your "Füchschen" (little fox)".

Oh, that a horrible world will bring so much sorrow and suffering to mankind! Only because a few idiots want this war, all the innocent people have to suffer. When will peace be ours again? I have noticed that the French people live more sensibly than we do. They are more appreciative and more family loving than we are.

Things are getting worse here in France as well, especially the food supply and everything is getting more expensive.

9, March 1941

I go on an early train to Montparnasse. The area is not unfamiliar to me. I find a place to stay and get some food stamps. Then I take a walk down to the beach to see the ocean for the first time. The water was smooth but a light breeze created a gentle surf. I collect seashells for the kids and take a few pictures. Then I climb up the bluff and watch a rather large ship leave for America. I see the sunset and the thrill of this majestic beauty is incredible. Then I buy a few souvenirs, a Norman fisherman, and soap bubbles for the kids. Then I had an excellent dinner at a very nice Servicemen's Center and later watched women in the market place sell baskets of mussels and oysters.

Went to the casino for a little bit and watched a show, the girls of course in the nude. I sleep in a primitive hotel, set my alarm clock for 6 am, go to the train, and am back in Vire 2 hours later.

10, March 1941

This is my brother's birthday! It is so sad, that we don't have a better relationship! I wonder if this will ever change!

I say hello to the old buddies and hear that everything is OK. Wool and sweat suits cannot be found anymore. I pay a visit to the Legalle family and they are glad to see me. I sleep in the Hotel d'Auton and plan to leave in the morning this time to Bucil. It is beginning to rain.

11, March 1941

Bucil is a poor little town. I drink a café au lait and eat some bread then I try to find the military cemetery, but I cannot find Rudolf

Gödtel's grave. I walk to Garennes, see the old mayor and receive his permission to look at some papers and books, but cannot find any clues or information.

Then I walk to Ivry la Bataille in the beautiful spring sunshine, always thinking of my loved ones, my German home and there always is the homesickness. There I find a Frenchman with a truck who gives me a ride to Dreux. I take the military train back to Paris and from there without too long of a layover, back to Corbeil. Although I have overextended my leave time by several hours, no one has even missed me.

12, March 1941

A new course is starting. To my surprise Captain Jetter assigned me as platoon leader. I have the feeling he may be of help to me.

16, March 1941

What a beautiful spring Sunday! In the afternoon I go for a walk along the banks of the Seine River. I find an empty bench, read in my book, and am in my world of thoughts, which are always turning home.

Papa relaxing by the Seine River

In front of me the picturesque valley of the Seine, the lovely town of Corbeil, nestled in the valley. I sit here for a long time in the warm spring sun.

When I get back at night I am called to the phone. It is Capt. Jetter. I answer by saying: "This is NCO Herzog". He answers: "Wrong! Make that Sgt. Herzog!" He congratulates me, but I am indifferent. A silent anger builds up in me. What should I get exited about? Now all of a sudden there is a big hurry to have to put on the new stripes. But I take my time. A French seamstress puts them on but does a lousy job. How long do I have to wait now, to become Lieutenant? Maybe another six months?

18, March 1941

I salute the major with my new stripes, as he just happens to walk by. He congratulates me but only halfheartedly and because it is a formality. I can tell his heart is not in it and he is not sincere. He tells me that after June 1st he will make a recommendation for me, before it would not be possible. Well, I know all about that and I am furious!

My only bright moments in this dark and miserable life are the letters of my beloved wife and my son as well as the sweet scribbling of my "Murschel". I keep everything.

25, March 1941

Slowly the park turns like spring. The food is still good. Tuesdays and Fridays we go to the movies. It's the only relaxation we have. They show mostly old movies, but that's OK. I like talking to the owner of the movie theatre and thereby improve my French.

1, April 1941

The weather turned very cool again and is very changeable. Lt. Hokloska is a very nice young man and likes talking to me and we get along quite well.

During the past few days the pact with Yugoslavia became effective, but two days later the government was thrown out by a coup in Belgrade. English sympathizers are at work. Young King Peter is crowned and the unrest and persecutions of the Germans is starting.

It won't be long before we will be moving in there.

5, April 1941

From time to time I send cigars to my father, and mother spoils me by sending her wonderful homemade cookies, which I loved so much as a boy.

6, April 1941

Palm Sunday

I wonder how things are at home? Now at this time my school kids are sitting in church being confirmed and I am not there. Rösel is in Sembach for 2 days to help Rettig's and Norbert goes to visit his grandparents and eats his meals there. I hear from them all about the delicious food and wonderful cakes they had for confirmation.

This morning early, German troops crossed over the Yugoslavian and Greek borders. Hard and bitter fighting ensued.

13, April 1941

Easter

I had made a request for a furlough in Paris for the Easter Holidays. Upon waking up I concentrated on my loved ones at home. My first sight is the wall to the right of me, where the pictures of them are hanging. Everyone loves the enlargement of Helga and they say: "What a beautiful child!" I am so proud of my two kids!

May heaven keep them for us, so we can have a lot of joy with them! I get ready very carefully and go for a walk amongst the lovely trees in bloom. Now at this hour they will be looking for Easter Eggs.

I am so very intensely connected with them in thoughts that I have to make an extreme effort to pull myself away. What's the use? In Paris I usually eat a very good dinner in the Café de la Paix. Even though it is a little expensive. In the afternoon I go to the Follies Bergere, where I saw a wonderful show with magnificent costumes. Tonight I will eat in the "Soldier's Center" to save some money.

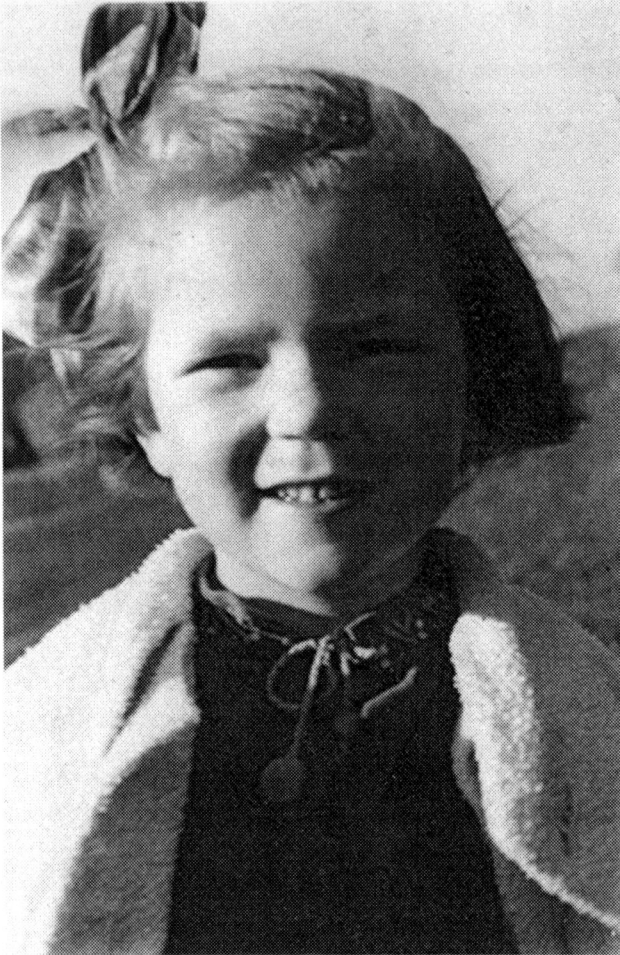

Helga at 5¾ years of age

14, April 1941

2nd Easter Day

I spend an afternoon in the lovely Bois de Boulogne. I watch the Parisians spending time with their kids and pets with blankets on the lawns and they picnic in the warm spring sunshine and it breaks my heart that I can't be with those I love. They are people just like us and again the insanity of this war comes to my mind again and how only fools could start something like this and involve all the innocent people.

The children romp and play catch; the young lovers kiss unabashedly, and take little boat rides on the small lake. Oh, if I only was in Bad Muenster and could take a boat ride with my family.

There are many soldiers. I stay quite a while and make conversation with a few old French people, who are all very friendly and nice. Later on I take the subway back to the city and at night see the theatre performance "Das Land des Lächelns (The Land of Smiles)", which was done quite nicely and left me deep in thoughts.

15, April 1941

I visit Breunling and we share old time memories, have to think of Feil. We have a nice dinner together in the Hotel Montcalmes. The afternoon program is to climb the Eiffel Tower. I get off at the Trocadero Metro Station and start climbing. I do not pause and continue this tremendous experience. The higher I get, the colder it gets, and the more tired I am. I grasp the railing and do not dare to look down the dizzying heights. I make it up with my last bit of strength. There is graffiti everywhere with thousands of German names, a lot of "Pfälzer's". The view from up here over this magnificent city is overwhelming and I stay a while.

I go with Zimmermann to the Montmartre where we want to see the famous old cemetery, which unfortunately is closed. We eat supper at Chez Weiss, an Alsace Lorraine restaurant and go back to Corbeil at 8 o'clock.

This was my Easter 1941.

16, April 1941

Yesterday I returned from Paris, today we begin the 5th training course. It would not be too bad here in Corbeil if it were not for the homesickness and no expectation for a furlough.

17, April 1941

One ray of light in this dark existence is always the mail from home. There are Norbert's letters and the sweet scribbling of "Murschel". Then I sit quietly by myself and try to imagine I was home again.

18, April 1941

The people from the training course have been grouped. I am supposed to conduct the officer's seminars for my organization. Finally this will be a job that gives me some incentive.

20, April 1941

I had mail from home. My parents wrote that they moved into the little room upstairs. Maybe they have it nicer there and more peaceful. Oh, how I would love to be home again to see my father's house with it's rooms and the garden, where I spent the years of my youth.

The war in the Balkan States began Palm Sunday and ended after 3 weeks.

My new Address is: Sgt. Eugen Herzog
L 06077/ A
L.G.P.A. PARIS

23, April 1941

Slowly the weather turns more spring like. Our lodgings are wonderful, the food excellent. Yes, our Otto, he knows how to cook! I received a darling letter from my little sweetheart. She dictated it word for word to Mama: "Darling Papa: We received the last card, the one with the little girl with the curls and the doggie and the boy hanging in the trees with his pants torn. The girl says to him: Why can't you get yourself down from that tree? Your package with the dates and the cup has arrived. I do not like to eat the dates. Mama and Norbert like them. I am looking forward to sleep with you when you get home. We are all looking forward to your coming, but me the most. Please send us some goodies for snacking. Now it's enough. Auf Wiedersehen my darling Papa! Greetings and kisses your "Purzelhund" (can't be translated, something like "cute puppy")".

Oh, what a sweet little precious girl. How she must have changed. I wonder if she still has her childlike qualities? This sad and miserable war, which robs me of the most beautiful years of their lives! But I do not want to complain, because I have my health.

30, April 1941

Once in a while I take a trip to the company in Lieusaint. I would not want to be there as it's a poor little town. At least here, on Sundays, Tuesdays, and Fridays I can go to the market and buy some things. I have sent about 30 packages home so far, fabrics, clothes, spices, cigars, magazines, coats, and clothes for the children, sweaters, stockings, etc.

1, May 1941

Memory of May 1st last year in Rüdesheim and a whole year has passed. Oh, what beautiful days those were. I still remember Café Reichsadler and the walk up to the monument, etc. Back then we had hoped I would be home a year later.

Instead this war continues unmercifully. There is bitter fighting going on in Tobruk. Why can't we make any headway there? A huge number of troops are at the Russian border. And now there is talk, that America will become involved.

3, May 1941

When will this war come to an end? I look forward to the day when I receive mail from home and I am happy when I know that all are well and healthy in Hochstätten and my parents in Sembach. My mother writes to me constantly and I am glad that they are happy in their little room upstairs. It breaks my heart to see the French people go for walks with their children.

7, May 1941

Although I do a good job in my position, make sensible and mature decisions they do not promote me any faster. It is the whole mentality and inner insincerity of the military.

8, May 1941

My Mother's Birthday, She Is 62 Years Old Today

I think of her, this good woman, who has bravely worked so hard all her life and has received so little reward. I can only wish her with all my heart, that she may have a long fulfilled life in good health and enjoy her children and grandchildren. I had sent her a package with coffee beans, which I had saved for this occasion and told her to have a nice afternoon with some cake and coffee with father.

Rösel wrote that Norbert had bought a blooming potted plant for his grandmother. They also brought flowers for Rösel for Mother's Day, which happened to be the same day. They are both so sweet and kind in their character, something that is inherited within. My sweet little "Murschel" said a poem which went like this: "On Mother's Day I come to you to wish you happiness and joy, the sun shall always shine for you and never should you be sad!"

12, May 1941

Today is sharp shooting. Before we left I received a long letter with a little note from Helga. The child writes so cute and draws her darling pictures. There also was some sad news that Fritz Hinkelmann fell in Tobruk.

14, May 1941

Inspection! Major Diffenhard and Major Lücke are in charge and we are all a little nervous. I wait in the sunshine on a bench outside until it's my turn. Then I give my presentation: "Structure of the Air Force". I did such a good job that Major Lücke shook my hand afterwards and Major Diffenhard expressed his appreciation to me later. He told me my class was excellent and he was pleased, that I covered the most important things. In the afternoon he is very friendly to me and I wonder if this will be an advantage for me.

16, May 1941

Today we have an easy day after we have a "slaughter festival". Our poor little pig! What a meal we had in the yard. We live truly high on the "HOG". There was talk of a possible furlough, but now a new course is supposed to start. I am so sick of everything! I heard by mail that Karl Krell is in Africa and Otto Kratz was in the fighting in Greece.

22, May 1941

A year ago I was in Halle!

The weather is getting nicer, more spring like and the trees are beginning to bloom. Norbert and "Murschel" write such darling letters to me. The boy does not write in a bad style, almost perfect spelling and I am well pleased. Only his punctuation needs some improving. It bothers me to no end that I can't be his teacher or have him in my classroom. I would be able to pass on so many things to him, that I received at that age; for example, the basics of geography, the German language and literature. This is all because of this miserable war.

28, May 1941

Tuesdays and Fridays we go to the movies. They mostly show old German movies. The cherries and currants are ripening. How I would like to be home and taste them from our garden. Actually my work is not too bad and I get a chance to go for a lot of walks. I have bought a raincoat for Norbert and a cute little hat for Helga.

She enjoyed the package with the pearls and sponge.

31, May 1941

My sweetheart writes how they spent Whitsuntide/Pentecost at home. Helga wears the new dress and socks I had sent her. They go on a trip to the top of the Ebernburg Castle, drink apple juice, ride on the merry-go-round in town, and go back home at 7 pm. The next day they want to go to the Altenbaumburg Castle and then want to walk to Huttental, which is quite a little hike. "Murschel" says: she won't mind to walk that far. After that, they took the train to Bad Muenster, rowed a little boat, and went the playground.

Helga and Norbert enjoying the playground

She is so darling with her letter writing, always writing numbers, and making drawings.

1, June 1941

One becomes so dull. I have not been home now for New Years, Easter or Whitsuntide/Pentecost. We get up later and receive regular bean coffee. We also have slaughtered a pig again and get pretty good meals. In the afternoon I walk along the Seine River and read my book. So the days are passing with not too much excitement.

3, June 1941

Rösel writes that she is still not decided, whether to send Norbert to high school or the middle school. On June 23, is the entrance test. This is a difficult decision. What are we going to do? I would so love for him to follow in my footsteps and become a teacher, a profession I love with all my heart. She asked his opinion. And yes, he would like to be a teacher, but wanted to be in my class for at least a year, but also heard that he might be able to get a scholarship. I am so undecided. In the meantime I get a letter in which Rösel writes, that he is sick again. What is it this time? I am worried again.

12, June 1941

My buddy Zimmermann is going to Halle for a five day course. Now I have the very nice room #8 all to myself, which I don't mind at all. The bed is not the greatest though; it is too hard. I would rather sleep on a French bed. Otherwise, everything is OK and the food is good.

13, June 1941

I always have to draw up new Service Plans. One perceives that there is no system here. To make a long story short, it is not satisfying any more to present my curriculum.

14, June 1941

The buddies from Halle make a very good impression. We often go to the Service Center for some good food and drink.

15, June 1941

I had requested a special furlough and hoped to catch a flight in order to be home for Norbert's exam, but my request angered the captain and it was not granted.

During the evenings I usually sit by the Seine and read my book "Um Mannesehre" by Schröder.

17, June 1941

Some rumors are going around about tremendous troop concentration in the East. Others think Russia does not look too bad but I don't believe it.

There are a lot of begging Frenchmen.

18, June 1941

None of my former pupils, who in previous years had sent birthday greetings, did not. This time only Johann Rettig thought of me.

I am still alone in Room #8.

19, June 1941

My Birthday

A couple of days ago I received a card from my mother and a package with cookies she baked herself. It was a beautiful day, I felt happy and cheerful. I go for a walk in the afternoon and sit in the sun in my swimsuit.

As of yesterday we have an almost tropical heat. 34C degrees in the shade and the nights do not cool down either. I sleep uncovered with nothing on. I wonder what it is like in Africa?

22, June 1941

Today The War With Russia Started

What insanity! What is going to happen now? We still have this terrible heat, a lot of French people swim in the Seine River.

23, June 1941

All day long I think of you, my dear boy. Today is the day of your big test. I wish you lots of success and that you may pass it. Surely you will be nervous, but Mama said, she rehearsed the lessons with you and you did real well. Today I received a sweet letter from her with the first rosebud for the season. Before falling asleep I look one more time at his picture, this good kid!

25, June 1941

The time of roses, strawberries, tomatoes, and cherries

How I would love to be home! Last night I dreamt that Norbert failed his test and I was very sad. Sometimes one has such days. I am waiting impatiently for news.

26, June 1941

Still very hot! After a thunder and lightning storm last night it cooled down just a little bit. At 10 am, 1ˢᵗ Lt. Rohr informed me, that I am being transferred. This sort of thing always happens too fast and unexpected. I finish packing a few packages to send home, pack and sleep for the last time in Corbeil.

27, June 1941

This morning by car to Paris, then at 5 am by train, a 2½ hr. ride, to Rouen. I was picked up and brought to the Hotel Dieppe, where I slept very well. Reported to Capt. Wolf and ate lunch at the mess hall. The apartment is beautiful. I did some sight seeing in town, the cathedral, the harbor, the destroyed areas.

It's hard to say, what this will be like, but I am very depressed.

29, June 1941

A summer Sunday! Oh, how beautiful is nature! I slept well in the little attic room and my first and last thoughts are my loved ones at home. Had some coffee in the Guard Room #19, instructed the French "Femme de Menage", and controlled the guards. However, the French cuisine leaves something to be desired! In the afternoon I read and wrote letters in my little room.

30, June 1941

Today is my first trip to the squads on guard. It won't take me long to get adjusted. It will take a long time though to get my mail now and I am so anxious to hear if Norbert passed his test. I meet people here I had known in Wiesbaden and Corbeil. I better not even think about furlough, I have become so complacent. What a crime is being committed here. I don't even know what my children look like. And all the other unreasonable demands that are made of us. Then people are amazed about the sorrow in the world, the many divorces, the unfaithfulness of husbands, etc. They should let us go home. The injustice, that has been done to me can never be rectified, not even a promotion. One is only a number here. I am just glad that I am out of this barracks atmosphere, for two years I have been aggravated with that.

1, July 1941

The trips to the control stations are far, but our Olympia car is in great shape and so is the driver. Occasionally we have to drive deep into Normandy. We were scheduled to go today, but gasoline is to be rationed. Also we are to listen to secret orders. The heat is horrendous especially in the car. We stop for a beer in the soldier's mess hall in Evereux.

3, July 1941

Today I did not go on a trip, but straighten the place up, tidy my closet and move my stuff in and make it comfortable and cozy for myself. There is also enough work in the office. But the food has to improve.

4, July 1941

They are really rationing the gasoline. Maybe it is desperately needed on the Russian front. They are making splendid progress crossing the

Duena and capture Witebsk. In the Ukraine our troops are advancing nearing the "Stalin line".

5, July 1941

Today we drive to the control stations #20 and #21. In Mortanie we eat lunch in a small inn. It is still terribly hot and on top of it, we had a flat, oh well!

If only the food at Madame Suzanne's was better. These women don't know how to cook. The salad is sour, the sauces terrible!

10, July 1941

When I give my class they are all amazed; they are not used to this kind of teaching. I am teaching right now about general promotions. I also want to give them a test about weaponry.

11, July 1941

I am so proud, that Norbert passed his exam. Rösel wrote in detail and I am so happy for him. He will start school in fall. Never will I forgive these idiots, that they have deprived me through this insane war of the most beautiful and important things in life.

12, July 1941

We have increased alert readiness. Why? Maybe it is because of the French National Holiday tomorrow? There is fear of parachutists.

14, July 1941

French National Holiday - Bastille Day

It is very quiet. Demonstrations are forbidden. Some fanatics wear red ties or carry red flowers in their lapel that's all.

16, July 1941

Today we were informed the major plans to come tomorrow for inspection. We figure we better check out control stations #17, #18, #20, & #21. It is a long trip and we get home late at night.

17, July 1941

At 10 o'clock precisely Major Diffenhart arrived. I gave my report and we inspected control stations #17 & #18. He was pleased. He should be and had to be approving. He was friendly, even invited me to eat with him. That was of course an honor. It was a lobster dinner for 5 Marks. I tried very hard to make a good impression and for the first time I saw the guy laugh. In the end he shook hands with me and said: Auf Wiedersehen!

20, July 1941

At home there will be strawberry season with all the wonderful fruit, ripe and ready to pick in the garden. The children are often in Sembach with the grandparents. Mother and father are still doing fine, thank God! Mother writes that Norbert has turned into a strong boy. He rode his bike to Breunigweiler to get a basket of cherries. Helga is tall and thin.

22, July 1941

Now I have nothing else on my mind but furlough. I imagine how wonderful this reunion will be how I will hug and kiss them, roughhouse with them and have them come to my bed in the morning. Oh, how I wish this time would come soon.

On my nightstand I keep an envelope with the little cut off hairs of my sweet child Helga.

23, July 1941

I am still hoping for the chance of furlough for the birthday of my little "Mouse". But now it is too late already.

24, July 1941

Today is the birthday of my little sweetheart! When waking up I thought of you, my precious little girl!

Helga on her sixth birthday

You are 6 years old today! I think of your touching morning prayer: "Wie fröhlich bin ich aufgewacht, wie hab ich geschlafen so sanft die Nacht, Du warst mit Deinem Schutz bei mir, Vater im Himmel hab' Dank dafür."

Translation: How happily I awoke this morning, slept so soundly through the night, you were with me with your protection, Father in Heaven thank you for that.

On a walk through the beautiful summer morning I thought of you at 8 o'clock and that you are now waking up and Mama and Norbert are congratulating you. I wonder what you will get for a present? Rösel wrote, that they are going to light 6 candles! I am with you all day, sweet girl. It would have been your nicest birthday gift to have me come home! Well, we will make up for it, won't we? In the evening I walked through the gentle summer wind and sat up until midnight at my window, staring into the night and almost faded away with being homesick.

27, July 1941

I bought a cute little alarm clock. Last night I had a strange dream. I went home on furlough and found Helga with her head all hot and burning up with fever and rapid breathing. I said: "Oh, my God, this child is sick again!"

I am so preoccupied with the family and something has to happen. My restlessness is so great that I feel I cannot stand it.

29, July 1941

Through the days between 21st and 25th of July, I went through hell. My sweetheart wrote of troubles and dark thoughts, so that I was just beside myself. I find myself tossing and turning through sleepless nights in bed. What is going on? Then there are many days without mail.

30, July 1941

I continually call the company for permission for furlough and I am told to be patient. I wonder if something is wrong at home. I have constant headaches.

31, July 1941

Quite often I am dizzy, that must be from all the worrying. The duty is not bad and I don't mind it. I enjoy driving around with our Opel Olympia. Then there are all the good buddies in my company. I am always looking forward to going to bed in my cozy little room. Today there was another meeting about furloughs. Of course I immediately and stubbornly put in for one. The captain finally gives his consent. I do not dare to believe its true. I'm not even looking forward to it, because I fear something will happen to ruin it. If only this torturing restlessness would disappear. Also there is no mail from home, but I have to be patient.

1, August 1941

It is 2 years now that I am involved in this miserable war. The weather continues to be bad. Now that my leave time is eminent I want to do my best to leave things in the very capable hands of my replacement, who will take over for me. I have to teach a couple more classes. My bag has been packed already.

3, August 1941

Today Lt. Meisner called me and said: "Get yourself in here, you can go."

Oh, the thrill! How desperately I have waited for this. I don't even dare to look forward to it, because I am afraid, something will happen to spoil it.

4, August 1941

Furlough From 5th Through 20th August

Finally! My suitcase is heavy with aperitif bottles. The other one is in Paris with the fur. I drive in a happy mood to Couches, from there by train to Rouen. Here I get all my papers and an exam by a doctor and at 4:30 pm my train leaves for Paris. I quickly go to the hotel to obtain my suitcase. Finally Breunling comes, we find the suitcase and he helps me carry everything, we then have a glass of beer and at 11 pm I get on the train.

5, August 1941

I find a nice compartment and meet a friendly Sgt., with whom I have a good rapport, we find a bench each in 2nd class and can sleep until dawn. We ride in pouring rain through poor little towns in Alsace-Lorraine and are in Metz at 9 o'clock, then at 12 o'clock to Homburg, Kaiserslautern to Hochstätten, arriving there at 7 pm.

First of all I see Helga. My God, how the child has changed. She looks like her Aunt Tilly. She runs towards me and wraps her little arms around me. Norbert comes running in the street and we finally surprise Mama, who had just arrived by train from Bad Kreuznach and did not expect me. She had given up hope, because we had been disappointed so many times. The children want to surprise her, I go into the house, and not having been seen by anybody, I sneak into the living room. The two pretend totally innocent and do not say a word, but talk Mama into going in the living room. A restrained cry of joy and she is in my arms. I hold her and caress her and we are overjoyed. She looks wonderful and my happiness is complete. Oh, my God, how richly you have blessed me!

We have so much to talk about, but the children need to go to bed. Then we are alone and belong to each other with a passion as never before. Oh, what a wonderful woman!

6, August 1941

Early in the morning the two wake us up. I hear a bright little voice crying: "by Papa, by Papa!" She comes to bed with us and we smooch and kiss one another 1,000 times. Norbert too, who looks well and healthy greets me enthusiastically.

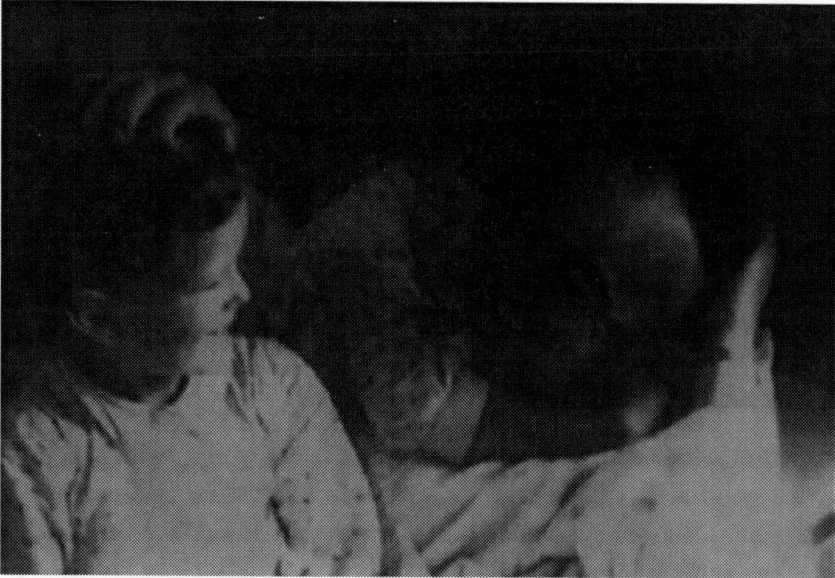

Helga and Norbert cuddling with Papa

They all out do one another to spoil me. My sweetheart is cooking all my favorite foods and they see to it, that I am comfortable. I experience a carefree wonderful day in civilian clothes.

In the evening we unpack and my treasures are admired. For Opa the gray suit and for Oma an umbrella and the silk, for Rösel a fountain pen and the 36 fur pelts, which she adored. We make little guessing games: "What's in here?" There's a coat for Norbert, for "Murschel" miniature chocolates. Everything is admired and everybody is happy.

I only wish the days would go by ever so slowly and I wish I could capture them!

7, August 1941

What a happy awakening! Norbert surprises me with his piano playing. He does so well with Mama helping him. We can even play 4 handed. My little darling wants to play too. "I make finger play," she says and plays with two fingers varying the keys. She knows how to write her name and is very proud of it.

In the afternoon I study a little with Norbert. I give him a subject for a composition and do some spelling checks. Oh, why could I not have had him as my pupil?

Today Helga gets the chance to sleep with Papa. After brushing their teeth Norbert says good night and "Murschel" cuddles in my bed next to me. We talk a little while until she gets tired. But first she still says her little prayer:

> **Du lieber Gott ich bitte Dich**
> **Ein gutes Kind lass werden mich**
> **Gib mir Gesundheit und Verstand**
> **Beschütze unser Vaterland**
> **Schütze Adolf Hitler jeden Tag**
> **Dass ihn kein Unfall treffen mag**
> **Er hat geholfen in der Not**
> **Erhalt ihn uns du lieber Gott.**

Translation:

> **Dear God, I ask you**
> **To let me be a good child**

Give me health and understanding
Protect our Fatherland
Protect Adolf Hitler everyday
That no harm may come to him
He helped us in the bad times
Keep him well for us now, dear God!

Then she turns to her side, her little head resting on her flatly folded hands, and soon I hear her even breathing telling me she is asleep. For a long time I look at the sweet little face with the peaceful smile. Oh, what unspeakable happiness!

8, August 1941

Rösel and I go on a beautiful trip to Wiesbaden and have a wonderful reunion with Gretchen. In the evening we see the movie: "A Man Rides For Germany". We have a lot of fun walking to the hotel in the pouring rain.

9, August 1941

We get up early, drink a lousy cup of coffee, and go to Gretchen's. Last night we finished a bottle of wine, which I had left there since New Years. In the afternoon we see the painter Born, where my sweetheart has a surprise waiting for me. She wants to give a belated picture for my birthday and wants me to pick it out. She saved up the money and keeps encouraging me, to be choosy. It's supposed to be for our beautiful home. We decide for a watercolor called "Pansies". She pays 25 Marks for it, sweet thing! At 6 pm we take the train back home and are met by our two kids at the station. This time Norbert gets to sleep with me. We talk for a long time in bed and I am proud, that he is so sensible. He has inherited the practical sense of his mother and that makes me happy.

10, August 1941

In the evening all 3 of us go to Sembach. I insist that the kids come too, as I want them around me every minute. We take the little wagon and quite a bit of luggage because we have to eat our meals there. We hope it will not rain. But as we get off the train, the sky is clouding over.

Helga wants to push the wagon, but because it was so heavy it tipped over in a curve, the handle hit her little fingers and skinned them on both her hands. Of course she cries but is very brave. We clean the road dirt from the wounds and wrap her hands with our handkerchiefs. I take her hand and she continues to cry for a while. Eventually I am able to distract her by pointing out all the snails along the way that have come out with the rain. Bravely she ignores the pain by continually calling: "Another snail"!

We get close to town when it starts pouring. A good thing we brought her raincoat and she looks just darling in it. A man we know from town takes her on his bike, but still her shoes and stockings get wet. Now this fear gets a hold of me again, that she could get sick. We stand under a tree for a while and then continue. The child is shaking and cold. At Tante Rettig, we get some hot water, because the pipes in the schoolhouse are broken and bathe her cold feet. Then we eat something and put her to bed. She seems happy and contented.

Then grandmother is coming and she looks the same. I am a little disgruntled because I reproach myself for having insisted to bring the child along. In the night we wake up from her crying. I automatically feel her head, because I am afraid she is running a fever. That's not it, but the pain in her hands. I try to calm her down and she is quiet for a while. Then starts crying again. I ask; does she want to come to our bed. Of course she does. I find some salve and spread it on the wounds, but she cries even harder because the salve stings. She rolls around and shakes her hands desperately. "Does it hurt this bad?" I ask. She finally says: "It does not hurt anymore". And goes back to sleep. A load has been taken off my shoulders.

11, August 1941

I say hello to friends and neighbors. I then go to the classrooms and see the miserable conditions everything is in. The children go up with me and look at books. I have some fun by letting Helga sit in the bench like a pupil and I ask her questions about the subject "How I get up in the morning". She raises her hand and answers me. It is touching.

We look for a certain book but cannot find it.

12, August 1941

Father comes to greet us and I am pleased that he looks so well. The children are spending the day at Rettig's. They feed the rabbits and help in the kitchen. In the afternoon I go to my parent's house. They are content and happy and I am glad they were able to work out the differences they had with my brother and Helene. They have a cute room and everywhere I can see mother's hand, the furniture, the pictures on the wall, the beds, and everything that is so meaningful to me. They are so happy about my visit. I walk through the garden with the children and everything reminds me of my growing up years.

13, August 1941

Today we want to go home. The child did not get sick, but she proudly shows everyone her injured hands where now scabs have formed. I walk one more time through the garden, all the rooms, which have seen our happiness, up to the attic and look across the peaceful little village, my hometown. How I love this place!

The parents come to say good-bye. We have a lot of stuff to carry. Father is more composed than the last time. Mother accompanies us. As we pass the big oak tree she leaves us. I know how she bravely suppresses the pain of farewell. She tries to smile with tears in her eyes as she embraces the children. O God, may the two of them live to a ripe old age without pain or sorrow! Then she turns and quickly walks back without turning around. From the old oak it is downhill all the way to the station. In the train our little "Mouse" leans her head against Mama and falls asleep. Opa came to meet us. They don't want to eat much, are tired, and just want to go to bed. The next day they can sleep in.

14, August 1941

Today we go to the circus. They have been looking forward to this for a long time. Mama wants to do some shopping while I take them. We enjoy everything and the two of them have a wonderful time. They see many beautifully decorated horses, which Helga loves. She comes up with an unexpected cute question: "Is the elephant dangerous"? She has only recently learned the word dangerous and uses it every chance she gets. At intermission we eat our sandwiches and pears, which Mama, as

112

always, has lovingly packed. They love the dressed up dogs and clowns. We go back downtown afterwards and meet Mama, Tante Mariechen, and Hilde. At night they tell the grandparents all they have seen and can't go to sleep for a long time.

15, August 1941

In the morning we romp and roughhouse in bed. What fun times! Norbert has grown into a nice boy. I study with him in the afternoon and find a lot of things lacking. Oh, if I could only be his teacher! My sweetheart does everything for me. She bakes cakes and my favorite, sticky buns. Oh, boy! They do not show how frugal they have to be. They send me to the garden to pick the last gooseberries and pears. Helga plays with her girlfriend Lilly and Doucy the cat.

17, August 1941

Today is a memorial service in church for Abraham Schmidt, who was killed in Russia. I dress in my uniform. In the afternoon the weather turned nice and we decide to go to Bad Muenster.

Quality time on the Nahe River

We take a rowboat for 1 hour. Norbert rows and Helga wants to try it too. We are so happy here and I have, for a moment in time forgotten that there is a war. We go to the playground, take pictures, have coffee and cake, and thoroughly enjoyed the day.

18, August 1941

The Big Day For Norbert - Beginning Of High School

Smart looking with his new backpack we go together to Bad Kreuznach. In the schoolyard he meets with some other kids his age and when the bell rings, they all pour into the building. I see just before he disappears, how he playfully grabs the arm of one of his classmates. That golden sense of humor he inherited from his Mama, her head used to be filled with thousands of little fun ideas and pranks and I hope he continues to look on the sunny side of life.

I go to the bookstore and buy a few books he needs, then take a walk up to the Kauzenburg Castle with a beautiful view over the city, and eat my sandwich, which Rösel packed for me. Then I slowly walk back to the corner, where we planned to meet. He wanted an ice cream so we go to the Salon Venezia. Starting tomorrow morning he has to go by himself. I was happy though, that I could be here for this important day in his life.

19, August 1941

One more day! Oh, I cannot hold on to the time, as much as would like to. Today I spend at home in bad weather. I bought a slate for Helga and she has fun drawing her little men, angels with wings and houses. How I would like to be her teacher! These idiots have ruined it all for me.

In the evening Rösel and I go for a beautiful walk to the top of the hillside with the picturesque little village nestled in the valley, where I have found my happiness. The smoke rises from the chimneys and nothing disturbs the lovely peace. We hold each other and talk of the good and the bad times in our 12 years together. Slowly it is getting dark and we walk back together like a young couple in love.
Tomorrow I have to leave.

20, August 1941

Farewell!

Oh, what a difficult day this is! Norbert says good-bye before he leaves for school. We want to make the most of this last day! I have to say good-bye to "Murschel", as we do not plan to take her to Bad Kreuznach. What an impatient little girl she is. She hangs on my neck, clings to me with her arms around my head and keeps calling: "Oh, my good sweet Papa!"

A sad farewell for Helga and Papa

She walks with Opa to the train and my heart is breaking, but I try not to show it. She jumps and runs and does not understand the seriousness of the moment. When the train pulls in the station she still sits on the railing and continues to give me kisses. Oh, my little sweetheart! She waves as long as she can see me.

In Bad Kreuznach we shop for a few things and I am always amazed at my loving wife, how she buys only practical and pretty things, then we wait for Norbert at the school and go to our favorite restaurant, Felsenkeller, where we get a good meal with ration cards. He shows me his homework, which he had already started and I think he enjoys the school. At 3 pm we go to see a movie. Then we slowly walk to the train station. Oh, the farewell mood is getting a hold of me. I try to suppress the pain in my heart as much as I can. We kept talking happily to each other, as to not make it any more difficult. We now have only minutes left. What is there left to say? Holding hands we realize, that we have given each other the most and the best in this beautiful furlough and we can only reassure each other of our love and to pray to God, that He may keep it this way for us.

Then comes the train to Saarbrücken. I embrace and kiss them one more time and tear myself away. From the window I can talk with them another 2 or 3 minutes, then the train starts moving. I grab their hands and they run a few steps along the train and I see tears in Rösel's eyes. I wave as long as I can see them, they get smaller and smaller, another curve and they are gone.

Now I am alone again. The train curves into the Nahe Valley and after 2 hours layover in Saarbrücken I catch the 10 pm train to Paris. I find a good seat, eat the two sandwiches my sweetheart packed for me, and quietly sit in the corner. What a horrible long night this is going to be on this hard wooden bench. At dawn I awake from a half sleep and see the dirty suburbs of Paris. At 7 am the train stops at the Station Gare de l'Est.

21, August 1941

I report back via telephone from Hotel Montcalmes, I leave Paris at 4 pm, and arrive in Evreux at 5:45 pm drag my luggage to the soldier's quarters, where my faithful driver Hartmann and NCO Schnitzbauer are waiting.

The first news is that I am to take over class #5. I also learn from a phone call that I am as of immediately, assigned to the regiment staff. What does that mean? Maybe finally I am a step ahead? I pack quickly and cannot take everything. Several things as well as a few bottles of brandy I leave behind in my closet.

22, August 1941

A sad good-bye from all the people I know including our cook Madeleine. Then we go by car to Couches, along the boring stretch to Caen. I am being picked up, and after a ten minute long ride, I am in Beueville. I report to 1ˢᵗ Lt. Dr. van Senden, as well as the other officers later. I get a very nice room at the mayor's house and the food is excellent.

23, August 1941

Sgt. Zöllner breaks me in on my new duties. Everything is quite confusing and I just hope I will be able to manage.

24, August 1941

Our Wedding Anniversary!

I see the ocean at Lion sur Mer for the first time. There is also a fancy party until 3 am. I hope this is not a preview of coming attractions! I wrote a long letter to my sweetheart.

2, September 1941

I get used to the duty and also learn to move around in the circle of officers. In the evening, I have an expensive lobster dinner. The commander is nice to me. I experience a lovely sunset in the evening on the southern coast of Britany. Went to sleep with a brilliant moonlight and an incredible view to the sea.

3, September 1941

We leave for Brest. What a dirty city! Before we get there we see through the fog, above the hilltops, a lot of barrage balloons, since the

English come here a lot. We drive down to the harbor, where there is tremendous activity and a lot to see: Military, POWs, tremendous truck traffic, so that we hardly get through. Everyone is working feverishly. High on the hilltop is the Navy War School, excellently camouflaged. Down below in port we recognize the war ships Scharnhorst and the Prinz Eugen. Soon we leave this inhospitable town and visit a flight command, where very young, sharp looking Lieutenants sit in their ME 109's ready to take off.

We go then to Morlaix and Brieux, where we inspect the installations. The commander drives like a maniac, 100 km speed and I hope he won't have an accident. We have to make the tremendous stretch of 500 km today and we keep going without stopping.

4, September 1941

I am happy to receive mail regularly from home. The class I have to give starts at 7:15 am. That's a little bit too early.

Now I have gotten to know the sea in quiet and stormy days! I have not gone in to swim yet.

8, September 1941

Helga's School Beginning

"Murschel", my little sweetheart! I was with you in my mind and thoughts first thing this morning. How I would have liked to walk to school with you on your first day. I would have taught you so much, if I could have been your teacher. I wish so much success for you, my darling, through all of your school time, my dear. May God bless you my dear child and I think you will go through your school time with ease, as I know you, because you are smart and intelligent. I can see you in your little knit dress and new backpack. Oh, it just breaks my heart that I cannot be there with you. I wish you the best, my little "Mouse".

13, September 1941

I drive with the regiment commander to Cherbourg for the day. We are there in two hours. From the hilltop we see the majestic sea in quiet repose. In the harbor the fortress and jetties are destroyed, also the Navy Arsenal. There are daily aerial attacks. Also while we eat lunch, but we do not go to the shelter. In the evening we go back a different way.

14, September 1941

24 years ago today I started my teaching profession, which has only brought me joy and fulfillment.

Today I am in charge of a group, which I accompany to Lion sur Mer. We spend the afternoon at the beach and a few of them go in swimming. In the evening it cools down and we go to a movie after I ate a tough steak in a French restaurant bought with coupons. At 10 pm we return.

24, September 1941

Today Kiev Was Captured

I enjoy so much reading the letters from my sweetheart, especially when she writes about the children. Norbert gets just average grades; sometimes, they are good ones. Helga, my little "Murschel", looks at school as a game. But that's OK. She draws her printed letters and little pictures diligently, but sometimes with big sighs.

28, September 1941

A rainy Sunday and the "gentlemen" drive as usual, to Lion sur Mer to go drinking. I am minding the place. Last night the English tried a landing attack by Lion sur Mer, two people were killed. We have alerts more often now. I love looking at the sea, especially with the roar of the surf and the evening stars shining over Le Havre.

30, September 1941

Quite often I am invited to the mayor's house for a glass of wine and a chat. I can improve my French and the people appreciate that I make an effort to speak their language and they are very nice.

2, October 1941

Yesterday I received a package from my sweetheart with her home baked cookies and two papers from Norbert with math and English. He is having a bit of a hard time, poor guy. Tonight I am on duty; the others go to Lion sur Mer to party. How I would love to go home again for 2 or 3 days.

Helga is the smallest in her 1st grade class of 15. She likes sitting in the front row. She had to tell the story of "Heinerle im Storchennest". (Translation: Little Heini in the Stork Nest") She wants to be the best in her class. She plays all by herself on the piano "So Nimm Denn Meine Hände". Translation: "Do Take My Hands".

She moans and groans about her homework though, oh, how cute she is, my little "sparrow".

3, October 1941

Today, Capt. Angrick returns from his furlough, now the boozing will begin again.

1st Lieutenant Komzak can quietly leave.

5, October 1941

Such a beautiful autumn Sunday and I have nothing from it! During the afternoon, I had some coffee on the lawn in front of the chateau with those silly "girls". As always in the evening, back to Lion sur Mer with the female assistants, and this eternal nonsense. Drinking schnapps, and beer with the girls bored to death. Did not return until 4 am.

6, October 1941

Of course we did not have enough sleep. Today the commander will be back and hopefully things will change. I heard from home that Rösel went to the doctor and she is well.

7, October 1941

I ride the bike to the ocean at Lion sur Mer. I always prefer to be alone. I watch the fishermen bring in their catch. What a gorgeous warm fall day we have.

9, October 1941

All the rooms in the chateau are to be painted an ivory color. Preparations must be made for winter.

Segschneider, Kühn, and Meisner made Lieutenant. I was passed by again. What is going on? I wish I knew. How can I have such continued bad luck?

Rösel thinks I might be able to get a furlough for the grape harvest, but I don't think so. "Murschel" wants to draw all the time. Where did she get that talent and enthusiasm for drawing?

12, October 1941

Again a Sunday with marvelous weather! Two female intelligence assistants having their usual coffee klatch.
Will I receive a furlough?

14, October 1941

I have received orders to work out a defense plan for the chateau. The commander does not give me much time, but he promised me a furlough afterwards.

15, October 1941

The plan is finished and just as I want to leave, the commander raises objections and wants me to make changes. I could go on leave later. Now that was the last straw. I am furious, but get to work.

I work so intently that I am getting headaches. Finally I finish it and race around from one place to the other to get everything taken care of. I have to bring a bunch of paperwork to the commander to sign. Now he is very nice to me and asks me smiling, if I want to go on leave now. Of course I want to.

Papa intently finishing his assigned paperwork

17, October 1941

I leave for the "Grape Harvest Furlough". It was kind of funny. I missed the first car, which was supposed to take me to the railroad station, but with the second one I make it. At 9:15 o'clock, I leave for Caen. There I take care of some orders, Sgt. Welch hands me my cognac bottles, my coat and my pistol, which he has kept for me. In the afternoon I ride to Paris. It is dark when I arrive at the Station St. Lazarre. I check out the trains for the next day and stay overnight as usual in the Hotel de France.

In the morning I leave without breakfast from the Gare de L'Est. I smuggle myself into 2nd Class, take my boots off and sleep until Chalons sur Marne. I arrive in Kaiserslautern at 8 pm, eat a salad, and make a phone call to Hochstätten with the message that the "uncle from Pirmasens" is coming. At 10 pm I get off the train and here is Rösel and Opa, totally surprised. She laughs and says: "Was that you who left a message, that uncle from Pirmasens is coming?" The joy was immense. The children were already sleeping.

I am tired, but unpack my treasures, my 6 bottles of cognac and liqueur. Then we go to sleep. How comforting this feeling to know, I am home again.

19, October 1941

In the morning Norbert comes in, can't believe he sees me and affectionately wraps his arms around my neck. He has to get ready to leave for school. He is so happy because Papa is home again. He comes upstairs one more time with his backpack to say good-bye.

Now comes my little "Murschel". Mama carries her in her little blue flowered pajama. I kiss her sweet little face with the warm fragrant skin and we hug each other affectionately as always. What a darling child! The little mouth does not stop talking. Too bad she talks in the broad "Hochstätter Dialect". She tells me all she is learning in school. Then we get up and have breakfast together, enjoying the good fresh rolls from the baker. We then sit down in the cozy room and she brings me all of her schoolbooks and worksheets. I think she will have an easier time learning than Norbert.

At 1 o'clock, Norbert comes home from school and I help him with his homework. I am not too happy with his sloppy writing though.

The weather is dreary and cold. I stay in the warm heated room. I must not think of the farewell yet. The grape harvest has not started yet.

Helga Herzog Godfrey

21, October 1941

For days Helga has a small wound on her knee, where she fell down. The wound has to be dressed, but she always makes a big fuss, and does not want anyone to touch it. She wants to remove the dressing herself and everyone has to turn around and not look, it is really silly. The wound is infected and pussy. We put salve on it and bandage it again. Afterwards, she runs around happily as if nothing was wrong.

She is so bright and tries to read everything she can find. In the evening we go for a little walk, down the old familiar lane and I explain everything and answer their many questions. I tell them how I met Mama and awaken in them love for their home. Then we go back in the cozy house and play some games. And then the beautiful evenings just the two of us together, my sweetheart and I.

22, October 1941

In the evening when the children were in bed, we went for a visit to the Kron's. At about 10 pm, the whole village is lit up bright as day. The English have dropped flares and the sound of planes is droning overhead. We quickly go home and wait. More and more flares are floating down from the sky and we are beginning to feel very uneasy. When we hear bombs explode close by, we wake the children. Norbert is in a deep sleep because he is always tired. "Murschel" is groggy, as we dress her. We wrap her in a blanket and carry her over to Laubenstein's basement. We sit in the damp, musty cellar, next to a big wine barrel. In spite of the fear and sound of the falling bombs, most likely in the area of Bad Kreuznach, she looks around happily and interested.

Finally after about an hour of us sitting there with the Laubenstein family, it gets quiet and we decide to get back home. The children snuggle back down under the covers and are glad to go back to sleep. I am now really worried and concerned about their safety at home.

23, October 1941

This morning, Norbert's train is delayed and we wonder if it is because of the bombing attack on Bad Kreuznach. He is coming home again, because of an announcement, that the train is 1 hour late. He hardly is at home, when the train comes in anyway. He runs as fast as he can to the station, but comes too late and does not make it. He comes back all out of breath and crying and I feel so bad for the poor kid. I write him an excuse for tomorrow.

My loved ones do everything to make things happy and comfortable for me, fixing my favorite foods, etc. Tomorrow will be the day of farewell again.

24, October 1941

Today I Have To Leave Again

I am down and depressed all day. In the morning Rösel, Helga and I go to Bad Kreuznach. There was no damage from the previous bombing attack after all. Thank God!

I pick up my uniform at the dry cleaners and while Rösel does some shopping. I walk through town with Helga. She wants to stop at all the windows, especially the toy stores. Later we meet Mama and go to Café Kiefer to eat cake and drink coffee. I take some pictures, and then we meet Norbert and go home on the 1 o'clock train. Then we just have the afternoon left.

I had bought a music recorder instrument this morning for Norbert. It is to be an early birthday present. I also ordered the first book of the history series he will be using in school. It is to be for his birthday as well.

All afternoon the burden of the farewell is resting on my shoulders. The little one constantly follows me around and wants to hug me. Norbert does not feel like doing his homework. Rösel has baked a cake for me and packed all my things, my sweet one. Later we play some more games and practice his recorder, which he has immediately taken a liking to, showing much patience and talent.

Later he comes in the room with red eyes. Mama asks him, if he has cried, but he shakes his head. I know that he did cry, because I have to leave again. He is so tender hearted.

When Helga sits at the edge of her bed later, and Mama tells her, that Papa has to leave tonight, she gets very quiet and the big brown eyes get moist. I listen to her little evening prayers, stroke her head, and kiss the rosy cheeks again and again. Then she turns to her side, folds the flattened hands together under her cheek, which is a habit of hers and goes to sleep.

Norbert wants to stay up and accompany me to the train.

My sweetheart snuggles against me affectionately and I know how sad she is. But we try to be strong and not show our feelings of despondency. The hours are rushing by. At 10 o'clock, the three of us must go to the station. But before I leave the house, I go back to the room where my little "Murschel" is slumbering sweetly and I once more gently kiss the rosy cheeks and have to forcefully tear myself away. At the station we still have a little bit of time, then the train comes in, I embrace them and get on. Rösel keeps holding on to my hand and walks along the moving train. I wave with my flashlight in the dark until the tracks turn the first curve. Oh this awful pain of these good-byes!

In Bad Muenster I miss my connecting train because of air-raid warning and spend an hour in a shelter. In Mainz I spend another hour in the shelter and it is slowly dawning. I dozed some and arrive at 7:30 am in Maastricht. At this time Norbert gets on his train to go to school.

25, October 1941

The trip goes fast and smooth the whole day through Holland and Belgium, a lot of factories with chimneys, coal mounds in the mining areas with everything black from the coal, the houses, the countryside and of course signs of war devastation everywhere.

In Vallenciennes, I get a bowl of stew, and then we pass Doucy, Arras and Rouen. The train is slowing down. I finally get there at night when it is dark. I call my unit and am informed, that I am to stay overnight in Rouen. That's OK with me because I am very tired. I drink a glass of wine, go to the Hotel Normandie and fall asleep right away.

At 4 pm the next day I am in Caen, where I am picked up. I report back and read something in my orders about a transfer. I wish I could go tomorrow!

1, November 1941

The French have a holiday. I have received my first sweet letter from Rösel, filled with so much love and longing.

2, November 1941

A clear and sunny, but cold late fall day! In the park the leaves are falling and in the chateau it is cold and the lighting is poor. The English have found our chateau and visit almost daily by their Spitfires. We are not flying the flags anymore as to not draw attention to the chateau. In the afternoon I go for a nice walk. I always enjoy being alone.

6, November 1941

Norbert's Birthday

Waking up in the morning I think of my dear boy. I wish him the very best, good health and success in school and for his future life. The whole day is a very special day for me and I think of him continuously. Rösel wrote and said, that she had to give him a little talking to and he promised the "blue from the sky" and that he will do better. He got an "A" in math, Mama and Oma both gave him 1. Mark, which he was very happy about.

For lunch, he wanted pancakes with grapes and plum cake for coffee in the afternoon. I wonder if next year there will be peace, and I can be there for his birthday?

On November 3rd school started again for Helga. The child complains about a sore throat. Hopefully she won't get sick. I have not heard yet.

I am still looking for shoes and wool. I finally found some shoes for Norbert and 1,000 grams of wool.

12, November 1941

There was a farewell evening before my transfer. In the officers club they "pigged out" and killed 3 bottles of cognac at my expense. Terrible! They put me on the spot to drink cognac, which I hated. Oh, my God, was I sick! Later on, someone dragged me to my room. Thank God the women left me alone. Finally, I could lie down on a couch and get some sleep. What a horrible experience. I was still sick the next day.

13, November 1941

A bad day! I still feel pretty miserable. I feel like there is a fire raging in my stomach and tearing apart my intestines. But I am leaving. Hurrah! I still have a few errands to do. I am all packed and go downstairs to wait for my transportation. I have a good talk with Sgt. Sitzman who is an understanding buddy. Finally the car comes and I have just enough time to say good-bye to everyone, then we leave.

Good-bye Beueville! I do not want to come back here anytime soon. The streets are wet from rain and we get to Paris in the evening. I get a room, eat some supper in the "Cou Cou", and go to bed tired and feeling miserable.

14, November 1941

In the morning, I meet a few comrades from previous assignments, and then I take the 11:30 am train to Troyes. It is freezing cold in the train. I meet a nice young lieutenant, a pilot, and we have a stimulating conversation about all kinds of things. I find my check in point is in a former high school. I have my luggage brought over and stay in a dirty hotel.

15, November 1941

Captain Bechler is OK. 1ˢᵗ Lt. Becker is a teacher and so is Sgt. Rose. So far, so good! The food is pretty bad though. Trying to find private quarters is a bit of a challenge. I decide after looking at quite a few places, for the Rue de la Paix #43 with 2 old ladies as my landladies. I think it will be comfortable and cozy. They start a fire in the fireplace and even bring me a hot water bottle for my bed. On the wall next to my bed I put, as always, the calendar from Norbert and the pictures of my loved ones.

**One of the pictures Papa carried during the
war of Helga, Mama, and Norbert**

This makes me feel at home right away. I have to be careful not to become gloomy and melancholy. Last week a man shot himself with his own gun. The reason: homesickness.

Oh, this miserable war is lasting way too long!

I finally received a postcard from my sweetheart and everything at home is all right. Thank God!

16, November 1941

What a dreary Sunday! Among the apartments I had considered, there was one I almost chose over this one, in the Boulevard Danton #22 with a nice bathroom. I don't know yet if I will stay here, even though the people are very friendly. The room is clean and I do have running water.

17, November 1941

I decide to stay here until at least 1ˢᵗ of December. I am assigned to the Flight Command's Night Officer. The long night duty is pretty miserable plus the food is not very good. In January we are supposed to get 140 German Air Force female personnel.

2, December 1941

I have not written for a while. The department commander was here briefly. I received some of my winter equipment and turned in some things like my overalls, ammunitions pouch, and flight cap. Will I be chosen this time? I have given up all hope!

The children have pulled out the Christmas Calendars and made an Advents Wreath.

Oh how I wish I was home!

10, December 1941

The weather has turned milder. I am shopping for Christmas presents for the children. It is so difficult to find something. I hope I will be able to give them some Christmas joy.

18, December 1941

I have a lot of work with the preparation of the Christmas party. I am in charge of the programming. I create a small men's choir and distribute poems and solo interpretations.

20, December 1941

We are rehearsing daily. Will I get furlough?

24, December 1941

Christmas Eve

There is a beautiful tree in the dining room; the tables are set with white tablecloths. Each soldier is receiving cookies, apples, cigarettes, a bottle of champagne per 4 men, and some chocolate, etc. The celebration is impressive. I have my luggage packed and I wait and wait and wait.

25, December 1941

1st Christmas Day

My furlough permit has been issued and at almost midnight, I check out with the captain. I happily go to my quarters and just worry that I might oversleep. At 6 am, I leave with my suitcase and packet. I sleep on a bench and although it is raining outside and pretty miserable, I don't care, because I am going home.

At 11 am in Metz, lunch across from the station, my connecting train leaves at 2:27 pm. Bensdorf, Homburg, and Kaiserslautern, where I unfortunately missed the last train. What rotten luck! I sleep in the station and spend a pretty miserable night. Finally morning comes.

This was my first Christmas day. Of course I had phoned my sweetheart.

26, December 1941

2nd Christmas Day

It is dark when I leave at 6 am. At 7:30 am, it is still dark when I arrive in Hochstätten. And there she is, my sweet loving wife. We embrace each other fervently and the joy of this reunion is immense. Only I know how much this means to her. Quietly we go home to the festive house. The tree is decorated; the house is cozy and warm, with the presents under the tree. I know how hard they worked to make this homecoming for me extra special.

Now Rösel gets the children dressed. Norbert can hardly wait to come downstairs. He greets me enthusiastically as always.

Then I shall never forget this sight in all my life: My little "Murschel" came through the door in her red velvet dress, her eyes shining and staring into the Christmas tree. There is a special glow on her little face and then she spots me. She stops for a moment and then flies into my arms. She does not say a word but just wraps her little arms around my neck, hugs me as hard as she can and gives me countless soft kisses. I have a hard time not to show my emotion and my incredible feeling of happiness. Then Oma and Opa come and we enjoy the Christmas spirit as we always have.

In the glow of the candles we sing all the beautiful old Christmas songs. I play the piano, Norbert his recorder and the others sing, with

Helga singing the brightest. Then we share the presents. I brought several special gifts from Troyes. For Norbert, a suit, roller-skates, a harmonica, from grandmother in Sembach, 5 Marks. For Helga a magnetic game, a puzzle, which she enjoys very much, a little Red Riding Hood dress and from grandmother, material for an apron, slippers and dolls, etc. For Rösel perfume and a silk scarf. For Opa gloves, cigars and a backpack, for grandmother walking shoes and other things.

We celebrate for so long that the night slowly turns into daylight. We blow out the candles and enjoy the rest of the day playing games and just being together.

I still so enjoy celebrating Christmas with my loved ones.

29, December 1941

The weather is beautiful, cold, and crisp. We go for a walk in the afternoon. The kids are having a good time, except the little one does not always mind. She cries and also starts coughing. Hopefully, she won't get the whooping cough that is going around.

30, December 1941

The doctor came and checked the child. He suspects whooping cough. Oh, dear Lord, I hope not! We have gone through so much sickness with the children. Norbert is coughing too; actually everyone in the whole house is coughing.

I find myself already counting the days to my having to depart, which I should not do. One should fully enjoy every moment of every day and not think of the farewell again. We make the best of every day. I help Norbert with his homework especially math. He is learning algebra now, and I just wish I could be his teacher. He would learn so much more. In the afternoon we go for walks. In the evening we play piano, games, or just talk.

31, December 1941

The last day of the old year. The one that was to bring us victory.

The mood is very dismal. The Russian front is collapsing. Our troops are suffering terribly in this brutal winter and tens of thousands are being killed or die of freezing and hunger. Wool clothes are collected, but they are much too late. Terrible news is reported. I am very thankful, that I am not stationed in Russia.

We do not have much winter weather, but everyone here is still coughing. We really seem to have the whooping cough here now. My poor little baby! She tries so hard to be fit and reads all day, most of all anything she can find in newspapers, magazines and signs. Tonight we gather in our cozy living room. We eat bratwurst and potato salad and glühwein (hot spiced wine). Helga goes to bed. Norbert wants to stay up to celebrate the New Year. People are quiet, sad, and depressed. An incredible sorrow has spread over the world.

We sit together, talk, and play games and soon it is midnight. When the New Year begins, we wish one another the best of everything and blessings for the coming year.

What will the New Year bring us? We hope for the victory and peace. That is our most fervent desire and much happiness for the year 1942.

P.S. A Copy of Helga's Letter:

Dear Papa;

I am looking forward to Christmas. Yesterday, St. Nikolaus came to school. I was not afraid. He gave me a little apple. It was red and good. My friend Anneelse got one too. Lieselotte Prinz did a pee-pee in her pants, she was so afraid. She was also afraid to go downstairs. Emil and Hans were led away by St. Nikolaus, because they are always bad. He took them to the bridge and then let them go again. Liesche Kuntz and Kätie screamed so loud, that Mama could her it in the house. We were drawing a picture of the St. Nikolaus.

I wrote a letter to Christkind, that it should come one day later when you come. Dear Papa don't worry I am not sick anymore. Mama made me stay in bed only one day.

We have baked Christmas cookies for you. We are looking forward when you come.

Come soon!

1,000 Kisses from your Sweetheart!

1942

1, January 1942

Furlough!

A New Year! What will it bring us? Will it bring us the fulfillment of our dreams and wishes, maybe the end of this miserable war?

It was quiet outside, no bells were ringing, as they usually would, no firecrackers, not a wintry landscape either. When the clock on the church chimed 12 times, Norbert set off one of his firecrackers. He wanted to surprise us. We wished each other the best of everything, as fervently as never before, happiness, health, and most of all, **PEACE** for the coming year. Rösel and I sneak up the stairs and kiss our sweet little girl, who was conceived in so much love. We sat together for another hour holding hands under the Christmas tree.

2, January 1942

Everybody in the house is coughing, especially Norbert, also Rösel and Oma. There is no perfect joy! Helga cheers up once the coughing attacks are over.

The child is very musically inclined, which delights my heart. She can play any tune on the piano. She also reads practically every difficult word.

Oh, why can I not be home to watch them grow up and develop. Oh, may this miserable, sad war be damned!

3, January 1942

With the 4 pm train, Rösel, Norbert, and I go to Sembach. Norbert wanted to see his friend Jakob. The schoolhouse is empty, uninviting, and cold. Norbert gets the key from grandmother and we build a fire in the kitchen to make it a little cozy. Grandmother is overjoyed to see us and immediately goes to the baker to get some fresh bread and rolls. We say hello to my father, who cannot hide his emotion and we enjoy a visit in their comfortable little heated room upstairs. I think they are quite happy there. Grandmother is happy to feed us and Norbert gets to sleep there.

Oh, home, precious home!

4, January 1942

Sunday! We slept late, until Norbert came with grandmother, who had already given him breakfast. Rösel, as always, fixes my favorite meal. We build a fire in the living room. Oh, how I would like to stay here forever. In the afternoon we visit our good neighbors the Rettig's, who serve us cake and a wonderful bean coffee, what a treat.

In the evening we see our good friends, the Gödtel's, who always out do themselves with their hospitality.

5, January 1942

Norbert looks very pale and coughs a lot. We are concerned. Later in the day we visit Uncle Friedrich, my father's brother, whose son Heiner is a navy captain, stationed on a destroyer at the Murmansk Coast.

We get home late. Mother also tries to always fix my favorite food.

6, January 1942

I meet a lot of village people who express their regrets, that I cannot be here as their teacher, because their kids are not learning anything. That makes me feel good.

I have organized books, magazines, and photos, take the "Grimm's" fairytale book for Helga with me and we start packing again. Mother in the goodness of her heart wants to give me everything, but I only accept a can of homemade liverwurst.

They fight back the tears when we say good-bye and I know she rushes back to work, crying quietly. Father stands in the street and waves with his hand before we turn the last corner. We had some new snow and the clear winter air refreshes us. I point out the beautiful colors of the evening sky to Norbert and the lovely wintry countryside.

The train is packed and when we arrive in Hochstätten, Helga has a terrible coughing attack almost to the point of throwing up. This definitely sounds like whooping cough to me. Completely exhausted, she grabs my arm and snuggles close to me, poor thing.

7, January 1942

The doctor still is not here yet. No gasoline! In the afternoon I go with Helga in the fresh air. What a bright, cute child! She asks me a 1,000 questions. She wants to hold my hand and looks so cute in her little brown coat. At home we put her red slippers on which I had brought her. Then I made a mistake and said: "Do you like the red slippers I brought you?" She answers quite indignantly: "But Christkind brought those!"

During the night she sleeps with me. After another coughing spell she says sleepily and slowly: "Handkerchief, Baba!" Then she folds her hands flatly together, tucks them under the rosy cheeks, and continues sleeping. Darling child!

In the daytime she seems OK, only she does not eat well. We constantly have to coax her. She loves playing with her dolls and reads everything she gets her hands on.

8, January 1942

We have a beautiful sunny day with light snow on the ground. We think it is good for Helga to get into the fresh air. Norbert works on his castle and his railroad station. I also give him some problems in math. He is mean and teases the child. Actually he should have gone to school today, but we let him stay home because of the cough.

I decide to go for a walk with Helga. On top of the hill the first coughing fit hits her. She wants to hide behind a wall, because she does not want people to see her. She is getting very short of breath and starts to stamp her feet. I blow her nose and she feels better; then she holds my hand.

I point out the beauty of the wintry landscape to her and we walk across a bridge, where I take a couple of pictures. I tell her the fairy tale of the "Tannengrossvater" (Grandfather of the Pines), which she listens very intently. Along the new highway she reads all the signs and points out to me where her Kindergarten is.

9, January 1942

What a horrible night this was. The poor child had such terrible coughing fits. Norbert continually coughed and Rösel and Oma have a cold too. Opa slept with Helga. When it got so bad that she had to throw up the mucus she hangs her head outside the bed all by herself and afterwards exhaustedly falls asleep. But she never cries. Only the next morning she is a little irritable.

My sweetheart does everything to make this time at home pleasant for me. She has baked donuts, which we all love. The doctor did not come again and the medicine has not helped either. How many nights and days of torture will this be for the children?

In the evening we light the Christmas tree one more time and sing all the lovely old songs. It is incredible, how musically inclined the child is.

After supper I get out the zither, my favorite instrument from my childhood and I get very nostalgic, as this is my last night.

Tomorrow I have to leave, this time maybe for a long time. We play cards, the game called "66". Oma knows it real well. The little one wants to play too. Oma gives her some cards and she slaps them on the table like an old pro. Before going to sleep I have to read her the fairy tale of "Snow White and the Seven Dwarfs". Then she says her evening prayer and I kiss the rosy cheeks with the fragrant skin.

Norbert promises me to work hard in school. He is such a dear, trusting boy, almost too soft.

Rösel and I sit together and remember the happiest times in our lives. She fights the tears. At 5 am the alarm clock wakes us.

10, January 1942

Farewell!

My sweet, precious wife has taken care of everything, as always. My bags are packed, my clothes are clean and my socks are darned, oh, how wonderful she is. She wants to fix eggs for breakfast and spoil me up to the last minute. Then I hear the child cough upstairs. I go up to the bedroom and hold her little head. She recognizes me but is too sleepy to respond. I kiss her rosy cheeks, her hair, her little hands, the feet she sticks out from under the covers and I tear myself away.

Then I say good-bye to Norbert, who bravely fights the tears. I hear the train announcement of the impending arrival.

For a long time I hold her tight and her tears are flowing freely now. I tear myself away, wave one more time and go to the station. Oh, how very painful are these good-byes!

I still have a little time before the train pulls in. Through the dawn I look to the picturesque hills with the vineyards and wonder, when I will ever come back home again. The journey continues from Metz at 2 pm, through the dreary Rhone valley and I arrive in Troyes at 7 pm.

How glad I was for the sandwiches my sweetheart had made for me. What a mood I am in!

11, January 1942

A dreary, sad, empty, and meaningless Sunday!

I am back to my flight command duty. 150 new Air Force female personnel have arrived. The captain is on leave. It will take 3 or 4 more days before I can expect any mail from home.

16, January 1942

I receive the first card from home. There is nothing much new. Everyone is still coughing.

19, January 1942

Today I bought a warm up suit for Helga. On the way I checked control stations #8, #9 and #10. The conditions are abominable. It is bitterly cold and slippery from the ice. I go to check point #12 with the last drop of gas. Oh, how freezing cold it was! My glands are swollen and I hope I did not catch a cold.

22, January 1942

The bitter cold climate continues. When we go to lunch, our eyes are burning from the cold. I hold my hands in front of my mouth so not to breathe the freezing air. The roads are slick with ice and it is hard to walk. What tremendous loneliness. Sadly I walk with my mess kit to the antiaircraft barracks to get my food. I look out the window into the dreary wintry landscape and think of my loved ones.

How are you doing, dear ones? My thoughts are constantly with you.

25, January 1942

On my nightstand are the photographs from Christmas. They help pass the dreary, boring Sunday. There are darling pictures of the children taken on the last furlough at home.

31, January 1942

Today is my father's 65th birthday! I had sent him a card with best wishes for a healthy and blessed old age for both of them.

Yesterday and today I went to the company to pick up the unit's pay.

I have to mention the bad speech by the "Führer" last night. This man is crazy! Now I have to go back to Romilly in messy snow.

1, February 1942

I had some mail from my loved ones, also a little letter from Norbert. He related the story of the one eyed horse nicely, only his script is very bad.

We have slippery roads from the frozen snow and it is bitterly cold. At night, I am glad to get to my heated room.

3, February 1942

My driver had to report back to the company, so I had to drive myself to the other checkpoints in this rotten French truck with wood gas and broken windows. I was totally frozen when I got there. I hope I won't get sick. Thank goodness I found a place, where I can get some eggs, also I was able to get a box of cheese. The roads were very slick and the trip hair raising and risky.

5, February 1942

It rained last night and this morning it is so slick that it is hard to walk. We had sweet cream of farina soup last night.

I wonder if Rösel is in Worms with Helga. Yes, I heard she has arrived there and she writes how very nice and comfortable they are there with Tante Mariechen. They are able to take hot baths and Helga's cough is much better. She plays with Hilde's dolls and is behaving herself. I am glad they are having a nice visit and some relaxation.

14, February 1942

I had some more mail from Worms. They are all well and happy. Norbert wrote me a sweet letter as well. Helga added onto Rösel's letter:

> "Lieber Papa; Ich bin in Worms. Es gefällt mir sehr gut.
> Wir bleiben noch 8 Tage da.
> Ich weiss nichts mehr. Gruss und Kuss
> Dein Julius."

Translation:

> "Dear Papa, I am in Worms. I like it very much.
> We are staying 8 more days.
> I don't know anything else. Greetings and kisses
> Yours Julius."

She seems to have inherited the sunny disposition and sense of humor from my sweetheart. I hope so.

15, February 1942

Oh, these miserable, dreary, lonely Sundays. At least I have a good radio station with nice music. I want to go to a French movie with French newsreels.

The planes from the nearby airbase fly overhead all day.

Helga eats well and I am glad to hear that maybe she will recover better there. Tomorrow they want to go home. They have been there for 14 days.

My good friend, Bolander, has died as the result from stomach surgery after being wounded in Russia. He was to go back to the Russian front afterwards. How very hard for his wife and child.

19, February 1942

I received the sad news that my cousin Salomon is missing in Russia as of December 6, 1941. He was around the area of Leningrad. How terrible, this uncertainty! If he fell into Russian hands, as an officer he was doomed. They would cruelly torture him to death.

My aunt writes: "We put everything in God's hands." If only he could have come home safely.

22, February 1942

Rösel and Helga are home now and they had 14 beautiful days there in Worms with Tante Mariechen. My little "Birdie" was not always behaving, but overall still pretty good.

28, February 1942

We drive with a French truck south from Troyes to Toussy, where the 4th Platoon staff is stationed. It is not a good trip. At 8 pm the truck broke down in bitter cold. Even though I have my coat on I am miserably cold. The truck cannot be repaired. We are stopped in the street until 1 am, when a French truck, also running on gas made from burning wood, towed us to Angillon, where the parents of the driver were very friendly, welcomed us, and made an omelet for us.

Then we wait and wait and wait, but the truck cannot be repaired. We have it towed to checkpoint #17 in St. Germain de Puis. Here we push it into a school yard and lay down in the cold barracks for 3 hours sleep. In the morning I telephone to headquarters in Bourges. No answer!

1, March 1942

Finally we find a mechanic who is able to get the truck going again. I hitch a ride to Bourges and stay there the afternoon. What a beautiful spring day! The first warm day in the year. I take a few pictures, look at the grand cathedral, go to the park, and later to our military facility.

I take a train back to Paris, change trains at the demarcation line through poor country, fallow land, and fields. I arrive in Orleans at 5:30 pm, change trains, arrival in Paris at 8:14 pm. I eat dinner at the Café de la Paix, very expensive, and stay overnight in the Hotel Provence across the street from the "Folie Bergere".

2, March 1942

I get a wake up call at 5:20 o'clock. I take the subway to the "Gare de L'Est" and leave there at 6:20 o'clock. I am tired and fall asleep on the train.

I am back to my routine. Thank goodness the driving with the old French trucks is getting a little easier as it is not so cold anymore.

5, March 1942

I had a dream that Salomon came home safely and somehow miraculously was spared. Oh, if only this dream could be fulfilled. It is raining today and I glue pictures in an album. My sweetheart writes to me now under the new air force number of my ack-ack unit.

7, March 1942

At home they had been so worried, because they thought I was in Paris during the night the English bombed the city so badly. They were breathing easier when they had some mail from me.

Norbert had to have some tutoring lessons in English, because he missed so many classes due to the whooping cough. He likes school and says: "School is better than vacation!"

8, March 1942

Helga tirelessly draws during school, filling her slate. Strange child! Her favorites are circus horses and brides.

At the moment, she is very naughty again, throws herself on the floor with temper tantrums, kicks, and screams for no apparent reason. Maybe she feels miserable because of being sick for such a long time.

Rösel has to go to the dentist with Norbert. Unfortunately they both have very bad teeth. I have sent them some toothpaste and soap.

9, March 1942

Norbert, my sweet, caring son, gets up real early in the morning before anybody else and starts the fire in the kitchen. I hope he stays like this, caring and considerate of others.

They received the slippers for him. I have been able to send quite a few things home, but soon there will be nothing to buy anymore in France and the people suffer from hunger.

10, March 1942

Today is my brother's 32nd Birthday. Oh, if only our relationship was improved. How tragic, this disagreement!

I have a lot of extra work with the transfer of the T-19 from Origny le Sec to Mesgriguy and a lot of organizing needs to be done. The cables have already been put in the ground, now comes the move. The trucks have already transported part of the equipment. Now I get the permission from Capt. Kessler for a vehicle and we go together. It is a 3 ton truck and we get stuck in a field with soft dirt. It takes us 2 hours of digging before we get out of there. That was tough and tiring work. The barracks and lookout point are already erected.

I had the unpleasant job of informing the local civilians that they had to leave the area.

At night I am always dead tired. I am just thankful that Mme. Levalle does such a nice job washing my laundry.

13, March 1942

Another beautiful spring day! At home they still have snow 2 feet high. They finally got some mail from me and were glad I was not in Paris, the night of the British bombing attack. Norbert, my good kid, asks every day, when he comes home from school, if there is any mail from Papa. I am thankful that my children seem to have inherited a faithful heart and are good natured. That makes me happy!

14, March 1942

I can now report to the CO, that the move has been completed. He was pleased with my good work. But what good does that do for me anyway?

15, March 1942

Mother went to Hochstätten. She was homesick for the children. She took a whole suitcase full of goodies: bacon, oil, 40 eggs, ham, canned sausage, bread, cookies, etc. It makes me happy, that she could help out my loved ones. Times are getting hard. They still have snow on the ground and it is quite cold. I hope she finds them all well and healthy.

16, March 1942

Today, Sunday, mother goes back home. She was happy, that they were all well. She was so delighted with the children and writes: That Helga, she is a darling little witch. She sat down at the piano and played the "Flohwalzer (Waltz of the Fleas)" with 2 hands, then "So Nimm Denn Meine Hände", and other tunes. She reads from the newspaper and writes a beautiful script. She had to write a page full of capital "W's" and she knows, that Willy is spelled with two "l's", and Wasser with two "s's". She also does math on her level real well. In the evening we played "Mensch Ärgere Dich Nicht" with 2 pairs of dice and she promptly added the points together.

Norbert too is very diligent and doing real well in English. He is so sensible and good hearted. Rösel hears only the best from his teachers. He is a well behaved boy and yesterday got his test back in German with an "A".

Nothing makes me happier than news like that and I would like to kiss him, the dear boy.

21, March 1942

The Beginning of Spring

We really have wonderful weather here, while in Germany they still have snow. I don't need to wear my coat anymore. In East Prussia they have 20 below zero Celsius temperatures. The Russian offensive has been postponed due to the weather.

Today we had sharp shooting for the first half of the unit.

22, March 1942

Spring is Here

In the afternoon I took a beautiful walk along the shore of the river all the way until just before the city.

Again I am in Troyes, go to the mess hall, where one can still get some half decent food. The days are getting longer and it stays light in the evening.

In the FLUKO (Air Watch Detachment), there is constantly building and repairing going on.

23, March 1942

Today the 2nd half of the unit is up for sharp shooting.

Papa honing his sharp shooting skills

Sgt. Reitmeier is easy on everybody. In the afternoon I buy stationary for the kids and have a few other errands to do. I always like to stop at the snack bar for a cup of coffee.

24, March 1942

Today I take the train to Romilly. Maybe I have to stay here for some time longer. Everyone envies me for the good life I lead. Really I am my own boss. But I still have not heard anything from my regiment about my promotion. It is really strange and I cannot figure it out. I have become just numb about it.

25, March 1942

What wonderful spring weather! Too bad, the French countryside looks so dreary and barren. You see nothing but notoriously gray houses, but I decide to sit in the garden and read. I also have some more work to do on putting photos in albums. This keeps me busy.

27, March 1942

I have found a place where I can get all the eggs and butter I want. Sgt. Hafke sees to it, that our room gets homey and comfortable. It is warm almost as in summer. I still have not heard anything about poor Salomon. I take a beautiful walk this evening and enjoy a magnificent sunset.

29, March 1942

Palm Sunday

The food is not good anymore in the mess hall. Nothing, but mutton meat and stew made from mutton. The French get grumpier by the day. I wrote a letter to Pfarrer Degen and asked him to say hello to my school kids, especially those who were confirmed today. Oh, if only I was home!

30, March 1942

So one day after the other passes. The "big cheese" at the ack-ack is a most unpleasant character. The food is getting worse, 3 boiled potatoes and everything is so unappetizing. We are looking forward to the new mess hall being opened. But hopefully I will get away from here soon.

3, April 1942

Good Friday

No one would know! The duty is as usual. In the afternoon it is cool and windy. Not even the food is any better today.

But I have experienced a great joy. I found out I am going to Halle on April 13th. How wonderful! Quickly I am going to inform my loved ones.

4, April 1942

<u>Easter</u>

It does not even feel like it! I bought some flowers, just so I have something green in my room. I am at home with my thoughts wondering, what they are doing. Surely the children will have checked out the nests in the garden to see what the Easter Bunny brought. I received a letter from my big boy in which he told me, that Helga still believes in the Easter Bunny. He also informed me of his report card. What an improvement even though he missed 21 days. In music, religion and penmanship he got a "B". The comments were: "conscientious, but withdrawn".

7, April 1942

Yesterday I had security patrol for 5 hours until midnight. I was dead tired. Tonight I am in my room. Around noon there was a fierce thunderstorm. Mother still sends me little packages with goodies, such as sausages and home made cookies.

9, April 1942

I have to go to a class in Halle and I am excited about it, because I plan to make a detour to see them at home. The FLUKO (Air Watch Detachment) duty is strenuous and everyone is tired.

I manage to pack also a bottle of Noisette, (Nut Liqueur) and I am scheduled to leave tonight. I am also able to bring them some eggs and butter and I know how they will appreciate these. Leaving tonight at 11 pm via Mühlhausen.

10, April 1942

The night is long. I travel together with Officer Spiess from Romilly.

11, April 1942

At the station in Hochstätten my little Helga-Mouse comes running down the road excitedly. She runs just like my mother. My goodness how the child has changed again since I last saw her. At home I unpack my goodies for them.

12, April 1942

What a wonderful day! In the morning we sit on the veranda, our favorite place in nice weather. The greenery is starting to sprout and will eventually cover the whole veranda.

We have coffee and play games; Helga is coloring in the new books I brought for her. With the 3 o'clock train, Rösel and I go to Bad Kreuznach and the children wave good-bye to us at the station. We go for a beautiful walk to the Rosen Insel (Island of Roses) where we have lots of happy memories. Rösel is wearing her new hat and looks very cute. She walks with me to the station, at 6 pm she goes back home, I get a bite to eat in the Felsenkeller and leave at 7:40 pm with an express train to Frankfurt, from there to Halle, where I arrive at 4 am.

14, April 1942

I have to get through a delousing. I meet old friends from Corbeil and I arrive just before the beginning of the classes. I move into room #26 of house #52 and everything is happening at once. There are 20 officers, 10 to 12 sergeants. I am very tired. It is very cold and we have to wear our coats. I am ordered back to the company in the afternoon and I pack in a hurry. I can get a train at 8:12 pm to Frankfurt and share the compartment with a couple of pilots.

15, April 1942

What A Wonderful, Unexpected Day

I take a "milk run train" to Hochstätten. Boy! Were they surprised to see me again. First Oma and Opa, then Norbert, the rascal, who was still under the covers, but was awake already. Then I go to Helga, my sweet little "Murschel". What a precious picture! She was still asleep with her cheeks rosy and the little mouth slightly open. The sleeves on her P.J.'s pushed up, her arms on top of the blanket. I quietly sat by her bedside, until she woke up. For one brief moment she looks at me with big eyes, then wraps her little arms fiercely around my neck. Oh, you sweet thing! She dressed herself then we had breakfast.

Mama was in Sembach, I telephoned and the children talked with her. Helga's cough is all gone, thank God, and in the afternoon we go for a walk up to the reservoir, where I take pictures of them.

Norbert, Helga, and Teddy

I point out the beauty in nature to them, every little flower we look at, the butterflies, we watch the busy ants and find a little frog, which delights them. Then we run down the steep vineyard and walk the Hauserweg back home.

Helga plays ball with the neighbor girl Irene and is happy and lively. I keep hearing her bright laughing.

I study some geography and German with Norbert and talk about the letters he wrote me. Then he plays his recorder for me and later, when it is time again for me to leave, they and Opa accompany me to the station. They happily say good-bye to me, because they know, I will come back again in a couple of weeks. At the Neuhemsbach station, Rösel picks me up with her bike. At the end of town, mother comes to meet us, too. She says they are both still healthy. It is dark when we get to the schoolhouse. We have a bite to eat with my parents, who are happy of course to see me again. Then we go to sleep in the children's room in the schoolhouse. In the morning I have to leave at 6:30 am with the bus. In Kaiserslautern a 2-hour layover then an express train to Metz, standing room only. At 7 pm I am back in Troyes.

17, April 1942

I begin my duty in the FLUKO (Air Watch Detachment) again. It will take a few days, before I will get some mail from home. I still read the "Trilogy" by Bruno Brehm, now the third book: "Neither Emperor nor King". I also spend my free time studying the French language, and trying to improve my school French.

22, April 1942

We were inoculated against typhus and as always I experience nasty pains in the chest and shoulder. I lay down on my bed, as this is my free day anyway.

24, April 1942

Today I have night duty. I talk a lot with the girls from the FLUKO.

25, April 1942

A free day today and I sleep late, but as always, I feel beaten up after a night of work and not being in any kind of routine.

The Sundays are very nice and soon the trees will turn green in the park and I can go and sit on the bench and read my book.

28, April 1942

Today I am mailing a letter to Capt. Angrick. It is almost 6 mos. that I am in this unit and nothing has happened. It is so discouraging.

The weather keeps improving and the days are beautiful. I wish I was home and could truly enjoy the awakening of nature.

30, April 1942

In my free time I often go to the day room to play the beautiful grand piano they have there. I am trying the sonatas again.

1, May 1942

There is no holiday here. In the east, the weather is thawing out from winter and the offensive cannot start yet.

My sweetheart writes that they are all very homesick for me. Helga writes touching little letters with no errors in her spelling. But often she is very naughty.

3, May 1942

I go for a wonderful walk outside of the city of Troyes, but they do not have forests like by us. Oh, how I miss my beautiful German homeland!

Mother writes me a lot and I am glad they are well.

4, May 1942

There are no more eggs to be had. Butter is also becoming rare and a kilo is now costing 5 Marks. We often go to a French movie; one good one was "Maria Stuart" in the French language. The French like to go to German films.

In Paris, assassinations of Germans frequently occur and the assassins are not being caught or prosecuted in spite of tough measures.

8, May 1942

My Mother's Birthday

She is 63 years old today. I wish her good health and rewards for her never-ending diligence, hard work and constant love and care. She received my congratulation letter. I unfortunately did not have a present for her, but I know she does not expect one.

She sent some sausage to me again, but she cannot send more than 100 grams at a time.

10, May 1942

Another Sunday! Not always is Sunday a free day. How pleasant is this FLUKO, because it is not stuck in a bunker, but where one can open the windows and have fresh air.

11, May 1942

In the evening sometimes, we go to the Soldiers Mess Hall to get something to eat. Most of the time it is always the same, a stew made with potatoes, etc.

12, May 1942

The division commander is supposed to come in the next few days. What will this mean for me, fortune or misfortune? I wait for this day with great unrest.

13, May 1942

I am supposed to take over the lecture of Sgt. Späth, who was transferred to Halle. Actually I wish the commander would attend my lecture, so he can see what I am capable of.

14, May 1942

What a day! The Division Commander Von Korff was here. What has this creep of a teacher, this Capt. Becker done to me? How can I ever forgive and forget this horrendous deed?

I am completely devastated and totally depressed. Never will I be able to forget this meanness. Is this just jealousy and resentment, that they just will not promote me, or is there a deeper reason for this?

Oh, if my loved ones only knew, just how much they have already humiliated me in the military.

16, May 1942

Now they are hypocritical and sugary sweet to me, maybe out of guilt? Oh, what low characters are these!

17, May 1942

Today Is Mothers-Day

Rösel went to Sembach a few days ago and brought some flowers to my mother. Hopefully there will be some mail in the next few days.

18, May 1942

I mail everything I don't need home, just in case there should be a transfer coming up for me. Most of all, magazines, books, empty bottles, etc. My mood is about as low as it can get. What is going to happen to me now?

I was able to get a pair of shoes and some slippers for Oma, also a pound of cocoa.

20, May 1942

Three years ago today I was drafted into this miserable war. How I have regretted this day! Today I received the news, that Norbert has tonsillitis with fever and was in bed for 3 days.

My little "Birdie" has written down a poem, which she recited for Mama on Mother's-Day. Sweet little thing!

Quite often she is not behaving though and Rösel said: "I get very upset with the child." Oh, how I wish I could go home again!

23, May 1942

Mother writes me every Sunday, so that I always get a letter on Thursdays. Fritz Rettig has received the EK 2 (Iron Cross 2 – similar to the Bronze Star).

24, May 1942

Pfingsten (Whitsuntide/Pentecost)

I think all day of home and all the wonderful trips we used to take on this very special holiday.

They would have gone to church this morning, as is customary. In the afternoon I buy some roses for the vase in my room. But I have become quite dull.

29, May 1942

When will this miserable war come to an end? In the east the big offensive is about to begin. Will it be happening soon? The Japanese are making good progress and have captured Burma.

30, May 1942

In our department is a girl, who has an incredible resemblance with my little Helga and I could imagine, that she might look like that when she is 20 or so.

31, May 1942

Today I have to take a guard detail of 10 men to the railroad station here to guard a transport of 600 Spaniards, who are to be fed on their way through here. They are to go to Germany as laborers. We see very different types of people: Teenagers as well as older men. Some with good new shoes others in rags and malnourished. They have to line up and then get a bowl of soup and a slice of bread.

1, June 1942

I wait now from day to day for my transfer, because I have put in a request. Just away from this company of pitiful characters and jealous people! Maybe I can be assigned to Scheuerpflugs's department? I would not mind.

3, June 1942

It has gotten very hot and I prefer to sit in the park and read my book, rather than go to the bars with the others to drink. This month I hope my transfer will come through. I am sending a lot of books home. I have been able to get some more butter, also some eggs, which I fry for myself at night.

4, June 1942

Sometimes I go swimming in the beautiful indoor pool and really enjoy it.

The English are flying missions to the Ruhrland with terrible bombing attacks. For instance our lovely city of Köln (Cologne) was hit badly and supposedly the whole inner city is destroyed with a death toll of 20,000. The people in the Reich are desperate and sick of the war.

6, June 1942

Mother writes that English planes have come to their area and a four-engine bomber was shot down close to Sembach. All through the night the sky was lit up bright as day from the flares. I am getting very concerned about the safety of my loved ones.

8, June 1942

Today I am ordered to the regiment. What does that mean? I hope everything will go well. The commander, Colonel Dr. Van Senden knows me and might consider giving me another chance? I hope so!

9, June 1942

My trip to the regiment: leaving Troyes at 11:35 am, arrival in Paris at 4:50 pm, arrival in Evreux at 7:30 pm. Met Capt. Angrick there and we drove to the lonely chateau. Such expectation and feverish restlessness. What is going to happen? The commander meets me in the hallway. He is cordial, shakes my hand and I am full of hope again. Then I participate in the opening party of the new snack bar. At midnight the commander breaks up the party. I sleep in a little room under the roof. In the morning I have an appointment at 9:30 am, but have to wait more than an hour, then his assistant asks me in.

A discussion, which lasted 1½ hours, followed.

11, June 1942

Capt. Becker tries to find out details about our discussion. It is better I get away from here soon. I am so looking forward to my furlough.

12, June 1942

What a scare! I received a telegram from Hochstätten saying: "Do Not Come, - Helga has scarlet fever". My poor little sweetheart! I pray to God, that He will heal her.

13, June 1942

Of course I am planning to go home anyway. If only the night was over. Tomorrow I have a physical exam and another inoculation. I run out to quickly pick up a cute little dress I have selected for her birthday, pack a bottle of champagne, and 2 lbs. of butter. I wait with great impatience until morning.

14, June 1942

I have furlough from June 14th until the 30th. The trip goes well. I arrive in Kaiserslautern at 6:20 pm, get a connection right away, and arrive in Hochstätten at 7:30 pm. No one meets my train, but they did not know I was coming.

Rösel sees me through the kitchen door and flies into my arms. Then they all greet me and I hear everything. Rösel has a sore throat.

Norbert got a diphtheria shot and ran a high fever, which always makes him hallucinate. He would grab Oma and cry: "The poor boy, the poor boy". Now he has an infected arm with thick, pussy blisters and is very pale. My little sweetheart is in bed upstairs sick with scarlet fever.

She heard my voice and when Oma said: "Who is here?" She happily says; "My Papa" and embraces me. Thank God, her fever is not very high.

16, June 1942

Monday passes mostly being with the child, reading to her, playing and talking. They are having great fun telling me about each selecting one of the little chickens as a pet. In fact, Doucy, the kitten, has taken a backseat.

17, June 1942

Helga's rash is already disappearing, only her throat and tongue are still bright red. Early in the morning when waking up, the little "Mouse" is calling: "I want Papa to come over here". Then she wants me to read fairy tales to her. I read the story of: "The Sweet Mush". She promptly repeats the entire story.

19, June 1942

My Birthday

They are all happy, that I can spend it at home. My sweetheart wakes me with a kiss. Her gifts, 2 beautiful shirts and some socks. Norbert gives me a belt buckle and 3 roses, my Helga-Mouse cannot wait to wrap her little arms around my neck and gives me lots of kisses, also a rose and a little bag of chocolates (from Mama of course)

My precious family! In the afternoon we have real bean coffee and cake, such rare specialties. They all compete to make this day extra special for me.

20, June 1942

Today I go to Ingelheim to get cherries. I am able to buy 2 suitcases full, 40 lbs. total.

Papa courting Mama on the Rhine River

Going through Bingen, many old memories of our young love in 1925, come back to me.

21, June 1942

How happy everyone is about the wonderful cherries. Helga wants to have her little plate full all day long.

Today, Norbert was supposed to go to a Hitler Youth festival in Rockenhausen, but I said: "NO"! Instead we go to the horse races in Bad Kreuznach. We see exciting races. It is very warm and carefree happy people surround us. One would think we are in the midst of peacetime, if it was not for the many wounded soldiers.

22, June 1942

Helga is beginning to feel better. She is still running a low grade fever, but her strength is coming back. After checking her temperature she will ask: "Is it a lot? Am I going to be well soon"? You sweet thing!

Norbert is doing well in school, which pleases me a lot. He is very nervous though. He has a lot of homework. They are into algebra and geometry, which does not come easy for him. Oh, if only I could have been his teacher!

The doctor came and prescribed heart medication plus eardrops for the child to prevent any complication from the scarlet fever. She does not like the eardrops, but is brave and lets us drip them into her ears.

24, June 1942

Every day Helga wants to draw and do math. She can now add the tenths up to 100. She understands quickly and easily. She also writes her Latin script beautifully.

25, June 1942

She is allowed to get up and sits on a pillow upon the footstool in front of a chair and writes a little composition about her illness almost without mistakes. In the evening when she is back in bed, she wants me to read her two fairytales: "König Drosselbart" and "Der alte Sultan". She laughed and had a good time, even though she is very weak and can hardly stand up.

26, June 1942

This is the end of Norbert's school year and his report card for the completed year, and now summer vacation begins. He grins from ear to ear when he sees us and we are all pleased.

But now we have to get ready to go to Sembach. My little "Murschel" is looking out the window stringing beads. It will be hard to say good-bye and she at first cries, because she cannot come with us. She then gives me lots of kisses and waves from the window.

27, June 1942

My sweetheart found the first gray hairs. Yesterday I spoke with Miss Schneider, Helga's teacher. She is very pleased with her and is the best pupil in class and often times "so cute". May God keep her sunny disposition and happy nature.

How I would have loved to take her to Sembach with us. My mother met us half way. We have a lot of baggage, but we have a bike too. In Sembach everything is the same. We immediately go to the garden to pick the strawberries.

28, June 1942

How wonderful to get rid of this hated uniform and put on civilian clothes. Father has aged and got very thin. Both of them come as often as they have time. In the evening we visit our friends, the Gödtel's. The neighbors Rettig are into hay and Norbert helps with the work. When we came home in the evening he was already asleep with his friend Jakob. He loves it in the country. Maybe he has inherited a little farmer's blood?

30, June 1942

Farewell

At 8:30 am we leave together. My parents are both here to say good-bye. At 9:26 am the train is leaving. My mood is very sad. I kiss them both and don't want to let go of their hands. Both have tears in their eyes. For a long time we wave with our handkerchiefs.

1, July 1942

What Stupidity, What A Silly Prank

I report back to Capt. Bachler, this uncouth excuse of a man! This dope wants to have nothing to do with me. So I pack my stuff and go to Paris. When I checked in with Capt. Dr. Küppers, I was in a hell of a mess. He screamed: "Schweinerei"! Has every bit of good sense left me? Why did I not just stay home since I was exposed to the scarlet fever? I am quarantined.

3, July 1942

Since yesterday I am in quarantine. No one can imagine my mood. My room was sealed and I am locked in like a prisoner. There is a sign at the door that no one is to enter and come in contact with me. These were the doctor's orders.

4, July 1942

I feel like I am going crazy and the day just will not pass. I torture myself with bitter reproaches. Why did I, a fool three times over, not just stay home? What does the regiment's commander think of me now? I read and write and stare out the window. I will never forget these depressing days.

5, July 1942

Sunday! It does not feel like it. Thank God I had some mail from home. Every line of her letter expresses her unspeakable longing. She dove into work to forget the pain of farewell. Norbert loves to ride his bicycle and he went to the woods to pick blueberries. Today is a very hot day.

6, July 1942

I slept well. Last night we had a fierce thunder and lightning storm; afterwards it cooled down. It is terrible, this imprisonment. When will they let me out?

I read a lot of stuff.

8, July 1942

I look out the window and I am amazed at how many Jews there are in Paris. They all have to wear the yellow Star of David on their coat sleeve. What a ridiculous order!

I try to pass the time with reading, improving my French and writing letters.

The fools are watching my temperature. How ridiculous! I am healthier than they are.

9, July 1942

Yesterday I got a letter from Opa informing me that the little "Mouse" is doing well. How happy that makes me. He writes:" Helga is just fine. She eats well again since the fever is gone. On Thursday, that is today, the doctor completes his treatment and she can go out again, since she does not have a temperature anymore and has no more complaints. She sings again and reads and draws."

10, July 1942

I wonder how things are going in Sembach? Now the delicious spice cake, which Rösel gave me, is gone, too bad. I still have some cookies left in my room. I just had to think how much Norbert is still so childlike, how he grabbed my hand 2 weeks ago in Bad Kreuznach and his teacher, Professor Köppers smilingly noticed it.

11, July 1942

Release From Quarantine

That damned military! I swear that I will hate and despise it as long as I live. When I think of the many humiliations and disappointments I have already endured. When will this torture come to an end?

When will this miserable war be over? There is no way of knowing. The Russian Offensive has begun. Oh, how much sorrow and sadness still lies ahead of us?

12, July 1942

Today it is raining and has turned cool. I think daily of my happiness at home. Helga wrote me a sweet little letter: "Dear Papa! I am completely well again. The doctor has given me some vitamins to make me strong. I have to get my school things together because I am going back to school tomorrow. Gruss und Kuss, dein Zückerchen (Greetings and Kisses, your Little Sugar)".

Oh, how precious are these letters.

19, July 1942

I Have Sunday Duty At The FLUKO.

We still have curfew. The Jewish Star on people's sleeves is becoming part of the picture in the streets. There are curfews for all Jews. They are not allowed in the subway, all public pools, all public buildings, the boulevards, and guesthouses, etc. They bear their fate with dignity and calm.

20, July 1942

A raid was being conducted last night against the Jews. 25,000 were caught and supposedly put into labor camps, the children in different camps. There are heartbreaking scenes! What is the sense of this? The bitterness and hatred of the French people is increasing, which is understandable. No one can understand these rules and actions that separate children from their parents.

21, July 1942

My mother is so happy, that the children are around her so much now, especially my little "Birdie". She says the child has grown some, but is very skinny. She does not like to do mathematics and will need some tutoring lessons to make up for the time she has missed.

22, July 1942

Today Helga goes to school in Sembach for the first time and she is looking forward. For her birthday she has requested a cherry cake without the pits. I hope my chocolates will get there in time. She gets enough fruits to eat.

23, July 1942

I still have not gotten used to the noise of the big city. After the night duty I cannot sleep very well.

Tomorrow is the birthday of my little "Mouse".

Tonight is a celebration of the 2nd year anniversary of the Paris FLUKO. Capt. Küppers has a good speech and there is a program of music by our own band. The songs of home, especially the Rhine songs cause everyone to feel nostalgic.

24, July 1942

My Little Girl's 7th Birthday

I wonder how you spent it, my sweetheart? On my nightstand is your picture and I am with you in my thoughts all day long. Before going to bed I eat the last chocolate cookie that you had sent me.

25, July 1942

In every letter the little "Mouse" draws pictures for me of brides with veils or mothers with baby carriages. She is very talented in drawing. The weather was nice on her birthday, Norbert picked some red carnations in the garden, and Mama had daisies, her favorites. Oma and Opa sent boiled eggs, which she loves, and my wooden box with the chocolates arrived in time. She wore the pretty little dress, which I had bought in Troyes and grandmother had cookies and candy for her. My mother had come for the birthday coffee and Helga arranged some cake on a plate for grandfather.

27, July 1942

Today she made the menu plan; pancakes with plums, coffee in the afternoon with blueberry and cherry cake. In the evening, rice pudding, with cinnamon and sugar and chocolate pudding with fresh strawberries from the garden.

Oh, if only I could have been there to enjoy these treasures. We all hope, that next year there will be peace and I can be there to celebrate their birthdays.

29, July 1942

How I hate working nights! This morning there was a parade from 10 am to 2 pm with Adolf Hitler's SS Body Guards on the Champs Elysses, which was very impressive. First class material and magnificent soldiers were presented.

30, July 1942

We exercise for the first time and take the subway to the country not too far from the zoo. On a long open field we do cross country marching. I have the command for one group and it is a piece of cake for me. Lt. Steiger is nice to me. If only he could be helpful with my promotion!

31, July 1942

Rösel asked me in a letter, if I still think of this day 7 years ago. Of course I do! That's when you presented me with a little darling daughter. Oh, just stay well, all of you. That is my only wish.

The harvest in the garden is completed. The children like it in Sembach better than in Hochstätten. My sweetheart would rather live at the edge of a city with a little garden, etc. Maybe this wish will be fulfilled one day.

Helga did a beautiful job reading in school according to her teacher and she praised her as a good example for the others. Norbert is a rascal. He has learned how to swim with an old inner tube.

1, August 1942

Now the first month after my leave has passed. I will never forgive myself for not having stayed another 2 weeks with my loved ones back then.

Here nobody gives a hoot. The FLUKO duty is extremely strenuous, especially the nights, in the morning I cannot sleep because of the noise.

2, August 1942

At home there was a very bad thunder and lightning storm. Today the children went with Rösel and my mother to church. Mother writes that Helga was being very quiet and good. The grandparents in Hochstätten planted the seeds of love, goodness, and kindness.

Helga plays with Ida Schwartz and her dolls and doll carriage. Norbert is working hard helping Rettig's with the farm work.

3, August 1942

Quite often Helga spends time with grandmother and grandfather. She seems to have recuperated from her illness very well. My mother wrote, that life has become easier for them with the new farm machines. Also the POW from the Ukraine is a big help for them. The two have more than earned it. How bitter and hard they have had to work in earlier days. They would not be able to do it any more.

5, August 1942

The curfew has been lifted, thank goodness! We can get out again, but it is still dangerous. We have to check in every 4 hours. Often I go to Paris alone to see the sights. I also try to buy a few more things.

6, August 1942

On July 25th and 26th Norbert and his friend Jakob went on a bicycle tour to Hochstätten, from there to Ebernburg and Bad Münster and back. That was quite a trip by bike and I was amazed at his endurance. In the morning he gets up at 7 am and is obsessed to work on Rettig's farm. He drives the reaping machine. Helga's bed is in the playroom.

7, August 1942

Rösel writes, that Helga is asking thousands of questions and the meanings of all kinds of words especially at night in bed and her thirst for knowledge is amazing. Sweet little "Chatter box"! Oh, if only I could be there!

8, August 1942

Rösel had the doctor come, which always worries me. I wonder what is wrong, she did not say. Finally I find out today. It was her complaint about her lower back. It's supposed to be a pinched nerve and not too bad.

9, August 1942

Slept poorly after my night duty. Then wrote a letter and went for a walk. I saw an exhibition by Arno Brecker and listened to a German concert in the square by the Champs Elysees. The French admire the military music and clap enthusiastically.

Tonight I stay home and read.

10, August 1942

For the first time, per my request, I was teaching some courses.

My sweetheart describes a day of work in Sembach. How diligent and talented she is. God blessed me richly when He gave me this woman for my wife. I just wonder if I am worthy of her. O Lord, give me the chance in this life to show my appreciation and carry her on my hands.

11, August 1942

Oh, I shall not forget this day as long as I live. Such a letter from my mother! What is going on? Oh, the shame and humiliation in the town. I just feel like crying. My good mother, who believes in me, is convinced this is just a bunch of evil gossip. How is this going to be clarified? I cannot sleep or eat. Oh, my poor, sweet wife!

12, August 1942

With what horrible thoughts I woke up. I am dead tired and feel beaten. I am just waiting for the next mail to give me some news. Oh, if everything would just get cleared up. I would like to pull the pillow over my head and cry like a child.

To numb my incredible homesickness I go to see a movie. It does not help.

13, August 1942

I wonder if I get some news today? I am not interested in exercising. If I live to be 90 years old I shall never forget this morning in the meadow, where I was totally absent minded, torturing my brain. What do I care about the exercising, the soldiers, this insane war, and the whole world?

I am just praying that my happiness at home will not be destroyed.

14, August 1942

Can I breathe easier and feel better? O God in Heaven, You have never yet left me in my despair and I do believe firmly in your help and guidance in this matter.

Today I had a dear letter from Rösel and one from Norbert, with a composition about his work on Rettig's farm. It is cute and I gave him a "B", because he always wants me to grade it.

15, August 1942

The letter of my mother gives me a little bit of hope, but I do not dare to feel good. I realize now how exhausted I am and how I have tortured myself. I fall into a death like sleep. What will the next few days bring?

16, August 1942

Today Norbert goes back to Hochstätten, because on Tuesday, school is starting again. My dear boy, stay well, study hard, and continue to give us so much joy as you have so far. Yesterday I sat by the pond in the park of the Tuilleries and read. But I just cannot be happy. These are terrible days.

17, August 1942

Yesterday I was in my thoughts all day with my dear boy.

There was another letter from my mother. Is there a glimpse of hope? Is this just common gossip? In the morning I went to church in my despair to seek consolation and found it. I would have never believed it, but when a man is in trouble, he learns to pray. I believe I have aged 10 years in these days.

19, August 1942

Rösel writes, that the poor boy cried at the station when he had to say good-bye.

The English invasion in Dieppe was repelled. We have increased the alert situation and are restricted to the base.

20, August 1942

Today Mainz was bombed. One third of the beautiful city reduced to rubble and ashes.

Rösel went, as she wrote, early in the morning to the train station to ship some vegetables in cartons to the grandparents and the little "Mouse" is still sleeping. Mama leaves a note on her blanket saying: "Mama went to the train station, get dressed and eat your bread". She answered back by writing a note saying: "Dear Mama, you should have done what I told you last night." What did she mean by that? Oh, if only I could see them again soon.

22, August 1942

The evening concert by the Evangelical Armed Forces Congregation was held in the beautiful Notre Dame Cathedral. Many French civilians attended. The presentations were excellent. I am very tired, because I had night duty (Officer of the Day).

I received a wonderful package in the mail with cake and a jar of homemade prune butter.

24, August 1942

Our Wedding Anniversary

We have been married 13 years now. 13 happy years! O God, keep this our happiness for us. I celebrated the day as well as possible. I know my love was with me in her thoughts and mind. Will we be together next year?

25, August 1942

Rösel and Helga went to Worms to visit Tante Mariechen for a few days. The little one was excited about the trip. She loves to play with Hilde's dolls and doll carriage. She is such a sweet "Doll Mommy". I hope she will become a domestic and talented little "Hausfrau".

26, August 1942

The war has been going on for three years. I had a bad feeling, that it would be a long and terrible war. It's a good thing one does not know, but I have lost the three most important years of my life.

27, August 1942

We have a terrible heat in Paris. Tonight I am going to the Casino de Paris. I hope to sleep well. I am still not at ease about the gossip story at home. O God, if only this will work out all right. My honor is in danger. It is 90 degrees in my room.

29, August 1942

Rösel wrote of an incident on their return trip from Worms, where the train derailed. Thank God, nothing happened to them. They were sitting in the car behind the baggage car, which had tipped over. After a delay of one hour they could continue. Their guardian angel was protecting them.

30, August 1942

Today was carnival in Sembach. Oh, what wonderful memories! Where have the happy times disappeared to? As shameful as my homeland has forsaken our people, still I am so attached to Sembach with the long lasting and impressive memories of my childhood. How I love this little village and how many nights did we dance until dawn.

31, August 1942

What unspeakable sorrow has hit our people! The English and Americans are flying night after night with their bombing squadrons over our cities destroying them. Mainz has been devastated, including the beautiful old cathedral, as well as Kassel, Frankfurt, Saarbrücken, all the cities of the Rhineland, Nuremberg, Ulm, and Stuttgart have been damaged badly. What is going to happen next? Everyone is afraid of the winter and the war is accelerating on a terrible scale. Oh, I am so sick and tired of everything.

1, September 1942

Three years ago today, the first disastrous shot fell, which triggered this unfortunate war! You reap what you sow! And yet we have to hope that we will be victorious, or else there will be unspeakable sorrow! How long is it going to last? The people are sick of the war; the provisions are getting worse, and the air raids more frequent.

2, September 1942

Helga's school is starting again today. The child is going to school for one whole year now and I have been cheated out of teaching my own children.

Damned be these idiots who have messed up my life! All the good and beautiful things I have wanted to teach my children, I have been betrayed.

4, September 1942

Why is the child so ill mannered? Rösel writes, that she does not behave and often cries the whole day. My little sweetheart! She so loves to play with dolls and would love to have a doll carriage. Norbert got used to Hochstätten very quickly, his friends, the chickens, the school, everything was again fascinating for him. "That's how kids are", Rösel writes.

5, September 1942

My sweetheart writes that while visiting in Worms they had an air raid and had to go to the basement in the night. They carried the child sleepily wrapped in a blanket downstairs and laid her on the straw mattress where she kept on sleeping. Later on, carried her back upstairs to bed and she never noticed anything different.

But why does she cry so much? Is it nervousness? She also does not eat well. This worries me. Oh, why could I not have her in my class?

6, September 1942

I went to church in St. Georges; the service was beautiful with musical interludes such as choir, organ, etc. An excellent young war pastor had an inspiring message. How wonderful I am always consoled and find new hope. Oh, my God! Do not let me become confused and lose my faith in you. May be everything will work out after all.

7, September 1942

Yesterday Rösel went with Helga and Norbert to the swimming pool in Bad Kreuznach. The little "Mouse" had fun in the kiddy pool and Norbert knows how to swim in the big pool. It breaks my heart that he learned to swim without me.

The days are very hot and humid and there is no relief in this big city.

11, September 1942

Norbert got an "A" on his math test. He is very proud of it and Mama, as well as Oma and Opa had to fork over 1 Mark as an award. But why does my little "Murschel" cry so much?

Rösel thinks she is nervous and afraid and this is since the scarlet fever. She is afraid to sleep alone and often gets to school late. She wants to take her to Dr. Gralka for a general check up.

12, September 1942

Helga does not enjoy math in school and does not seem to have a talent for it. Otherwise she is very bright.

I went to the bird market today. Oh, how my father would have enjoyed this. I remember how much he liked canaries. I am still looking for a few things like a raincoat for Rösel, wool and butter.

14, September 1942

15 years ago today was my first teaching day after teacher's college. How very happy I was. All of my dreams were fulfilled.

But today is a different story. Oh, my God, what have I done to deserve this? Why do you punish me like this?

15, September 1942

Today is one of my sad and desperate days. In addition, Rösel writes, that she had nightmares about my promotion. How strange. I will never forget how I walked around the yard with a miserable headache, thinking I will go crazy, brooding about my misfortune.

16, September 1942

My Sweetheart's Birthday

She is now 34 years old. O God, keep her for me! Keep her well and healthy and let us enjoy our children. All day long I was with her in my mind and thoughts. I write until midnight. This is my last night in Paris, my last time in the Hotel Montcalmes. Good night, my dear ones.

17, September 1942

I arrive in Corbeil at 7 am. From 7 to 8 am, I thought of my son, who is going to school at this time and the homesickness completely devastated me.

In the evening at 8 pm I get back, dead tired without hope.

18, September 1942

The terrible night of my nervous breakdown! Pain in my chest, is this a heart attack? After seeing the doctor I find out they are supposed to be mental disorders. I am prescribed several medications.

Zimmerman made Lieutenant, this 22 year old punk! Where is the justice in this world?

19, September 1942

I participate in a class in hand-to-hand combat. The song "Blue And Sunny The Days" comes in my mind.

We have a beautiful fall day. I am so closely connected with nature, that I feel a physical pain in my soul, not to be able to be home. I march through the field with my thoughts elsewhere and at night I fix up the dreary room # 7 as homey and comfortable as possible to make it my place.

20, September 1942

I Have Lost Paradise In Paris

This morning the first lecture. The afternoon is terribly cold and I suffer from being homesick. I feel so alone and lonesome. I go with my book to the hillside above the Seine River, sit down at a bench, look over the neglected and overgrown gardens and give in to my sad mood. The song "The Last Rose" comes to my mind.

I have had no mail from home for 5 days now.

21, September 1942

Hand-to-hand combat again. The weather is cool and I am chilly. I look at the young Eifler; he has made it. I could have been chosen with him and I could have gone home at Christmas in my lieutenant's uniform.

Oh, well, what is the use? I will forever remember this field, the old Chateau; the gardens overgrown with weeds, the last lovely autumn flowers.

No dinner today, only a cold supper portion. Capt. Jetter comes every day. He is very friendly and jovial with me and at one time I thought he might have been instrumental and able to help me. But I do not believe it any more. I try to do my best at least while he is here. We are being worked very hard, throwing hand grenades, etc. and after 3 days we are exhausted. I hope I don't have to stay here.

Finally I get mail again regularly. Rösel writes, that she was in Sembach for a few days. Also, that the child does seem to be very nervous. She did not want to go to bed and is afraid of everything. Also she gets to school often late and cries a lot.

24, September 1942

The grandparents, Rösel and the children, these good, hard working people have gone to the fields to pick up ears of rye and wheat, that were left by the machine and taken them to the mill. They received 70 pounds of flour from the milled grain.

25, September 1942

We had another pork meal, which was a feast. Of course everyone is drinking too much and the jokes are getting out of hand. This is not my "cup of tea" anyway and I can't wait to get out of there. At 1 am the captain is leaving and so do I for my night duty, which is very strenuous and I am tired.

26, September 1942

Today, Saturday, our duty is only ½ day. I am disinterested and spend most of my time in the chateau playing the piano or I go for a walk through the dewy field. In the afternoon I get some coffee, write and read, then go to bed at 9 pm.

28, September 1942

We had another instruction class in hand-to-hand combat. The days are awfully long. I will never forget these impressions: The hard damp bed, the old chateau with the dirty lunchroom, the out of tune piano, marching without joy or a song, and the painful thoughts.

30, September 1942

My little Helga-Mouse hates math, but why? The fault lies probably with the bad situation in the schools. The package for my sweetheart's birthday only now arrived. She enjoyed the chocolates, the little evening bag, and the raincoat. She reminds me that last Sunday was carnival in Hochstätten. Oh, the happy memories! "Try to have a little joy" she writes. Also she writes: "How grateful am I that I can still write to you. Look at all the horror and sadness this war is bringing upon mankind. Compared with that, your problems are small, aren't they? You have given me so much joy."

Oh, my dearest, how brave and sensible you are.

1, October 1942

Now that September is gone; I wonder how long it will be before I see them again. Helga is envious, because I sent so many gifts to Mama. In the meantime the little cactus pot, the balloons, and other miscellaneous things have arrived. So many things I still want to send them. I cannot find shoes for Helga anymore though.

4, October 1942

Pastor Degen's wife died. This will be very hard for him. He is so helpless. Their son Hansi came too late. He only found his mother's grave piled high with flowers. My colleague Jakob Herzog, who is in Russia, has not been home on furlough for 20 months. I cannot complain. The people are getting very angry and disillusioned about this war lasting so long and no one appreciated Göring's speech tonight.

5, October 1942

There is another promotional celebration. What feelings of desperation and disappointment for me! When will they celebrate my promotion? Probably never!

Norbert has become very mature and independent. He is also getting better grades in math and every time he gets an "A"; he wants 1 Mark from Oma and Mama for his savings account. Rösel raises them well, especially to be frugal.

7, October 1942

My sweetheart writes that my "Murschel" had to write 100 times for punishment: "I am not allowed to eat in class."

Oh, you sweet little bird! She wrote me such a darling four page letter, in it she says: "I hope you will be pleased with me, dear Papa, because I have written you a very long letter."

Oh, if only I could be a little "Mouse" and observe how she acts in school, or better yet, have her as my pupil.

8, October 1942

The sergeants and NCOs have a special course. A lot of my old time buddies are among them from the Unit #7 in Troyes. How that cuts into my heart when I see the lucky ones, who have made it now. Späth has been chosen already and he will be a lieutenant by Christmas. Oh, this is so bitter! Will I ever remember later on, how I felt in these days and weeks?

9, October 1942

The area commissioner of the Armed Forces has requested my address. What is that supposed to mean? I am very restless and worried for the safety of my loved ones. Dear God, why are you punishing me? I have lost all my joy and happiness, and seem to have aged 10 years.

10, October 1942

Last night, after an unsuccessful "Evening for Comrades", all the worst aspects of the military became evident and all unimaginable dirty jokes and weaknesses of character were displayed. So much so that I was shaking with disgust, this course will come to an end today. I am glad I will be off for 3 days.

11, October 1942

This is a Sunday, and Sgt. Seitz and I put in for a day of furlough. We want to go to Biaritz. This pitiful excuse of a man, Lt. Vogler does not give us permission. This narrow-minded twit made lieutenant.

In the afternoon I go to Paris, eat in an expensive restaurant, went to see the Music Hall D'Etoilles and stay overnight in a nearby hotel. Tomorrow I go to Le Havre.

12, October 1942

Le Havre!

What a terribly dilapidated city! Dirty, cluttered, fish smell everywhere, and evidence of terrible poverty. Half of the city has been evacuated and there are coastal batteries in the harbor. The mess hall is small and pitiful. We see many sailors. I took the incline railroad up the mountain. At 5:10 pm I depart from Le Havre.

18, October 1942

I have not written for a while. This is just another one of my depressed Sundays. It is cool, cloudy, and the leaves are falling from the trees. Fall is coming!

Rösel is upset with me, because I have written to the superintendent with a query to research the possibility of deferred military duty in order to teach school. She is not in agreement that I should be called back, she thinks it is better that I stay. Of course she is right, as always. I never get smart and a lot of this is probably my own fault.

19, October 1942

Today I received a letter from Maj. Dr. Scheuerpflug, which consoled me a little, but still did not get my hopes up. How can I be persecuted like this by ill fortune?

Only I wish this miserable war would be over.

21, October 1942

The nights are cold and I could not go to sleep until 3 am. I put on my socks and was then able to go to sleep. In the new course, I meet people I have previously known. They all feel sorry for me and cannot imagine what is wrong. Why am I not promoted?

23, October 1942

Rösel went with both children to the pediatrician, Dr. Gralka. Results: both of them are extremely nervous, Norbert eats too fast, and Helga has no appetite at all. Both of them do not have their proper weight or height. Now there are new worries.

24, October 1942

I am so sorry I wrote such an offensive letter to my mother, accusing her of causing this gossip in town, that I had requested to be sent back home. Of course they would love to have me home. I will ask her forgiveness in my next letter.

25, October 1942

My little sweetheart! She wrote to me two darling letters and wants to have an answer soon. Only her script is not very good. She tells me about her 2 pigtails. Oh, how I would like to see her in her new hairdo.

28, October 1942

Today I slept late because I expect to see Capt. Jetter. I stayed all day in my cold room and glued pictures in the album. Of course he did not come. At night I got a package with cake and a dear letter.

29, October 1942

It has been pouring down rain all day long. Of course the captain did not come again. I wanted to ask him about the query. What should I do?

31, October 1942

Another course is ending. I heard from my mother and her letter created a new concern for me. O God, when will I finally see clear and can breathe easy again?

Norbert is ill mannered and Helga cries all day long. Norbert loves school though and that is important. But he has very little energy and wastes a lot of time. Besides he has a fresh mouth. Now is when he needs his father.

1, November 1942

Outside, the yellow and brown leaves come tumbling down from the trees. I shall always remember the dirty room with the out of tune piano, the chateau's moat, the open field beyond, and the dreary days with rainy weather. I want to get out of here.

5, November 1942

Today I started thinking of the day 12 years ago. It was a cold starry night when I took my sweetheart in our Opel to the hospital, there she gave birth to our son. Will he be the joy of our lives later on? We can only hope and wish that he will stay healthy in body, soul, and spirit. He has given us much joy, but also so many worries.

6, November 1942

Norbert's Birthday

He is 12 years old today. I thought of both of you while standing by the window in this cold Chateau St. Pierre. The rain is still coming down in buckets.

7, November 1942

Yesterday Capt. Jetter said: "Things are looking good for you." Stupid me, I looked at it as a good omen, because he said it on Norbert's birthday. His gifts were a box of chocolates from me, from Oma and Opa, 40 Marks, from Mama, a sweater, from grandmother, 5 Marks.

8, November 1942

We have alert and curfew. We cannot leave the place. Reason: American troops have landed in Algiers and Morocco. Does that mean a change and hopefully a shortening of the war?

I sent a soccer ball to Norbert, which I was able to get for him.

10, November 1942

My little "Murschel" has an inner ear infection. Is this due to the scarlet fever? But she wrote herself and said that she was feeling fine and had no fever.

11, November 1942

I Am Sick

It started last night with high fever around 40C. I had a miserable night with chills and shaking in that cold room with no care. Aspirin did not help and I did not sleep all night long. In the morning I went to the dispensary and saw a doctor. His diagnosis: a bad case of the flu, but at least my lungs are clear.

12, November 1942

I am not any better yet. The fever is still about 40C. In the morning, I take aspirin and quinine, plus I have no appetite. Do I have an attack of dysentery? Where does this come from? Quite a few other buddies have it too. The dispensary is crowded and I have to take a charcoal product and try to sweat it out.

13, November 1942

The fever is slowly going down, but I still have to stay in bed. I did not write home, as I did not want to worry them. I hope my little sweetheart is well again.

14, November 1942

After the doctor saw me today he lets me get up. I feel very weak though. In addition I still have this dysentery and cannot eat much. What caused this, the food or a cold?

15, November 1942

I get up and try to get back to work. Tomorrow I want to try and go to Paris. I have a few more things I want to buy. I have sent home some rationing stamps because I know they want to buy some things for me for Christmas. It is the same situation in all European countries; there is not much to buy anymore. Last year I could have bought a blue fox fur for 150 Marks, now it costs 650 Marks.

19, November 1942

The war situation is deteriorating. The Americans have dug in Algiers and Morocco. Additional troops have landed in Tunis. Benghasi has been lost and Rommel has been defeated in Africa.

20, November 1942

The weather is still cold and wet. Everyone are catching colds. Yesterday Rösel went to the doctor with Helga and he had to open the eardrum, which must have been very painful, because my poor little girl screamed bloody murder.

We heard that in North Africa the entire French Armed Forces took up sides with the Americans.

23, November 1942

My "Murschel" writes such sweet and touching letters, in which she continually asks me for a doll carriage. "Such as one of these I would like to have" and she encloses different drawings. She has her heart set on it. But I don't believe I can fulfill her wish, since there is just nothing to be had anymore.

24, November 1942

I had another letter from Helga. "Dear Papa, I will write to you very often, so I will get mail from you too. Is there not such a doll carriage in all of France?" Again, drawings upon drawings!

At home winter has arrived. Because of the time change it is not so dark anymore in the mornings when Norbert has to leave. He has not had very good grades lately and I should be there now. He is missing out on so much.

26, November 1942

The French people become more hateful, which is understandable, but there is no excuse for pushing a young German female soldier in front of the Metro train last week.

I did not get to see the captain all week. If only I knew for what reason they are making it impossible for me to become an officer? It is very strange indeed.

29, November 1942

Another Sunday! I went to the market to try to find some gloves and a sweater for Rösel. It will be a poor Christmas this year.

Helga is well again, thank God and she will not have any after effects with her hearing.

There will be no presents this year, but that's OK. If only I can come home and we will have a little tree.

30, November 1942

My little "Mouse" writes such darling letters: "My ears are all well again. My chicken has not laid an egg yet. Last night I dreamed, that I went to the post office to mail a letter for you and when I opened the door, you were standing there. Just now Mama found my Advents Calendar. 10,000 kisses from your Herzemäuschen (Little mouse of your heart)".

Dear God! Just keep my happiness for me, which is so pure and beautiful.

1, December 1942

I was able to get a pair of very pretty gray leather gloves for Rösel and a pair of woolen ones for Oma by trading lots of cigarettes. It was an all day job though.

2, December 1942

Today I will be able to finish my Paris photo album. That was a job. Now I can take two photo albums home at Christmas to show them. The other pictures I cannot glue in anymore, because there is no more glue to be had. This will be a job for peacetime. Oh, if only that was here.

3, December 1942

The political situation is not good. The Americans are in North Africa, and the Russians have begun a tremendous winter offensive. It does not look like this war will be over any time soon. I toy with the idea to put in a request for a transfer to Germany.

4, December 1942

I receive another cute letter from "Mouse" in colored letters. She writes about putting her shoes, as is the custom, in front of the window on "Nicolas Day" and hoping for some goodies and not pieces of coal which you received, if you were bad.

5, December 1942

This deceitful trick of Lt. Zimmerman. This smooth talking rogue wants to actually cheat me out of my furlough. The villainy in this world has become so great, that there is no more trust and faith in anything. I am incensed and demand an appointment with the captain.

6, December 1942

Today the captain is supposed to come. He himself is going on furlough. I will tell him everything. Now the lieutenant has thought things over and had come to tell me, he will take care of everything and get my leave time after all. I am getting to the point of just not caring anymore.

8, December 1942

I'm in Paris. There is an air raid! The Metro subway is closed. I missed the train and stayed overnight in the Hotel Süd.

In the evening again, this fear creeps up inside of me because of a certain letter. What a night! Should I despair in my God? I have given up all hope.

9, December 1942

What a wonderful resolve. O God, you have not forsaken me after all. I hope that everything will work out.

I pack and leave at 5 pm for Paris again. In the middle of the night, I walk up the steep road to the Air Command P 21 A. I spend a cold night in an unheated room.

10, December 1942

I get up early and find out, that I may have to report at any hour. My last hope for a Christmas leave is gone. In the afternoon, a recall back to Lieusaint. I won't be able to go until early in the morning, which means another night in this miserable cold room. I cover myself with my coat and catch a cold anyway.

11, December 1942

At the Austerlitz Station I leave my luggage until afternoon, then I get my papers, take the 6:15 pm train to Etampes, where I am picked up.

12, December 1942

This was again a big disappointment. I was supposed to start working in the registration, but did not even have to introduce myself. Supposedly this was a misunderstanding? So I go back to Paris.

14, December 1942

The children are so looking forward to my coming at Christmas, but they will be very disappointed. I do mediation duty until 9 pm. I am back in my room #7, which has been before the silent witness of my heartbreaks.

The first letters are arriving from my sweetheart with all of their terrible disappointments. When she told Helga, that I cannot come, she started crying. But when Mama consoled her by saying, that many "papas" cannot come this year, she wipes her tears and smiles again. Dear sweet child.

16, December 1942

Norbert is a little more controlled. They could have still let me go, but no, they are stubborn. Only if I could get out of this unit. Today Norbert received his report card. I wonder how it turned out? I wonder if he was happy or sad?

In the meantime, I sit here in my dreary room and stare out the window into the pouring rain.

18, December 1942

I cannot seem to be able to get control of this unspeakable homesickness. Today a decision will be made. I have to be ready to be called at any hour. Where will I be sent?

19, December 1942

I could have left this evening, had they let me go. The 3 pounds of veal meat that I was going to bring to my family I gave to our cook. That would be the least I could do.

I know how we all feel. 25 men are supposed to come and with whom I will leave. Finally at about 8 pm they arrive and bring me mail from Rösel but not from my mother.

20, December 1942

This morning at 10:40 am I should have arrived in Bad Kreuznach. Dear God! What do you have planned for me? The weather is spring like and I sit all day in the mess hall, while I am in an incredibly sad mood.

21, December 1942

Today I was in the day room, when I was called. The decision has been made. I am going to Montpellier immediately.

I packed in a hurry, said good-bye to Corbeil. We drive to Paris. We have a layover until evening and leave from the station Gare de Lyon on the express train that goes to Lyon, Nice, and Monte Carlo. We travel all night via Dijon to Lyon. The night is clear and starry and I get no sleep, but some hot coffee in the dining car in the morning. I have marching provisions for 4 days. Arrival in Avignon, I have to change trains to Nimes and we arrive in Montpellier during the afternoon.

23, December 1942

The first impression is shattering. The accommodations are pitiful. I report immediately and request a furlough and of course was rebuffed.

Well, this is it! I just feel so bad for them at home, because they had hoped until the last minute. Now all of our Christmas will be sad. I unpack my blanket and strip of canvas. The food is disastrous.

Why do I have such bad luck?

24, December 1942

Christmas Eve!

I am at home with my thoughts. How I do wish you the very best, all of you. How will I spend the most beautiful of festivals? I work from 7 am until 10 pm.

In the evening between 6 and 7 o'clock, I go to the little square in front of the building and walk around in a circle, trying to imagine what you are all doing at home.

25, December 1942

Christmas Morning

Today I worked again the whole day. Also tomorrow, then a regular duty in three-day intervals is supposed to start. I could not sleep at all last night because of the noise of the drunks. These people just have no soul, mind, or feeling.

I hated to sit in that damp French cellar with the artificial light, when I could be enjoying the candle's warm glow and surrounded by my loved ones at home. I only have a few Christmas cookies left from my mother.

26, December 1942

2nd Christmas Day

Between 8 am and 9 am I walked again outside, wondering, if my mother went to Hochstätten. She was looking forward to it for some time now to see the children again.

Yes, she came yesterday and left today at 4 pm. She brought cookies, 10 Marks for Norbert and material for an apron for Helga. She enjoyed listening to the children sing and play. Afterwards, the grown ups stayed up until 1 am.

28, December 1942

Now I have regular duty in shifts. The weather is clear but cool, the days are sunny, but at night it is cold. Helga has told her brother that she knows now there is no "Christkind". So this magic and dream of her childhood is gone too. How sad! At home they have snow and the kids are sledding down the hillside. Norbert wants to make another calendar for me, the dear boy.

30, December 1942

There is a trip to Palavas on the blue Mediterranean. What a lovely sight but a cold wind is blowing. I visit the coastal artillery at the naval post.

Papa in center with buddy and Italian soldier

In the evening I observed an exercise with tracer ammunition. Later on, I eat a wonderful baked fish in a little bistro. Truly a delicacy, after being hungry so many times, and getting such mediocre food.

31, December 1942

So now this old year can take its leave, this year, that has brought me so many disappointments. Everything up until the furlough in summer was OK, then right away two unfortunate strokes of fate: The worrisome news my mother wrote me about from Sembach and my apparent deletion from the future officer's list. This caused me so much stress and pressured me so, that I lost weight and became extremely depressed. The one situation has been cleared up and just maybe I will be lucky and still make officer in the New Year.

We celebrated a little this evening. 1st Lt. Hieke made a little speech. We had a pitiful tree, sang "Vaterlands Lieder (patriotic songs)", and drank some red wine. At midnight we congratulated one another and I sneaked out and got lost in the beauty of the southern starry skies and sent up my fervent prayers to my God, those of thanksgiving and for His guidance. Oh, may my prayers come true!

191

1943

<u>Excerpts:</u>

On January 1ˢᵗ, of the year 1943, I received mail from home, from both Rösel and my mother. They gave me a report of Christmas.

<u>Rösel's letter dated 24, December 1942.</u>

It is 9:30 pm Christmas Eve and Norbert just went upstairs to bed. Helga is asleep for 1 hour already. She was blissfully happy with her new ball and a new doll. She took both to bed. She got over your not being here easier than anyone else and consoled herself and us by saying: "We have to be happy because Papa wrote he will come in a few weeks." Norbert took it much harder. He did not want to eat supper and was very quiet and solemn. But when he saw the soccer ball from you his eyes got big and shiny with surprise. He does not want to take it in the street though, as to not get it dirty.

How I felt, well, that you can imagine! I played all the old Christmas songs on the piano, but I was not able to sing any of them. We missed you so much.

I want to thank you most of all for your love, you know that I do not want or need more than that. I only wish, that you will come home to us well and healthy. Let me embrace you as always on this special day and do not forget me.

My sweetheart lit the candles on the tree and as always, slipped through the back door. The children came in and experienced the everlasting magic of the rather big Christmas tree this year. They sang as always, all the familiar Christmas songs and said their little prayer of thanks.

Her words: I looked for you all evening in my thoughts from Paris all the way to the deep south and I could not find you. Because I know, how the loneliness makes you sad, so I am sad too!

<u>Other Letters From Rösel</u>

<u>Rösel's letter dated 20, December 1942.</u>

On Christmas Eve we will be together, although we are far apart. You will be sitting among us and I will be with you. I will sit next to your hard bed, because I cannot imagine any other room around you. We then will be very close to each other and light a little candle for each other in our hearts. It will be bright around us, even our hearts will ache. And when I light the candles on Christmas Eve, you will come to us, won't you?

Rösel's letter dated 31, December 1942.

The time is rushing. Only another half an hour and we stand at the threshold of a New Year, a year, of which we know nothing. It lies before us in complete darkness. What will it bring us?

We hope and pray that we may end it in good health as we begin it. The children are both healthy this time. I wish for you everything one wishes for a beloved human being and that this war will not tear us apart. I will kiss our children and wish them the best.

Rösel's letter dated 2, January 1943

We stayed up until midnight. I wished my parents a Happy New Year. I then went with the last ringing of the bells upstairs to Norbert. He was awake immediately, being such a light sleeper. We thought of you. Then I kissed Helga who was sound asleep and 5 minutes later I was in bed.

1, January 1943

The New Year 1943

The New Year began with a simple party at the FLUKO. After the Lt. made a short speech, I try to collect myself and concentrate totally on them at home.

A lot of superficial people all around me probably just thought of drinking and do not have the soul that thrills me in moments like this.

At midnight I tried as hard as I could to concentrate on my loved ones in Sembach and Hochstätten. I sneak away down to the front of the building to be alone for a few moments. I look at the starry night sky above me and I am in deep thoughts by myself. I wish with all the passion in my heart, which is so much part of me since I was a child, all the best for my loved ones, for me, and for all the suffering humanity. Oh, if only all these wishes would be fulfilled. Always people wish good things for themselves and still there is so much sorrow in this world.

What will you bring us, year 1943? I put it all in your hands, O God! You have helped me so many times before.

3, January 1943

The duty is boring. I have a lot of time to read books, write and think. The buddies are nice guys and I consider them valuable human beings, especially Pastor Eiber is my kind of guy.

5, January 1943

We have a trip to Marseille. This experience and the memories, as well as my photos are very meaningful to me. It took us 4 hours by train to this huge, very impressive city. The cathedral Notre Dame de la Garde, the view to the downtown area, the old and the new harbor, the Rue de la Croniche, the crime ridden section at the harbor, and the return trip in the evening.

There are more such trips planned in the future.

7, January 1943

Two small packages came from the family. One from Rösel with cookies and a cake, one from my mother with a can of home made liverwurst, 1/2 pound of butter, etc. How they all worry about me. At home they have snow 2 feet high and it is very cold. Here the weather is sunny, but the nights are cold.

12, January 1943

Today I received a calendar from Norbert, which he made for me with so much love. I go for a beautiful walk through the southern countryside that's just like Italy. Too bad I did not have my camera with me.

15, January 1943

We have strange weather, thunder and lightning storms as by us in the summer time.

I wonder if they have taken down the Christmas tree at home. My mother writes Helga is a sweet and talented child. She reads and writes far ahead of her classmates. With her grandmother she plays the game "Mühle". When she plays with Opa, he has to place the game pieces the way she wants them and of course he has to lose.

19, January 1943

At home the snow is melting. We are always so tired because of the long walk to the chateau. Rösel writes, that Helga is getting a fresh mouth and Norbert does a lot of ice skating. Today I went to Palavas. The Mediterranean is cold and is a magnificent blue color, but very windy. I have enjoyed some wonderful baked fish in one of the hotels.

23, January 1943

Why do I feel so down and out, and often so depressed?

27, January 1943

There are tremendous worries about the eastern front. Stalingrad is on the verge of being lost after a heroic fight by our 6th Army. Fight to the last man! What a terrible misfortune and sacrifice for our people. There are quite a few people from Sembach killed or missing.

31, January 1943

My Father's Birthday

He is 66 years old. I sent him a birthday card in time, wishing him many more years of good health and happiness in his "Golden Years". He has earned it so much after a life so filled with struggles.

5, February 1943

I still have not heard anything about my leave time. I was supposed to go home on the 8th. Today I received a letter from Rösel in which she wrote that mother had called the doctor for my father. What does that mean? I am really worried. Is he sick? He is losing a lot of weight and the doctor was not too clear.

6, February 1943

My furlough is approved, thank God! For 18 days from the 8th to the 26th of February. This morning I went for my physical exam, and then do the last preparations. I cannot take too much this time. At night I am so tired, but wound up at the same time, that I cannot go to sleep. In addition to that, I have pain in my muscles and joints.

My train leaves at 3:30 in the night via Nimes, where I have to wait for 1 hour to catch the connection to Paris.

7, February 1943

I try to sleep on the train in spite of the pain and the stomach-ache. When it turned light I saw the lovely countryside near the Cevennen, with the deep crevices and bare rocks. For hours the train rides through tunnels and pretty hillsides. Finally we are in same flat country again. It is getting dark again and as we are passing Fontainebleau we are headed for Paris. At 10 pm, 19 hours after starting this trip, I arrive very tired at the Gare de Lyon in Paris. I right away go to the Hotel Montalb to take care of Lt. Hieke's orders, find a room in the Hotel Central, but cannot sleep all night because of the pain.

I want to get home as quick as possible.

8, February 1943

I quickly go once more to the Hotel Montalb to pick up a picture that has been kept for a ½ year for me. I then go to the train station Gare de L'Est. I leave at 8:05 am, on the by now a very familiar stretch to Metz. I arrive late in Kaiserslautern. I have to wait 2 hours for the train and have time to eat and drink something. I telephoned Herr Metz in Sembach to ask how father is doing, then to Hochstätten. Shortly after 9 pm the "milk train" leaves for the Alsenztal (Alsenz Valley).

At 10 o'clock I see standing by the lit up crossing barrier, my sweetheart and Norbert waiting for me. The reunion is wonderful, but both are shocked when they find out, that I don't feel well. I know now, what it is: It's a reaction to the terrible pressure on my nerves. I have suffered too much these last few months. Now my nerves have given out.

Oh, how wonderful I feel just to be home again. They left the Christmas tree standing so I could still see it. "So Papa can enjoy it", according to "Murschel". She is already sleeping, the little "Mouse". I soon go to bed happy, warm, secure, and safe.

I can hardly sleep with the pain. What is this? I sit up for hours and still have the discomfort in my stomach and a terrible restlessness. I hope I won't get seriously sick.

Norbert leaves in the morning for school and then the little one comes to greet me passionately. Oh, what a joy to feel her dear little soft arms around my neck and the tender kisses on my face.

My sweetheart takes such good care of me.

9, February 1943

I stay in bed. Maybe with this wonderful care I will be well soon. Rösel brings me a wonderful breakfast: Fresh rolls from the baker with real butter, a soft boiled egg, coffee, etc.

Around noon I get up. Gone is the hated uniform and on with the civilian clothes. I sit in the cozy living room, listen to the radio, read the newspaper, and help the children with their homework. Later when they are in bed we take down the Christmas tree.

"Christkind came to get it", we tell Helga the next morning, but she does not believe it anymore. That's too bad. But she still talks about Christkind, as if she still believes. Her girlfriend Wilhelmine has told her the facts. We had to take the tree down, because it was losing all its needles, but I was glad that I still got to see it.

Every day I am served my favorite meals and for my breakfast the wonderful rolls.

13, February 1943

This afternoon we all go with the 4 o'clock train to Sembach, I of course in civilian clothes. I insist that we take the kids. We have a lot of baggage, but that's OK. It is raining and foggy.

I am a little worried and concerned, because I do not know how father is doing. Quickly we have heated the kitchen nice and cozy, where I like to be so much, and in the evening, we go to my parents. With great uneasiness I quickly climb the stairs. How will I find him? When I open the door my mother stands at the table working, father sits in a chair. He has gotten very thin in his face and does not know how sick he is. I take a deep breath and greet them. Both are surprised and happy. Quickly mother has made something to eat for us and we sit together for a long time.

We talk about all kinds of things. Helga is allowed to sleep with grandmother, which makes her very happy. In her blue pajamas we play the same old silly games. I kid her and pretend to be envious of her bed and say: "Will you get out of this bed right now"? And of course she squeals and says: "No! No! No! I am staying right here!" She sleeps against the wall and feels safe and secure.

We go back to the schoolhouse, built a fire, and put a hot water bottle inside the bed in the children's room.

In the morning I wake up from the sound of clattering dishes in the kitchen. Norbert has his friend Jakob over already and soon my little "Murschel" comes with grandmother, her little face beaming all over. After breakfast I start tidying up, build a nice, roaring fire in our comfortable living room and get busy sorting out books. I am filled with a deep abiding peace and look forward to our old happiness.

14, February 1943

At noon time we go to eat at my parents and mother has fixed a nice dinner for us. We visit some friends and enjoy our visits with Gödtel's, who always out do themselves in their hospitality for us. I feel better every day.

15, February 1943

We are still in Sembach. I play the piano, look through my books, and straighten up the magazines and newspapers. At noon we always eat at my parents and then supper at home. Helga wants to sleep with grandmother every night, but she often bothers father who is a little nervous, with her constant questions and loud reading, even though he loves her a lot. He is often irritable and cannot go downstairs anymore, because he is quite weak. Most of the time he lays on the bed or sits in a chair and the days are very long for him. At night he cannot sleep, because of his restlessness. Also he has a pain in his chest. What is wrong with him? I decide to call the doctor.

Otherwise he is cheerful and talks about the war and politics, does not really act sick.

16, February 1943

The Sembach villagers are in a very bad and somber mood, too great were the sacrifices of sons and husbands in Stalingrad. There are 6 of them missing in Russia. Some people give me dirty looks because I am still sitting in France. It is not my fault.

At night I speak with the doctor and I am very worried about his diagnosis. It is a malignant tumor on his spleen, which can spread to other organs, such as the liver, etc. There is no point doing surgery at his age. I thank him and hang up in great shock and deep sorrow. This is it! A terrible sadness comes over me. This means I will be losing my father this year. These are the sad facts. How often have I feared this moment and how have I wished, they could still have many good years together. 66 years is much too young to have to die.

Now I want to make good use of these last hours of our being together. I want to surround him with all my love. I ask him about his young years and I let him tell me about his military time, which is a special nice memory for him. I show him his certificate of the world war, which later on I want to frame. He likes the idea and says: "Yes, I'd like that! Something like that is nice to keep for later on." We look at old photographs, Richard and I with our Russian prisoner of war, Jeffim. He reads with emotion, what my mother wrote in back of the picture 25 years ago: "Has he not grown into a handsome young boy? He gives me more joy each day and if he stays healthy, we have not fought in vain."

He is so proud of me, because he and I look so much alike and I have inherited so many of his characteristics, also because I became a teacher. Of that he always was proud. I have never disappointed him and was in general, well behaved.

Later I would like to have his photos from the war, which mean so much to him, his beautiful watch, and his cane from Russia. Also his special award, the EK2 (Iron Cross 2), as well as his postcards from the war.

I keep looking at his dear face with the trusting blue eyes, his broad head, kind of like mine, the large nose, the little mustache, the gray hair, and the bony hands. How strong these arms used to be and how they could tackle hard things in his work as a farmer. Now his hands are shaky and have turned thin. How I would like to hold these hands and stroke and caress them, but shyness keeps me from doing that and a man cannot get that sentimental. But I want to see if he runs a fever and feel his pulse. He keeps very quiet and does not know that I just want to hold his warm hand.

We talk a long while of earlier happier times. Later he shows me his feet, which are swollen very badly, probably full of water. I am brave and try not to show my emotions, but Rösel knows, what goes on inside of me. A song comes to my mind:

> Oh, love as long as you can love
> Oh, love as long as you may love
> The time will come the time will come
> Where you stand at graves and weep

17, February 1943

Today I take Helga-Mouse with me to the schoolroom for an hour or so. I forgot to mention that we met her teacher, Miss Schneider, on the train. She said smilingly: "Helga can stay out of school for a few days, she won't miss much. She is a sweet, happy child, sometimes so cute and unspoiled." That makes me happy of course. So she gets to sit in a bench of the 2nd graders with Miss Trude and very soon, after getting over a little shyness, gets right into the class activity. The teacher discussed the subject area of the chimney sweep and the little rascal keeps raising her hand and gives the best answers. Then she got to write. I gave her a blackboard and she wrote in clear and neat script her sentence: "Der Schornsteinfeger ist schwarz (The chimney sweep is black), and he has a ladder, etc."

An hour later I went back downstairs. Never will I get over it, that I could not teach my children as my pupils.

At noon we go back to my parents house for dinner. Mother has made fried crullers especially for me. Father hardly eats anything. What is this? Otherwise, he is cheerful and we talk a lot. They relate the incident, when they had sat me down as a baby at the edge of a field, while they were working and the ants crawled all over me and I started screaming. The way he tells the story, it warms my heart. Then we look at a picture of me, age 4, with a balloon, which was taken in Kaiserslautern. I still have the little picture standing on my piano.

I tell him, that on my walk to and from the train station I always look across the way to where his fields are and I can see the four little trees he had planted. I know it pleases him to hear my interest in his world and he says very lively: "So, you have an interest in those four little trees?" I try to talk more about the things that are dear to him. Then I take several pictures of him with Helga, then mother, and he looking out the gable window. He has no idea these will be the last ones. They are sacred to me.

In the afternoon he struggles to walk up to the schoolhouse, as he always had. It is difficult for him, because he is so weak. I will never forget the sight of him, as he hobbles in on his cane, a scarf wrapped around his neck. He sits at the table in the living room looking at pictures and smiles at the children. I sit down at the piano and play some of the old familiar songs like "Long Long Ago" and others. I notice how he takes his glasses off and wipes the tears from his eyes.

Slowly I get ready, because we want to leave on the 6 o'clock train. Does he know that he might be in the schoolhouse for the last time? By the stairs he stops as always and it is here I shake his callused, faithful, hand and because I promise I will come up one more time, before I have to go back, he is composed.

How often have we said good-bye this way? Back in June he cried and said with a shaky voice: "Come again soon!" And every time he stands there and waits, until I have to turn the first corner. Also this time too he stays there on his weak legs, watching us walk away. At the old city hall I turn and lift my hand in greeting, then we are gone.

Silently we walk to the station. I am unspeakably sad. Not even the children can cheer me up. Helga carries her little pail of honey. It is dark by the time we get on the train.

18, February 1943

Helga just loves her dolls. "Christkind" did bring her a doll carriage and all day long she rides her dolls around in that carriage. She says: "My baby sleeps until noon".

This morning I rode with Norbert in his train to Wiesbaden. He sat with me in the same compartment. His classmates are fresh and act up. He is quiet and well behaved. At the station I say good-bye and admonish him to pay attention in school. In Mainz, I see terrible destruction from the last bombing.

Humanity has gone insane and destroys the cultural possessions of one another. In the evening I am happy to be back in the circle of my happiness with the family.

21, February 1943

I have recuperated so well because my sweetheart takes care of me so lovingly. Every morning she spoils me with breakfast in bed, rolls with butter and a boiled egg. How wonderful, just like in peacetime. I think they have saved up to treat me royally. In the morning we all go with Oma and Opa to church, in the afternoon in lovely spring weather we take a beautiful walk to the Altenbaumburg Castle. I breathe with great contentment the clean, pure air of the country and forget for a few hours the burden of the war and my personal problems. The lovely valley lies before us as well as the silhouette of the ancient castle, dating back to the 11th century and at my side my beloved wife and children. We walk slowly and enjoy the spring day. Oh, how perfect was this day.

In the evening we pay a visit at Oscar Beck and Tante Ella, who treats us to wine and cookies. We talk for a long time about politics, about the deplorable and disgraceful state of affairs of the party and the somber mood of the people.

22, February 1943

Only a few short days are left and my heart is getting heavy already. Every afternoon we go for a walk, this time up the mountain to the reservoir.

Afternoon walk through the hills near the reservoir

The children are in high spirits and play "horsy". We look down on the peaceful and picturesque little village. In the evening I get the zither and we sing all the old folk songs and Helga sings the loudest with her clear and pure voice. Later we visit Laubenstein's and then go to bed. We belong to each other in a love that gets more beautiful every time.

23, February 1943

I took Norbert to the dentist, Dr. Wallau, because he needs braces to straighten his crooked teeth. He has to wear them for two years. We go for another wonderful walk to the "Ackerberg" hill and while the kids are playing; Norbert is riding his roller skates in the street, and we sit in the warm sunshine on a rock and think of the farewell. In the evening we do a little magic and I show them a few tricks. I have learned to make a coin disappear and "tearing" off my thumb. Everyone figured out how I did it, except Helga. She screeches with delight and keeps asking in a singing voice: "But HOW do you do this?" Opa laughs so hard, that tears are rolling down his cheeks. Happily we end this evening with a glass of wine and pastries.

24, February 1943

Tomorrow I have to leave. Norbert has to go to Rockenhausen for a "Hitler Youth Seminar", which I am not very happy about. He too has to pack for 3 days and put on his uniform. Then we go all together to the station. Helga is happy. She never feels terribly sad saying good-bye, because I divert her with happy and carefree talk. She sits on the railing at the gate and keeps saying; "Auf Wiedersehen" and gives me lots of kisses. Then she waves until I cannot see her anymore. Norbert stands by the train window and looks out. He is so handsome and grown up. I am so proud of him. I know he is fighting his emotions and tries to be strong saying good-bye as the train stops in Rockenhausen. He quickly walks through the gate, does not turn around anymore, and is being met by his group leader of the Hitler Youth. He turns around and waves and I take a picture of him. Then Rösel and I continue to Sembach. We take our luggage on a cart for the ½ hour walk to town. Several things we still have to take care of.

Then we go to my parents to eat. So it is at this time, that I see my father for the last time alive on the evening of February 24, 1943.

He does not know just how seriously ill he is. He sits at the table and does not really look sick. Mother is composed. She has fixed my favorite, noodles and stewed blueberries. To please us, father is trying to eat some, but he has no appetite. He gets a lot of company from friends and neighbors. They all bring him something. He is very thin and bony and extremely weak. I keep looking at him as to memorize every little detail, as I know this evening is the last time I will see him. His blue eyes, the thin lips, little mustache, and his hands have become very bony and they shake.

He speaks very sensible about the war and he is convinced that it is lost for us and will be detrimental for our people. Later he said in a sorrowful tone of voice: "My life was one single struggle".

When mother says something that he likes to hear, then his eyes get bright and shiny, such as when she said, "How all people see a great similarity between him and his sister". I have to keep looking at him, still so alive, his dear eyes, and I listen to his voice, which seems I have never done before. Why have I not been kinder and more understanding to him in earlier years? Now I reproach myself.

As long as I want to prolong this visit, the good-bye is inevitable. I want to be brave and not show my emotions. I would love to hug him, stroke him, to show him my childlike love for him, to safely take him to the dark unknown afterlife. But I have to compose myself. So we say good-bye. Rösel watches me and knows how I feel. As I want to shake his hand, he struggles to get up from his chair, because it is something special to shake the hand of his son.

Even though Rösel tells him, to stay seated, he insists and supported by his cane he shakes my hand. For the last time I feel the pulsing of his callused fist, that had worked so hard all his life and he gives me a few good pieces of advice: "Just don't volunteer, leave the door open." Those were his last words to me.

He meant I should leave the door open, so that the stairway would be lit up, as it is already dark when we leave. In the doorway I take one last look at him. Oh, who can imagine, how I feel?

Mother goes down with us into the front yard and she wants to know, what we think. She too feels no hope and she starts to cry. She is shaking all over and I tell her she will catch a cold. She says: "Oh, if only he would get well again."

For one hour, I am together with my loved one and she knows how heavy my heart was in this difficult hour. I could not sleep the rest of the night and constantly had to sit up.

25, February 1943

Travel Day

I got up at 3:30 am. Rösel made coffee. I ate some of mother's cake and started walking to the station at 4:10 am. She can still hear my steps in the quiet night, until I turn the corner by the old city hall, then I am alone with my thoughts.

My sweetheart slips back into the warm bed and accompanies me in her mind. Above Sembach, I turn around and look at the sleepy little village one more time and across to where the dark pine trees grow and I plead with my God, to whom I have so faithfully prayed as a child, that He may turn everything to the best. Over there lie father's two fields that he loves so much. Should he never be able to walk there anymore?

At the station I still have some time and meet a couple of Sembach people. I have ½ hour layover in Hochspeyer, almost 2 hours in Landau. I write the first postcards home, eat some of my cake and get some coffee. Then I catch the express train to Mühlhausen, sit in 2nd class, and I try to sleep. The morning breeze wakes me up and I huddle under my coat. I arrive the next morning at 7:30 am in Montpellier, get a cup of strong coffee and eat some more of mother's cake.

Then I report back to the Lt. Depressed, I unpack at the cold unfriendly chateau. Outside there is the spring sun. I made the mistake and lay under a palm tree with a blanket. The ground was still too cold. I caught a stuffed up nose and an infection of my eyelids. I had night duty that night.

27, February 1943

My brother Richard has been drafted.

P.S.

It was father's wish, that we should become reconciled.

Papa's brother Richard

28, February 1943

There is nothing new here, except the feared Mistral. The strong wind has arrived. After a talk with the 1st Lt., he thinks it could go fast with my father. He might not survive to April. His father-in-law died of cancer in the liver.

5, March 1943

Daily I think of my father. Mother will keep me informed. If only I could be with him these last weeks.

10, March 1943

Richard turns 33. We still have the strong Mistral wind.

22, March 1943

I move in with Sgt. Huter and Sgt. Schwister. The room is much nicer and I finally have a closet. Rösel was in Sembach last Sunday. She wrote about my father, the same as my mother did. She thinks it would be best if he could take his leave from this world and not have to suffer, since he can't be healed anymore. When I mentioned that he could sit outside in the springtime, he said: "If I am not under the pine trees by then."

25, March 1943

I ask that father may get well again, but do not believe that's possible. The last news was not encouraging. In the meantime I have read the books, which I had taken with me from the library.

1, April 1943

Norbert wrote a very good long report to me about his time in the "Hitler Youth" program in Rockenhausen, which was excellent. He had a lot of fun.

The days are passing in the same routine. The night duty is not too bad, because I can sleep some.

3, April 1943

I took a wonderful walk around the chateau area in the evening, passed the waterwheel, the vineyards, and through the southern countryside. I enjoy seeing the spring flowers, the blooming violets, the fragrant pines, and cypresses. The blue sky is clear and silky and I think of my beautiful German homeland and my young years, when my father planted the seed for the love of nature in my heart and more than ever, I am with him in my thoughts. Still, I am very sad.

4, April 1943

Recently I have sent many letters, in which I talked about my beautiful growing up years and the love of my homeland. These were meant especially for father and he read them with great joy. "He is a nature lover", he would say to my mother. One thing I missed out on, was to ask him more questions about his military time, his experiences of the WW I. I know too little about that. He always wanted to go to Metz with me by car. This will not happen anymore now.

5, April 1943

The Telegram

At 7 am, Sgt. Heide woke me: "There is a telegram for you". Oh, my God! With my heart pounding I read the words: "Father's condition grave, we expect the worst. Rösel."

I immediately request to speak to the 1st Lt. to ask for leave. To my horror that pig headed bureaucrat has no intention of letting me go but insists of waiting until my father has died. Such outrageousness! Tears of fury and anger rise up in me. How can anyone be this cold hearted? This miserable parasite! But what good does it do me to be upset? I think of my father all day long.

How is he doing? Is he conscious? Is he suffering? Is he asking for me? Will I get there in time or will I come too late? Oh, how can I have any interest in my duty? In the evening some "big wigs" are coming, Col. Schuler plus Maj. Küppers and others. I give my report, but what do I care about these people.

During the night I try to telephone and get through to the FLUKO in Kaiserslautern. I ask them to find out if my father is still alive. Oh, could I be with you in your last hour, you poor sweet man!

6, April 1943

The Day Of My Father's Death

It happened at 12 o'clock midnight. Rösel has been informed as to what to do. I have received a message over the air traffic service that my father is dying.

Can anyone imagine, how I feel? In the afternoon I want to be alone. I sit in the park of our chateau on a rock. The "big wigs" walk by, no one takes notice of me. I plan to see the 1st Lt. this afternoon. In the small grotto by the windmill I am finally alone and all my penned up grief and the pain of my soul erupts and I am sobbing unrestrained. For the first time I should lose a dear person, so close to me. In my despair I keep praying: "O God, release him from his pain, if he is suffering! Take him home to you today, if you have not answered my prayer to be able to be there with him." It is with disconcertment that I ask myself, how one can wish, that one's father might die? It just would be best for him. On the way back through the vineyards and passing the little forest, I keep on whispering: "I will never forget you, my dear, precious father. I will always honor your memory."

At 3pm, I go back to the bureaucrat and appeal to his humanity. He thinks for a long time and only when I assure him, that I will be back in time for the gas protection class in Paris, he agrees to let me go.

Now I quickly pick up my papers, for the train leaves in 2 hours. It seems impossible, that I am going to make it. Quickly I run to the chateau to get my orders and gas mask. A buddy is taking my luggage to the train and waits for me there, because I still have to have a physical checkup. Everything works out only the tram is late and I am standing on pins and needles. The 1st Lt. takes his time with the signature and says hatefully: "You won't make the train anyway." Still I run without stopping to the station, just reach the train, which is a little late, ringing wet, jump on, and ride towards home.

Slowly nighttime is falling. At the same time, while I am on this train in the Rhone valley, my father dies. Of course I don't know it yet. In Mühlhausen I have a two hour layover, I drink a hot coffee and continue at 10:15 to Strassburg, Rastatt, Karlsruhe.

7, April 1943

It is pouring rain. In Karlsruhe I get a bite to eat and reach Kaiserslautern at 6 pm in pouring rain. I take a bus to Sembach and meet Otto Nebel. Hastily I ask him: "Do you know anything about my father?" He told me: "He has died!" A piercing pain stabs my heart. Why, oh why could I not be there in time and still find him alive? I am afraid of the moment I will see him dead and cold.

It is still daylight and mother is in the stable working as always. She looks up for a moment and when she sees me she runs into my arms crying loudly. I keep holding her and she keeps crying. Then we go upstairs to the front room, where he is lying. Strangely composed, I walk into the room. In the back against the wall is the bed. Under the white sheet I see a body, strangely small, as it seems. I lift the sheet and look into his face, so pale and waxen. His chin is tied up with a tie and his faithful blue eyes are closed forever. His mouth with the narrow lips and the little moustache is severely closed. His chin was full of stubble because he could not be shaved anymore. His hands are folded and they have dressed him in his tuxedo, which he wore at the wedding of his two boys and after that never again, it is brand new.

I would like to kiss him on his forehead. Oh, why could I not have been here last night with him, squeeze his warm hand, stroked him and tell him of my love for him, so he would still be able to feel it! Now it is too late!

For a long time we both look at him. How haggard and bony his face has become. How thin are his fingers and arms, that were once so strong and that I always admired so much. His fingernails are blue, his cheeks sunken in and his dear large ears are of a bluish color. But most of all, what is so shocking and unnatural, that everything is so cold and stiff. I touch his forehead, his hands; I stroke tenderly over his gray hair and just cannot bring myself to leave.

And now mother tells me how he has died. My sweetheart sat up with him for 2 nights, when he was in kind of a coma and hallucinated. He kept looking at the ceiling as if he was searching for something and he did not recognize anyone. The minister came and read a psalm to him, which he was not able to hear. Very rarely did he have a lucid moment and the last clear sentence was: "Has Rösel gone?" He always had a great rapport with my sweetheart and that is of great comfort to me.

Maybe he would not have recognized me and still I would have liked to have been there until the end. My mother, the nurse, and my uncle (his brother) took turns taking care of him. While mother rested a while, my uncle was with him when he gently went to sleep forever. As he told us, he took a deep breath, then his faithful heart stopped forever. His right hand slipped down from the blanket precisely at midnight from the 6th to the 7th of April 1943.

We want to be grateful, that he did not have to suffer and was not in any pain. Rösel had written me that the doctor said there was a chance of a blood clot in his bloodstream and that it could have caused a stroke. He did not want to give him injections for pain, because he would get used to them and he wanted to wait to the end with that. Well, that was not necessary anymore. I tear myself away and quickly go upstairs to the little room, where both of them had a few happy years together. There his bed was stripped and empty. Never again would he sleep in it. It breaks my heart, realizing, that my mother does not yet realize just how lonely she will be.

Then I call Rösel and she will come tomorrow with the children. Mother fixes something to eat for me and we speak of him, whom we all loved and have lost now. She answers my question, how she had met him, so many things of the their young lives together, their love and their marriage, and things I never knew. His dear picture rises up in me newly transfigured.

She had met him after his military time, at that time he was a hired hand at the Mehlingen mayor's farm and was so well liked because he was diligent and a hard worker. Everybody liked him in town and she did too, because he was such a handsome strong young man and always dressed nicely. He wore his reservist cap, always a clean shirt and liked to smoke a good cigar. That's when we met and got to know each other and fell in love.

She then told me also about the problems, his temper, the difficulties that developed after a visit of his parents with hers, and about the pride of her father. He did not want his daughter to marry a hired hand. She talked further about their subsequent marriage and my birth.

Also, she told of his young years when he contracted typhus at age 13. He carried a heavy sack of wheat all the way from the train station by himself and got sick from being wringing wet and over exertion through a thunder storm and how he could not go to school for 6 months.

Now I cannot speak to him anymore or ask him any questions. How I regret the opportunities that are gone forever. For a long time we sit together on our couch and talk, then we go to sleep. Mother is in the kid's room and I in the playroom. I got a hot water bottle for her, because she is trembling from excitement and the cold. Now she is a widow!

8, April 1943

I meet Rösel and Helga at the train station. I finally see them come. Rösel in her brown raincoat and "Murschel" in her little rain coat, because it is pouring. Next to them there is a soldier. And lo and behold, it is my brother Richard. I am a little uptight about this first meeting. I had written him, but there was no time for him to answer. First my little "Murschel" runs up to me to greet me, then I say hello to my sweetheart, and then the two "enemy brothers" are standing across from each other. But there is no other kind of thought except we quietly look into each other's eyes and shake each other's hand. Let us forget about the old quarrels. It was father's wish that we would reunite and forgive one another and now at his death this should occur.

We walk home together. He tells me about his rough training and I know, that he too is heartbroken about father's death and in the meantime he has grown up and became a man and understands, that father at all times meant well. He will stand at his casket and the tears will freely flow.

My sweetheart has thought of everything for the funeral. Tomorrow, Oma, Opa, and Norbert will come. I still have some things to take care of. The death certificate has to be issued, the casket has to be selected, and the carriers secured. They should be his friends and classmates. Then the mayor has to be notified.

His obituary is in the paper this morning. Every free minute I have, I go to my parent's house. There are only hours left when I can still see his beloved face. I cannot help but stroke his hair, his pale cheeks, and his cold hands.

It is terrible to realize that a beloved person is simply gone and will never wake up again. This means farewell forever. I take a picture of him. Tomorrow he will be in his casket already. His body will be given to the earth and will decay and nothing will be left of him, but the sweet memories. His picture will forever be alive, the continuation of the forever alive soul as I understand it. The casket will not be finished until tomorrow, so he still has to lie in his bed.

My sweetheart is practical as always, mother is sad but composed, and Helga plays with her girlfriends. We have decided not to show the children their dead grandfather. We want them to remember him, as they last saw him.

Again it is evening and tomorrow, we are going to have to bury him. That means farewell forever!

9, April 1943

Friday

Today we buried my father at 2 pm.

At 8 am the casket was brought, a natural oak with white interior. Our neighbor Rettig and the carpenter bedded him into the casket, his last place of rest. He fit in it so well. How straight and stiff are his legs and how lightweight is his body that used to be so strong and heavy. Somewhat unfeelingly, the carpenter turns his head until he is lying straight. Then my sweetheart comes and gives him the last service of love by decorating his casket with flowers and evergreen. Into his hands I put the daisies, which I have brought from Montpellier as a last greeting from his son who loved him so much. Now he lies there so dignified surrounded with the flowers, that it is almost festive, so peaceful, as if he were just sleeping.

Continually, flowers and wreaths are arriving from relatives, friends, and neighbors. The sympathy in the village is great and that is so comforting. On the casket there is a beautiful spray of white carnations and a total of 34 wreaths. My aunt from Kaiserslautern has been here since this morning and she mourns her beloved and only brother, together with her son who was killed in Stalingrad. Shortly before noon my in-laws are coming with Norbert. I appreciate it that they are giving my father this last honor. Norbert walked passed the open door without taking one look at his dead grandfather. It is better this way.

Shortly after noon the house fills up with funeral guests from close and far away. With a heavy heart I dress into my tuxedo and my sweetheart gets herself and the children ready, then we go to my parents house. All the rooms are filled with people, many brought a last greeting of flowers, and many stand crying at his casket. When my in-laws walked in, mother embraced Oma crying loudly: "Now I am alone, aren't I?"

Uncle, his only brother has tears in his eyes, when in a sudden surge of sorrow he tenderly puts his hand on his head and shakes him gently. They loved each other a lot, these three. Their growing up years must have been good ones.

Ever closer comes the hour when the casket will be closed. In the yard there are many black dressed people. We all stand around him and everyone speaks so well of him. When I said, how he had to work so hard all his life, even Richard turns away with tears in his eyes. So he has forgiven him, thank God! Now the bell is ringing for father. Down below, the men's choir is assembled to honor him with a last song, and Pfarrer Degen, the pastor arrives.

The funeral procession is waiting in the yard and the time has come, where his casket has to be closed. Mother takes one last look at him, crying loudly and I stare into his waxen face with burning eyes. Now the lid has closed above him, the four screws have been tightened and four men carry him downstairs. When they pass through the doorway, mother cries out: "Now you are leaving me!"

Downstairs in the yard, the casket is put onto two supports. The weather is dry but cold, while yesterday it was still snowing and raining, real April weather.

We have mother in the middle, Rösel at her left and I at her right. This way we are standing on the steps, the children behind us, and then the others. The men's choir begins the song, which he himself has often sung at funerals: "Sleep Father Now In Eternal Peace". For 50 years he was a faithful member of this choir. The men are doing a wonderful job and when in the 2nd verse they get to the part: "Thank you for all the love of a father, for all your trials and tribulations". A big lump gets in my throat, but I try to control myself. But then when I turn around, I see my little "Murschel" with tears streaming down her face. Overpowered with fervent love, I would like to hug her and hold her close to me.

When the song is finished we go downstairs slowly, the casket is lifted up onto the hearse, the wreaths are loaded and the funeral procession starts moving. My eyes are focused on the hearse and while the church bells are ringing, we walk through the village, up the dirt road to the cemetery outside town. The lane he rode so many times with his horses and wagon as a hard working farmer. Then we go through the gate. At the end of the cemetery's gravel road they stop the black clad horses, which pulled the hearse. The casket is lifted off and carried up a ways to the freshly dug grave. Someone had decorated the inside of the grave beautifully with fresh pine branches. Now the carriers slowly lower his casket, remove the ropes from under the casket and the minister begins to speak.

He selected the scripture from Matthews 25, Verse 21, describing him as a faithful and diligent man: "Well done, good and faithful servant, you have been faithful with a few things; I will put you in charge of many things. Come and share your master's happiness".

Now indeed we are standing at his grave, something I have thought of often, what it would be like to be the mourner, rather than one just participating in someone else's grief. Thousands of times I have sung with my school children and the men's choir at funerals, most of the time not particularly involved. Our children are standing behind me and I wish I had been holding their hand. What an experience will this be for them and will it stay in their memory?

And now Pfarrer Degen begins his message, describing my father as a hard working, honest, and upright human being. He gave the most important dates, also that he was proud and pleased, that his oldest son enjoyed the respect of the town's people as the teacher of their children, with his younger son following in his footsteps. Also that he served for 4 years in WW I, however his health suffered in the Russian winter in 1916-17, he had a stroke in 1936 necessitating him to use a cane and since then, became a broken man in spirit. It was painful for him to see his friends still able to work hard. He said, that my father did not realize,

217

just how serious his illness was. During the relatively short time he was sick, he still went to church regularly and enjoyed his choir attendance and competing in different singing festivals.

I remember when he looked down from the church balcony with his shining eyes, when I directed Max Bruch's "Helden Feier", or when I conducted a theatre evening with my school kids and the choir. How proud he was, that his son was able to go to a teacher's college.

Richard gave his father a lot of worries, but later on he was forgiven and was content with his destiny. We were all comforted, that he could leave this veil of tears and did not have to suffer very long. He had always said: "If only I could just go to sleep one night and not wake up in the morning."

All these things Pfarrer Degen described in his beautiful talk. My mother, who had been crying quietly into her handkerchief, calmed down and just kept sighing once in a while. Now the men's choir sings their 2nd song: "Farewell". Then the minister says the blessing and the people disperse. We stay a while longer and toss flowers and evergreen bouquets down on his casket. I tell the children: "Throw a flower greeting down for grandfather", which they do. They are so sensible and sweet; I would like to hug them. After the minister has expressed his sympathy to us, Frau Landmesser, the cemetery's caretaker, begins to shovel the dirt on top of him and the sound of that first shovel of dirt crashing down on his casket tore into my heart.

Now they cover him up and we shall never see him again, only the memories will remain, such as his last good-bye and his last handshake.

Slowly and sadly we walk home and everyone meets at the house for a snack and coffee and cake. After everyone has left, we stay for supper, and then accompany the in-laws to their train. I then thank them that they came. It touched them, that there was so much sympathy extended to father and they could see, how well liked he was in town. At sunset we walk back and I look across the way over to the dark pines, where he is resting, as I will for all times to come from now on.

Norbert can stay tomorrow, but on Sunday he is going back to Hochstätten to Oma and Opa's house.

10, April 1943

Mother slept with us last night, this most difficult one, the first night without him. She has probably cried herself to sleep, when she was alone. Now she has new worries: Richard was ordered to join a replacement troop of a grenadier regiment, which is to be sent to Russia. What dreadful news.

Today there are a few errands to take care of. Rösel has changed things around in their room. Father's bed has been moved out and a dresser put in its place and above it she hung the old family pictures. After cleaning the place my mother will move back in alone, as a widow.

In the afternoon Alice and Jakob come to visit. He has quite a saga to tell. He was wounded in Stalingrad, but lucky, to survive and be sent home. How fast this day passed!

11, April 1943

In the afternoon Richard has to leave for Wiesbaden. My poor mother! When she shakes his hand, she strokes with a tender gesture over his sleeve, and then she has to let him go.

A little later, we walk part way with Norbert to the station since he must return to school tomorrow. We wave when he turns around. He is such a big boy now and we can let him go alone. Helga sleeps in her little baby bed, which she just barely fits into and before saying good night, she hugs and loves her grandmother, sweet thing!

In the afternoon we went one more time to father's grave, standing there in silence and reverence, with the small hill piled high with beautiful wreaths and flowers in brilliant colors in the evening sun. We had bought the plot next to him for mother later on.

12, April 1943

This is my last day of furlough. I straighten things in the library up in the attic room and do a little math with Helga. I am surprised, how fluently she is reading and what an excellent memory she has. My sweetheart packs my luggage, bakes a cake for me, and gives me all kinds of goodies to take. Also ham, eggs, butter, sausage, etc., so I will have good supplies to last me a while.

In the evening we sit together for a long time, before going to bed.

13, April 1943

The day to leave! My mother gets up very early, because the bus leaves at 7 am. Quickly I am packed and the time comes to say good-bye again. My little "Mouse" is still asleep with rosy cheeks. I quietly call her: "Little Mouse," she blinks her eyes, stretches, rubs her eyes and reaches up to my neck with her little arms, gives me kisses and says Auf Wiedersehen! Then mother says sadly: "Oh, yes, always the good-byes". I embrace her, console her, but she cries. At the door I hug my sweetheart, get on the bus and see driving by, Helga in her little red jacket by the window, waving.

Then the bus takes me through the village to Kaiserslautern, where I take the express train to Metz. I eat lunch in a hotel across from the railroad station, walk past the old barracks, where father served 40 years ago, get my ticket to Paris, and arrive there at 8 pm.

I find out that the gas protection course did not take place after all. I go to the FLUKO to telephone and report back. I then get orders to return early in the morning and stay overnight in the Hotel de la Terasse.

14, April 1943

The long, long trip straight through France, further and further south through the Rhone valley. The trip is terribly long and the train is moving at a hellish speed. I read my book that I took with me and eat the sandwiches, which my sweetheart made for me and I look out the window at the lovely valley. In the evening I have to change trains in Avignon and one more time in Tarascon, where I stand at the platform for a long time in bright moonlight and finally arrive in Montpellier at 11 pm. Dead tired I fall into bed.

15, April 1943

I check in with Lt. Jagsch. What an incredible outrageousness! He did not believe me that my father did not die until the night of the 6th.

I will get his death certificate. I am infuriated about the bureaucracy of these stubborn idiots.

19, April 1943

Mother was yesterday, a Sunday, at his grave. She wrote: "I cried myself out. I had no idea I could be so lonesome for him. I had to take care of him, but this is all taken away from me. But work is the best medicine; it lets one forget the pain. When one stops to think, how so many young people have to die, who would so like to live, like Hermann Schäfer. One should allow father to have his peace. He had his care and a decent funeral. After Easter I will go to Mehlingen to visit my sister and also to Breunigweiler."

20, April 1943

I move to the Avenue D'Assas into a much better room. I fix it up to make it homey. My roommate is Schafitel, a teacher's son from Swabia.

22, April 1943

Excerpts From Mother's Letters

"Now I cannot show father your letters anymore. The packages that I sent you, he always wanted to pack them and tie them up, I never did it good enough. It is so difficult to be alone. One can never confide in someone anymore. It is not cozy in my little room anymore. The Mehlinger's had admired his casket. Tante Elise said she had never seen such a nice funeral."

23, April 1943

Rösel writes, that she did "spring cleaning". They want to paint the bathroom. Oh, everything is so senseless and we miss you so much. Yesterday the Easter Cards for the kids arrived. Helga read both of them, as always, aloud. Today she said: "Mama, now that I don't believe in the Easter Bunny anymore, can I help color the eggs?" I promised she could. Norbert will still hide them.

25, April 1943

Easter

We have beautiful warm spring weather and nature is at its best with flowers and trees blooming everywhere. I go to the chateau to be alone and in my thoughts I am at home. Will the children be looking for the Easter Bunny now?

Mother writes: "It is Easter Monday. The weather is stormy outside and our house is so empty and lonely. I am afraid! Yesterday I went to Mehlingen. I could not stand it here anymore. Saturday I bought a flowering plant and took it to his grave. Oh, how I miss him! If only this war was over and Richard was home.

I often have to think about how angry he was, when he saw me working so hard and running around. That made him so depressed and he was so weary of his suffering."

26, April 1943

Easter Monday

Here a holiday is like any other workday. One gets so numb!

Rösel sent me a package with Easter Eggs and a cake, sweet thing! She writes: "Today, according to tradition, we will take a walk to the Altenbaumburg Castle. You remember we always did this on Easter. It is so beautiful walking through the fields with everything in bloom. The plums, the cherry and apple trees, and then the blooming lilacs on top of the castle. The intoxicating fragrance is everywhere.

After returning, mother is setting the table for dinner. How wonderful it would be if you could share this meal with us.

How I would like to be close to you in the white church in Montpellier."

28, April 1943

Rösel also sent me the thank you notes from father's funeral. She also thanked me for the dear Good Friday letter, in which I expressed my appreciation for her understanding in honoring my sorrow.

She writes that she will go to Sembach tomorrow and take Helga with her, but she can only stay until Monday or Tuesday, because Norbert's school is starting again.

The brown chicken has hatched 3 chicks and the children are overjoyed. Norbert was in Feil and brought back 3 Easter Eggs and 5 Marks.

30, April 1943

We were issued tropical uniforms, not that nice but practical. I also need my sunglasses; the climate is so different from home. So far this spring has been a period of time mostly filled with the illness and loss of my father. I will hope and pray that the future will have in store for us, only happy things. Maybe peace will come soon! We will not give up hope.

Mementos of my father:

His medals;

> EK-2, Cross of Honor for fighting on the front.
> His 2 Military Reserve pictures and his pipe
> His pins for his 25th and 50th membership of the men's choir
> His picture albums from WW I.
> The cane from Russia

His favorite songs:

> Hymn: "Great God, we praise you…"
> Choir: "Holdriola."
> Oh, mother, give me your Blessings
> As it was at home
> Soldier songs: "As I stand at midnight dark.
> In the field of early morning

Folksongs:

> We're parting now with sound and song
> In beautiful meadows

1, May 1943

On 21, August 1944, some of my diaries were lost in an attack with French terrorists near Livron south of Valence in the Rhone valley. I will try to reconstruct the events between 1, May 1943 and 15, August 1944 in a condensed form from memory. Details may have to be omitted.

May 1943

I am still in Montpellier and we are still living in the Chateau Font Trouvee. In my memory, is the long walk, the ride on the streetcar, the short footpath through the pine forest to the chateau, and the room with stone tiles.

NCO Trifflinger and Sgt. Lublasser are acquaintances from Troyes. NCOs Gossen and Pfister, 1st Lt. Hieke and Lt Jagsch are on the terrace sunning themselves. Slowly it is turning warm again. The soldier's mess in Montpellier, and the food in the Café Rompel are just average. My friend Sgt. Schafittel handles the mass of notices in the FLUKO.

There is supposed to be a move again to Rue de la Loge in the city. The trip to Toulon!

June 1943

The citadel is being fixed up. A new house will be available in the beautiful avenue behind the chateau for the non-commissioned officers and sergeants. I get a nice room, which I share with Schafittel. I have a good bed and there is a sink to be able to wash. There is a nice garden with flowers. The mosquito net, one cannot do without. In the evenings I relax with a good book by the open window or on the veranda. They are working hard on the citadel remodeling. The dining hall is supposed to be ready soon. We will be moving soon.

A Sunday outing to Palavas.

The day room is large, but not comfortable. In the morning I usually go for coffee and two slices of bread with jam. Soon furloughs are to be given again.

I still have not gotten used to the idea, that we should have another baby. I should look at my brave, little wife as an example. She has accepted it and is prepared. What a wonderful mystery about motherhood.

22, June 1943

The Furlough

Aside from a lot of miscellaneous items I want to bring my loved ones, the most important one is Max, the turtle. I talked Sgt. Rompel into letting me have him, which was no easy task. The last few days I had kept him in the garden and yesterday he disappeared. I searched everywhere and finally found him hiding under the flowers. Because of the heat, I often poured water over him. He will be such a joy for the children.

At the last minute I reached my train. I was wringing wet because of a missing signature. I always go on leave with such high expectations and later on feast on the memories.

Two weeks away from this miserable military, away from southern France and homeward bound, and the wheels are rolling home. Oh, what a feeling! All the soldiers are in a happy mood.

23, June 1943

Left Mühlhausen at 10 am, arrived in Sembach, or Hochstätten (I do not remember). Anyway, the joy of the family was tremendous. My little wife looks pale. No one knows of our secret!

24-30, June 1943

Wonderful days in Sembach! Helga is a sweet little darling. She is beginning to look more and more like a Hoffmann (Oma's family name), but in her characteristics, especially in her talents she resembles me. She still likes to come to my bed in the mornings to smooch.

One day I decide to take the turtle to school. The children are excited and show a lot of interest. Then he is to stay in the garden. Nothing is more beautiful than to go to the garden with my sweetheart in the evenings. She picks strawberries for me and I have a little chat with the neighbors.

In the evening we visit father's grave. It is well cared for and the deep love of his family surrounds his spirit.

1, July 1943

Half of my leave time is over already. Then I begin to already think of the good-byes. My sweetheart is wearing her hair up and it looks lovely on her. We enjoy something like a second honeymoon, except more beautiful than ever.

6, July 1943

We go to Wiesbaden to visit with Gretchen and Mariechen. In the afternoon I see 1st Lt. Weber to inquire, if I can put in a request for the female Air Force Training School for air messaging as a teacher. He sees no problem. As soon as I get back I will put in for a transfer.

7, July 1943

We are going back to Sembach with the kids, because Norbert has a school vacation. He is happy that he was promoted to the junior class of high school.

8, July 1943

Farewell

Early in the morning I leave by bus. Helga is still asleep, but then wakes up and wants to wave good-bye from the window. I get a good train to Strassburg and Mühlhausen, where I get a bite to eat for lunch. In the evening I continue via Belford to Montpellier.

10, July 1943

I present 1st Lt. Hieke my proposal for the transfer. Of course he denies it, this stubborn bureaucrat and even Jagsch tries to talk me into staying. That's it: "They are just taking advantage of my work and talent here". They want to make me platoon leader for Master Sgt. Hager.

12, July 1943

As of today I am platoon leader of the 2nd Platoon. Thank goodness a change of pace. I drive out to the chateau again, where Sgt. Merlich lives, and lies around in his bathing suit all day. It is lovely in the sycamore grove with the chirping crickets, and the peach, almond, and apricot trees.

14, July 1943

I go on the first trip to the different checkpoints in a rented French car. The driver is grumpy because he has to wait a long time everywhere.

15, July 1943

This is the second part of the round trip. There is a good atmosphere at the checkpoints; the people are orderly and decent. But there is still much work to be done. But I do not care for Körner as secretary and I will appoint someone else.

18, July 1943

Now begins the best part of my time in Montpellier. Everyday there is something new. The platoon moves into house No. 21, the first floor. There I have my first conference meetings. I reject Sgt. Körner as secretary and 1st Airman Scheller is recommended to me. I choose him and it was a good choice. He is a respectable, careful, and diligent person quite to my liking. We fix up the platoon meticulously as we need it.

When I come back to my room at night, there is nothing greater than sit on the veranda and read.

I work out the plans for the check up points and I am careful that good work is done. My people soon know to appreciate me, I conduct my classes well and see that things are in good order and the people grow together in a valuable comradeship.

25, July 1943.

The terrible heat! The first grapes and daily on the road! We will be receiving a new wood-gas burning truck (truck burns wood which produces a vapor gas for the engine to operate).

30, July 1943

We do daily trips in terrible heat to the checkpoints with a new wood-gas truck. We take along rations for 10 days, a supply of drinking water, and munitions, etc. We have a good rapport with the people of the village. I love driving our good Mercedes KFZ.

I like to drive to Checkpoint #10 to NCO Küster. Everything is spic and span. A stonewall has been built around the barracks. Sometimes, we are able to get something to eat there.

1, August 1943

I look forward to mail from home telling me that Rösel is OK, as well as everyone else.

3, August 1943.

We climb to the "Pie St. Loup" near Cazevieille. We stopped at the "Robbers Cave" and the quite dilapidated French apartment houses and now, new barracks are to be built there.

5, August 1943.

I have a lot of work at Checkpoint #11 located on a high mountain. The people there subsisting on military field rations for weeks now. This cannot go on much longer. The work at the barracks has become very labor intensive. Supplies have to be brought up via horse drawn wagons.

6, August 1943.

We drive to Beziers with material including posts, barbwire, boards, tar, nails, stoves, camouflage colors, etc.

7, August 1943

Everything at Checkpoint #13 is always in order. The climb is from St. Drezery. The view in the distance is beautiful at dusk.

10, August 1943.

I love to go to Palavas, swim in the blue Mediterranean, and eat baked fish. I watch the people at the beach and how happy they are. I lay on the beach for hours. One can swim out but has to be careful of the undertow.

We make friends with the French drivers.

14, August 1943.

In between some beautiful quiet days in Montpellier, I pursue my favorite pastimes.

15, August 1943

Sometimes my driver Kern and I sit on the highway, mostly at night, because the truck has broken down and it has to be towed. We have made some friendships with French drivers.

18, August 1943.

Many trips to Sete using Route #20 with a wonderful view down to the sea.

20, August 1943

I am happy. This is so much better than in the FLUKO. I don't have night duty anymore and I can divide my time, as I want to. The food is good and the view over the Mediterranean Sea incredibly beautiful.

22, August 1943

I like to visit Checkpoint #14 with NCO Spatz and can stay overnight there. Of course on the floor of one of the houses, which is under construction as a new barrack. The trip by bus is over Lunel.

23, August 1943

The bus trips to Beauvoisin, with accommodations in the schoolroom. An old mill tower is located nearby.

25, August 1943

In Lavalle, is a beautiful chateau, where the paratrooper company is billeted. The accommodations are on the chateau grounds. Two blonde children are busy playing.

1, September 1943

We are to move to the citadel. We feel uncomfortable there. There are pretty gardens in front of the House #21. We make daily trips to the citadel in order to arrange the barrack's dining room.

2, September 1943

I like to drive to the Checkpoint #18, Grau du Roi. NCO Fründ, a down-to-earth farmer from Westphalia who is in charge. I always stay there one night with the mosquitoes and the sound of the sea. The watchtower is built upon the house's terrace.

4, September 1943

At Checkpoint #21 in Agde, the defensive emplacements are being built with materials delivered partially via trains, bicycles, and trucks. While there, I try to do some shopping for the family.

5, September 1943

I am happy to have such good news from home. My sweetheart is feeling well. If only I could see her. Norbert will know of course what's going on.

I will try to look forward to this child, that God has blessed us with. I just hope everything will go well!

10, September 1943

I am moved to the citadel, and was assigned a comfortable room with NCO Meier.

12, September 1943

Together with Scheller, I organize our business office. NCO Meier is very busy acquiring material for the guardhouse. Always in Beziers, negotiations with construction site supervisors take place. Tremendous loads of materials are hauled, but the building of the guardhouse will not be finished. Now comes an additional order that most of them must do their own cooking. I observe Lt. Effler, as an immature boy and Lt. Scholz, just the opposite. I work very hard; Hieke can see the results. I wonder when he will submit my appraisal?

22, September 1943

I had a slight car accident near Generac with minor scratches. From the "smuggle" trip, I was able to obtain soap, some chocolate for the children, and two kilos of almonds and raisins.

1, October 1943

The mess hall is finished, the dining room walls are painted with German landscapes in the style one would see in an old farmhouse. The food has improved and in our rooms we have stoves for heating. I develop a friendship with Schafittel, a teacher's son from Swabia. One can still swim in Palavas.

6, October 1943

Today I submit my application via Lt. Colonel Hieke to headquarters in Lyon. What success will I have?

15, October 1943

I hear and see nothing about my application. It will probably be lying in someone's drawer for a long time.

20, October 1943

We take a lot of trips to Sete. There are tremendous defense fortifications being built, along the whole Mediterranean coastline. An army of workers put up barbed wire, laying mines, gun emplacements, and bunkers. The French are angry having their beautiful coastline ruined.

1, November 1943

I sent something for Norbert's birthday, but don't remember what, most likely some books and a letter.

6, November 1943

Norbert 13 Years Old

Today is the celebration for the initiation of our new dining room. Col. Janson is here too and it turns out to be a fun party.

For you, my dear son, I wish you the best, good health and success in school.

7, November 1943

I report to the commander and he is sympathetic about my situation and promises, to do his best in the matter.

10, November 1943

It gets colder and we build cozy fires in our rooms. Scheller also sleeps with us. NCO Stefan Schmitt has the attic room.

1, December 1943

At Checkpoint #15, NCO Hentschke is in charge of repairing the mill tower.

2, December 1943

In Lavalle, the parachute division there has been transferred to Italy. Our people have moved into the chateau.

3, December 1943

The work at guardhouse #10 is completed. Around the barracks a one meter thick stonewall has been erected.

We can still get grapes. I will never forget, how many wonderful blue and white grapes I ate. We usually bring back baskets full during our trips. Once we towed a Frenchman and to show his appreciation he gave us two baskets full of grapes. How often we have eaten them on the road. The trips to the third platoon's checkpoint.

In Narbonne, I submit an application to Sgt. Leidenschwanz to deliver coal to checkpoint Bedarieux as soon as possible. It was a long return drive through the night.

6, December 1943

There is a trip with M/Sgt. Hager to the Pyrenees via Perpignan, St. Louis. Then with the incline railroad we climb up through the magnificent snowy mountains. What an incredible panorama. Freezing cold in Latour located on the Andorra Border! We are across from the Spanish city of Puigerda, ablaze with lights. Happy people! Back to Bourg-Madame, where we stayed overnight.

At night with the help of the border guards we smuggled coffee, oil, chocolate, tobacco and soap over the border with a sled over the hard frozen snow. The bitter cold, even in bed. Returned in the morning after a very long drive.

I have so many memories of Tiefland. Now I saw for the second time the wildly romantic Pyrenees.

A few weeks ago we did the terribly long trip again by car with Sgt. Leidenschwanz and S/Sgt. Winkler to the godforsaken Outpost #29, in Montford across from Mt. Canigou. There is a dreary loneliness up high on the bare mountain. But they have cared for themselves. They have slaughtered a cow, have rabbits, geese, have collected chestnuts and potatoes, and have enough firewood for the winter.

9, December 1943

I drive to Canx to deliver materials.

10, December 1943

I drive to Murviel. There's trouble with NCO Buchschatz's transfer from Pie St. Loup to St. Martin.

11, December 1943

Now there are only a few weeks left to the "Big Event"! My sweetheart writes so bravely and confidently, that I am completely relaxed. Everything is prepared. When her time comes for delivery, she wants to go to the Clinic Martha Petschel. If only I will get a furlough. I am looking for baby clothes, jackets and little hats and was able to get some things.

Often together with Schafittel, we have a glass of red wine and our daily evening meal. Often we also eat in other locations. Everything is very expensive and the French are ripping us off.

12, December 1943

How cozy it is in our room when the fire is burning. Some of the men I have recommended to be promoted have become NCOs.

Daily we take provisions in the morning to the checkpoints; there is always the weighing and dividing up, but I enjoy it. With many difficult supply trips I often pitch in myself.

Checkpoint #11 is still not finished. #12, on the hillside of St. Martin is OK. The barracks from the #16 were moved in six trips by truck to #14, and the constant back and forth with #15 located in Beauvoisin. The trips with the Opel Olympia.

14, December 1943

We had a delicacy, smoked eel. Some to eat myself on the 18th and 19th, some for the mess hall, and some to send home. They will arrive in good condition. There are only a few days left until Christmas. The beginning of January our baby is supposed to be born. I can hardly wait.

The children write such sweet letters.

20, December 1943

The disappointment! In the evening while at my office, I receive word that I will be transferred. 1ˢᵗ Lt. Kröger of my unit spoke to Hieke and ordered that I be immediately reassigned to Lyon. I am angry over this! Why not before! It is way to late.

21, December 1943

My orders are that I am to move to Lyon and I am not too happy about that. Such bad timing! I pack and say good-bye to Montpellier. On the Lyon bound train I meet the teacher Mr. Müller from Neukirchen.

Arrival in Lyon-Perrache, drive by truck and welcomed at Alai-Francheville. A nice room in a beautiful chateau; "acquired" by the commander. I have a good bed, there's heat, good food, and good comradeship. Also, 10 nice military female personnel are stationed there.

Captain Becker goes on furlough.

22, December 1943

Preparations are being made for the Christmas party and I make myself useful. A Christmas program which has a lovely atmosphere. 1ˢᵗ Lt. Schönmehl, 1ˢᵗ Lt. Dammertz, and Lt. Haferkamp work together with me. The duty is pleasant. The commander does a good job planning this Christmas festival. He seems to be the perfect example of a "man of the world". His pride and joy is the physical map on the wall.

23, December 1943

There is a rehearsal for the Christmas program and I do not rest, as I want to make a good impression.

I receive a wonderful Christmas package from home.

24, December 1943

Christmas Eve

In the afternoon there is a mood of Christmas already. Outside the wintry weather, frost, cold, and fog. In here, the cozy warm house with steam heat and good food in the dining room.

In the afternoon we prepare for the festival in the evening. I rehearse with Private First Class Hase, two pieces for the piano and the violin. At 5 pm, in the dining room, there is mysterious activity. At 6 pm, everyone stops working.

All the men and the 10 female personnel assemble. Then the Commander, Col. Janson enters in a happy mood. Everyone takes their seats and first of all there is a festive dinner with soup, pork cutlets and vegetables. For dessert pudding, every man gets a beer, cognac, and liqueur. Then the Commander gives a very nice speech, while the lights on the tree are lit and we sing together "Silent Night, Holy Night".

My thoughts of course are at home and at this hour I need to be alone and go to the park and let my mind and thoughts drift back 800 km north of here, where my loved ones are celebrating the festival of love and are thinking of me. That is what we had planned to do, to be close in our thoughts at this hour.

The tables are set beautifully, there is a gift for each man, a basket of cookies, nuts and chocolate, a bottle of wine, cigars, cigarettes and a book with a handwritten Christmas greeting from the commander. Pine branches on the white cloth tables, the fragrance of Christmas; in short, I have not experienced such a Christmas given to the troops during this war. We sit according to our place cards and then the program takes place.

Poems, songs, and musical interpretations, then the second part, which was more humorous. A big success was Private 1st Class Kroll as St. Nicholas (like Santa Claus), with a big sack full of presents for each of us and for each one of us a fitting poem. Medals were presented to the commander and to some of the men.

My table companion was the fabulous Eris Förster. Soon the atmosphere was exuberant. Lt. Kröger and I played as an intro, Händel's "Largo". At midnight the female personnel had to leave, the men stayed until 1 am.

I had to go back outdoors into the starry night to let my thoughts drift back home and think of how you will probably blow out the candles by now. How the Christmas fragrance will still fill the house, but how you will now sleep sweetly, my beloved.

And soon, very soon your big hour will arrive, my sweet wife.

25, December 1943

A beautiful, bright winter day! Outside there is white frost on the trees and the grass. At midday, my free time begins. In the evening at dusk I go on my old familiar walk under the overpass along the little rushing brook. At 7 pm, I leave for the city to go to the military cafeteria and eat a wonderful Christmassy dinner with turkey and salad.

How good I slept and how wonderful the cookies tasted which Rösel and mother had sent to me. Every evening I light a candle on the fireplace hearth and burn a little pine branch. This way I have the fragrance of home in this place.

26, December 1943

It is fun to work here. I go into a lot of trouble to design a big, new strategic map, which covers the whole wall. I put in little flags and other designs. Tonight I am working until late into the night. I took a few photos today. My buddies here are very nice to me.

I still have some cookies left including a small gingerbread and the pine aroma. These were two wonderful days!

In the afternoon, we went into the city to see a movie. It is a rarity to be able to go to Lyon. The trip includes an electric train, an incline railroad, and a streetcar.

27, December 1943

I often work on the wall map past midnight.

28, December 1943

We have classes about the geological structure of the earth, which was excellent. The commander came to observe, it was a success.

29, December 1943

We have a field training exercise by marching to the new FLUKO at Fort St. Foy. I plan to take my military skills examination.

30, December 1943

We prepare for the New Years Eve celebrations.

31, December 1943

The entire afternoon was spent practicing for the New Years Eve celebration. Two attractive dancers for the evening are the charming Eris Förster and M. Dietrich, with 1ˢᵗ Lt. Schönmehl as master of ceremonies. At 8 pm, we get together for dinner and then we have an extensive and wonderful program. The French ladies are invited and are amazed about our beautiful celebration. The evening gets to be more and more fun, but very soon it will be midnight. The mood is high with cognac and champagne.

1944

1, January 1944

New Year

What will it bring us? I hope and pray the fulfillment of many wishes! At midnight, I slip out of the door to be alone and I look up at the immense starry sky and concentrate all my thoughts on my loved ones at home. My most fervent wishes accompany all of you, especially you, my sweet wife. It won't be long now, until our baby will be born and I wish you the very best for the coming weeks, if only everything will go well.

Norbert made another calendar for me, cut out a wooden Santa Claus, and painted it. Helga has written a sweet little letter to me.

The early morning belongs to me. I go for my walk in the clear frosty winter air along the little brook. I think how they are now probably attending church in Hochstätten, singing the old familiar New Years hymn "Help, O Jesus, let it be a good beginning of the New Year."

2, January 1944

From now on I am in a state of the highest expectation. Any day the "Big Event" can happen. Actually I am quite confident.

3, January 1944

Every evening I go for my walk under the bridge by the brook, smoke a cigar and let my thoughts drift homeward.

I have asked Lt. Kröger several times about leave time. My sweetheart thought I should try to take it starting January 5th. What if I come too early?

My shopping has been all taken care of. I have bought some cute little jackets and hats, bibs, etc.

4, January 1944

My big map is finally finished after arduous work. I have glued it neatly to the wall and attached all the tactical signs carefully. I am proud of it and the commander is pleased.

5, January 1944

The Lt. asked me if I wanted to have a furlough, I said: "Yes, for a specific reason". He smiled and said: "Well, then go ahead for that specific reason today!"

I was due for a leave for some time now.

6, January 1944

Our Baby Sigrid Has Arrived!

8, January 1944

If only I knew what was going on at home? Why haven't I left yet? My Sweetheart wishes for me to be there.

10, January 1944

My college friend Krause says: "There is a telegram for you!" Quickly I go to my office. Capt. Becker meets me and says: "Let me congratulate you on your baby daughter."

That's it! A tremendous feeling of joy and happiness fills my heart. A little daughter! Just what Rösel had wanted. For a long time I hold the telegram in my hand on which it says: "Our Sigrid has arrived". With all my great joy I try to keep calm. If only my sweetheart and the child are healthy.

Now I quickly get on with my leave time. The papers are ready soon, I just need the signature of the commander he is very busy. I check out quickly with him, also the doctor, and then go downtown to the railroad station. Smooth trip through the dark of night, in Mühlhausen, I cross the tracks to catch an off limits train to Badenweiler. From there by express train to Mannheim. I had a confrontation with a railroad official. It doesn't matter. Anyway, without authorization, I take an off limits train over Ludwigshafen. It is horrible how Mannheim has been destroyed. I arrive in Neustadt. Oh, if only the train had wings!

11, January 1944

In Kaiserslautern I have time to telephone. I get a connection to the Clinic Martha Petschel and I hear the lovely voice of my sweetheart, telling me that everything went well and that we have a sweet little baby girl. Oh, my Lord, how I thank you!

Rösel would like me to come in the morning, when I have had time to get cleaned up, shave, etc. I know she wants to be proud of me. Caring as ever, she tells me, where my clean clothes are, and what to wear, etc.

At 10 pm, the children are at the station because they know I am coming. Norbert and Helga are excited about the new baby sister and Oma and Opa also have smiles all over their faces. We spend a happy evening. We keep laughing and talking and I can still see Helga sitting on the kitchen chair, her hands clamped under her thighs, laughing so hard, that her little face gets all crinkled up.

The evening passes in the happiest of moods and it is time to go to bed; tomorrow will bring great joy.

12, January 1944

I go to Bad Kreuznach in Norbert's school train. Sister Martha receives me very cordially and she gives me satisfying answers to my questions. Then I am allowed to go through the double doors, where I know my sweet happiness awaits me.

And there she is, laughing at me, radiantly healthy and happy, the symbol of a young and blessed mother. My heart seems to break with overwhelming happiness.

For a long time I hold her and cannot say a word, all choked up with emotion. My precious sweetheart! Oh, my God, You have blessed me beyond expectation. But when will I see our new baby?

And there she is, sleeping so sweetly and healthy into her new life, with chubby cheeks and the tiny little fists with the fingers so perfectly formed.

I find out that everything went well and how brave you were, my precious wife. She went with Oma to the station on the morning of the 6th, confidently and not in the least bit worried. The delivery went normal with the good care of Schwester Petschel and I know she was in the best of hands. I stay there all day long and from now on every day.

13, January 1944

We have again a happy reunion after being expected with great anticipation. How I love to see our baby nurse. Then I can see her blue eyes.

15, January 1944

There is not a day I do not go to visit. The children also want to come.

16, January 1944

Today Norbert and Helga came to admire the new little baby sister. Helga is in awe of her and Norbert also seems to like her.

The in-laws are happy too, although at first they were not too thrilled. Rösel has company from cousin Ella, Frau Dexheimer, etc. Everyone brings gifts. Tomorrow Rösel gets to go home. I have the best impression of the clinic's food, her care is excellent, and everything is spotlessly clean. For the time being, Rösel can still nurse the baby, but soon she will get an additional bottle. She still sleeps the whole day and I love looking up at the corner window, where they are.

17, January 1944

Today we pick up mother and child by car and bring them home. She is carefully wrapped with pillows and blankets. At home, the very best care will await you, our sweet child. We want to do everything to love and cherish you and create a happy childhood for you just as the other two have enjoyed. That we promise, you darling child!

Some things trouble me though. Rösel was in a dampened and gloomy mood a few times and in tears she said once: "I don't know, I have such a heavy heart. When I look at the poor little thing, I feel as if this child will have to go through a lot."

Oh, dear God, such feelings cannot have any basis. We have conceived this child in fervent love and welcome her with all the ardor of our hearts. Keep our happiness alive!

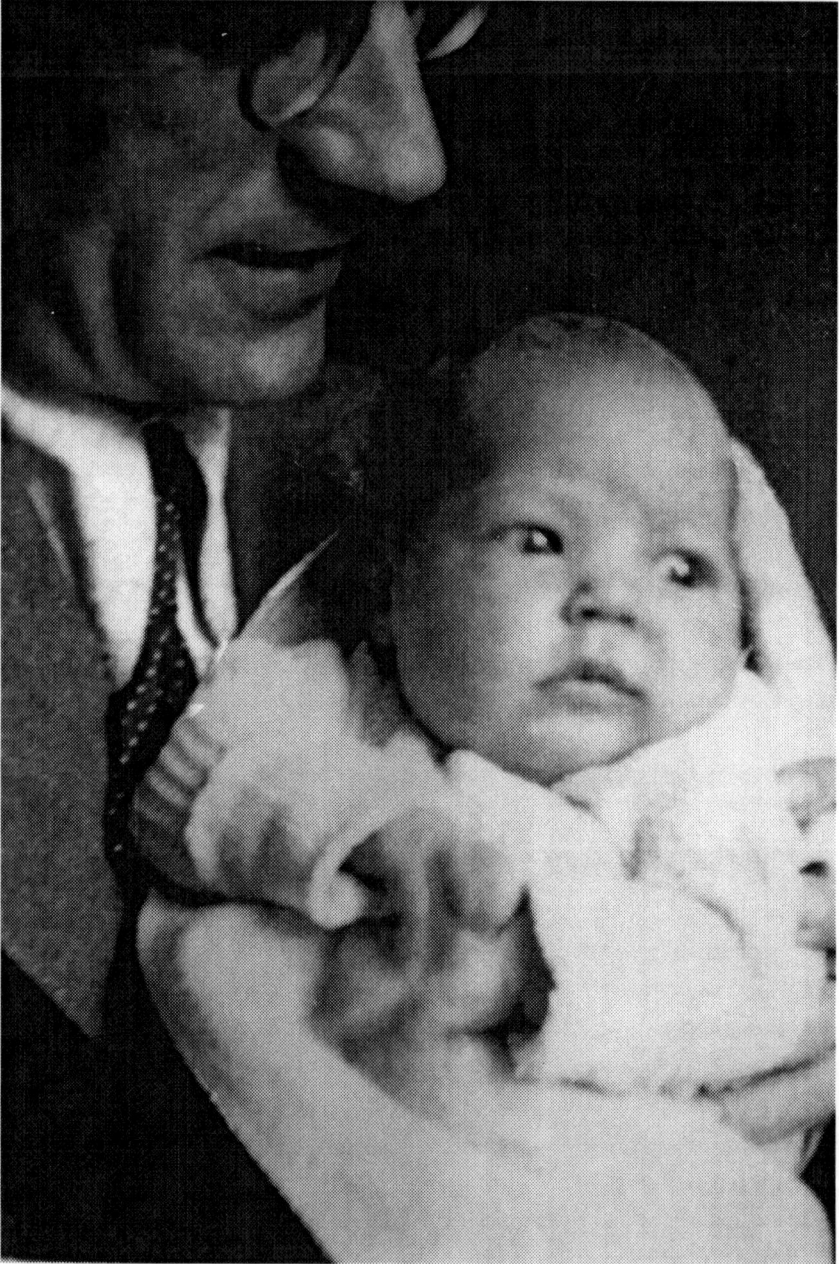

Papa's new daughter Sigrid

18, January 1944

How wonderful and lovingly Rösel cares for the child. How sweetly she is lying in her bassinet. She grows and develops, is very quiet and almost never cries, but sleeps all day.

On Sunday, she will be baptized and the Sembacher grandmother shall hold her and be her godmother. Of course she is excited.

23, January 1944

Sunday! Baptism Of Our Sigrid

In the morning, Else from Cologne, comes with Klaus surprisingly. Grandmother comes too. At 2 pm the minister, Pfarrer Zinn, comes to the house. He has become a friend of the family. And now our child receives her name: Sigrid Ingeborg

With dignity and seriousness, the festive act takes place. Grandmother is holding her. Our friends then stay afterwards for coffee and cake. A good bean coffee that was stashed away for this occasion, a cigar and good conversation with the minister adds to the pleasant afternoon. In the evening we are together and Klaus takes care of the entertainment, Well, I must say, our children are better behaved than him.

The planes are roaring above us! When will this misery end?

24, January 1944

Grandmother goes back home to Sembach.

25, January 1944

I go with Norbert to Sembach to get the fully packed baby carriage. Grandmother helps push it up to the old oak tree. Richard was there on furlough too. He looks well and I wish him the best. We have completely reconciled.

29, January 1944

The Hour Of Farewell Has Come Again

Early in the morning, I believed I would miss the train. A fast good-bye by the front door, then in a rush to the station, where I found out I would have had enough time.

Via Darmstadt, there was an air raid in Bensheim, and then via Mannheim, Karlsruhe, and Freiburg. With a delay across the Rhine River, arrival in Mühlhausen at 8 pm, then a smooth trip back to Lyon.

31, January 1944

This birthday, my father had not lived to see. Oh, if only he would have been here to welcome his new granddaughter.

I close this month in my diary in the firm and confident hope that the "fates" may continue to smile on us with sweet blessings.

1, February 1944

Now my time in this division will be over soon. As much as I like it here, I would still like to go back, but not to Montpellier. I would though, like to be moved as platoon leader in the 17th WFR either in Annecy or Thonon at Lake Geneva. That would make me happy.

2, February 1944

To work with Capt. Becker is more thorough and systematic than with that young inexperienced Lt. and he is very nice to me, or is he two faced? Often Dold and I go with him at night to his apartment because there is always the danger of terrorist attacks.

4, February 1944

How beautiful are these evenings that remind me so of frosty winter nights at home. Every week on Thursdays, we have field exercises, we have to march heavily armed with our compass and maps.

This is healthy and we get back pleasantly tired.

10, February 1944

As of today, we eat in the officer's mess. Becker is very ambitious and independent and wants to make major. The commander is running around a lot and loves good food and drink. What a way to go through the war!

12, February 1944

Every morning, I am the first one at breakfast. It sure is different to dine at this refined and pleasant table, than with the enlisted men. Occasionally at night we get together with a cognac, cookies and cigars, even radio, music and dancing. Is it "Dancing on the Volcano"?

15, February 1944

I sleep in a pretty room upstairs, which is cleaned by a cleaning woman every day. Close and I room together. At night I always love to read a little in bed, snack on some almonds and cookies and then go to sleep.

16, February 1944

Often the commander comes and we plan and modify the big map. There is a lot of red tape, with daily notices of appointments, etc. The regiment requires maps and card files in three copies of all sentry locations. Drawings with visual perimeters of these sentry locations have to be made. I draw and write all day long until late in the evening.

Once Capt. B. has invited me to his apartment for a cigar and was very nice to me, but I had the impression, that he was somewhat of a hypocrite. No teacher is well liked in the military.

28, February 1944

I want to get back to the company soon, but they still need me here. Sgt. Sachse only helps out at Lt. Kröger's.

10, March 1944

My sweetheart writes the child develops well. "Her big blue eyes have so much expression, showing her soul, and her fat little cheeks are too cute".

Today is my brother's birthday. He is stationed deep in Russia at the middle front near Kowel. If only he is safe!

12, March 1944

I go to Etampes as a courier. All my plans are ruined because of train delays and all the errands I have to take care of for the outrageous Capt. Becker. I have to run all over Paris just because of a forgotten letter. The long trip and I myself have no time to do anything for myself. I barely have time to get something to eat. I stay overnight in a hotel near the Arc de Triumph. The next morning the return trip, which went according to schedule, of course, what a mockery!

15, March 1944

I have been able to buy a silk blanket and a little fur cover made from rabbit skins for our little "Mouse", also good wool stockings for Helga and Norbert and a model of the "JU-87" for Norbert. I packed those things and give them to buddies going on leave to mail for me there.

20, March 1944

Transfer to Marseille to the 21st WFR. I do not need to express what mood I am in. The commander receives me one more time, slick as an eel, friendly and tries to give me hope. But I just want to get out of here, away from these hypocrites.

The one honest and true friend I have here is Dold. To him, I bid a heartfelt good-bye. We walked around the town, telling each other our problems and concerns. He knows the military and the ruthlessness within. He also predicts the ending of everything, which is not good, but he is a smart and sensible man. Together with Sgt. Staats, I pack and we go to the train station.

With a heavy heart I leave.

21, March 1944

Early in the morning we arrive in Marseille. We ask directions to La Pomme and drag our luggage to streetcar No. 15. I report to Lt. Meyerhofer, another slick and arrogant individual. How can I have such bad luck with all these company bosses?

I am to go to the FLUKO in Toulon. Oh, I hope not! That would mean I would never get home again because the invasion is expected here.

22, March 1944

The decision has been made. I do not get sent to Toulon, but to Oedipus in Aix en Provence. For two nights I pragmatically slept here and had my meals here. Maybe it will be better here, the city makes a good first impression, a small spa, or health resort.

23, March 1944

Found a nice place in the city in a lovely building, a former student home. I meet Sgt. Zimmerman, whose job I am supposed to take over and Sgt. Seitz, two nice buddies.

The food is only mediocre; the evenings are beautiful with sub tropical vegetation, balmy air, a lot of cypress trees, and a good bed, but no closet.

25, March 1944

To work, we always walk about 10 minutes to the barracks, which are very primitive. There is Col. Vollbracht, holder of the knights cross, an unpleasant kind of a guy and a bunch of young officers, who are really punks.

But I don't worry about them and enjoy the beautiful spring climate.

6, April 1944

Easter

A wonderful day! I wonder how they are doing at home?

One thing, that makes the day a little special, in the afternoon we get some good bean coffee and a platter full of cake, with music by the house band in the yard. We have not enjoyed anything like this in a long time.

8, April 1944

Rösel writes: "Sigrid is the joy of our lives. She already knows her bottle".

14, April 1944

There is no greater joy for me than walk through the little town of Aix en Provence, sit down at a restaurant, read, write home, or just watch the world go by.

15, April 1944

I was able to buy a little dress and some underwear for Helga and our little "Mouse". Duty is not too bad, thank goodness.

20, April 1944

The fact that today is Hitler's birthday does not interest me in the least, but because of this occasion, we get coffee and cake in the afternoon. That is OK with all of us!

25, April 1944

Rösel writes: "Our baby is so good and sweet. She just eats and sleeps and hardly cries at all."

I still have not given up on being transferred to the Air Force Female School in Wiesbaden. How wonderful it would be to be so close to home. I wonder if there is a chance of this working out?

4, May 1944

Too bad we have to say good-bye to beautiful Aix en Provence soon.

6, May 1944

We say farewell to beautiful Aix en Provence. With an old bus, we ride across country to Courthezon on the Rhone River.

Late at night we arrive at our new quarters at Monsieur Courtil, a primitive place with a straw mattress, no closet. My roommates are Sgt. Ascher and Sgt. Hackbart, the latter with an incredible sense of humor, both good buddies.

7, May 1944

I take a look at the town. Our company surely has tried very hard to find lodgings in this dilapidated town, for the men, offices, dining halls, etc. Well, we will get used to it. I have had to get used to so many different places. There won't be many changes. My first impression of La Merthe, it is a million Mark project. Why this enormous expenditure and extravagance? Such a terrible waste! Nothing was conserved; the walls made of expensive cork and are soundproofed, expensive equipment and machinery, a giant weather map worth 18,000 Marks. We can only enter the sanctum with tennis shoes.

8, May 1944

Today is the 65th Birthday of my dear mother.

10, May 1944

The duty is the same as in Aix en Provence, only no chance to sleep. New sleeping rooms are supposed to be built. There are an unbelievable number of officers running around. They have nothing else to do, but have drinking parties, often until late at night. I meet the unpleasant Lt. Most, this "punk", who least deserves to be an officer.

15, May 1944

I am just so happy, that I always have good news from home: "Our little baby girl develops so wonderfully."

16, May 1944

A grueling heat has begun.

20, May 1944

I have a good relationship with my two roommates. We don't care for the two tough guys, Brinkman and Frank. There are too many evil oddballs of our nationality and that's very disturbing.

Frank has stolen duck eggs from our hosts. Why should they not call us "barbaric"?

22, May 1944

We get a lot of asparagus soup, but that's OK and we don't complain about the food.

We enjoy a lovely evening in the shady backyard under palm trees and sycamores. The people are hospitable and friendly and we talk about all kinds of things, politics, the relationship of our two nations, etc. I am so grateful of my knowledge of the French language and I know an understanding between our two people would be possible, if our "Prussian Militarists" would not ruin everything for ourselves.

28, May 1944

The female Air Force personnel have arrived. Nothing to brag about! They rush into the stores and buy everything they can get their hands on. With many, you see the lack of upbringing.

There are the daily buses, which most of the time do not operate, with the female personnel fighting for the seats, silly cackling, and giggling. I am quiet most of the time.

31, May 1944

"Oh, what a darling baby our little Sigrid is. I wish you could see her. The other two are very misbehaved. We need you everywhere!"

1, June 1944

What a lucky thing we can get fresh fruit in large quantities. We buy wonderful cherries, 2-4 lbs. everyday. I have been assigned a female helper; she is a stubborn East Prussian character. The duty at the command post has become entertaining and some friendships have formed already.

5, June 1944

After searching for a long time, I have found a farm, where I can get a few eggs twice a week. We buy an electric cooker and fry eggs and onions in our mess kit. I have plenty of red wine. Of course I drink it in moderation, while others drink in excess.

6, June 1944

The Invasion

When it became cooler in the evening, I went out and took a wonderful walk around the town. At home now, it must be pretty during this time of the blooming lilacs.

10, June 1944

There was the first heavy bombing attack on the transport services in Avignon. There are strong over flights on our positions. For the first time I hear the awesome roar of the four engine bombers and see the formations of the silvery shining planes above us.

We are in the one man foxholes and the icy fear creeps up our backs. What if they drop their bombs right above us? But this is not meant for us. They pass us by.

Down below in Avignon, black smoke mushrooms up and the vibration of the detonations carries up all the way to us. There is a roaring and rushing sound like I have not experienced so far. What terrible fear the people must have experienced!

12, June 1944

In our house at the Courtil's, new water pipes are installed. That's how we Germans are. They move in as the "Big Lord's" and as if they never want to move again.

15, June 1944

This day is the first time we hear about the **V-1**.

19, June 1944

My Birthday

I cannot believe I am 41 years old. My sweetheart sent me a sweet letter, also the children, as well as a package with flowers and cookies. Yes, I am getting old with quite a few gray hairs.

23, June 1944

My sweetheart writes: "When I wake up in the morning I hear this blissful sucking and grunting sound. The little "Mouse" is awake, but does not move. Whenever this child cries, something is wrong with her."

25, June 1944

After the cherries, we have plenty of peaches and apricots. Also the heat! The sky is hazy and the air shimmers, the cicadas chirp in the cypress trees day and night, the Italian workmen are working naked from the waist up in the sandpit. What a country! Stones, thorns, rocks, vineyards, and azure blue skies!

30, June 1944

I have been transferred from the 21st WFR to the 3rd Air Traffic Regiment. Is it good or bad luck?

Lt. Most, the "punk", has no care or understanding about my problems. My two buddies and I discuss the political situations. We are in agreement, that this war is lost for us.

The invasion continues to be successful. We cannot stop the British at this point. The terrorist attacks on Germans increase.

1, July 1944

Is there anything better, than to fry two eggs with onions in my mess kit at night with a glass of good French red wine? Then I like to sit under the trees in the yard and talk to the family Courtil. How happy these people must have been at one time.

3, July 1944

Why this tremendous work and preparation? One French woman asks me: "Have the German women come for repopulating?" I did not know what to answer her.

4, July 1944

The first transports of females have been returned to the Reich. I ask the Lt. if I cannot accompany one of the transports to Mainz, the answer is no; instead he sends one of his friends with a suitcase full of stuff to Schlesien.

There are farewell parties every night with drinking, singing, music, and laughter. Truly a "Dance on the Volcano"!

5, July 1944

The last night of farewell parties for the female helpers. Major Schobinger has a good-bye speech and there are some tears.

8, July 1944

There is heavy fighting in Normandy. Our troops fight heroically. Caen is totally in ruins. Where is Rommel? What is going on with Rundstedt? Is there a crisis? Will the Anglo-Americans push through? We are convinced of it!

16, July 1944

An expensive command post is erected. We have 16 dive bombers, have not lost one yet, but have the daily heavy over flights by the enemy. When we stand at noon, only for 5 minutes, by the wall during the changing of guard, our shirts stick to our bodies. How often I jumped out the window to go to the cantina, to bring back tomatoes, peaches, pears, and apricots in my helmet. We have now an air raid siren.

20, July 1944

Today the breakthrough at Avranches happened. This is an impending disaster!

The Assassination Attempt On Hitler

Oh, if only it had been successful!

What needless suffering! The poor humanity could have been spared. The assassins General Field Marshall von Witzleben, the Generals von Hase, and Beck, plus many others are executed by hanging.

22, July 1944

Every day we are busy with the machine gun fortifications surrounding our position. Machine gun nests and gun emplacements are improved upon, clear around the whole base. All French vehicles have been requisitioned to transport sand.

24, July 1944

The British make incredible progress and their tanks are all the way up to the city of Brest.
What is going to happen? Is this the beginning of the end?

26, July 1944

The food is good; my favorite is noodles with bacon, that is delicious.

I will never forget the view down to the Rhone valley and the church tower of Avignon in the glistening heat.

27, July 1944

We continue to have heavy aerial attacks on all central points of traffic in Southern France such as Nimes, Tarascon, and Montpellier. Soon the most important railway connections will be destroyed.

Will an invasion possibly take place in the South? Often we run up to the underbrush behind the cypress forest, when the sirens start sounding. Jaschinski, Fischer, and I have our special hiding place, where we feel safe. From here we watch the silvery shining planes high up, flying in formation move above us and down below in Avignon we see only clusters of flames and black smoke. One bomb after the other, thrown in rows, comes crashing down and we hear and feel the vibration of the detonation all the way up here.

There is no sight of our "jabos" (dive bombers) hunters. The cowardly officers run around like chickens with their heads cut off. But at night they have to have their boozing parties, the disgusting creeps.

28, July 1944

The noble French daughters from the richest families of Chateau Neuve have to do maid service for us. This too will change, I am certain of that.

1, August 1944

Rösel writes: "After our little "Mouse" was restless for a few days, she got over getting her first two teeth without any further disturbances. She looks so sweet. The other two continue to be naughty and misbehaved. Helga cries a lot for no reason and Norbert will not listen to any reasoning. I cannot discipline him anymore. Oh, how much do we miss you and how much we need you! Sometimes I cannot help myself but cry my heart out. Then I look with enjoyment at our little sweetheart, who gives us so much delight every day. Her eyes are more and more expressive and sometimes she looks at me so lovingly."

4, August 1944

Every night we go up to the hedge, where the machine gun emplacement is located. We are amazed at the old soldier, Brinkman, at the eagerness he does his work, while the others, including us, do not kill ourselves. We rather mock these needless measures. Things will change, that we are sure. We wonder if the planned bunker will be finished in time. Now they think of it, when it is too late.

I wonder how the Italians feel working here? I know they despise us. There are many hardworking men here from the organization named Tott. One of the men is 72 years old.

Our poor, stupid people! I pity them all! They work hard and are faithful. They are basically good people and then everything goes down the drain, just because they are too trusting and simpleminded. They allow themselves to be led into this disaster.

5, August 1944

Maybe it is a good thing that I am not in Marseille now, if there is an invasion down there, no one will make it out.

6, August 1944

How ridiculous to work on this machine gun emplacement. There is no material, no nails, and everyone has to put in their 2 cents worth. We have to do a field exercise under the command of Major von Büren. Not bad, but this idiot of a colonel has to mess it all up and the whole thing becomes a comedy. We are so disgusted about everything.

The Americans are pushing into France!

7, August 1944

20 years ago my father went to war (WW I). Are our people condemned eternally to tumble from one war to the other?

I am thinking whether it might be advisable for me to report to "Alligator", "Butterfly" or "Mouse" to get out of this "witches caldron". I have a feeling that something is going to happen here very soon.

8, August 1944

We notice the contemptuous looks of the French Baronesses at lunch. They know they will not have to do slave labor for the German big shots here much longer. The farmers transport the sand in a composed and serene manner. How much longer will this last?

9, August 1944

With the daily air raids I am here or there, either on the cold stone tiles or on the hot sand under the bushes and I see above me the countless planes of the American Air Force proudly cross the skies. Such a tremendous war power was greatly underestimated. Down below in the plains, the bombs are falling and the earth is trembling all the way up here.

No rain, just heat, drought, and dust on the olive trees. The grapes are ripening.

There is feverish work on all positions. The terrorist attacks in Southern France are increasing. The other day an airwoman was pushed in front of the subway train in Paris and killed.

10, August 1944

Rösel writes: "I wish you could see how our little "rabbit" uses her hands. Yesterday she grabbed one with the other. When she sees her bottle, she pats her covers excitedly. When I change her, a feeling of well being goes through her whole little body. She grimaces, stretches her legs as straight as possible, and straightens her hands along side of her."

Tante Sannchen wrote a few days ago: "Last Sunday I was in Hochstätten and could admire your little Sigrid. What a darling! She got her first tooth a few days before. The whole family stood around her baby carriage and she was happy with all the attention."

Something is in the air! We were advised to send all things we do not need home. I was able to give Brucker a package since he is going to Stuttgart.

12, August 1944

Daily there are systematic attacks on our positions in Marseille, Toulon, and Montpellier. Are these the previews of coming attractions? In the north, the 7th German Army has been defeated.

The Americans are in Tours, Orleans, and Chartre. If they push up to Dijon, we will not get out of here.

14, August 1944

A Low Level Attack On Our Position!

The day I shall never forget! The attack was carried out by six to eight "P-38 Lightnings". At 6:20 pm there was an over flight, then they turned into the sun and we all rushed out as fast as we could. I decide to run up to the one man foxholes, and all hell breaks loose all around me.

I jump into the closest one man foxhole as if the devil was behind me.

Behind me is "HELL"!

What does one think of in minutes like this? I see my family before my eyes and I frantically and desperately try to think that I have to survive for them. In such moments one learns to beg and pray for ones pitiful life, and yet, one fears for the worst. Should my life come to an end here, this pathetically? 10 minutes later everything is over! I am alive!

I hear someone calling: "Here is someone wounded!" Down below there is only dust and smoke to be seen. Three are dead, and four or more are wounded. Sgt. Hübner is buried alive.

Most of them had run through the garden and it was just there where the bomb had fallen. The crater was not very deep but the explosive effect was worse. The three dead men were terribly mutilated. Strangely all three of them had their heads blown off. Poor Baumgarten, he was so full of life and did not think of dying, and Holtz the same. Behrends has a wife and three children.

How good it is that the family will not know the details of their terrible and pathetic deaths. Also how a life is so perfectly worthless in war.

Our position is in bad shape. The roofs of the buildings are destroyed, the walls collapsed, all the windows with the frames ripped out, inside everything is broken, water 3 feet high and all the work rooms with all the expensive equipment are just a heap of rubble. It is impossible to work here now. But we say: "Thank God, we have been spared!"

Through the ruins I make my way back to my room. Devastation everywhere! Under the rubble and debris I find some of my things, such as my wet, battered suitcase, my briefcase, and the backpack. Everyone is rushing around frantically. We have orders to pack up and deliver all military things to headquarters our personal things should be shipped home.

Feverish clean up is under way. Roll call with announcements as to the missing. Many are there with blackened faces, torn uniforms and still under the shock of the death of their buddies. In the darkness a couple of caskets are quickly constructed and the body parts of the three killed are gathered and placed into the primitive boxes. Poor Baumgarten's leg had been torn off as well.

The speech of Lt. Most was callous and insensitive. This immature creep even indirectly blamed the dead. It is outrageous! We are furious!

Slowly it is getting dark. Of course there is no way to even think of sleep. We have an emergency maintenance. This night for sure, another attack by the "Maquis" is expected.

All around us on the hillsides, fires are burning; what does that mean? Is this a signaling of the terrorists? I sit all night in the machine gun stand with the Saxon barber and stare into the night. Oh, how miserable I feel. The night stayed quiet in spite of some shooting. Close to morning I fall asleep in spite of the cold.

The invasion begins; the first ships sighted are from Corsica in the direction of the Southern French coast.

15, August 1944

The whole day consisted of the most basic of necessary duties. Mock still runs around with his bloody shirt. I am totally exhausted. I have not slept in two nights, nor eaten, at night it is freezing and in the daytime we have the heat. Our French personnel have disappeared; the Italian workers are also gone. The work on the bunkers was in vain. Now we experience the air raids and fear them. This is the third night without sleep.

16, August 1944

In the early dawn we take a bus down to Courthezon. Good-bye La Nerthe forever. The remains of the gun emplacements will be detonated within the next few days. The enemy has landed in Antibes, St. Raphael, west of Nice. There is only one panzer division for the defense. This is the beginning of the end!

We are assigned quarters in a house where the offices were before. All day long we have low-level attacks aimed at the streets in the village. Often we run to the meadow into our one man foxholes. We just want to get away from here, as far as possible.

17, August 1944

I prepare for all eventualities. In my trusting suitcase, that has accompanied me to so many places, I pack everything that I can discard in an emergency, such as my extra uniform, etc. In my briefcase I pack all the things that are precious to me and that I do not want to lose.

I pay a visit to the very nice French family Courtil, and give them the suitcase, the package with the bottle of oil, that had cost me 30 Marks, plus a bottle of the very expensive and special Montbazillac cognac. These two bottles I hope to be able to pick up in peacetime or have them send them to me. Will that ever happen? I hope so.

The enemy has pushed into the northern part of Toulon. The comrades in Marseille and Toulon are already cut off.

18, August 1944

We work in the villa, but the next day we move to the casino in the middle of the village, which is camouflaged well under the palm trees. We are dead tired, because we have not had any sleep in days.

19, August 1944

I unwillingly became a witness to the tyrannical Col. Vollbracht, when he screamed at the major in front of all the soldiers. Patience! Your glory will soon come to an end.

I once more visit these nice people, the Courtil's. I thanked them for their kindness and expressed my hope they would not suffer any ill effects and also one day maybe in better times, we would see one another again.

In the night we were awakened at 4 am, we were to turn over all laundry and pieces of equipment and we are only to take what we need to wear, such as summer uniform, walking shoes and hats. In this process my dog tags were lost. In the yard a giant fire destroyed new equipment, clothes, shoes, boots in giant piles. All of our munitions were detonated in the open field. The fires crackle all through the night. The expensive broadcasting intercom was hacked to pieces with axes. Why not load it up on a truck and save it? It is a crying shame! No, there is no way we can win this war. With what great enthusiasm these kids destroy these valuable technical installations. These are products of the Nazi education.

At dawn there is nothing left, but messy heaps of rubble and piles of gray ash. That's another thing our poor people have to pay for.

20, August 1944

We tried via Lt. Mock to requisition French trucks and cars in vain. The French know what is going on. The cars and trucks have mysteriously disappeared in the night or are not useable. In the afternoon they pass out red wine and the guys get drunk like crazy. The cognac bottles are thrown into the river, no one cares. But how do we get out of here?

Sixty men have to walk out of here. The rest of the twelve men under my command are to wait for cars from Company #2. Such bad luck! I am standing in the dark entrance to the village, from 8 until midnight. I am passed by with hundreds of trucks, cars, tanks, and armored scout cars, also artillery vehicles fully loaded with soldiers. Everything is heading in the direction of Lyon. What is going on? Is this a planned removal or a panicky flight?

I call out to every vehicle, but my people are afraid, that no one will pick us up and they will have to stay behind. Major Schobinger has left us with the frivolous remark: "Well, by walking you can get home as well!"

Our cook was crushed to death between a tank and a tree and buried wretchedly along side of the road. Finally close to midnight a truck comes full of soldiers and luggage but we luckily get a seat. We just have to get out of here. The trip is slow with many stops. By 3 am we have not made it past Montelimar with the convoy. We stop shortly because the driver is overtired. The wood gas truck is lousy, but the driver is excellent.

We had trouble with the alternator; we got lost, and were alone on the road. In a short time our fabulous driver had it repaired. Behind a small village we park for 2 hours and I lie down along the side of the road and sleep some. We sleep as well as in the best bed. At dawn we quickly get going again.

21, August 1944

Another day to remember; the attack! We have no idea what this day will bring us.

Suddenly there is a hold up. Supposedly a destroyed bridge up ahead. Thousands of vehicles are jammed up ahead for miles. In a village with a steep road we wait about an hour. There are terrorists all around us as well as the machine gun fire from the mountains. I go with a few people up a hillside to check things out. The guys decide not to get any closer. Finally we continue on but have to come to a stop every 100 meters or so. A bunch of officers pass everybody in a car recklessly and inconsiderate, loaded with boxes of cognac, coffee and French women. Disgusting!

Everyone is afraid for their pitiful lives. On top of the hill about 2 km before the bridge we have to make another stop. There is an attack by low flying fighters. We run into the fields along the road well camouflaged, but still have continual strafing by diving aircraft. There are a lot of vehicles on fire or burnt out. We finally make it to Loriol. We run into a Bistro to fill our canteens with water, and buy some coffee and fruit. The heat is unbearable! We are wearing only our thin camouflaged uniforms and the helmet. At noon we gain a few meters.

Behind Lorial we finally reach the destroyed bridge. The crossing is another story and a half, no point in its description, it is well set in my memory.

Then we get to the town Livron and we are told an especially dangerous route is up ahead. We crouch down on the truck, all weapons ready to fire. Suddenly shooting from the right, we leave the vehicles and take cover in the ditches.

To summarize the main points, the coward, Capt. Unger. The scouting troop with the poor overweight infantry Lt.; who was killed ten minutes later. A half hour later, we smoke out the guerilla hideouts. The houses up on the hillside are in flames. Only single rifle shots. Have the attackers been beaten off? We continue on.

We have numerous air attacks now. We continually are lying in the ditch. We have nothing left to drink. The skirmish flares up again. Suddenly severe and intense shooting from everywhere, bullets explode all around us. Is this artillery or mortars? We have no explanation. The shelling is so heavy with bullets whistling past my head, that I keep ducked down and get no chance to shoot back. Where is the opponent? We do not see him.

Capt. Unger hovers behind a house with his machine gun, white as a sheet. Oh, and such people have become officers! The two females are shaking in the ditch and crying. The Red Cross convoy gives us some protection. Now we are shot at from a cornfield behind. Am I destined to lose my life here under these pitiful circumstances? If only we will not fall into the hands of the terrorists, there will be no mercy.

The first dead and wounded. The Sgt. from the medical team finally manages to shake up the Capt. who is in a kind of a daze. There is only one possibility to get through and that is to retreat. We run breathlessly through the field. Sparks are dancing before my eyes, my breath is whistling, but every second is precious. That ridiculous Capt., who was incapable to lead our group, has long disappeared up ahead. How can one have any kind of confidence in such superiors?

Finally a small train comes up with three cars. After a short discussion with the train conductor we go back to Livron. Wild shooting is going on there and the Russian Battalion cannot help us either, so we get back on the train and head for Valance, still no water available and we are all dehydrated.

The people on the train are not very well armed, only a couple of Italians in the open freight car ready to shoot. We are confident that we will get through. But we are concerned, that the guerrillas have blown up the tracks. Now comes the moment of truth, but briskly and efficiently the little engine steams up ahead, what a good little train!

Today, where I write this, it all seems sort of ridiculous. Back then in those fearful moments it certainly was different. No one wanted to get tortured to death by the terrorists. Now comes the critical moment; over there on the street stands our whole convoy in bright flames. My backpack was burnt with all my clothes and pieces of equipment, my gas mask, my tarp, the field rations, my brown briefcase with all the things I did not want to part with.

What I Lost Near Valence On 21, August 1944:

- My camera and all my photos, including those of the children,
- The birthday roses from the children,
- New Year's calendars from Norbert
- My alarm clock and the picture of my parents
- My travel kit with contents,
- 3 diaries, No. 8, 9 and 10
- The letters of the children,
- My military passbook and dog tags
- My 6.35 mm pistol
- Helga's locks of hair
- A flashlight
- The Death Announcements of my fallen friends.

Although it hurt to lose these things, right now it is really irrelevant and secondary. We are overjoyed, that we are alive. We don't know how many dead and wounded there were. Who did not make it? Who fell into the hands of the terrorists?

Later we heard that across from us were Canadian Parachute Troops that's why we had this grim resistance.

We arrive in Valence in the dark. Stay overnight in a large dance hall on straw. My throat is dry and raspy. Luckily I was able to save my canteen and we finally get some water. We are so tired that we fall onto the straw and immediately go to sleep. Outside we hear rifle shots, but we don't care, just sleep.

Not for long though and we are brutally awakened. Outside a dangerous, concentrated attack by the terrorists on the city of Valance. Fighting troops are organized to defend the city. Does this misery not stop yet? We have become complacent and accept our fate of the inevitable. We stand around and wait; finally they let us go back to sleep and the night passes quietly. Oh, how badly we needed sleep.

22, August 1944

I ate something and had a cup of hot coffee in a small café, washed at a fountain with no soap and decide to try and join up with any group, since we are totally scattered and dispersed. There is hardly anyone left from my company.

At noon I find a uniform coat, one of a pilot, it does not matter, it fits. A friendly Austrian Lt. from Vienna gives me a ride in his car through the city.

I get lunch in a small restaurant outside of the city. The French people watch with interest the spectacle of the thousands of troops pouring through their town. They say: "They are not fighting!" Without showing their hatred, but outwardly indifferent and even at times friendly and helpful they are amazed about the sudden change of things.

Now the Germans are leaving their country, where they were "guests" for four years and the "liberators" are coming soon.

They are hoping for their freedom. I had a chance to talk to a few Frenchmen. One says: "You won't get through anymore. The Rhone Valley has been closed off at Lyon". But we still hope.

In the afternoon I manage to jump on the running board of a car and I am lucky. It's a machine tool outfit well equipped with material and they even have a kitchen truck and have not lost anything yet. So I can ride along with them. In the evening we stop in a village 12 km south of Lyon. The vehicles are taken to a big park.

Had a conversation with two women who were feeding their babies. I was able to get a big plate of wonderful noodles. Even found a piece of soap. How glad one is for such small luxuries. Forget about shaving though. How peaceful is the quiet park.

Under a group of pine trees in the middle of the lawn I fix myself a bed. I find a blanket and a tarp, use my hat as a pillow and so I get to sleep wonderfully. In the morning it is getting cool. I get some hot coffee and bread, also some sugar from the comrades, and then we continue on.

23, August 1944

We make it to the freight station in Lyon. At the last minute I decide to go to the railway station, maybe I can catch a train.

I see Capt. Becker and I don't care if I see him or not. Later, also the commander. Your glory is over with!

At 3 pm I am able to get on a crowded train, that makes many stops. I was able to buy a comb from the restroom lady. At dark we reach Macon. Here we have a layover in the middle of nowhere. Only the engine leaves and no one knows why. On the next track a train with Russians. The many Slavic looking faces; the sad Russian songs. What are these people all thinking of? They are "cannon fodder" for our interests.

Across from us another train full of French Militia with their families; all of them escaping to Germany. Their faces are sad, because they cannot stay in their country anymore. They have bet on the wrong horse and their destiny is now closely connected with Germany.

We are stopped all night long on the tracks. Has the French locomotive engineer deserted us? Anything is possible. Guards are posted on both sides of the tracks against assaults, but nothing happened. We are just so extremely thirsty and have to be very frugal with our water.

Excepts From Rösel's Letters In August:

"Our little Darling is so sweet. I wish you could see how she laughs. It is touching to see how she opens her little mouth when I approach her with the Dentinox bottle to spread on her gums for the teething pain. She tries with both hands to direct my hand to her mouth. I was at the pediatrician with both Helga and Sigrid today. He said: "Be glad, you have two healthy children." I am so happy.

Our little "rabbit" has two teeth now. She gets cereal and vegetables and gains nicely."

Thoughts About My Children

Why was I not able to influence my children, to sharpen their senses for all things that are good, true, and beautiful? Rösel does more than her share, but they should have received something from me too. Will I be compensated in our little Sigrid one day?

24, August 1944

Retreat From France (Cont'd)

The night was terribly long and I could not sleep. Where would we be able to sleep anyway? Some find a place between the railroad tracks or next to them in the field. I find a place between the feet of others. In the railway cars are a lot of civilians as well. At dawn we get another engine and we slowly get moving until we stop again somewhere else.

Now this is getting a little ridiculous. I see convoys upon convoys over there on the road and I quickly make the decision to get off this train and others follow me. I jump onto the running board of a moving truck. Someone is trying to tell me to get off, but I stubbornly stay on. It is a truck with a damaged clutch. In spite of it we make headway heading north closer and closer to the border.

At noon we reach Chalon. Here I decide to get off and wait for a better opportunity. In a good restaurant I get an excellent meal and suddenly, what a surprise, I meet a man from Sembach, Willie Weissman.

At a street crossing I jump onto the running board of a truck and I am lucky. It is a whole convoy from a supply base unit commanded by two officers, who really seem to care for their people. A still young Capt. constantly patrols up and down his convoy like a police dog. We have a short rest stop in front of a village along the road. I am able to get a belt from a buddy. Even though it is too big that's OK.

Close to evening we reach Dijon. There are supposed to be terrorists here. We have our arms ready to shoot and wait, until an armored panzer scout car can join us.

The villages have been burnt down because they were hideouts of the terrorists. The Capt. is smart and never stays overnight in bigger towns, but small villages. The vehicles are camouflaged well, and then food is passed out. I am also very well taken care of. We sleep in a gym hall on straw. We eat our canned sardines with friendly people on a farm across from the gym. How wonderful we sleep on the straw.

25, August 1944

We make good time through the beautiful Burgunderland, up and down villages with poor houses, green meadows with Holstein cattle. We drive past Besancon, which is picturesquely nestled along the hillside. In the evening we arrive at Belfort, with memories of the glorious victory in 1871, of which I have read so many stories. We pass the old forts and come across a clean small town just before the Alsatian border. The captain again drove up ahead to arrange for accommodations. When we get there the schoolroom floor has already been covered with straw. The cars are hidden under sycamore trees in the schoolyard and secured for the night. Soon we will reach Germany.

In the morning we receive from the captain new military pass books authorizing him to give us transportation to Germany. At 10 am, we continue.

26, August 1944

The French workers, cooks, and waitresses are dropped off, as we cannot take them across the border.

Finally we cross into Germany. What a feeling! We are in the beautiful Alsace Lorraine. In Sennheim the Capt. releases us. He was more than decent and considerate to us!

We catch a train to Mühlhausen. At the station a friendly woman gives me pears and apples. I am home again!

I reach Neustadt, dear old Neustadt! 18 years ago I spent a happy time here. I can either stay here or go on to Kaiserslautern. I decide to continue my trip. I get there at 10 pm and stay at the military center across from the railroad station. In the morning, I telephone the flight command in Sembach and find out that Rösel is in Sembach with the children. Lt. Müller gives me my marching orders for Trier, where I am to report.

I take a train to Neuhemsbach, then walk the old familiar way to my dear home. I look a mess and hope no one will see me in town. I have not shaved in 2 weeks, am dirty and have nothing with me except my tarp, helmet, and rifle. I meet Frau Schneider, the family Hanbuch, and at the schoolhouse, family Metz.

The First Homecoming In 8 Months

Overwhelmed with joy, my sweetheart runs into my arms in the hallway. How sweet and young and pretty she is. Helga stands there, almost timid, but anxious to hug me. She looks very skinny. Then my gaze drifts toward the baby carriage in our old kitchen and now comes the strangely unforgettable moment, that will be forever in my memory: There is our child in the carriage, tall and thin, with tanned skin, looking into the world with big eyes and is chewing on a cookie. How strange, how strange!

What is going on inside of me? How do I come to call out: "Is that our child?" I do not know what made me ask this ridiculous question, but I do not know this child. Eight months have passed and she has changed so much. You cry my dearest? Oh, I know what goes on in your heart. Without a word I pull her into my arms. I want to pick up the baby, but she turns away and starts crying.

All of this is because of this lousy, miserable war!

Then I watch how this little human being is bathed and changed, gets her bottle and put to bed. She has lost a lot of weight in the last two weeks due to a virus, that caused vomiting and diarrhea. The doctor advised not to give her too many vegetables. Now there she is in the same little crib the other two have slept in and where they were sick and caused us so many happy, but fearful hours as well. How I would love to slip in on tiptoes later, but Rösel would not allow it. The child should not be bothered anymore now. Often she lies quietly in her bed for hours, does not cry, and just plays with her hands.

Pretty soon afterwards, mother comes and as always is happy to see me. Her golden heart of a mother is touching. Oh, may she live a long time still and live to see the end of this miserable war.

"What do you look like?" Yes, it is high time that I wash and shave and look like a human being again. Get rid of these rags, my sweetheart will wash everything.

While Rösel is getting lunch ready, Norbert comes. There he is, my big boy, so strong and tall. My goodness how he has changed! He is not a child anymore. His naked knees are strong and tanned and his hairstyle has changed. Mama can ask him to do all kinds of errands and he is responsible and takes good care of things.

The afternoon passes with talking and being busy with Sigrid. Now I can see for myself, what a good baby she is. In the evening, Alice comes and so did Ernst Gödtel.

Oh, how wonderful to sleep in my bed again! If only we could be together again for good, here in our own home, where we have built our happiness.

28, August 1944

Of course I stay in Sembach for the whole day. My sweetheart takes care of my laundry and I go to the garden and visit with Rettig's and Metz. Norbert can skip school this one day, in the evening he leaves.

Helga is skinny and tall, but healthy. She resembles my mother a lot, the way she walks, and other characteristics.

29, August 1944

I have to catch the 5 am train. Oh, how hard it is to say good-bye again.

Helga slept in the front room, where all the furniture has been stored. Drowsily she wraps her arms around my neck and says with a quiet voice and in her typically slow mannerism: "Wiedersehen!" Yes I want to see you again always again and again after the many, many farewells we have gone through. My sweetheart is standing in the doorway and I keep looking back, waving, until I cannot see her anymore in the dark.

In Kaiserslautern I have to wait for a train to Saarbrücken. I have nothing but my helmet, my tarp, my rifle, and a shoebox with the most important things. My mother gave me an old shaving kit, which still works.

The main railway station in Saarbrücken is destroyed. We pass through terribly bombarded factories and railways. We hang around Mettlach all afternoon. Finally a train arrives. Thank goodness it starts to rain, because this will diminish the danger of the "jabos" (dive bombers). Everyone is terribly fearful, but we make it OK. We reach Trier in the evening. We report to the front assembly point near the railroad station. There are a lot of scattered soldiers.

30, August 1944

We take a train to Metz, report to the Bayernkaserne. This place is meaningful to me. 45 years ago, my father stayed here and through this gate he marched in and out. This was the first time for him to be out in the world and away from home. He, who in his strict and simple surrounding and upbringing never got to travel anywhere, it had to be the first significant experience. His spirit surrounds me and a deep sorrow grabs a hold of me to have lost him. Why did he have to die so young? It was always his dream, later on to come back here together with me. I look up room #45 in the big building. What may he have experienced in those two years? How often did he look out this window longingly in the direction of his beloved home?

I meet a lot of people I know, almost all of the company from Troyes. I am not in a hurry to get away from here. Sgt. Nietsche wants to give me a ride. Not a chance!

I go downtown, go in a café, have coffee and after a long time, some cake, enjoy a good dinner in a restaurant across from the railway station and fix myself a bed in the Bayernkaserne. There is an air raid at night and we have to get up and go to the shelter.

31, August 1944

In the morning I look at the beautiful Dom Cathedral in Metz. The parade ground, which father had mentioned so often and I thoroughly enjoy exploring this lovely old German city, which will not ever be German again, but be French from now on forever.

Again, I get a good meal at noon and have the opportunity to buy a new cap and some socks. In the afternoon I go by truck with Lt. Lindemann, another "punk", to the destroyed FLUKO, where hundreds of machine guns were destroyed by an attack of the Americans. A half hour later, I report to a Lt. Most. When I look at that cynical, despicable face my stomach turns. And I am supposed to stay here with him plus another 50 scattered men.

We are sent back to Metz and there are divided again. Sgt. Lindner picks out his friends and we are divided into service at the bunker. Things are queasy and uncomfortable.

The Americans supposedly are close to Metz. There are a lot of unpleasant officers; only one seems to have any sense. He divides the guys into groups by age. The older ones will go by foot to Merzig. I am with this group, older than 40. We march at dark through the German Gate and I think how often my father has marched through here.

Memorable was the SS Officer with the face of a criminal. Why don't you conduct your own war, you criminals! The misery of refugees on the roads!

The "party big wigs" have left town days ago. And now the poor betrayed farmers of the Pfalz area with their meager belongings, head back, accompanied by their wives, children, and old people in wagons and carts displaying a bleak and gloomy mood. Why have they relocated these people prematurely in Alsace Lorraine?

When it gets daylight, we are close to Bolchen. I am able to hike well, but not everybody. A friendly Lothringer picks us up and gives us a ride in his truck. We get all the way to Saarlautern, find a gasthaus, get a good meal, and rest a while. We have a lot of time and are in no rush to get to Trier. There are air raids all day long anyway and we constantly have to run to the shelter.

The local people are terribly frightened and at times panicky. They scream and run for miles into the fields. In the pauses between alarms we try to sleep a little in the meadows between the bunkers. At night we are able to get a decent meal and even private quarters through a Red Cross nurse. Unfortunately the night is interrupted with continuous alerts and we get no sleep at all. But somehow the night passes.

1, September 1944

In Saarlautern, we catch a crowded train at 5 am. We are lucky, it is raining, and that diminishes the danger of low flying attack bombers, until we arrive in Trier. We leave our stuff at an inn near the station and I report to Col. Hanstein at the assembly place. Result: We are sent to Darmstadt. That's all right with me not too far away from home.

In beautiful sunshine we ride through the Mosel valley to Koblenz. I have a lot of running around to do to secure an overnight stay; but the buddies are glad I take care of this for them.

I have a plan. In the morning I will go to Bingerbrück. First I send a telegram and ask Rösel, to meet me there. Whether the telegram will get there is another question. I awake early and go to the station.

2, September 1944

At 9 am I arrive in Bingerbrück. Rösel is not there, is not on the next train either. It's a long and boring wait. I go to the soldier's relief center across from the station on Koblenzer Strasse, get a bite to eat and wait for the next train. It is supposed to be here at 2 pm and it is now 4 pm and it is not here yet.

I finally give up and take the next train to Hochstätten. All afternoon a refugee train with Germans from Luxembourg is sitting on the tracks. As the train pulls in I happen to see my sweetheart at the gate. She sees me, with a look of complete shock and surprise reflecting in her face. She and the children were there to see Uncle Gustav off, who was home on furlough and is going back to Italy. And there is also the baby carriage with our little "Bunny". How sweet she looks in her blue hat and that tan skin. She looks at me with big eyes and of course does not know me. They are all so happy to see me so unexpectedly. Why have I lost so many precious hours? I should have gone there directly and immediately. Of course, Rösel did not get the telegram.

The child has gotten used to me and does not cry anymore, but laughs and kicks with her legs. She has recovered from the virus and is gaining weight again. What a joy for me to watch what a happy baby she is. She lets Mama change her without fuss and with a great appetite, drinks her bottle, holding it all by herself. She is not in the bassinet any more, but the green baby bed, where the other two have slept in also. How touching it was to see all of them kiss her goodnight. Never has there been a more fervent wish for God to keep them well for me as Rösel folds the child's innocent little hands together, saying: "Gute Nacht, schlaf gut, träum süss, der liebe Gott behüte dich und morgen früh wieder gesund aufwachen." ("Good night, sleep well, dream sweet, the dear Lord watch over you, and wake up well in the morning."). I know she says this every night to our darling and prays to God to keep this child well for us.

Deeply moved I go downstairs with my wife, with whom I feel so very closely connected. And how rich am I to have found such a woman.

We eat supper, the children want me to talk about things, Helga shows me her schoolwork, and late at night we go to bed overtired. Our baby, the little "Bunny", as we call her lately, is sleeping peacefully.

3, September 1944

I have to leave at 5:30 am. Helga is in Opa's bed, a little drowsy, but she wraps her arms around my neck, kisses me and then I say to her: "Close your little eyes, go back to sleep, sweetheart, it is still dark outside."

Then Rösel walks to the train station with me. The train is on time I quickly embrace her; we wave to each other until the night separates us.

I meet my buddies in Darmstadt. They were not as lucky and had to sleep on a floor in Mainz. We are all much too early. The huge assembly place is teeming with scattered soldiers of the Air Force and other service branches, with men of all ages, especially officers, this cowardly pack that deserted us so shamefully in France. These gluttons and boozers, how I hate them! These fat, empty, and meaningless faces. Every few minutes one sees another familiar face. We have nothing to do, just hanging around. No one knows where we belong and no one cares about us. But the rifles, they take away from us. We cannot be newly equipped. Poor Germany!

4, September 1944

Still no decision! We have daily air raids. We run into the woods miles away, this is our only salvation. The allied bombers do carpet-bombing on the beautiful cities of Mainz and Worms. The sounds of the attacks are dreadful to listen to. At night we are thrown out of our beds. It is too dangerous to stay here since this is a military airfield. After several tries I manage to get a coat from one of the comrades.

5, September 1944

Parts of the waiting masses have been reassigned. We are divided into "Enemy Aircraft Warning Service" and "Security Guards". I would really like to stay with my buddies from Troyes. Daily we run up into the woods to hide out during the air raids.

7, September 1944

Finally a change! A new marching company has been put together of about 140 men. I have the command and I have orders to take the company by foot to the Fritsche Kaserne. Finally some responsibility!

Papa, 1ˢᵗ. row center

A lot of people have trouble with their feet. I let them go by streetcar. The rest of them march up the cobblestone streets past the railway station and through the city to Ludwigshöhe. I let them have a rest period, which everyone was thankful for. Arriving at the new Fritsche Kaserne, I have them line up and present them in good form to the Adjutant Lt. Wehr.

At night I have to take them up to the position "DACHS", at night back down again. They still don't know what to do with us.

8, September 1944

The food is not too bad. I sleep most of the time in the cellar of the Kaserne. Daily there are heavy flyovers and we run into the woods because there is not enough protection from bombs.

9, September 1944

It was hard saying good-bye to Lindner and Hech; they were good buddies. Today one troop including Meixner went to Arnheim, Holland. Others go to "Mountain goat" (Taubensuhl), or "Honeybee" (Bitburg) or "Meadowlark" (Cochem) or "Owl" (Birkenfeld). I myself would like to go to Koblenz or Kaiserslautern. Finally I learn of the decision; first there was talk of me going with 8 men to Metternich near Koblenz and I was very happy. But then comes the disappointment, Stetternich, near Jülich. I don't like that at all, but there is nothing I can do about it. The decision is irrevocable. That means in the afternoon the small group heads for the station. I look at the beautiful main railway station, not knowing, that just a few weeks later bombs would level the city of Darmstadt.

We leave Darmstadt at 2 pm. We have long waiting times everywhere. People are hanging on the running boards and riding on the bumpers between the cars. The train finally makes it to Bad Kreuznach. Here I get off.

Of course I take the opportunity to go home. The comrades try to find a place to stay overnight. I reach a train to Bad Münster and from there I walk in the night with a young soldier from Hochstätten. I cannot describe the happy feeling in my heart, to see them this soon again.

I knock at the door around midnight. The door finally opens and my sweetheart says, as if she had been expecting me: "I thought it would be you!" She whispers as to not wake the others and standing there in her nightgown, even though she had a little cold. We go upstairs immediately. Helga sleeps with her in bed. We carry her to the other room without her waking up. She sleeps so soundly and peacefully, the little rascal with a smile on her pale face. To my question, how our little one is doing, Rösel tells me she is sleeping in the bathroom, because she had a bath. There is so much to talk about. The others don't know yet, that I am here.

In the morning a happy reunion!

10, September 1944

Rösel brings me the little "Mouse" all wrapped up in a blanket, while she calls enticingly, Papa, Papa! She is trying to get her used to me. But she just stares with big blue eyes questioningly. She does not know me.

In an earlier letter, Rösel had written me: "I wish you could see how she touches your picture above her bed every evening, stroking and caressing it. When I say: "Papa?" she immediately looks at the picture". But when I want to pick her up, she turns away, makes a funny little face, and starts crying. I have to give her time.

Now we go downstairs to the cozy warm living room, Helga smooches with me, Norbert has matured a lot, and the little one makes us all happy. Rösel is not aware how I secretly and with great joy watch her when she picks up the baby and plays with her. Then the little darling squeals when she is held up high and she just loves to be cuddled.

In the afternoon I have to leave. I try to catch a ride and with that in mind we all start walking. Sigrid is in her carriage with the little rabbit fur blanket I had bought in Lyon. The child is able to sit up already. Rösel changes clothes. How attractive and young she still is, my pretty sweet wife. We walk down the old highway, but only very few cars pass and none of them stop. As I am deciding, if I should try to catch a train, that's when a truck stopped. I quickly say good-bye to Rösel, Norbert, and Sigrid. Helga, the little chatterbox, has stayed behind at the end of the village. I get in the truck and by the little bridge I see Helga sitting on the railing with her girlfriend. I call out to her and she waves at me until I can see her no more.

I meet up with a couple of buddies and we get an excellent dinner at the Hotel Lahneck in Stolzenfels and perfect beds for accommodations. At the last minute, Mayer was able to get our rations at the station in Bingerbrück.

11, September 1944

Slept well, left at 9:12 am via Koblenz. In Andernach we had a succession of three different air alerts. For more than an hour, the flyovers of heavy formations lasted. We could see the four engine Flying

Fortresses, and it was a very uncomfortable feeling listening to their horrible, cruel roar.

The train stops in the middle of nowhere. All passengers had to get off. The first time, everyone takes cover along a dirt road, close by, is an ack-ack artillery unit shooting wildly. At the second alert the train is pretty protected by trees. This attack is not meant for us though. The formations are heading across the Rhine River to Bonn and Cologne. Those proud cities are at this moment reduced to rubble. The sad thing is, there is hardly any industry or military left. They were all at the Russian Front.

What an insane heroism, whatever for? Tens of thousands are at this moment losing their lives and their homes. We hear, only the Cologne cathedral was left standing, though damaged. It is heartbreaking how this beautiful city has been destroyed. And yet, new life arises out of the rubble and ruins.

We get a pretty good meal in the Domcafe and decide not to continue until late at night because of low flying air attacks. The proprietor has put up some tables and chairs in the September sun and I can get a cup of coffee.

I then walk through the ruins into the city. Everywhere I see the same picture. Heartbreaking! The bombs have destroyed many 6 to 7 story high buildings and in these attacks whole rows of houses were leveled in an instant. And of course, thousands of innocent women, children, and old people have died a horrible death. Many have been buried alive. Shaken and distressed, I walk back.

At 9 pm, I get a train to Düren, where my sweetheart had spent her growing up years. She had asked me if possible to go to Lindern, her hometown. In Düren we have to get off the train, because of an air raid. Everyone has to get into the cellar at the station. Then we continue and when we get off it is pitch dark and no one has a flashlight and we don't know where we are going. A young woman takes pity on us and shows us the way to the military installation in town. It is late, but we can still get a cup of coffee and sleep on straw bags.

12, September 1944

We report to Capt. Haumann, he seems OK. Work, food, and accommodations are decent. We are supposed to stay here for the time being.

13, September 1944

The day is long and boring. In my free time I put a small table under the dark pine trees and in the lovely autumn sunshine I write a long letter home. In the evening we suddenly received orders to dig one man foxholes. There is the fear that the Americans will push through here.

14, September 1944

I am supposed to stop a truck on the street, in order to take equipment to Cologne. I am called back to find out that I am to move with a few other guys to the Wassermann post in Kleinhau in the Hürtgenwald (Hürtgen Forest) as reinforcement for the fighting group there.

That's all I needed! I am cursing my bad luck, which is to no avail. Schmitt is sent to Bonn far away from the fighting. Well, we shall see! I have been able to get a hold of a blanket and a towel. We get ready. Our troop consists aside from myself, Sgt. Sand, NCO Sauer and 7 Privates. We march from here to Jülich. There we encounter some "party big shots" that terrorize the population. People are in a helpless rage.

At the railway station there is a mixed crowd of all kinds of people: A lot of scattered soldiers and Hitler Youth, adolescent boys that have been ordered to dig trenches. In Düren we get a train to Obermaubach. I suggest we stay overnight here because it will be difficult to find the way up to the post in the dark.

Most of them stay in the small restaurant. I was going to look for a room, but could not find anything. Lottes and I sleep in the barn and fix us a comfortable bed and slumber well in spite of the grunting pigs.

15, September 1944

We head by foot through the poor little village, through some woods and a wide meadow, always uphill. On the right and left there are craters from bombs, those craters could be used as foxholes. How sad, that I will not be able to go to Lindern. An hour later we see the first houses from the top of the hill. That is the town of Kleinhau. We also see the landmark a 40 meter high water tower. Now comes the not so pleasant reception; suddenly Meyer detects low flying planes behind us. We turn around and with shock I discover four P-38 Lightnings coming out of the rain clouds flying very low over the rooftops directly toward us. Not a minute is to be lost. The closest house is about 100 meters away, the post up ahead another 100 meters. What to do? We cannot be rational at this point; the planes are right on top of us. We quickly throw ourselves into the potato field next to the road, others in the ditch.

And already the on board cannons and machine guns are hammering. I believed, my last moment had arrived and thought sadly, is this how I should be losing my life now? I lift my head and see that three of the Lightnings have already passed the military post, but the fourth one turns and it looks as if it is coming back on a second run. I scramble to my feet and in a breathless run, reach the first house, and stand with the protection of the wall behind me. The plane's pilot apparently had changed his mind and continues on. Thank God!

That was the beginning. We arrive at the post and meet Sgt. Müller. Most of the others are "punks", only about 2 or 3 decent people. What am I supposed to do here? I am getting tired of being pushed around from one place to the other. We have nothing else to do but stand guard every 2 hours, taking turns, partially at the entrance to the village and at the post. We are fed and housed in the village. I have very nice quarters in house No. 37 with the family Scholl, who own the bakery. I would like to write to these nice people later.

We can tell we are close to the front. From far away the thundering of the ack-ack can be heard. In the Hürtgen Forest the machine guns are hammering. We sleep in the bunker. The equipment is to be detonated, after the enemy has entered the area. Those are the division orders. What nonsense! Then it will be too late.

The news from the front is not encouraging. A breakthrough by the Americans is expected. Are we already closed in?

Oh, what a mood we are in! At 24:00 hours I am thinking of you, my dearest.

16, September 1944

Your Birthday, My Sweet, Little Wife

I wish you the best, most of all good health, happiness, and that we may soon be reunited in a peaceful time again. It promises to be a beautiful fall day. The leaves have turned red and gold, but why can't I be with you, my beloved? All my thoughts are with you and may my love protect you.

At noon I go to the house where my quarters is located. There are a whole bunch of women, who all talk too loud. There is an ill-mannered youth of about 16, who is flopped down on the couch all day and sleeps. My Norbert is a different kid; that I know!

In the afternoon I go in the pine forest along the street to Hürtgen. I hear the rumbling of the grenade explosions, but I don't care. I have to be alone with my thoughts.

At 4 pm I am invited for coffee. They have the typical black bread for this area with butter and jam. Into the coffee I put the last cube of sugar I still had from home.

I know that you too are with me in your thoughts and mind, my dearest. What do I wish for you? That all of us together can celebrate your birthday next year in peace and that this wretched war may be over.

17, September 1944

Every 5 hours, each one of us has to do two hours of guard duty. In the evening I stand at the entrance of the village by the gasthaus. Anyway, there is much to see. It is raining and foggy. The situation has not yet been clarified. We are to blow up the tower when the enemy is in position, then we are either killed or become prisoners. I do not want to become imprisoned!

The Sunday meal was good; we even had pudding for dessert.

18, September 1944

Tonight, I am startled, by the whistling of an artillery shell. It seems to be passing right over my head. How quickly I leaped behind the barracks wall for protection. Only now, it becomes dangerous here. The artillery continues shelling all night, but we feel safe in our bunker.

19, September 1944

Blue And Sunny The Days

Duty is not too bad. My host family has baked plum cake today. Oh, what a feast and it reminds me of my growing up years, when mother baked fresh crunchy plum cake every Saturday, while the plum season lasted.

All day long the planes are above us, especially the Thunderbolts. What are they up to? Every night there are attacks on the main roads. The population of the village sleeps in the bunkers. We have gotten used to the howling and roaring of the shelling. When I hear the whistling, I duck behind the wall of the bunker.

I stand guard in the pouring rain. How glad am I for my coat and the tarp.

20, September 1944

The front is moving. Reinforcements are ordered. How we feel sorry for the people who are opposite the Americans through the nights in this horrible weather. The mood is more than depressed among the people. They feel like a lamb led to the slaughter. The military is not armed very well and hardly trained. Yesterday their commander was shot by mistake.

We do not receive mail anymore. The post is to be kept secret. We receive instead of German arms, French rifles and hand grenades, as well as a Czech machinegun.

21, September 1944

The night stayed relatively quiet, even though the captain expected a break through by the Americans. My relationship with my host family grows more affectionate all the time. They do more than expected. They offer me coffee in the morning and afternoon. The town of Kleinhau is to be evacuated. The artillery gets worse every day and night. Our batteries are deployed very close to us. The Marauders circle above us with a great roar. If they drop bombs on us we will be sacrificed. They are greatly feared planes, but they turn away, thank God! They may have been looking for our artillery and could not find it.

The damage in town is extensive. The people all sleep in their basements. Telephone and electrical lines are destroyed, the street, the gardens, and meadows are torn up and riddled with craters, many houses are damaged and there have been a few fatalities, one Sergeant, who sacrificed himself to save three playing children.

22, September 1944

My host family is crying, when I see them. A grenade hit their garden and broke all of the windows. The furniture was thrown all over and the shock is still in their bones. All the people curse Hitler and the Party who are the criminals responsible for this miserable war.

I cannot expect these nice people to cook for me anymore, but they still do it. A police force from Düsseldorf has arrived to help out. Everybody is so sick and tired of everything.

The four artillery cannons and tanks are ordered up front. The infantrymen march through the village with bazookas; they are well-trained soldiers. A lot of animals are killed. In spite of the misery I had to laugh, when I saw the mayor trying to collect pieces of his pig that was killed in his garden. In the dusty street hunks of fresh killed meat from pigs and cows are lying around. One man is standing cursing in front of his stable, that now is just a pile of rubble.

In the evening, while I was in the schoolhouse talking to the teacher's wife, ten to twelve mortars passed overhead and detonated near by. It was a direct hit on our installation. When I returned I could see the damage. Half of the barracks is gone, the latrines riddled and the tower damaged. No casualties thank God! Why don't they just blow up the tower, then we could get away from here. Normal duty will not be possible now, because the lines and equipment are destroyed.

During the night we had an incredible artillery attack and the howling and exploding of shells just didn't stop. The people in town do not leave their cellars. It is raining day and night, the wind is howling and from the woods across the way, machine guns and mortars are hammering. What bad luck to have been sent here!

<u>24, September 1944</u>

<u>An Incredibly Sad Sunday</u>

All morning I am lying on my straw sack in the bunker brooding. My host family has cooked for me one more time. They have to get ready to evacuate. Orders from the High Command.

In the next few days, the village will become a battle zone. In Grosshau a direct hit has destroyed the church. Three of our men have to dig mass graves. Who are they supposed to be for? Between the exploding mortars, we try to get back into town as fast as possible. I desperately cling to the hope to get out of here alive and constantly think of my loved ones at home, especially our little baby. How much I love her all of a sudden.

I imagine, how she wants a "hanky" at night, because without it she can't go to sleep. She grabs the "raggy" as she calls it in both hands and holds it in front of her face and that's how she goes to sleep. I remember, how 2 weeks ago, when she cried; I kissed her tears away and my sweetheart said: "We just cannot stand it when the child cries". These scenes are so vivid before my eyes and I think I would just die of heartache.

I say good-bye to my host family and they are crying. They had to pack a couple of suitcases very quickly and all unnecessary things have to stay behind. They tell me to go back to the house and help myself to the pot of soup with the meat. Also they left me a half of a plum cake. In the pouring rain the people are loaded up in busses. Now the village is empty, the houses are open and some of our German soldiers, what a shame, are starting to loot.

In the middle of the night the new mechanized equipment arrived but without fuel. Oh, well! That was to be expected. The brave guys drove through the worst and most concentrated hail of artillery shells. Well, nothing has been accomplished, because shrapnel has damaged some of the equipment parts.

What will happen with our provisions? It's a good thing we have "requisitioned" some supplies such as butter, canned sardines, fat, potatoes, jam and cheese. We also have a couple of chickens and rabbits. From now on we have to cook for ourselves and that will be primitive.

25, September 1944

Finally! The M/Sgt. received orders to have five men march from here to Cologne and I am one of them. They finally realized that they have to newly equip us. Thank God! We quickly get packed and get on our way, across the little meadow, through the woods, always down hill through dense under brush. We are in a happy mood. We hope the comrades staying behind will make it home alive. I have not had mail from home in some time but I am confident, everything is OK.

The wet branches hit me in the face; we pass another crater, pass a swampy meadow, rest for a little while by a tree trunk, and reach the town of Obermaubach. Here we feel safe. We get coffee in a gasthaus and I eat some of my plum cake with it and then try to find accommodations for the night. After an hour or so I am able to secure private quarters for all of us for the night. I enjoy the good bed in a private house after a chat with the friendly people. In the morning they fix a nice breakfast for me.

26, September 1944

We go to the train station in the pouring rain. In the waiting room I eat the last piece of plum cake. We board the train and finally arrive in Düren. We climb across the wreckage to find a place to get something to eat and drink. From here we catch a train to Cologne.

What is going to happen to us? Right now we really don't care.

27, September 1944

We slept during the night on straw sacks in a small bunker, while we are passing through here. There has been a very heavy and devastating bombing attack on Cologne. The bunker is shaking and we experience hits very close. This beautiful city is in the process of being leveled. More and more soldiers are arriving, all of them scattered, not belonging to any units anymore. They come from France, Belgium, and Holland.

30, September 1944

Today a decision is made: I am transferred to Trier. In the afternoon departure from the main railway station, I look at the silhouette of the majestic Cologne Cathedral, which miraculously was left standing amongst all the ruins and rubble. It breaks my heart to see this beautiful city absolutely destroyed.

In Koblenz, I get on a streetcar and get off in the old familiar Stolzenfels. The owner of the castle, a lovely lady, is finding quarters for us: Three men up at the castle, Lottes and I with the friendly family named Bach. The Nazi mayor's wife has arrogantly refused us, but the poor workers wife has willingly accepted us. How touched I am to be included in such a homey and cozy family atmosphere, with an ordinary, friendly, talkative woman in a tidy kitchen and two well mannered girls. The little one reminds me of my Helga, sitting in the bathtub, embarrassed that I saw her. Later on, the two are sitting in clean, flowered pajamas at the table staring at the guests.

We eat something, talk, and later on, sleep in the people's beds. The lady sleeps with the girls in the children's room. It's been a long time, that I had such a good night's sleep.

Outside I hear the sound of the rain and the slapping of the Rhine River's waves against the bank.

1, October 1944

We awake late and that's OK. We do not have to rush for anything. We drink coffee and then go to the Hotel Lahneck, where we are to meet the three others. I reproach myself that I have not tried to go home, but that would have been very risky, because yesterday Bingerbrück had a very heavy bombing attack.

We sit on the beautiful Hotel Terrace with the high windows and look out onto the muddy waves of the Rhine River. I write letters and read. We eat an excellent lunch here; we even have pudding for dessert and then walk up to the Stolzenfels Castle. How wonderful it would be, if I could stand up here on a sunny day with my beloved at this magic castle and enjoy this magnificent view down to where the Lahn River flows into the Rhine.

They all praise their quarters and the host families, and joke with the charming castle owner. In the afternoon we stop a truck and catch a ride back to Koblenz. We have to wait until 11 pm. At the station we eat some of our field rations, get into the 2nd class train compartment and make it to Trier without any incidences. I could even sleep a little.

An ack-ack soldier takes us to the high bunker at 2 am, where we stretch out on the hard benches and catch a couple more hours of sleep.

2, October 1944

We report to Maj. Schneider at the casino. We are supposed to stay here for the time being, that's OK, I guess.

3, October 1944

I am assigned to Group #1. Accommodations are in a large hall with high windows and a hard bed. The new buddies are OK. The food is pretty good and I am pleased. The duty in the FLUKO is not bad.

4, October 1944

A low flying attack on the Mosel Bridge. Our ack-ack is defending bravely. Surprisingly, there are still some good cafés and restaurants here.

8, October 1944

The situation on the front is not favorable for us. In the east as well as the west, there are big offensive measures planned. The bridgeheads are in Aachen and Metz. Will Metz be able to hold? We all hope, that everything will go quickly before the war is carried on into the Pfalz area, my home. The hinterlands have been heavily bombarded and the Rhine Valley and large railway stations have been hit badly.

I wonder where my brother Richard is? Is he in Kurland? If yes, he will not get out of there. I also do not get any mail from home anymore.

9, October 1944

I intend to ask the major, if he would grant me a temporary duty assignment to get home. My buddies suggested for me to do that. The major cannot say more than no.

10, October 1944

Today I meet Major Schneider in the yard and ask for the possibility to go home for one or two days. He thinks about it for a minute, how to combine a temporary duty assignment with it and says: "You can go for three days." I am overjoyed, immediately go to personnel to have my orders issued and go to the 19:58 train.

In the hotel across from the railway station I get a bite to eat, pancakes with applesauce. I am on time for the departure, but I have to wait 2 more hours until a steam engine is secured, then finally we get going, the windows carefully darkened. Around midnight I arrive in Turkismühle, there a layover until 5 am. The time just will not pass.

The waiting room is crowded with refugees, crying children, tired women, and soldiers. One lays the head on the table and tries to sleep. Outside in the hallway soldiers are laying on the floor, trying to sleep. Finally at around 5 am, a new morning is dawning, a train comes. We reach Bad Münster via Idar Oberstein and continue on about 8 am, arriving in Hochstätten at 9 am.

Oma is the first one to greet me by the barn door. They are all surprised to see me again. Norbert is in Sembach. Rösel greets me in the entrance hall. In the small, cozy kitchen they have hot coffee for me, then we make a fire in the living room. And now there is my little sweetheart. Rösel brings her wrapped in the brown blanket. She looks at me with big eyes, not recognizing me, and she says temptingly: Papa, Papa! I want to hold her, but she turns away. I have to be patient.

I watch with amazement, how the child drinks her bottle hungrily all by herself. She has gained some weight and is a happy baby. After her meal she is put back to bed and we leave her alone. She develops normally and wonderfully. It is so cute when she knows it is time to eat and even sees her bottle, how she kicks, wriggles and pounds her little hands and whines with impatience, but never cries. Such a big appetite! Then she lies on her back, holds her bottle with both hands real high and sucks contentedly. Every afternoon Rösel takes her outside into the fresh air. This is good for her and she has not been sick yet. When she smiles, she shows the four little teeth, which is just darling. Our joy is immense, when the child wakes up and immediately laughs and waves her little arms. She knows people now and I am allowed to pick her up now.

Helga is tall and skinny. They tell me she is very ill mannered and cries a lot, but I must say, while I am there, she is sweet, affectionate, and eager to learn. She wants to write, draw and have "dictation". Anxiously she writes down every sentence and is thrilled to have no mistakes.

Norbert is still in Sembach. We called to tell him that he should come later with grandmother because we have company. He understands, and they will come tomorrow.

11, October 1944

I had a good night sleep, we build a fire in the living room, and I enjoy the homey atmosphere. I can now experience for myself, how our little "Mouse" chirps like a canary, as Rösel had written in one of her letters. When lying on her back she kicks her legs, laughs, and enjoys her little life.

In the evening grandmother comes with Norbert. How happy she is, my good mother. She is the same and still the years have left their mark. Norbert is a quiet and sensible boy.

We take care of the little one and bring her to bed. Happily she "talks", we cover her up, arms under the blanket after Mama folds her little hands and says her evening prayer. Then we leave her alone, she follows us with her eyes until we turn off the light.

Opa claims that Helga is behaving and obedient, does not cry and listens only because I am here.

13, October 1944

Today I Have To Leave

Since riding the trains has become very dangerous, we want mother to go home either late at night or early in the morning. At night though it is too dark for her. When Norbert went up last week he had to get off the train and run into the fields because of aircraft strafing.

My mother so enjoys our little girl. In the afternoon we get ready, as I want to go to Bad Münster by foot. We take the little "Mouse" in the baby carriage. She is happy, smiles and shows her four little white teeth. As of a few days ago she makes us laugh by wrinkling her nose, putting her head back and laughing, thereby imitating one of Rösel's old acquaintances from Lindern. Now she sits in her carriage with her blue hat, looks at the chickens and pounds her hands on her blanket.

It is a warm sunny day and Norbert takes his roller skates. Suddenly a couple of Thunderbolts are circling above us. Are they looking for the railroad tracks? Quickly we go behind a hedge and cover up the baby carriage with a dark coat, as the white is too noticeable. The child is quiet and we duck behind the bushes. Helga is trembling with fear. The little one does not know yet, why her life and so many others might be endangered by an insane humanity. I remember a part in Rösel's letter, where she wrote recently: "Poor thing was so frightened, when low flying planes flew over the roof tops, that she could not calm down for some time."

I suggest now, that we say good-bye here. This is too risky. Hastily we part and it's so hard, as always, to leave them, my loving wife, the good mother, and that little innocent child. Rösel waves until I am around the next curve. Norbert wants to accompany me with his roller skates. He is such a well mannered and mature boy and we talk like two good friends.

For a moment I am contemplating to use the opportunity to talk to him about the facts of life and sexual things, mostly because I am sure he knows, at almost 14, how this little baby sister came about. But then I shy away from the thought. One thing I am not too happy to hear is that he and his friends are walking on Sundays with girls his age. Are these worries starting already?

We come to the town of Altenbamberg. I advise him to turn around and go back, but he wants to come with me to Bad Münster, takes his skates off and walks with me a while. Finally, shortly before Ebernburg I tell him to return, otherwise it will get dark. He puts his skates back on, kisses me in a trusting childlike way and heads back, turns around twice to wave and then disappears behind the next curve. This has been another good-bye, as there have been so many.

I get a train right away, but only until Heimbach. Here the train does not continue and we have to walk to Turkismühle. Just great! I get together with another soldier in the pitch dark. Near Neubrücke a train loaded with ammunition was attacked and destroyed. There was a horrendous roaring fire with continuous explosions.

It is a long walk, something like 12 miles to Turkismühle. We take turns carrying the heavy suitcase with fruit for a young woman, her reward of three cigarettes. Finally we get there. A crowd of people, the waiting room is destroyed, all the windows smashed. A few boring hours of waiting, we continue to Hermeskeil, where the station was bombed the day before. We have to go on walking. Thank God it is raining, so the "jabos" are not to be feared. At 10 pm I finally make it. I am thankful for those three days.

15, October 1944

Mother writes, that my aunt from Kaiserslautern has been bombed out and has moved to Sembach. No more school, Sigrid weighs now 16 lbs.

16, October 1944

They have not received any mail from me at home and are worried. Rösel writes: "Norbert's school has been closed since Sept. 18th. Our little sweetheart sits in her highchair now at mealtime and wants something of everything."

22, October 1944

On October 18th, Himmler's appeal for the formation of the "Peoples Army" was proclaimed. All men from 16 to 60 are to be armed.

My brother Richard is in Riga, Latvia. Herman Hanbuch is killed in action. Oscar Zapp is wounded and in a Russian prison camp, all from my small home village. Bombs fell on the railroad bridge in Bad Münster.

The turtle, Max, has tried to bury himself in the garden and they put him in the cellar in a sand pile, so he can hibernate for the winter.

5, November 1944

Mother writes: "Helga is here with me. She is a good girl and behaves herself. She wrote you a big letter yesterday. Your schoolhouse has been turned into barracks. Two rooms on the first floor have been confiscated for the military. It is getting crazier all the time".

I ask the Lt. for permission of a temporary duty assignment and after a short hesitation he says OK. Quickly my papers are taken care of. In the evening I leave by train from Trier and surprisingly the train is heated. Layover in Hermeskeil until 3 am, then from there to Bad Münster. I get a connection right away and arrive in Hochstätten at 6 am.

They are all still sound asleep. If only they knew I was standing in front of the door. For a minute I wonder if I should wait until they wake up, then I decide to knock. Oma opens up. First she thinks it is the company from Kaiserslautern, then the great surprise and then comes later, a little sleepy, my sweetheart.

6, November 1944

Norbert's Birthday

How happy am I that I can be the first one to congratulate him. What a handsome young man he has become. My gift to him was a mosaic puzzle of Germany. We unpack it and begin to put it together. He loves it and I am happy, that he is so knowledgeable in geography. He kisses me in a childlike manner and says: "Thank you, Papa."

And now the sweet little "Mouse" comes. Again she stares at me with big eyes. She has changed and looks chubby and healthy. I talk to her, call her little names and try to pick her up, but she wrinkles her nose, so we can see the little white teeth and looks like she is going to cry. Now the magic word is: "Don't cry!" and Rösel picks her up and says: "Where is Papa?" and "This is Papa!" She sighs and looks at me more quietly. Then she gets her bottle, which she drinks with great appetite and we go downstairs where a warm fire is burning. How cozy! She lets me hold her and I carry her around the room and show her different things, like the radio. When she hears the music, she moves her head back and forth and jumps continually.

At noon we have a good dinner, because of our big boy's birthday and after all he is the center of attention today. During dinner we have a lot of fun with that little one. Thank goodness for bibs. Carefully she eats soup from a spoon and absolutely loves the potatoes. As soon as the mouth is full, she drums with both hands continually on the table until the next spoonful is offered. Also a mixture of cottage cheese, cookies, and sugar is put away. Then she is put down for her nap. What a good baby she is!

Later Opa and I work on the darkening shades, which need repairing and in the afternoon we repair the tire on Norbert's bike and I am surprised and pleased how good and talented he is with technical things.

After our baby gets up, I cannot wait to hold and cuddle her. She knows a lot of things and I ask her, as I did with the others: "Where is the light? Where is the music? Where is the radio?" The birds capture her interest and when I say: "Where is the birdie?" she looks out the window and points. One never tires to kiss the tender fragrant cheeks and memories of the other two at that age come back.

In Norbert's honor, there is a birthday coffee and even a cake, a rarity at this time and I know, how they have struggled to be able to bake this. We are so thankful, that he is only 14 and not 16 or they would put a weapon in his hands. What a crime is committed here on our young people.

At 7 pm our little "Mouse" goes to bed happily, I pull out a bottle of my French sweet wine and we talk away the evening. Later on when we turn on the light in the bedroom, the baby wakes briefly, turns over, and continues sleeping. She is a very light sleeper, so I have changed the light switch, to a quieter one.

7, November 1944

I awake in the darkness from happy sounds of cooing from our little sparrow, as we call her. I hear my sweetheart whispering to her: "Little Mouse!" and each time she answers with a delightful cooing sound. Now I am completely awake and enjoy Rösel and the little sweetheart.

That morning I watch how she gets her bath. What fun! She has no fear of the water, just like the other two. Rösel has made sure of that. She wriggles with her firm little fleshy body like a fish and she has to be very careful, that she does not slip out of her hands. Constantly she smashes her hands down on the water and kicks with her little legs with exuberance. All the while she "talks" and patiently lets Mama wash her head, instinctively closing her eyes. Finally she is lifted out, does not cry, but lets Rösel rub her skin dry until it is glowing. Then she gets dressed in clean clothes, gets her bottle and goes to sleep.

That afternoon I got a little upset with Opa. For a couple of days, she does not want to sit on the potty anymore, also does not want to be held to go "Pee-Pee" anymore. Now Opa was holding her for some time without her doing anything and then, all of a sudden, she wet his pants. He gave her a little pat on the rear end, she started to cry so bitterly, that it cut into my heart and she just would not calm down. The crying came so deep out of her little heart, that it upset me. I kiss the tears from her eyes, the dear salty tears, and we use the magic words: "Don't cry!" and slowly she calms down. Our good mood is gone for the evening and Rösel is upset and Opa of course feels badly and is sorry.

At night we have so much fun watching her standing on the red sofa, holding on to the back and jumping up and down. Standing up she stretches her legs real stiff, standing on her toes. We cannot stop laughing. Soon she will be walking and is now almost 10 months old. I say good night and already long for the next reunion. Norbert watches with a condescending smile, but he loves his little sister.

We eat supper, during which I am very quiet. My brave little wife knows this already, knows that I am thinking of our farewell. Then I go with Rösel and Norbert to the station, the train is supposed to be delayed. Indeed we sit there on the waiting room bench, Rösel with a scarf over her head and Norbert in his blue raincoat and we try to joke and make the hour of farewell easier, which it never is. The minutes are precious, that we still have time to talk and I am glad, that the train is late. Finally it comes. I kiss them, who are so dear and precious to me. How I miss my little "Murschel", who is still in Sembach. Then I wave to them until the darkness surrounds me.

I get back to Trier at dawn and I am thankful for these wonderful days at home.

9, November 1944

No speech by the Führer, as was originally announced. Thank goodness! What would he have to say anyway, this windbag!

The people are infuriated about these adventurers, who have started this insane war.

12, November 1944

During the night we had shelling of the city. I am now in the Group #3 with Lt. Kuhn, who is a decent guy. In a letter, Rösel tells me that Sigrid has been a little restless as of a few days. Is she teething? I hope she won't get sick.

17, November 1944

Rösel picked up Helga in Sembach. She was there for three weeks and had fun and a good rest and gained some weight. My mother loves to have her there and caters to her every whim. She slept in father's bed. She has so many characteristics of my mother. She is a good hearted and good natured child, and was homesick for her little baby sister.

My brother Richard made it safely out of Kurland. Thank God! He is now in East Prussia. He has been lucky a few times.

Rösel writes: "The child during the last few days is very restless, especially at night. In the evening it is hard for her to get to sleep, she seems to be in pain. Her left cheek is always red and it looks like the 7th tooth is trying to come through. In the daytime she is fine, smooching with Opa. No one else could come near her. She is very frugal with her affections.

20, November 1944

I am still able to find a few restaurants in Trier with good food. Sometimes I even get a piece of cake without coupons.

Trier is slowly being evacuated. The head of the Nazi Administration District is putting pressure on the population. Some of them move to Thüringen.

All military personnel whose ages are prior to 1906 are to be reassigned from the Air Force Courier unit to replenish the infantry.

1, December 1944

The city hall received a direct hit. Two shrapnel pieces hit right next to my bed and all the windowpanes were bashed in. They smashed through a steel helmet and a closet and ripped off Sgt. Neunkirch's right foot. Poor guy moans and is white as a sheet but is very brave. Everyone went to the cellar to sleep. There were two other wounded and no one can sleep upstairs anymore.

2, December 1944

We all move into the damp FLUKO cellar, but we don't mind because we feel safer there.

In a letter my mother writes: "There is nothing that can be purchased anymore, so I cannot make any gifts. It is not advisable to go to Hochstätten because of the danger of the planes. We have had the first snow already."

5, December 1944

Rösel writes: "It is so sad, that you do not receive mail from us. It takes all the joy away from writing."

Trier is becoming lonelier and more dangerous. One is glad to be able to make the way to the FLUKO and back, since there is no place to take cover. We continuously have to expect attacks from the artillery.

6, December 1944

Rösel writes: "Sigrid is so cute. She knows when she sees her coat and hat that we will go for a walk. And she is so proud, when I put something pretty to wear on her and she looks at herself from top to bottom. Yesterday we had fun again with her bath. She likes her little fat legs and pinches them. Her appetite is excellent and her favorite is boiled potatoes.

8, December 1944

Today supposedly a big miracle is to happen, which will alter the war situation instantly. Poor stupid humanity! They cling to a piece of straw and continuously are deceived. The people cannot do anything about the impending doom anymore but run weakly into their own disaster.

10, December 1944

Slowly it is becoming very dangerous in Trier. Feverish preparations are made for the move to Wittlich. A temporary command has been there for weeks. The work is moving very slowly. I have not had any mail for weeks. Nothing comes in and nothing goes out.

The buddies try to forget the misery by drinking too much Mosel wine. The FLUKO cellar is damp and cold but we feel secure there. We have visited the high bunker. Here I would not worry about even a direct hit. The city is deserted and only a few people stick it out.

14, December 1944

This Is The Day I Consider Especially Blessed

Twenty years ago today I came to Hochstätten. It was a day, for which I am thankful my whole life. For twenty years we know each other and fifteen years our wonderful marriage has lasted, although five of those, we have been robbed and those years can never again be recovered.

Mama and Papa as newlyweds in 1929

But many happy years I hope to spend with you, my dearest wife and mother of our children.

There is a tremendous troop movement in the Eifel Mountains, especially near Bitburg. What does that mean? Could there possibly be an offensive?

16, December 1944

It is impossible to buy anything for gifts anymore. Almost all stores are closed, the windows boarded up, Trier is a dead city. We have the ominous feeling that something is going to happen here soon.

19, December 1944

The Day Of My Wondrous Salvation

I will be thankful for this day, as long as I live! The miracle is, that you O God have given me the message to move when I did.

On this day, we had several air raids. In the Esperstedt House on Hosenstrasse #18, suddenly there was a radio message, that fighter planes were approaching Trier. Why all of a sudden, do I experience this strange restlessness and feverish haste to pick up and get out of there? It is insanity!

What made me run as fast as my legs would carry me and when I had reached the optician's shop, I heard a horrible, tinny rushing sound and all I could think of was: "O God, bombs!"

Then just behind me there is an awful horrendous noise. A tremendous air pressure throws me across the street, there is a rumbling and crashing sound from every direction, and all windowpanes and glass are flying through the air. Further more, the roof tiles are thrown into the street and the detonating sounds keep on. Then I realize with horror, this is a carpet-bombing. Will I reach the casino? O God! How does one feel at such a moment? I do not remember how I made it around the next corner. At the moment I reach the entrance of the bank building there is another horrendous noise in the yard of the bank. I throw myself down, and then get up with bleeding hands and unfortunately there is a wagon in the way. I fall over boxes and other equipment. Another soldier comes from the other side trying to reach the entrance as well, slips and falls on top of me. At the entrance of the stairway we both are on the floor. I scramble up panting and race down the stairs completely out of breath. Down below the door is torn open from the tremendous air pressure, the whole cellar is shaking, and the people are thrown around. There is finally some protection on top of us. A few more explosions outside. Then silence!

After a while we venture outside. There is terrible destruction everywhere. I only want to see the Hosenstrasse and the blood in my veins seems to turn to ice, when I see, that the house No. 18 is leveled and has been reduced to a pile of rubble and so are the neighboring houses. Terrible! Everyone in there is now buried alive. The next day Mrs. Espenstedt has been dug up dead from the wreckage of her house. Had I stayed just two minutes longer, I would have been killed as well. And the whole road I breathlessly ran down had been hit. All the houses in the Palaststrasse were destroyed and nothing left but a chaotic heap of rubble.

A burning feeling of happiness fills my heart. You have so wonderfully protected me, my God and I know the prayers of my loved ones have sent some special angels to save me!

I turn away in shock and walk with deep thoughts through the destruction and look at the horrified faces of the poor people and see the sad wretchedness. How many casualties there were, we do not know. I know that in the Schifferkeller (cellar) where I have often found shelter, a direct hit has killed 70 to 80 people.

The poor postmaster was thrown against a stone pillar, where he fell dead with a fractured scull. In the streets there is broken glass a foot deep. It was indeed a carpet- bombing across the whole city. What a shame for the beautiful city of Trier.

This was only the beginning. They will continue to come. Our group is the first one to move.

20, December 1944

Move to Wittlich! In the morning at 5 we leave from the casino. Some of the guys leave by bicycle, the females with a lot of luggage and a few men by train from Trier West. The bags by horse and wagon and after some waiting we actually leave. In Wengerohr we change trains and then on to Wittlich.

The first impression is not bad. The accommodations and offices are in a former Forestry. The rooms for the females are nice. The food is pretty good and we will stay overnight in the schoolrooms in town.

On December 6th at 5:30 am Rundstedt's "West Offensive" began between Malmedy and Luxembourg (The Battle of the Bulge). The first success was a complete breakthrough through the American lines. Will they make it to the Atlantic?

We notice an increased activity of armed action all around Trier. The Americans were completely surprised.

21, December 1944

There was a tremendous attack on Trier. Whole city blocks are gone, the cathedral is badly damaged the casino is burning.

We have the first snow. I walk in the wintry forest with a boundless yearning for home. There are all those beautiful memories of my childhood and the knowledge what my own children have to do without. How very sad that makes me.

The night in the school is cold, no heat and all the windows are bashed in. The offensive seems to be successfully moving ahead and the American Army at Bastogne is encircled.

23, December 1944

Third great attack on Trier (100 British Lancasters). Mostly the center and western part of the city are hit. How sad about this beautiful city.

Attack on the railroad station in Wengerohr. We watch a plane being shot down and see the pilots parachute down.

I looked at the cellars in the city. They will not be sufficient for direct bomb hits. The people hope that Wittlich will not be attacked as it is supposed to become a hospital city.

24, December 1944

Christmas Eve

The package from home has not yet arrived!

At 3 pm the heavy attack on Wittlich. I had just gone up to the woods when I observed the approach of several formations of four engine planes. I see a column of smoke, which is the sign of attack and then I hear the whooshing sound. The few of us who were there run as fast as we can uphill. Every minute is precious. I get caught with my belt hooks in a thorny hedge and desperately try to get loose, without success. I remember thinking: "Is it here and now that I should die?" I finally tear myself away. All around me are explosions that are coming closer all the time. We run further away from the Forestry; there is a little pause, then a new wave hits and this time even closer. I am laying flat on the ground expecting the inevitable, dull and humbly at the same time into my destiny. But I want to live, dear God, I want to still live for my family. O God I do not want to die yet, I am still so young!

15 minutes later it gets very quiet. The formations of planes are leaving our air space and as we look down below we see Wittlich burning and thick, black mushroom clouds rising up everywhere over the city. Our place is a mess! A bomb hit directly in front of the door. The wall is smashed in, the roof destroyed, all windows ripped out, the interior badly damaged.

The buddies and females, who were still in the house, received only light injuries. Some were buried under debris and we were able to dig them out, unharmed, thank God!

We were so lucky.

This Was My Christmas

I walk around and think of home. We had planned, that at 5 pm, when "Christkind" comes, we would think of one another and would be together in our thoughts.

Evening comes and the sun sets red as blood in the west and under the pine trees in the snowy winter forest all by myself, I celebrate with my loved ones this sad Christmas.

The evening does not bring much of a Christmas mood, just clean up work. At 7 pm we sit quietly and sadly in the dining room with a few candles burning. There is coffee for everyone and a few cookies. Capt. Romfeld says a few fitting words and someone starts singing "Silent Night Holy Night". There are a lot of teary eyes and my friend Paul

Haardt, who is very concerned about his family, turns away sobbing with his body shaking uncontrollably.

Then I do my night duty. All night we put up new patrols. The city is still burning. The roaring of only a few planes is still to be heard. It is bitterly cold and all night I think of my loved ones. Are you well? How was your Christmas? Oh, may you sleep sweetly until tomorrow.

A gloomy winter day is dawning.

25, December 1944

1ˢᵗ Christmas Day

I go to town. The destruction is terrible. Sorrow and tears everywhere. The people dig desperately through the rubble of their homes that are no more than a heap of ruins. The streets are riddled with bomb craters. In the afternoon I am back in the crowded bunker. Mostly there were women, children, and the elderly. When the earth starts trembling, one woman falls from one fainting spell to another, while her little girl keeps screaming.

Oh, you miserable criminals, you, who are at fault for all this wretchedness, you will pay for it one day.

At night I quickly decide to ask the Capt. for permission of a short leave and after thinking about it for a minute, he approves. In a feverish hurry I get ready. Five days! Who could describe my feelings?

I get a car to Bernkastel. There is Christmas mood everywhere. Candles glow on Christmas trees, children's muffled voices behind carefully darkened windows and I have the best kind of Christmas mood. I decide to walk across the Hunsrück Mountains. In the night I ask for the direction to Morbach. A car approaches and gives me a ride over the high road to Morbach. I get a friendly welcome at the baker and his wife, a cup of tea and a piece of cake. They are ordinary warmhearted people who talk about their son on the Russian front. They make a bed for me on the couch in the living room. My heart is calming down and I thank them for their kindness and look forward to the next day with anticipation.

At 6 am I go to the station and get a train to Simmern, anyway I am making progress.

26, December 1944

2ⁿᵈ Christmas Day

Today I will be with you! The train is terribly slow. Close to 9 am before the "jabos" are coming, we get to Simmern. I go downtown and cannot get a cup of coffee anywhere. At the end of town I finally find a little place where I can get some coffee, also, a truck, where there is room along with a bunch of soldiers and then we get going. We keep watching the sky, but we are fortunate. I get off in Rheinböllen in hopes of getting another ride, but no luck. So I walk about 9 miles to Stromberg. It's a beautiful, clear and frosty winter day, blue skies and bright with snow and it is fun to walk. At 2 pm, I arrive in Stromberg. I can get a simple meal in a gasthaus with a bad apple wine. I see Marauders circling above Bad Kreuznach. What are they up to?

I get a ride to Schweppenhausen; walk from there over Windesheim and Hargesheim to Bad Kreuznach. My left foot hurts because the leather of my boot has hardened from the snow. It does not matter!

But what has happened in Bad Kreuznach? I cannot believe this little insignificant town was bombed as well. Smoking rubble everywhere and the familiar smell of smoke in all the streets. Salinental and Bad Münster was hit bad as well. From the bridge by the swimming pool up to the Felsentor one Marauder crater after the other. The overpass of the train is just a heap of rubble. I climb across the devastation and discover with a shock, that the bridge to Ebernburg is destroyed as well. That was the Marauders work that afternoon. I decide to crawl across the ruins of the bridge over pilings and bent metal; I hope I will be OK. Deep below the rushing water of the Nahe River. On hands and knees I carefully continue, swinging from one girder to the other. Drenched in sweat I finally reach the other bank. The rest of it is easy. From there it is just a stone throw to Hochstätten and I am not the least bit tired anymore. I find out from a friendly railroad worker, that nothing has happened there.

And there is the dear house and when I knock, my sweetheart says unsuspectingly: "Come in!" Looks at me with big eyes and cries: "Well, I'll be!" Then we are in each other's arms and everyone is embracing me at once. And there is the sweet little baby and the Christmas tree.

I kick off my boots, bathe the sore foot, and wash myself. O God, I am home again. Who can describe this feeling of bliss?

Norbert and Helga greet me with great joy. Norbert as he gets older, a little more reserved, but Helga is still the little smooch she always was with her cute pug nose. And now the little sweetheart! She has gained more weight and shows off what she has learned: "ba-ba", (for Papa), "ga-ga" (for the chickens) "kat" (for cat).

At the table we all have fun watching her eat. When the potatoes are steaming hot and we blow, she blows also. She is always happy and pounds her hands on the table. She gets thinned cereal (like Cream of Farina) in her bottle, which she drinks all by herself. Then she gets a little white hat on her head, which is getting too small, her rubber pants and finally her sleeping sack up to the shoulders. When we ask: "Where is your sleeping sack?" she grabs the sack with both hands over her chest and laughs, that we can see the little teeth. Then we carry her in her bed, lights out and soon she is asleep.

Helga was determined to sleep in my bed, but was content, when we convinced her to sleep with Opa, and she happily crawled into his cozy, warm bed.

Oh, how wonderful to be under my own roof again.

27, December 1944

Actually Christmas is over, but for me these days are always Christmas. It is cold and we stay inside. The children tell me about Christmas Eve, this year not as peaceful as usual because even on this day, bombs were falling and did some damage in Schenk's and the nursery. They tell me what all they put in my package and I know how hard they tried to please me.

All day long everything revolves around the dear little child. She gets held, carried, takes her naps, and grows like a little weed. Soon she will be 1 year old. She does not walk yet, but that's OK.

Norbert reads a lot of books. He brought quite a few from the Sembach library, books I myself had read with great enthusiasm when I was his age. Helga wants me to give her "dictation" all day long. Right now she reads "Anderson's Fairytales".

They have gotten used to the circling dive bombers in the daytime and at night the over flights of bombing squadrons and the people are used to going into their cellars.

After the child is put to bed, which has been lovingly warmed with a hot water bottle and gets her mittens on to keep her little hands warm, we talk until late.

Every morning, that she wakes up healthy is a gift for us.

28, December 1944

Rösel has told me, how rudely a colonel has confiscated our apartment in Sembach and ordered my mother to leave. What is going to happen to our beautiful furniture and my books? Patience! Different times are coming.

Ice flowers (frost) on the windows. In the afternoon we all have to go to the cellar in Laubensteins. The little "Mouse" gets wrapped in a blanket and I hope she will not catch a cold.

At night we light the Christmas tree, we still have a few candles left from last year. I show the little one the bells and baubles, then with shining eyes she looks into the sparkling, magical light of the tree. I constantly want to kiss her little head.

We eat cookies, drink eggnog I smoke a cigar and enjoy the peacefulness of our home.

29, December 1944

It gets colder every day. Norbert "eats up" Karl May's books. There has not been any school for a long time because of the air raids. The damage is tremendous. The boy is 14 years old and his knowledge is greatly lacking in many areas. How I would like to make up for it!

Helga likes to play with her girlfriends. She is very frightened of the planes and is the first one to run into the cellar. Both of them love their baby sister. We pack suitcases with clothes and other important things. Some of them we put in neighbors cellars, some we bury in the garden.

It was on this furlough that my "Murschel" went through a bit of a trauma with her pet goose, named Liesel. She had all the chickens and the goose tamed, so that they would let themselves be petted by her. Well, it was decided that since the goose was getting pretty old and did not lay eggs anymore, she should become meat on the table, which was a rarity.

Opa told Helga, that Liesel ran away, so not to sadden her too much, but she went looking for her all afternoon and calling her, after the goose had already been slaughtered. That night when we had some delicious white meat for supper, she was still crying over the loss of her pet she thought ran away. I was told later on, that Norbert told her the truth and created a whole new drama, which caused her to get sick and cry for days.

In the evening, putting little Sigrid to bed, we observed that as soon as she was put down on her sheet, she felt so comfortable and cozy, that she turned her head to the side, cuddles into the pillow and blinks her eyes until she is asleep. At night though she is extremely sensitive to any noises and as soon as the light is turned on she turns over and threatens to wake up. She is very good sitting on her potty, although for the most part not successful yet, we put a stool in front of her with a book or her bear.

At night we play games and the in-laws and Rösel complain in their presence, how the two older ones are often misbehaved. Their reaction is totally different: Norbert gets obstinate and is insulted. Helga is genuinely remorseful and embarrassed. She is sorry, that I had to hear this. When I ask her in the kitchen: "What is this I have to hear about you?" she cries bitterly and it hurts me in my soul. I hold her, stroke her hair, and then she promises to be more obedient. Oh, I know her tender mind and soul.

Norbert, who has quite a different nature, acts glum and dejected. I ask them both to get back to the games. Norbert is reluctant, while Helga is quickly reconciled. Slowly Norbert becomes more trusting and in the end we are all happy together again. They don't want to go to bed and the hours are so precious. It's finally 11 pm when we turn in.

30, December 1944

Today is my last day. The children are around me all day long. I carry and hold the little "Mouse" a lot. She wants to look out the window and at the Christmas tree. I want to touch the sweet soft cheeks with my lips.

The two big ones put out seeds for the birds in front of the window and watch the golden orioles and finches.

Helga plays "store" with her best friend Wilhelmine. When it turns dark we light the candles one more time and sing the dear old Christmas songs.

In the afternoon, the planes were close and some bombs fell in the fields. I quickly picked up the baby from her bed, wrapped her in a blanket, and carried her to the neighbor's cellar they have asked us to share, as it is bigger. We have taken care of the most important things, such as packed clothes, dishes, photo albums, etc. and have distributed them in various different cellars of neighbors.

The preparations for my leaving have been made. I would love to stay for the New Years, but that is impossible. At 7:30 pm, I say good-bye. Only Rösel and Norbert accompany me a ways. I take the bicycle and we walk. What do we have to say to each other on the way? As always, the same: "Please be careful, be well!" At the Lettwald Forest, we say good-bye. For a long time I hold their hands in mine. "Do not cry, my dearest, I will come back!" Norbert is brave as always then I get on the bike, I look back one more time and wave. I am to leave the bike at Heblich's in Ebernburg. When I get there, I have a little problem. All these houses are deserted, the windows smashed in, grenade fragments, and rubble everywhere. Finally I can get the bike stored by Mr. Scholl, and can quickly call from the railroad station to leave a message for them to pick up the bike the next day.

For an hour I wait in the crowded station for a train. Miraculously one actually is able to leave with destroyed tracks and all, until Turkismühle. I find a truck there that gives me a ride in exchange for cigarettes. We cross the Mosel Valley and at 5 am I am getting off in Binsfeld. From there I have about 14 miles to walk to Wittlich. I get under way and at dawn I pass a bunch of people, old men and worried looking women, on their way to early mass.

The rising sun is turning the snow to a pretty pink and in the distance there is the sound of heavy artillery fire.

31, December 1944

New Years Eve

I am still dreaming of home! A towing vehicle passes and gives me a ride, but on the hillside the truck gets stuck due to the slick road and even the snow chains under the wheels do not help. I continue on foot for an hour or so until another car picks me up and takes me all the way to Wittlich.

I arrive at 9 pm. The weather is cloudy, thank God! I report back to the Capt. In my absence another accident happened. On December 29th, a V-1 accidentally hit in front of our FLUKO, killed Sgt. Reichard, tore a huge crater, and leveled the pine forest. Now the FLUKO is to be moved to Bernkastel.

A great joy is waiting for me, my Christmas package packed with so much love and care. There is a bottle of eggnog, a Christmas Stollen, a bag of Christmas cookies, a dear letter with photos of the children, a homemade calendar from Norbert, and from Helga, a letter with colored letters, and a bookmark. A picture with the happy little "Mouse" in her "da-da" pants, two homemade sausages from mother and more. Everything is packed in colored paper and decorated with fresh and fragrant pine branches. Now New Years will have meaning for me!

The evening is dreary; the comrades are down. A lot of the females have been discharged. It has become too dangerous. We stay in the cellar. I eat a couple of cookies and drink some of my eggnog, but do not feel like celebrating. No water, no lights, Wittlich is a dead city. Somewhere more bombs are detonating. A crime on New Years night! Some of the remaining females are crying.

But I am far, far away with my thoughts, at a place where I know my happiness lies and where I have been only yesterday. I pull out Rösel's Christmas letter one more time and she writes: "I would like to ask you, please help us pray that you will come back home to us; won't you? Sigrid says: "ga-ga", when she hears ducks or sees a goose, an egg, or a boiled potato. Her favorite food is boiled potatoes and sausage. When Opa gets the seeds to feed the chickens and they have picked up all the grain, she shows Opa, where to get more. She is such a darling and has 7 teeth now. Once in a while she gets restless and uncomfortable but never cries".

So I am connected with you and will make the step over the threshold into the New Year, hoping it will be a better one.

1945

1, January 1945

New Year! Will You Finally Bring Us Peace?

Unshaven and unwashed being without water; I go up to the Forestry. Are they now sitting in church singing the old familiar New Years hymns? Help, O Jesus, stand by us!

The low flying planes are approaching again and above us are the machine guns hammering and the bursts of fire from the aircraft armaments. We all take cover. Now the cartridge cases crackle through the branches of the trees.

In the afternoon the 2nd attack happened. Capt. V. and I duck behind the closet, the windows are blown out, and we are sure the house would collapse on top of us. But we made it once again. That was my New Years Day!

2, January 1945

This morning we buried poor Reichard at 8 am. With our helmets on we march to the cemetery. The sun rises red as blood on this cold winter day. A few fitting words from the chaplain, a couple of shovels full of dirt into his grave, that's it! His wife and children could not be here. How sadly some lives come to an end.

In the cemetery there are about 30 caskets of killed civilians still from the attack on Wittlich, mostly women children and old people. What a crime to humanity! The city is still smoking from its ruins.

In the afternoon I walk to the Grunewald Hospital. What a relief for the nerves; this walk in the pure, cold winter air. I feel secure here. What a tragedy; all these badly injured. Constantly new ones are brought in from the Bastogne front.

The Rundstedt Offensive has come to a stand still. This will be the bitter end.

By the baker's family, I can warm up, drink a cup of coffee, and write a letter.

3, January 1945

It is very eerie for us here to do our duty. We are sitting like on a stage. All the windows and doors are knocked out, no electricity, just candles. When a dive bomber arrives everyone runs to the forest. We get no supplies, everyone is sick of duty. Thank God it is snowing, that means fewer dive bombers.

At night I go together with Lottes to the city to pick up my laundry. The cleaners are of course closed, the windows are smashed in; I crawl through the broken door. I search through the clothes and indeed did find my things, of course unwashed, but truly a miracle.

In our cellar every night there are a few civilians, who do not dare to go home anymore to sleep. How secure I feel in my little corner!

4, January 1945

We are still here, but sitting on pins and needles. Fortunately it is still snowing and cloudy most of the day. That saves us from the planes most of the day. In our free time we go up to the forested hill as far away from the city as possible.

The duty is not bad. I enjoy transmitting the conversations for the captain. At night it is cold at the switchboard and I wrap myself with blankets and keep my coat on.

5, January 1945

I volunteer when I hear that a courier is requested for Wiesbaden. That will bring a change for me.

I am to contact the General Command No.12 with a letter to negotiate the situation with Bernkastel. This is quite an honorable task. Quickly I pack my things in such a way, that they can be easily taken along by my buddies in an emergency and put everything into the closet.

I leave Wittlich at 5 pm, walk to the intersection, and get a ride standing on the running board of a truck. How cold my ears and hands were. In Neuerburg, that's how far they went, I walk for a short stretch then get another ride to Alf, then walk again for a few kilometers in the slippery snow. I regret having done this. Will I have to walk through the whole night? It is getting dark and finally in a curve a truck with a trailer full of rocks and soldiers stops. They take me as far as the Mosel Bridge near Treis. After I paused for an hour, I walk to the other side, and then for another 1½ hours, I walk via Müden to Moselkern and arrive about midnight.

Maj. Weiss is still there. He is very nice and friendly. Why could I not have had such officers? I have had very bad luck in that respect. The letter is being evaluated and replied to, I can eat something and can sleep in a bed.

Early in the morning I go with the courier Sgt. Dicken to the railroad station.

6, January 1945

Sigrid: 1 Year Old! Sweet Little "Mouse", How I Think Of You

We go together with a lot of delays and stops, because of the many destroyed train stations to Winningen on the Mosel. From there we cross the river by ferry and then by foot up the mountain through the beautiful snowy landscape to Waldesch. On the way I meet Bollenbach from Hochstätten, who is with a prison detail. He gave me an apple and we talked briefly about home. In Waldesch we got some coffee and something to eat and continued on in spite of heavy enemy flyovers.

At this hour (it is 10:30 am), I have to think of my sweetheart and our little "Bunny" a year ago.

Finally we get to Rhens, which is badly destroyed with one bomb crater next to the other. At 12:30 pm we get a train to Bingen. After a stop over in Boppart for tanking up water and putting on coal, we continue. The passengers are frustrated, because the train is freezing cold.

Bingerbrück is a sad sight. Shortly before Mainz we get an air raid alarm and everyone flees into the fields along the tracks. We finally make it to Wiesbaden, eat, and stay overnight in the Hotel Taunushof.

How well I slept. My prayers for this day and night are for my little Sigrid.

7, January 1945

All day long I was busy taking care of my orders and instructions. Had to go to several different offices of the General Command No.

12, had discussions with Lt. Haas, then Maj. Krahm, also with the Airborne Command.

The result: **The Party is mightier than the Armed Forces!** No military units have the authority to requisition office space in Bernkastel. A sad state of affairs indeed!

Nevertheless, I receive the written authorization to go to the Airborne Command and notify the Capt. He is pleased with my results.

In the afternoon I go to town, stop for an hour during the evening at Hausers, these are the dear old familiar surroundings, so typical of my sweetheart's family. Wendel and Elsbeth are also there.

In the evening by train across to Mainz, where there is an air alert and I spend an hour in the bunker, then stay in the Hotel Richter in a freezing cold bed.

8, January 1945

I get up at 6 am, go to the station, the train is 1 hour late and it takes forever to get to Bingen, there, a layover until 9 pm.

Do we have to expect "jabos" (dive bombers) again? In Boppard I decide to get off the train close to midnight. I find accommodations with a friendly family of an old teacher and bookbinders.

In the morning I enjoy a cup of hot coffee and a piece of the good sausage, still from mother. Then I begin my lonely march up the winding road through deep snow. Way down below in the valley is the picturesque town of Boppard nestled along the Rhine River. The winter air is clear and crisp and I continue undauntedly, but it is getting more and more tedious. It is very slippery and a lot of drifting snow and I start to sweat from the strain.

The road is endless. It's a total of 30 kilometers, but by using shortcuts I get it down to 22 km. Two hours later I am at the peak of the mountain and reach the little town of Buchholz. At the local gasthaus I get a cup of hot coffee and something to eat. Played the piano a little bit and then continued on my way always through deep snow. Finally the road begins to descend and I stumble over gravel and thick underbrush. Down deep below flows the Mosel River and along side the charming little wine villages.

Finally at 5 pm, I am down below in Brodenbach, wringing wet with perspiration, cross over by ferry to Löf, no train leaving from there, so back to walking. In Moselkern I find out, much to my disappointment, that the division has moved to Weiler, only a few men are left. I stay overnight and get a good night's sleep.

9, January 1945

I have time to sleep in. In the afternoon I go by truck through the destroyed town of Cochem up the hills to Weiler. It was a dreary accommodation in this poor village. All the offices were crammed together in a single room inside the only inn in town. The people are poor and there are a lot of long faces, since a lot of the guys have not found a place to stay, they had it much better in Moselkern.

1st Lt. Knab is asking me: "Do you want to go to Elster for 6 weeks as an instructor?" I agree, although I am in a predicament, because Maj. Weiss had talked about wanting me as an aid. Which is the better choice?

Where will I stay this night? I find some friendly farmers and can stay in a warm room on a straw sack spread across several chairs and cover myself with my coat. I sleep wonderful and cozy. They previously offered to me some potato salad, just like at home.

10, January 1945

We leave at 8 am. Thank God I have several blankets, because it is bitterly cold. After just a few kilometers I am frozen stiff sitting on the gas tank in back of the open truck. In Dreisch, we get a cup of coffee. We load up a few more soldiers and then in a fast tempo, get under way, constantly on the look out for attack bombers.

I am afraid I did myself in and am getting sick. I have a terrible cough and cold feet as never before.

Planes are approaching again, so we run up to the snowy forest, where there are already a bunch of civilians.

After that, I quickly get my paper work done, pack in a hurry, and say good-bye to Wittlich. I am glad to get out of here. For a while I can ride in the military ambulance, then walk 15 more minutes to the station Wengerohr. Here I wait for hours on the cold bombed out platform. I keep walking up and down the tracks to warm up my feet. I even go to the railroad crossing gatekeeper's shack. But it's cold there too, with the windows blown out. No one can give any kind of information. Poor Germany!

The train from Trier is supposedly 2 hours late. Well, we are used to waiting. Then comes a hospital train and I manage to get on with a bribe of cigarettes and can sit on my backpack in a small aisle. We manage to get past a few stations then comes the first layover near Cochem, where the tracks were damaged. The train stopped from 9 pm until 7 am. That was awful!

11, January 1945

Unfortunately we are getting into daylight with a greater danger of the dive bombers but we quickly get to the main railroad station in Koblenz. What a horrible sight is this city. At the station only one single set of tracks is still intact. Driving through the city there is not one single house that is not leveled or left undamaged. Why do our poor people have to suffer like that?

Only the "Deutsche Eck" is still standing. The backpack is heavy, but no one stops. I walk across the Pfaffendorfer Bridge, which surprisingly is still standing, to Ehrenbreitstein and up the hill to FLUKO in Urbar. The town is pretty badly destroyed, but the FLUKO is in a good area and several well built tunnels have been constructed there. I would like to stay here. I also get the chance to meet Lt. Stinner; this distinguished human being.

In the afternoon, my paper work is completed for transfer to Darmstadt, where I have to introduce myself. My luggage is kept in storage for the time being. I head back to Koblenz on foot at around 5 pm.

We are told that the train is indefinitely late. We have a two hour wait on the cold platform in the freezing cold. Below in the destroyed waiting room, some soldiers build a fire on the floor, which looks spooky through the open ceiling into the night. The only working person there furiously steps on the fire to put it out, because, according to him, it can attract the planes.

Around 9 pm the train finally arrives. I am freezing and my whole body is shaking and I cannot feel my feet anymore. In the cold train in spite of the icy wind that blows through the open windows, I must have dozed a little bit. Until we hear the order "Everybody off the Train" in

Bingen. Thank God, a heated waiting room. Here I fall asleep and before I know it it's 5 am. Now we get from here to Darmstadt without a hitch.

But what has happened to this formerly proud city?

12, January 1945

In the last air raid there were 30,000 killed, most victims suffocated and burnt. **What kind of a horrendous war is this**? Only facades and chimneys are left standing. A dead city! But miraculously the streetcar runs again on 2 tracks, but very few people are living amongst the ruins.

In the Cambrai Kaserne (barracks) I meet after a long wait Lt. Höcker, this icy cold North German; a fish blooded lawyer, a military pig of the worst kind. I waste a whole day, putting a plan together, eat a lousy lunch, keep on working until the "High and Mighty", who has not the faintest idea about any of the methods of training, is finally satisfied with my outline. People like him cannot have any kind of power in a new state. They became our misfortune with their stupidity. How I hate these obnoxious, belligerent, and ignorant military characters.

I finally manage to get away. And for that, I had to undertake this very difficult trip. Quickly I go to the streetcar stop and catch a tram that takes me to a good train to Mainz where we have another layover. I can stay in the gasthaus across from the station, then the next day take a crowded train with upset civilians, crying women, cursing soldiers, with many stops and ice cold feet all the way to Bad Kreuznach, because my plan has long been formed: I will look up my family.

How glad I will be to walk the 12 km from Bad Kreuznach to Hochstätten. The 16 year old son of Hanni Putz walks along with me. He wants to go to Hochstätten too. It is very hard to walk in the slippery snow and we do not make good headway.

Poor Bad Kreuznach! Everywhere the black burnt house walls stretch up to the sky and in Bad Münster we can hardly get over the ruins and sometimes have to crawl on hands and knees through the bomb craters.

The boy is brave, but getting tired. It is so cold, that my breath is forming ice crystals on my ski mask. We walk across a little bridge through a garden, climb up many steps and come to the train tracks, which we follow to the railroad bridge behind Ebernburg. I carry the boy's suitcase since he has gotten very tired.

Shortly after midnight I turn the corner by the church and see in the moonlight the dear old house with the green shutters, where I know my happiness resides. I just hope and pray they are all well and I find myself restless and a little worried. After all it has been weeks, since I have received any mail from them.

I knock softly as to not frighten them and Oma opens the window upstairs and soon after, the door opens. "I am here again!" I say. Soon my sweetheart comes in her robe and I hear that they are all well. But that shortly after my last furlough the dear little one had the chickenpox. She was running a fever, but otherwise not too bad and also did not break out very much.

I do not want to disturb their nights rest and also do not want to wake the children (Helga sleeps with Oma) but I go into Norbert's bed. How funny, when I push him over a little he sits straight up and asks half asleep and indignantly: "What is going on here?" I whisper to him: "Be quiet, Papa is here, go back to sleep. Tomorrow I will tell you everything." Then he is happy, turns to the wall, and continues sleeping.

In the morning Helga comes, happy as always and the sweet little baby. Sigrid recognizes me and lets me love her. Norbert told me in the morning, how he is helping with the building of the tunnel.

13, January 1945

What a beautiful day! I am so happy that they are all well. The Christmas tree has been taken down, the living room is warm and cozy; my sweetheart sews on all my missing buttons and washes my laundry.

We have so much fun with the baby and I am happy, that the two older ones like her, even Norbert plays with her a lot and tried to get her to walk. She loves to sit on her potty, with the stool in front of her and her toys and tirelessly takes them out of the box and then expects someone to put them back into it. So funny is when Rösel asks her: "What do we ride in when summer comes?" She says with a high-pitched voice: "r r r rad" (wheel)! She is learning more and more words, she just cannot walk yet, but that's OK. For the heavy little body the legs may not be strong enough yet. Helga wants to write and read to me; in between she goes sledding and sliding on the ice with her friends.

Helga "Ice Sledding"

Norbert is wearing a Hitler Youth Belt, which I am not too crazy about. The influence of the family is evident and I like his very mature thinking. Helga is still very much a child but very sharp, alert and eager to learn. At night we play dominos and Mühle, which she plays with great enthusiasm. Then they have to wash and go to bed.

Norbert is very superficial with his things and not too meticulous and very quick with washing up. Helga on the other hand is careful and meticulously washing herself from head to toe.

Something else, the complaints of Oma and Opa about the children are only partially justified. After all they are children, who have to express themselves and often make old people nervous. One cannot forbid them to talk, sing, or be a little noisy. No child at that age is virtuous in nature and doesn't have to be.

We are together until late at night; we share things and talk about happy things. We wish this time would last forever, but the hours are slipping away. In a few hours I have to get up again and I do need at least 3 hours of sleep and Rösel even more so. At 3 am we get up. Everything is prepared. The sandwiches she made for me are ready. She makes some coffee, and then comes again the farewell. Very carefully I kiss the sleeping darling on her forehead, then Norbert, who I love to ruffle up his course hair and my "Murschel", who always hugs me so tenderly in her flowered pajamas. Then I console my brave little wife with the vague assurance that everything will be all right and I will come back.

How could it be, that we have deserved this kind of destiny? We tried to be good people and did not want this criminal war.

Up by the church I turn around one more time. I know she is standing by the door crying. Then I begin my difficult march through the snow. I will have to figure on 2 hours at least.

14, January 1945

Opa's Birthday

He is 70 years old. Last night I wished him the best. He is such a good, kind, and decent human being and more than earns it. May he be able to spend many more years in the circle of his loved ones.

At 6 am I arrive after a tedious march through snow and slick roads in Bad Kreuznach. I am sweaty and glad that I can rest a while in the little room at the station, which is heated a little bit. Outside on the platform, the people have been standing for hours, waiting, freezing, cursing, or they are patiently waiting like sheep. Indeed a train leaves at 8:30 am. But only until Gaulsheim, there everybody gets off.

The enemy planes have tried to destroy the bridge yesterday, but have attacked the railway and village instead. What a crime!

I get a ride at the intersection. In Bingerbrück there is a layover because a large vehicle blocks the road. I walk passed the destroyed railway station and I climb across tracks, bomb craters, turned over train cars, and locomotives. Just let me get out of here!

There is nothing left of Bingerbrück. Where is the railroad station? Actually the walk would be pleasant in sunshine and the beautifully glittering snow if it were not for the horror all around me.

Shortly before the Rheinstein Castle, a convoy passes me and I can get a ride until we stop in St. Goar to watch as hundreds of Liberator planes proudly fly across us, leaving their contrails behind. No one stops them in their fateful and ominous trail. Where will they bring death and destruction today?

Yes, this is America! What a crime of insanity, to bring our people into such misfortune.

I can have a ride until Boppard. I wait until the air raid is over, get a bite to eat and get a ride on a truck all the way until Koblenz. Quickly we get across the bridge. Thank God, the sky is overcast and no planes at the moment. At 5 pm, I report back to Lt. Stinner. He did not even know I was gone for a day. I could have stayed home another day.

15, January 1945

While still in Urbar, I have two nice days to myself. The food is good I have a decent bed. I have no duty and if there are any air raids I go with all of them to the tunnels. There is a nice day room where I can read and write.

I request some Official Regulations Manuals and think about, how I will arrange the lessons.

17, January 1945

In the afternoon a truck comes with Sgt. Lambert. I can ride with him. It is getting dark. From Niederelbert I climb up the hill through the snow. There in the moonlight I see the silhouette of the barracks, where I shall stay for 6 weeks. I get a good bed with sheets, a bowl to wash, a cup, etc. There is no running water.

21, January 1945

The life is lonely up here and I am homesick for my loved ones. The poor girls are to be pitied. They have difficult jobs and work hard at it. The food is lousy, to put it mildly, and this cook does not know the first thing about cooking.

The Russian Offensive

The Russian's have tremendous successes! Breakthrough on all fronts! Warsaw, Litzmannstadt, Kalisch, etc. are lost.

22, January 1945

It snowed heavily through the night, ½ meter high and we have a beautiful winter landscape. The post is camouflaged very well. Our room is cozy. We get wood, make us a fire; we have good light and good beds. I also was able to get a closet for my things. In the evening I look forward to read in bed.

23, January 1945

It has snowed again through the night. On the way to the communications shack I walk through snow ½ meter deep and the snow falls into my boots over the top. The feet are always cold anyway, especially at mealtime in the unheated dining room. We have to wear our coats.

The Russians have overrun the upper Schlesian (Silesian) industrial area and have captured Posen, Thorn, Insterburg, and Tilsit.

I wonder where my brother Richard is and if he is alive and safe?

24, January 1945

I still have some cake and cookies from home. I will be very frugal, so I can still enjoy them for a while.

I give a daily 2 hour long lecture about aircraft recognition; including latitude and longitude grid procedures, as well as the structuring and subdivision of the Armed Forces for the radio operators. Everyone is excited and enthusiastic about my lessons, but what good does that do me? My efforts in this war have never been recognized or appreciated.

25, January 1945

All men born 1900 and earlier (up until 1897) are to be drafted into the Armed Forces.

27, January 1945

The Russians have taken Elbing and the beautiful city of Breslau. Oh, how is this going to end?

The German Territorial Army has been assigned. The English destroy one city after the other.

28, January 1945

I ask Lt. Stotz about a short leave time. I have nothing to do anyway. After thinking about it for a minute, he approves. Oh, how excited I am!

I am going to surprise them again. Even though I have not had mail in a month, I have the secure feeling, that everything is OK.

In the afternoon I walk to Montabaur, which is a treacherous way. I slip and slide over the frozen snow and hardly make any headway. The eyes are sensitive to the blinding brightness of the winter day, but it's a healthy march to the pretty little town. At the station I meet NCO Massierer. My right boot does not seem to be in good shape because my foot is wet. On the platform is a group of Russian prisoners. The train is ½ hour late. There is a tentative alarm, but luckily we make it out of the station. The train arrives at Limburg on the Lahn without difficulty.

Via the Frankfurter Route to Niederhausen, there I have to change trains. Then via Erbenheim I arrive in Wiesbaden at 11 pm. I walk up Ringstrasse, when I get to the Ring Church there is a full alert, but where should I quickly go? I find a cellar across from the church and sit there for 2 hours with these poor people, who are tired, hungry, and exhausted; mostly women with their children wrapped in blankets, until we get the all clear. How this humanity has to suffer.

29, January 1945

At 5:15 am, my train leaves for Mainz and there is the connecting train, overcrowded, but no engine. It's the same old misery, we wait for more than an hour with cold feet, and it is getting daylight.

Will we get hit with dive bombers again? Finally at 8 am we get going and finally make Bad Kreuznach. How sad to see this familiar town so badly damaged. I meet the 2 Bollenbach boys and ask about Hochstätten. They tell me everything is all right. Oh, how I will love to walk home for the next 2 hours.

In Ebernburg, I was able to cross the Nahe River by foot on the ice, as it was completely frozen over. The two bridges in Bad Münster are being reconstructed. What hard working brave people! But what is the sense? Shortly before Hochstätten there suddenly are planes above me. They are dive bombers and formations of bombers. I take cover under the trees. Afterwards I walk up the street, turn at the church and then see the dear familiar house with the green shutters. At the window I see Oma's face and soon afterwards Rösel opens the door. How wonderful to see her sweet loving face.

Where are the others? Opa is in the cellar with Sigrid, Norbert, and Helga. When things calm down and the roaring of the planes subsides, Rösel brings the little "Bunny" to me. She blinks her eyes, looks at me, but does not cry, but reaches out to me with her little hands, lets me hold and love her, sweet little thing. Only when Rösel goes to the house for a minute and I am alone with her, she starts to cry with her sweet deep voice. She is still surprised and not used to me yet. There comes Mama again and the tears stop.

And then comes my "Murschel", so tall and skinny and uninhibited, calling out: "Where are you coming from?" She laughs and greets me with her old familiar affection. And there is my boy, my big boy, who is so mature and sensible. He laughs and is happy to see me. Oh, dear God, keep them for me and with it my happiness.

Tomorrow I would like to go to Sembach, but we do not know if there will be a train.

In the afternoon Helga wants me to "dictate" to her. We write words starting with the syllable "un". She tries very hard to write with a beautiful script. Norbert on the other hand does not show any interest in learning much to the disappointment of Rösel and the grandparents. It is such a misfortune, that there is no school for him anymore. He has too much free time and a lot of precious time is wasted. In the evening Helga wants to sleep with me, a repeated promise and we have to keep it. How happy that makes the little rascal.

How much joy and pleasure has been denied to me in these last 5 years. Never to be retrieved.

The sweet little "Mouse" is already sleeping wearing her white mittens and little nightcap. Helga and I smooch with each other. Oh, how I would like to hold them and love them forever. In the morning the little chatterbox wakes me by kissing me and talking like a book.

30, January 1945

We keep busy with the darling baby (I have a new pet name for her: "Laufele" (Little Walker). What a good healthy appetite this child has. When she has had enough of her pureed vegetables, which Rösel puts in a bottle with a large nipple, she pushes it away and then wants to walk. We hold her by the hand and she makes fast little steps, or we hold her by her upper arms and then both legs move as fast as possible.

How cute she looks in the pink skirt, which reaches all the way to the floor. When she sits on her potty, she loves to empty her box with toys. Rösel's purposeful work has paid off, the child is almost trained and that after just 1 year. Only after a nap is her diaper wet. She does not nap anymore in the morning, just after her noon meal for about 2-3 hours. If only the bombing planes would not come so often.

At noon we walk to the train station to meet someone and Helga comes along. She loves to toddle along with me asking a thousand questions. She wants my opinion about the school cellar and says precociously, she had heard this from Oma: "But what if there is fume poisoning because of the stove?" I calm her down and say: "You must always pray, then everything will be alright." Then she squeezes my hand a little harder. How thin and petite she looks in her blue knit suit and the blue cap.

She likes to play with her little sister and loves her dearly. She continually talks to her, just as my mother would. She has so many characteristics from her, the way she walks, the way she holds her hands, etc. She is soft and kind and pleasant like her.

Norbert is helping to build the tunnel, which is to protect them from shrapnel and any kind of shooting. It's basically women and children, who do this hard physical work.

We have to save on everything. Because matches have become so rare, Opa has been making fidibusse (long thin wooden sticks for lighting fires), a word that amuses Helga tremendously. Salt is difficult to get, the flour is dark, things like shoe polish and soap is literally impossible to find.

In the evenings we are happy together and I tell them funny stories about my classmate Gillman and Professor Stoffel, which gets them all laughing. Helga wants to play games and she is very good at it. I pull out the zither, which has such fond memories of my childhood, especially as Christmas time is so closely connected with this instrument. We play all the old familiar songs, like: "Guter Mond du gehst so stille" (Good Old Moon, You Go So Quietly) und "Weisst du wieviel Sternlein stehen" (Do You Know How Many Stars There Are).

This evening we have another fun time, when the little "Bunny" is undressed, standing on the sofa. She is holding her teddy bear, which is about her size, wrapping her left arm around its neck. With the right chubby little arm she waves intensely and squeals excitedly. We laugh so hard that we cry. She does not get influenced whatsoever, but keeps on waving faster and talks with such enthusiasm, that her little head gets bright red with the strain. Then we all say good night, give her kisses, she is wrapped in a blanket and carried upstairs.

Tomorrow Norbert and I want to go to Sembach.

31, January 1945

Father's Birthday

He would have been 68 years old today. What a good thing, he did not have to live to see a lot of things. We get up at 3 am, I take a map and a small backpack, and then we walk to the station. The train is supposed to leave at 5:13 am. Of course it is late. We walk 2 or 3 times through the quiet streets of the village. I hope it won't get too late so we still get up there before daylight.

Finally at 6:30 am the train comes. No windows, it is cold and unheated and we sit closely together to keep warm. Everywhere are the signs of this miserable war. Alzenz has been hit bad. In Winnweiler we get off and decide to walk. In the pharmacy we try to buy Vigantol for the baby's teeth. They are still closed. I show Norbert Winnweiler and the important buildings there. How interested and attentive he is and what a handsome boy he is in his gray coat and the blue hat. We get a ride and make it up to Sembach.

Dear little familiar village. We walk up the Almengasse and everything looks so strange as if I had not been there in a long time. There is the garden, the garage, and the house of my parents. Oh, how I would like to be a child again. And there is my mother. How old she has become. Her neighbor points us out and at first she does not seem to recognize us, then a smile crosses her face, she claps her hands together, rushes towards us to embrace us. What joy!

Quickly we go upstairs into the kitchen. First we drink a nice hot coffee. Then I look around the house. Strange people are here; who are victims of the bombings in Kaiserslautern.

We go up to the schoolhouse. Mother tells me about the episode with the rude colonel, this "punk". She had to be insulted by him. Be patient, dear mother, times will change. All our furniture has been put together in the bedroom. I check out my books and they seem to be intact. In the cellar everything seems to be all right. Our two front rooms are used to stage drinking parties by the "gentlemen" of the National Socialistic Party (Nazi) staff. The large schoolroom is used to accommodate military; the small one is an office. If only the schoolhouse and our apartment will weather the storms of these times. I go with Norbert to the library in the attic and pick out a few books then we go to eat at grandmothers. My mother has cooked us a good beef broth soup and made pancakes from the dark flour and served them with homemade currants in a jar, the way I love them.

In the afternoon we visit the families Metz and Rettig's, our good neighbors, who have not gotten over the loss of their son Otto at the Russian front. It's a good thing mother does not realize the seriousness of the situation in the east; still she is quite worried about Richard.

I had a short visit with my friends, the Gödtel's. I was offered, as always the best hospitality and treated to wine and homemade sausage. Almost all homes in the village were quartered for soldiers. Ernst and I had some serious discussions about various subjects and according to him there are a few fanatics here in town as there are everywhere.

Mother is now finished with the feeding of the animals and cooked a good supper for us. We go to sleep together in the little room upstairs, which is the way I remember it. Father's bed has been put back up there and Norbert and I sleep in the extra wide bed. How peaceful, how cozy and calming to sleep again in your parents house, to sleep so sound and comforted as in your mother's arms.

We had set our alarm clock to 3 am. The backpack and the briefcase are packed. Norbert was able to get some lamp oil and 1 pound of salt, all rare things, and mother has packed a can of homemade sausage, a large piece of meat, a can of fat, ham, etc.

Shortly after 3 am we are ready to leave. Mother wants to make coffee for us but we do not accept, but say good-bye to her and wish her the best. The good, kind woman! She would give everything for her children. Then we leave into the dark night. It is very slippery, because there was a freeze during the night.

I had figured a 2-hour walk to Winnweiler. It is not easy to walk because we step into water a lot and the route is treacherous. Norbert is holding up bravely, he is my big dependable boy. I carry the briefcase and his raincoat; he is carrying the backpack with the lamp oil. Slowly our eyes have gotten used to the dark.

Soon we are in Wartenberg and we pass the time with comfortable talks like good comrades. I tell him things from my growing up years and some of the history of the town, about the old mill, which we are passing, and where we used to get the bread in WW I and I am pleased, that he is interested in everything. He listens attentively until he spots a tractor along the roadside, which was hit by dive bombers and of course he has to investigate it.

Slowly it is becoming daylight and the early morning is dawning. I ask him if his feet are wet. We are both tired. Partially the street is free of snow then it is easier to walk. Soon we see Winnweiler in front of us.

1, February 1945

It is daylight and we are 20 min. early at the station. Of course the train is delayed again. We sit in the dark waiting room closely together and we are feeling the cold because we are sweaty. Hopefully it will not be too late, because there are no trains in the daytime with the danger of the air attacks.

About 7:30 am the train finally arrives. It is not heated of course and without windows, some of them boarded up. Norbert stands by the window and looks out. I explain things, show him, and name all the villages we pass through. Shortly after 8 am we arrive in Hochstätten. They are all happy especially about the gifts.

I have observed and become witness to the two big ones aggravating one another with the typical sibling rivalry. Often I can see that Helga, who feels being at a disadvantage like all kids at that age, sulking and grumpily saying: "He got…." and "He gets to…" Norbert himself, not too affectionate as it is, hits her, teases her, calls her names and loves it when she is insulted and starts crying. So the three adults constantly have their worries. But that will change too. Be patient, my dearest, your troubles will be rewarded one day.

I use the time to do some math with Helga, which is not her favorite. Add, subtract, and multiply. She is doing quite well and the little rascal is happy about my approval. She continues to be the little "village broom" and slips out every chance she gets. Norbert works again on the tunnel bunker. The little "Bunny" sits in front of her stool, recognizes her ball, and calls it: "balllll". Furthermore, when she wants to get up from her potty she says: "auffff (up)". She is getting quite heavy to hold, is well nourished, but with the age of 13 mos. cannot walk yet. Her little legs seem to be a little weak. That's OK; she has time. Also sitting up she is not too good at yet. When she is in her bed or baby carriage, she stays put until she is picked up.

The time for the farewell is approaching again. My laundry is done, my sweetheart mends and sews on buttons until the last minute, and so I am all taken care of again.

I find out a car is leaving and I hope to be able to get some transportation. I stop by at Frau May's, where the Sgt. of the military convoy lives. He is just eating dinner, but tells me he will be leaving within the hour and I can get a ride. At 2 pm I am ready to leave. The little "Mouse" was put down for her nap and Rösel says: "Give Papa a kiss!" I touch her with my lips, the peachy fragrant skin, kiss her little head, her sweet face, one more look into the baby bed and then say good-bye to the in-laws and promise, if at all possible, to come back on March 18, when Norbert has his confirmation.

By the manse the trucks are waiting. The drivers are in a good mood, they had some wine to drink and sing and yell good-bye to a lot of the people in town. I say good-bye to Rösel and Helga and they are brave as always. I still see my sweetheart in her gray coat and Helga in her blue hat waving until I turn the first corner. Norbert hangs onto the truck and rides until the end of the village standing on the running board. There he says good-bye and walks back with his friends.

And again I leave behind my precious home and enter into an uncertain future for an uncertain time. But my heart is full of happiness and wonderful memories that will get me through a lot of rough times,

The young guys are drunk and their driving leaves something to be desired. In Bad Kreuznach, which is already heavily bombed, there is full alarm. I am restless, but we keep going to Sarnsheim. Here the convoy stops and I continue by foot through the beautiful early spring sunshine. In front of me in the distance I see the Niederwald Denkmal (memorial) and wonderful memories of field trips with my school classes come to mind as well as weekend visits with the family. Oh, if I could go on such trips again with my loved ones.

I cross the bridge through the heavily destroyed Bingen, have about an hour wait and go to the restaurant Father Rhine, where I get a good glass of wine. Then my train leaves for Mainz. As soon as we enter the station, there is an air raid alert again. Quickly into the nearest cellar, that was my luck as Mainz at this hour was hit so badly, that it was nearly leveled. The poor civilians! The earth trembles with each impact.

Finally at 9 pm we get the all-clear sirens and we run outside. The city is burning in many areas, no fire engines, no water, what can we do to put out these horrible fires from this destruction? The night is lit up like day and sparks are flying every which way. The railway station has been hit hard and there is no way I can get over to Wiesbaden now. How will I be able to catch my train at 4:35 am to Limburg? So I stay the whole night, just like the other soldiers and hundreds of civilians in the freezing cold air raid shelter hovering in a corner and try to doze.

At 3:30 am, another Sgt. and I manage to get a ride on a truck just in time to meet the 4:35 am train at the main railroad station in Wiesbaden. Via Niederhausen, we arrive in Limburg at 8 am and stand by the road for 2 hours. No vehicle comes by. We start walking and come to a little town of Staffel. Here low flying planes again. We are able to get a bread roll, a wonderful rarity, then keep marching, have to take cover in some woods and witness a heavy attack of Marauders on the town of Nassau, why this little insignificant farming village? We are about 12 km from Limburg. A car gives us a ride to Montabaur arriving at 4 pm. I am in no hurry.

In the evening we get to the post. Nothing has changed. I could have stayed an extra day and no one would have even noticed or cared for that matter. It is just as well, because that day, a very devastating attack was launched on Wiesbaden and I might not have survived. A guardian angel was with me again, as so many times.

Lt. Storz is obliging as always.

3, February 1945

I did not have to work the whole day. Our barrack's dayroom is cozily warm.

4, February 1945

It is cold, we have snow, rain, and it is stormy. I wonder what my loved ones are doing this Sunday at home?

5, February 1945

Lt. Storz has a new job for me. I am to instruct a group of young girls of the BDM (Bund Deutscher Mädchen, i.e. Association of German Girls) in telecommunications. I am looking forward to this. I go with my necessary luggage and see the group leader for a discussion of the most important things I'm to teach. I am to stay there and get private quarters. I am to begin the lectures in the morning.

6, thru 9, February 1945

I Instruct The BDM In Montabaur.

This morning I met the group of eighteen 16 year old young girls, who are very curious and eagerly awaiting my lecture. A leader began with a short speech and a song, and then I begin with my class about military dress, rank, service grades, uniform rank designation, and the physical basics of long distance voice communication.

At noon I am finished and have the afternoon off. After a good lunch at my host family I go for a walk or in the café, where I can still get some cake. In the evening I get to sit with the family in the cozy warm kitchen and later read my book in bed.

Every day the lessons are interesting and the girls are enthusiastic and eager to learn. They really appreciate my teaching.

On the 9th, the snow has completely melted and the mild spring air is delightful.

The money situation is getting ridiculous. For a pack of cigarettes they want between 10 and 20 Marks, for a bottle of wine up to 50 Marks. There is continued demoralization.

A fantastic sum of over 5,500 Marks has been accumulated. More importantly to me, are the musical contributions by the work girls, the helpers, and the art-loving Lt. Storz. The girls play Beethoven's 5th Symphony, the Pathetique, and works by Schubert, Chopin, Brahms, and Bach. They are the intelligent daughters from educated families. There is nothing to drink but bad cheap booze.

11, February 1945

By radio, the message is delivered, that I am to return immediately. I regret this and the girls are very disappointed, so is the leader of the group. I finish my prepared lesson and do an example of operating a small switchboard of 10 lines and explain to them the FK 16.

Then I say my good-byes and receive their appreciation, have another good meal and take my time getting back. My backpack has already been delivered.

12, February 1945

At the last minute, I receive another radio message that I am to stay 8 days and instruct the future wireless operators in physics. I like the idea and gladly stay another week.

13, February 1945

Today, once again I skip eating my normal rations and want to eat again in Montabaur.

14, February 1945

I have a daily lecture of only 2 hours, which I try to present to my pupils in an interesting and gripping manner. Although the subject is difficult, the girls are trying very hard.

The weather is clear and we have dive bombers all day long. The soldiers of the post are ordered into their one man foxholes to man the machine guns. Luckily, we are camouflaged very well but the mood of the people and the soldiers is devastating. No one believes the regime's idiotic claims of victory anymore. The Russians are 80 kilometers away from Berlin, Stettin has fallen, and they are deep into Silesia.

In the west, the Americans will soon begin a new air offensive, which has already started in a devastating form. The air attacks on all German cities as well as villages have increased and the farmers do not dare to go into their fields anymore to work. This will result in a famine of the worst kind.

It is unspeakable how the people suffer, how they still work, do without, and are plunged into deep despair over their loved ones, their sons, brothers, husbands on the front lines, who are slaughtered by the millions. Why is there no end to this cruel murdering?

15, February 1945

In the afternoons I am free and after lunch I go for a walk and observe the excellent camouflaging. On such a walk I can think my own thoughts. Later I go to the bakery, get a cup of coffee and some cake.

17, February 1945

Today is my last lesson for the future wireless operators. Lt. Storz, who comes in once in a while to observe, is pleased. Tomorrow I will leave.

18, February 1945

Too bad I have to leave. I did enjoy this time here, also staying with the nice family, the Chalon's.

I walk to Montabaur and shortly before the city there is another air raid. I wait until the countless formations of four planes in each group have passed overhead. Where are they going to bring more death and destruction? Around 5 pm I can get on a truck across from the school, which drives straight through to Cochem. That was lucky! There I wait an hour for another vehicle to Alf, where I stay overnight in soldier's quarters. It is cold and dirty and at 7 am, I am standing in the street again.

19, February 1945

Left Alf at 8 am, and make it to Traben. I stood on the running board of the truck for 15 km but did not care, at least I am moving. I get a good cup of coffee and bread with jam in the Hotel Gräfinburg and an excellent dinner with meat.

At 8 pm, I arrive in Wittlich, marching with my luggage up to the Forestry School with mixed emotions. I really did not want to come back here. I report back to Capt. V., and as always, Lt. Stinner is friendly to me. I sleep well and will get back to my duty tomorrow.

20, February 1945

I am doing switchboard service again in the bunker. At least I feel safe here. The afternoon is free and I walk up to the Children's Sanitarium, which has been turned into a field hospital. I sit in the sun and read, when a friendly nurse brings me a cup of coffee and a roll.

22, February 1945

I am doing duty every 24 hours. There are tremendous flyovers. More than 2,500 enemy planes have been sighted today with their course due east. Where are they going and what devastation will they bring again? Through night duty I can sleep a few hours.

25, February 1945

I am transferred to station Zeisig. This night we are to be picked up by truck. Some of them have left already. At 5 am, we are awakened; we still get a few things such as razor blades, toothpaste, stationary, a bottle of wine, etc.

I get on the open truck with four other buddies. We pass the field hospital and drive through the cold, fog, and icy wind, until darkness turns into daylight. We drive up and down hillsides and dangerous curves, first north then west to Urschmitt.

26, February 1945

In a friendly farmhouse, where there are only two women and children, I can wash up and shave. I get ready to report to Lt. Knab. Finally at 9 am, he is ready to see me. Why do I always have the bad luck to run into these kinds of superiors; who are not only ignorant, but could care less about an individual. Of course my request to be sent to Koblenz is denied without any reason or further comment. What kind of people are these? Major Weiss too, only has a polite smile for me.

I am very disappointed! There is no food, no accommodations and no one gives a hoot. But they very quickly find work for me. I go looking myself to find private quarters without success. These are poor villages here with pitiful houses and tired, desperate people. There is gloomy anguish and hopelessness everywhere and an unspeakable fury at **Hitler and the Party.**

27, February 1945

I stayed overnight in the dirty barracks with no possibility to wash. Everything is dirty and unappetizing. In the afternoon I start my

24 hour duty doing analytical work. What a terrible nerve wracking situation. I have never experienced anything like this.

Everybody yells and screams at once, so one cannot understand a thing, and I think my head is going to split. This will be a long night. Thank God I can sleep a little, because I am one of the older ones.

28, February 1945

The Americans have broken through in the west and have taken Bitburg. That is too close to home. What is going to happen here? I have orders to leave by truck to the post Biene. In spite of the danger I am strangely calm and have the feeling that I am going to make it.

But what if I am captured by the Americans and taken prisoner, or if we get a direct hit on this vehicle, which has 40 boxes of hand grenades loaded on it? It is a dreadful trip with a truck with defective brakes and no lights. We are only moving at crawling speed. We pick up a field kitchen in Weiler, end up in the ditch a few times, and thanks to some helpful buddies get pulled out again.

What a tangled knot has formed here. That would be something for the dive bombers. The closer we get to the front the heavier the artillery fire and it is getting more and more dangerous.

The roads are a mess with chuckholes from frost damage everywhere and partially destroyed by tanks. There is a convoy of wagons with horses, no wonder we don't make any headway. We finally arrive in post Biene at 2 pm. It looks very bad. In the afternoon the company already has 7 wounded. The equipment has been prepared for detonation, including the demolition of most of the barracks. The men are dead tired, apathetic, and depressed.

Lt. Smolka, a 23 year old "punk" as Company Chief.

Explosions are heard all around us. A temporary shelter is set up for the new group's evaluation; which has no training in close up combat, but will be merged with the infantry and are to defend the post. I don't envy them.

At 4 pm we finish the loading up of the trucks and I try to hurry everyone, because the artillery attack will get heavier in the morning. **The Americans are only 2 km away from here!**

We get through OK to Spandahlem, over the dangerous high roads, driving very carefully. We have one breakdown and lose about an hour. At 6 am we arrive in Wittlich. Here I make the mistake and do not call the division, but decide to take the equipment to Zeisig. It turns daylight at 7:30 am on a bright sunny day and I stand on the running board keeping a lookout for dive bombers. We are lucky, not a one is to be seen. We get to Zeisig at 8 am and take cover in the woods.

At 8:30 pm I go to the commander, but he is not available yet. We are very tired the strain of the constant lookout for planes and the hard physical work has exhausted us.

1, March 1945

A Very Bad Day

Why do I have such bad luck in this military? Instead of receiving recognition, I get strong reprimand from the commander. This arrogant, stupid, 28 year old person, whose mentality reaches no further than the military narrow mindedness. Oh, these ignorant, presumptuous people. The time will come, when they will be knocked off their pedestals. That is my only consolation. I calmly let his reproaches wash over me and what he throws into my face cannot insult me. I am above such humiliation and degradation. He threatens me with a field court martial and a disciplinary report placed in my records. I don't care.

In the afternoon Lt. Zeller is questioning me. Why did I not just go for a walk yesterday? I would have been away at the right time!

2, March 1945

The heavy flyovers! Thousands of four engine bombers! In the evening, attack planes appear over the village.

It is getting colder and snowing again, dirt and mud everywhere. There is no point in polishing boots anymore. There is no polish for the boots anyway, no more soap, no salt, no matches, and soon no food anymore.

In addition to that, the idiotic speeches of our **"Beloved Führer" who dribbles that there will be a glorious victory entering into history at the end of this war.** Is that man not insane?

These criminals! The people are consumed with a helpless rage but have to continue to endure and suffer. It is the most horrible time in all of our history. The unspeakable tortures; the incredible sacrifices, the deprivations, and the nameless fears.

Now the beautiful city of Dresden has been totally destroyed by bombing. We have no more cities left.

3, March 1945

I try to find a place to stay in town. In the cold and dirty barracks, 25 to 30 men sleep in one room. I find a small room in House No.14. The people are nice and the bed is clean. The place has a wonderful smell that reminds me of my childhood at home, the smell of apples and smoked meat. It gives me such a homey feeling and that's why I decide to stay. The night duty is hard on the nerves and I am very tired.

4, March 1945

In 2 weeks, my boy is supposed to be confirmed. I will not be able to come and that will be hard.

I have checked by radio, what is going on at home and find out, that yesterday morning only 1 kilometer outside the village some bombs fell. I am greatly concerned and worried. O God, be with my family and keep them safe from harm!

My host family is very nice and friendly. We have not been able to get bread for the last two days, but crackers instead. The food is bad. My jar of honey from Christmas is empty now too. I just wish I could get out of this mess.

The Americans have advanced to Trier, the English are in Neuss and Cologne was attacked with artillery.

A cold and sad Sunday!

5, March 1945

Five years ago I moved out of Gensingen, and the children were there. How long ago that was!

Tonight, my host family invited me for supper. There was good food just as there would have been with my parents at home. The memories of my young years of beautiful days and hours are rekindled. You would have cooked like this, my dear mother.

Excerpts From Rösel's Letters:

From a letter of January 5ᵗʰ:

Three or four times I was standing at Sigrid's little bed with my heart pounding. She slept so peacefully, while the planes were roaring overhead and I prayed, that we would be kept from harm. Now our little sweetheart will be 1 year old tomorrow and she is sick. She must have caught a cold, when we carried her outside right from her bed. Now the poor little thing has the chicken pox. Her fever is down tonight but she has no appetite. She is so disfigured with the pockmarks and her eyes are so tired.

From a letter of January 8ᵗʰ:

Our little "sweetheart" is much better today. Yesterday, on her birthday was probably the crisis and the pockmarks are starting to heal. She says your name a lot and points to your picture. She loves it when I powder her. Yesterday she slept peacefully all through the night.

O Lord, my God (this is my prayer at the end of this writing) keep my happiness for me!

From a letter of January 28ᵗʰ:

Our little "Mouse" is so precious and gives us more joy each day. It is so cute, when she talks to her bear. A new word in her vocabulary is "Bach (Brook)".

6, March 1945

What a misfortune it was that I had to go to Zeisig. There is no way to talk to this petty and narrow minded Lt. Knab, a person, to whom eating and drinking are the most important things and who is unable to have any kind of human emotion, he is nothing but a fossilized creature. There was no reason why he could not have transferred me to Koblenz, no obstacle whatsoever, but now it's too late.

Stumpf also, is in the true sense of the word, stubborn. What do you mean, confirmation? Is that so important? I have to stay and would have liked so much to be there for my boy's big day.

Over there the American tanks are rattling along in direction of Koblenz. I leave my baggage at my quarters; but take my combat equipment to my post. We man the machine gun stands and the assigned one man foxholes.

The 24 hours up on the hill in rain, sleet, and snow are awful. Trembling with cold, I walk back and forth 10 steps each time. Where are my thoughts? As always, with my loving family. My brave wife! Norbert, the quiet and good boy, my skinny, talkative "Murschel" and the squiggly, little "Mouse" and those dear and kind old people, Oma and Opa.

I keep a constant look out for any signs of the enemy. The roaring of the countless tanks and vehicles in the distance does not let up. Will they come here? I only have a machine gun with 300 shots of ammunition. A terribly long night descends upon us. At 1 am, Sgt. Dietrich comes to relieve me for 2 hours.

Over in the barracks we lie there like sardines in a can on the floor, chattering with the cold. The mood is irritable, many are grumbling and cursing, rudeness on one hand, good comradeship on the other. These are signs of the times.

At 3 am I go back out on the hill in the pitch dark. How glad I am for my flashlight. If only morning would come.

The rattling over there on the road has not stopped for one minute. With such tremendous and superior strength and massive equipment, our poor people should fight against this? Insanity!

I am glad to have some water left in my canteen. How many nights have I already spent not sleeping in the last 5½ years? The morning does not want to pass either. Finally at 2 pm we are relieved. After 26 hours, frozen stiff from being outside, we have to get right back to regular duty.

Everything has been disassembled and made ready to be destroyed. In the afternoon the company is to move, marching destination unknown. The detonations have been prepared.

7, March 1945

As the afternoon passes, the situation gets more critical from one hour to the next. Twice I have repacked my gear. What should I leave behind, the box or the backpack? I don't really want to lug the heavy backpack.

Finally, close to 7 pm, they begin with the detonations, when we hear that enemy infantry posts are stationed just a few hundred yards across from us in the woods. It's a crying shame, how all this expensive and sophisticated equipment gets blown up into the air.

It is pathetic to think, that the poor people who have worked and sacrificed for the ammunition, the barracks, telecommunication equipment, the new artillery gun that just arrived 2 days ago; everything is going up in flames.

In the meantime, we retreat backwards across the meadows. The backpack with things, which I can do without, I have taken it to my host family and asked them to keep it for me. Hopefully, to be able to pick it up sometime after the end of the war. I had a little bit of the good eggnog left from Christmas, which I finished up, I would have still enjoyed it for some time, being very frugal with it.

We assembled in Klidding, and then we march together to the little town of Beuren close by and decide to stay overnight, which was a good idea. I found quarters with friendly people, who gave me something to eat, hot coffee, and a wonderful bed to sleep in. I am so appreciative of their kindness.

8, March 1945

We have decided to leave at 7:30 am. The people give me coffee, I had a good nights sleep and feel refreshed. I with NCO Hoffman and many others that join us, including some of whom I do not care for. My best buddy is Bertina and the lawyer Hartkopf from Cologne. Near Brenn on the Mosel River (what a wonderful view), over there is the bridge of Eller, which has been bombarded so many times. We hope to cross over the river. This will not be easy. We divide into groups of six, rather than all at once. This should be better. We march to Neef where we hope to cross the river. This is a big worry. With the help of a couple of soldiers, we are to transport boxes with ammunition. We try it with a small boat pulling it across on a steel cable. Luckily, it is foggy.

In spite of all the misery we have to laugh, when we have trouble getting the boat to the river's edge and the two sweaty men pull it over to the other shore. Over there two others try and manage to beach it. It took three trips to get all of us across.

In a house we find two bottles of wine and we march for four hours uphill over terrible roads, toward Genderich, through marshy and muddy fields, wet meadows, and woods. We often have to stop and rest a lot. I have to admire Bertina for his tremendous will power to carry his heavy backpack. It is 4:30 pm when we get to Genderich. A man on the road, who was in charge of a few French prisoners shot himself, because they escaped.

We get a bite to eat in an inn and some coffee. There is no place to sleep, so we continue on to Moritzheim. But we had to return, as there was nothing available. In a house in Genderich I can sleep on a bench in the warm kitchen. I am also able to get a good supper at a neighbor's house; who had just killed their pig. I also had a conversation with a black bearded custom's agent.

The night passes well as we are very tired.

9, March 1945

We continue at 8 am over the high road in direction of Kastellaun. Passing us in the opposite direction are many workers from the east and POWs.

We join an old Sgt. we know, who is heading for the intersection in Bell and then on to Buch. Why did Bertina and I not continue to Kastellaun alone? We will come to regret this!

In Bell's only inn, we can get a beer and our marching portion of food. All villages in the area are crowded with retreating German soldiers.

We walk through the evening sunshine through the woods to Buch. We report in the schoolhouse to the Lt. and most the buddies are here already. I find some straw and we find a place in the schoolroom to sleep, after which, we get some warm soup. I sleep very poorly, it is very noisy, no lights, no darkened windows.

10, March 1945

Today my brother Richard is 35 years old. O Lord, protect him and bring him home safely. We have not heard from him in months. How is he doing? He is in the heavy fighting in East Prussia. Perhaps has been captured by the Russians. If only he will come home alive.

I spend all day today with the hospitable teacher Miss Jantzen. I did a makeshift cleaning of my messy boots in the village pond, got a chance to wash and shave, and took a look at a bomber which destroyed 4 or 5 houses when it crashed. What an incredible plane with four engines, it must have cost a fortune.

Then I have a nice conversation with my colleague and find that I am longing to talk about the teaching profession. We agree with our opinions on important issues. Also she is a bright lady, who has traveled a lot, even to America, and agrees that Hitler was the biggest national disaster that could have happened to our people. **How much longer do the people have to suffer?**

In the afternoon, Miss Jantzen insists, that I have coffee with her and a neighbor brings over some cake, very nice. She even arranges a place for me to stay with another neighbor and I am already looking forward to a bed and a good night's sleep. In the evening as I am having a cup of tea and some supper, Bertina comes by for a chat, then we hear the alert whistle. This is for us and we are fuming about this revolting situation. Forget the expectation of a comfortable night of sleep.

At this point we are just so impassive and resigned, that we accept anything that comes along. Indifferently we get ready to leave again. What is going on anyway? Nothing good, that's for sure. Oh, we are so very tired. What about all the loud mouth promises of a day of rest?

We thank the nice people and thank them for their hospitality and stand in the schoolyard for 2 hours. No organization, it is disgusting. They count and recount the men and it takes forever to list all the weapons. What a circus! The decision has been made. Our whole company is to be integrated with the infantry.

We were afraid of that. The mood is depressed. Of course the two Lt.'s are not included and stay behind. Finally when it gets dark we leave to an unknown destination. We are too furious to talk.

Resigned, I trot along with the others through the pitch dark night. Now it begins to rain, just what we needed. I just don't care anymore. At the crossroads of the Bell-Hunsrück high road, we stop. Here we wait 2 hours. A Lt. from the infantry is supposed to come and take us over. The people grumble and are angry and the mood is terrible.

In order to keep warm, I keep walking back and forth in the pouring rain, back and forth, I don't remember how long. Lt. Stumpf dismisses us with a couple of pitiful words. Oh, what little contact these people have with their subordinates. The people are silent and cool about it. Finally the Lt. comes with 100 men from other various units tossed together and now we head west on the high road. But, where are we going? In the direction of Morbach?

While now en route, a very difficult decision begins to take shape in my mind. I discuss it with my good buddy Bertina. By the crossroads at Kirchberg I have already lost the troop, but still struggle with my decision. I turn to the left and several times I almost turned around, plagued by pangs of conscience, I stop. Try to think things through. I continue walking, almost hesitantly, I then make the final decision to keep on walking. If only I could have said good-bye to Bertina.

I do not remember how long I walked in the dark a motorcyclist stops and gives me a ride. I look at my watch it is 6 am. Where did the night go?

People start walking to church. This is Sunday, I forgot.

11, March 1945

I ask several people, if I can sleep some at their place, most refuse, finally an older lady takes pity on me, but she wants to go to church first. I follow her, sit in the last pew, wet and dirty, and let this Catholic Mass, which does not mean anything to me, pass me by.

Being protestant, I am used to my own kind of church service. Freezing I leave the church, after the constant, monotonous mumbling of the praying people got too much for me, I waited outside for the friendly lady. She gives me some bread and hot coffee and shows me to a bed. How wonderful! Immediately I fall into a deep sleep. Two hours later I am awakened by the rumbling sounds of dive bombers. I get ready, thank the friendly lady for her kindness, and go down to the crossroads. Finally a truck comes, towing a vehicle. I can stand on the running board, but since there are no fenders, I get splattered with mud from top to bottom. I don't care.

In Simmern, where a terrible attack of carpet bombing has wiped out the entire railroad station and all the tracks, I get off, manage to get on another truck and make it to Argenthal. As I am back on the road hiking, suddenly Lt. Stinner and Sgt. Haupt are approaching from behind and pick me up. What a coincidence! I feel comfortable riding with them, the old buddies from Trier, people I know.

We make a stop at the relatives of the Lt.'s in Rheinböllen and are welcomed hospitably. The time passes quickly with eating, drinking, and good conversation. I begin to feel up and happy again.

I am sure Lt. Stinner will help me. We stay until 4 pm in the afternoon. Volksheim is our next stop. We find private quarters in this clean town, which reminds me so much of home. Oh, if I could just stay here.

At a farmhouse with a friendly lady, I get to enjoy a wonderful supper of fried potatoes, bacon and eggs, red beet salad and homemade red wine. Then a soft bed with red checkered sheets. A real farmer's bed! Oh, how tired I am and how wonderful I sleep.

12, March 1945

The next day I am to continue on to Kastellaun, but my trip will go past Hochstätten. No one can stop me from that. After a few rides with military trucks, I am back to hiking again and not too far away from home anymore. Oh, what a feeling! I don't even care what people I meet will think of what I look like.

It is 11 am, when I step into the hallway. I open the door, a loud scream of surprise by Rösel and Oma at the same time and then there is Opa too. They are in the middle of house cleaning for the upcoming confirmation. How completely calm and unsuspecting they are, just as if we were in the middle of peacetime instead of war. It breaks my heart to know that I will not be able to be there for my son's confirmation.

I eat something, am very tired, serious and quiet. Then I go upstairs. Helga is in bed with a cold. The sweet little one is awake and looks at me with big, blue eyes, trying to recognize me. Sweet child! I cannot tear myself away. When Rösel is asking her: "Is this Papa?" She looks at me first, then at my picture on the wall and then there is a new word: "Hand". She means my hand, recognizing it on the picture. When asked: "Where is your ear, your eyes, your mouth, your nose? She points with her finger correctly. A new word in her vocabulary is: "Aug" (Eye)

At that moment the geese are quacking downstairs. Immediately she calls out: "gack-gack". She is holding on the railing of the bed, hops up and down, and squeals. She is never in a bad mood, always happy.

While she sits quietly and plays with her blanket, I unpack and repack. My old cardboard box that has been through so much is emptied, toothpaste and other items I have always dragged along, I leave here and the backpack, which I got new in Alk is refilled. My sweetheart puts in clean clothes and underwear, darns and mends, gives me a jar of jam, boiled eggs and sandwiches.

I am just glad I left the totally rusty machine pistol in Alk. I am not going to bog myself down with things like that.

My big boy in the meantime cleans my muddy tarp, the shoemaker repairs my boots, and so I am just about ready in the late afternoon.

There are no planes today, thank God, so we do not have to go in the shelter. For dinner we have boiled potatoes and bacon sauce. The baby eats like a lumberjack. I take a look with the children at the tunnel they are building for their protection. They are doing a good job, but still have to do the breakthrough in the middle. My most fervent wish: "That the war may just pass them by here quickly and they will be spared from any kind of horror."

The afternoon passes with preparation for my leaving, but I still find time for the children. Helga does not eat well and is too skinny and short for her age. I love the three of them, all the same. My big boy is supposed to become confirmed this Sunday. How mature he has become. The tailor brings his new dark blue suit; it is his first tailor-made suit, which he will wear in church for his big day. How much I would like to be here for this day of honor. If only he will not be drafted into the German Territorial Army, that is my fear.

Helga plays hopscotch in the street with her friends. I go for a walk with the little "Laufele". Constantly the little mouth opens and she tries to speak. Her walking is not too good yet, but she is advanced in her talking.

The hours fly by and the parting draws nearer. I will take the bike to Ebernburg. Norbert walks up ahead at 5:30 pm. I still eat some scrambled eggs and have to admire my brave wife. Saying good-bye, I have to continually kiss and love the little "Mouse". I put my cap on her and she blinks up to the rim, her mouth wide open, so we can see the little teeth. "Give Papa kisses" Rösel tells her. She touches my cheek so incredibly softly with her little mouth and I force myself to hide the pain of farewell. After saying good-bye to Oma and Opa, I walk together with Rösel and Helga through the town pushing the bike. What do we still have to talk about? Nothing more than to reassure each other of our love and not doubt, for one minute, that we will see each other in good health later on. But I have the feeling it will be a long time this time. At the little bridge we say good-bye, Helga fights back the tears, sweet child.

I get on the bike and turn around often to wave, until I cannot see them anymore. Here is the familiar old road, the trees, which I know so well and every bend in the road. Oh, I want to see you again, my precious homeland and then stay here forever.

I catch up with Norbert shortly before Ebernburg and am amazed he had gone so far already. I give him some good advice for next Sunday and let him recite the psalm he has to say before the congregation, which is Psalm 91, Verse 1: "He that dwelleth in a secret place of the most high shall abide under the shadow of the Almighty. I will say to the Lord He is my refuge and my fortress, my God in Him will I trust". I listen to him; I try to have him improve his pronunciation some. I bring to his attention the meaning of this day and tell him to have faith in God; which has been so vividly impressed upon him through his growing up years by his Mama and grandparents. I try to prove to him, how a strong faith in the guidance and direction of the Almighty can visibly intervene in one's life. I kiss the big boy and wish him the best. He takes the bike and turns around. "Auf Wiedersehen, Norbert!"

Post Script About Norbert's Confirmation.

It did not take place until March 30, 1945 because the Americans had captured Hochstätten on March 13[th,] the day after I left them. I know this from a letter that Norbert had written and which I did not receive, until November 1945.

End Of Post Script

I walk across the narrow railroad bridge and just then a train approaches from behind. I quickly climb onto the trestle or I would have gotten hit. Very closely the train passes me by, but I have made quite a shortcut. Wringing wet, I arrive with my heavy backpack in Bad Münster, where I have a lot more time than I thought, since the train is late. Finally there is a train at about 10 pm. I can go to Simmern, where the Red Cross offers hot coffee, walk 20 minutes to the tunnel, where the connecting train was taking cover, and waiting. Miraculously it is heated and I can go to sleep for a couple of hours. At 7 am I arrive in Kastellaun.

13, March 1945

I am to report to Marching Company #2 of the Troop Consolidation Camp Helm. Everyone is pushed over to the Army. All day I just hang around, my mood is not good. What is written in the stars for me?

I leave Kastellaun with a marching group of all kinds of thrown together people. My foot bothers me, which was already sore in Bad Kreuznach from the newly repaired boot. We walk in rows and I am one of the oldest. This immature "Punk" is pushing us. I don't care! I am very down and depressed. It seems that I am the only Air Reconnaissance person with all these picked up people. The typical picture of a disintegrating army. We stop in a wooded area until the dive bomber danger is passed. In the dark we continue on another 3 or 4 kilometers. By then there are over 200 men.

There is a constant counting, writing down, and dividing up. I just don't care! We sleep in a barn. I curse these criminals, who treat human beings like animals. At midnight there is an alert. 100 men are selected, get weapons, and are moved to the front lines. I was spared and we continue sleeping.

14, March 1945

I get some coffee and some good farmer's bread across the street from a nice farmer's family. I am not bothered by anybody, can sit in the sun, and read. That's how I pass the whole day. At night we get new details. There are only 50 men left. We leave for Hundheim.

15, March 1945

We sleep in another barn. The German Territorial Army, mostly kids and old men join us and are trained how to use bazookas. What insanity!

First of all, 15 news reporters are assigned to the field replacement battalion. So we take our baggage and march over there to the woods. With me are four buddies I remember from a previous assignment and with whom I have a good rapport. We take a rest here and there, I eat some of the sandwiches, which I took along and drink some of Opa's wine I still have. We arrive at the next town and here we receive weapons and are sent to the 9th Grenadier Division. I just let everything wash over me and my hope is dwindling.

We are to go to Blankenrath, oh, my God, all the way to the front lines. Weapons are handed out. Then the alarming news, that the American tanks have entered the Mosel Valley.

One should have observed our "brave staff", how they got up and started running. In front of the village a dive bomber attacks. Across the way there are explosions and detonations. All villages are overcrowded with military. We finally find a dance hall without lights, where we can sleep on some straw. It is freezing cold and I pull my coat over my head, put my flashlight and glasses in my hat, and try to go to sleep.

16, March 1945

We start up at 5 am. It is still dark, but the early morning sun is turning the sky red. We keep on marching. Spring is coming. All around me there are a thousand voices of birds giving a morning concert. We cross the Hunsrück high road and the closer we come, the more violent and severe the shooting becomes. Soon we reach the crossing, where there is a sign to Kirchberg. I had no idea that I would be going through here the same day so close to home.

But now we continue on a road, without cover and mercilessly subjected to the dive bombers with constant explosions and detonations to the front, the right, and the left. Over there, most villages are burning, even the little wooded area where we had just taken a rest.

With all the misery I had to laugh. A young Swabish boy, just 18 years old, freshly appointed from the substitute replacements from home, was already sick and tired of everything. He kept throwing his baggage piece by piece into the ditch and with a furious Heil Hitler; he slung his gas mask into the nearest tree.

We just enter a village as a few heavy impacts hit with horrible noise into houses and streets. We are used to it and I just duck mechanically. But this one time there is a bursting metallic sound and with a great whistling sound a shell hit only about 2 meters away from me. Only because I immediately threw myself down behind a low wall, my life was saved. A rain of dust, dirt, bricks, and stones falls on top of me and all around; the walls are covered with splinters. I was saved once more.

Women and children wander around aimlessly and crying from their houses and cellars, which are all damaged badly with all the windows bashed in. This is not a very good outlook with our division stationed here.

We look up at the dairy and we find some of our soldiers tired and exhausted lying on the ground sleeping. They don't even react to the attack anymore. A few more explosions close to us and we make it to the dairy by leaps and bounds. I meet the commander, a decent young major, named Seefried. I tell him of my wish, to be sent back to my old unit and he thinks indeed, that might be possible. I don't dare to hope, as I have been disappointed too many times.

And now begins the time of waiting again. From 8 am to 2 pm, I stand in the hall of the dairy and wait for some kind of decision. I am taken to the major. He has long phone conversations with different units. He informs me, that a transfer is denied. I somehow knew that it would not work out. He sends me to the V-Staffel (Supply Echelon). He tells me it is a pleasant duty and promises to request me back at a later point. I am to ride with the courier, who is lying overtired on the floor, to the echelon. Two more hours pass, then I get on the passengers seat on his motorcycle and in a wild ride we make it up to the edge of the woods and are safe.

Papa having fun posing as driver with his buddies

I get to the new echelon and meet my buddies of the gray uniforms. I take a deep breath and somehow feel quiet and secure. I sit under a tree not far from the well camouflaged trucks, eat some of the hard boiled eggs Rösel packed for me, and the afternoon passes. I meet the young leader Lt. Engelschall. I report later to the sergeant and suddenly, close to evening, there is some movement over there on the road. Everything is moving back; vehicles, bicycles, soldiers on foot, without interruption. Everyone is in a hurry, because the Americans supposedly have broken through, which means for us to get up and move. We are just about the last ones to leave the forest in the dark.

In the curve, the four horses are still lying there with the horrible wounds in their backs. They were shot in the afternoon by dive bombers. It is the terrible enemy Air Force that breaks our resistance.

We drive in a convoy across the high road, downhill to Kirchberg, through the next few villages, always heading south. In a wooded ravine we camouflage our vehicles and stay the rest of the night. It is very cold and I find myself a cow barn where I can sleep for a few hours. In the early dawn new orders: Quickly reload and throw away unnecessary equipment. What a waste! Then I get special orders to drive my truck back to Oberkirn, where equipment of the division is to be loaded.

17, March 1945

We cross the hills to Rhaunen, passing long convoys of French prisoners. They are holding up white flags and for them this is the hour of freedom and liberation. No one pays any attention. We have orders to somehow get to Waldmichelbach in the Odenwald on our own and anyway we can. With the help of a good map, I plan the route and everyone is relieved that I am taking care of it. I am undecided if I should dare to make a detour through Hochstätten or Sembach. It might not be too wise though, because the Americans are supposed to be in Meisenheim by now which is much too close. Soon we are in Kirn, then on through the Lauter Valley.

By Lambertsmühle, a dive bomber attacks and we take cover. The Lt. wants to go through Kaiserslautern, but I talk him out of it. Too dangerous, it's a big city, too vulnerable to air attacks. Instead we go past Otterberg, Baalborn, (oh, just over that hill is Sembach, my home town, where mother is). If only she knew! Then we go through Mehlingen, my birthplace and no one can keep me from stopping there. My uncle and cousin Ottilie are completely surprised. Hurriedly they pack some sandwiches for me and I tell them to give my regards to my mother, then I have to continue on. What do I see? Bombs in Mehlingen; this benign little village! The schoolhouse is gone, only rubble reminds me of the place, where it once stood.

From there we head to Worms. A totally destroyed city and my heart is bleeding! We can hardly get the vehicles through the ruins and rubble. At 7 pm we cross the Rhine River. How fortunate that all day the sky has been overcast. It is evening and after a long search we find some lodging with friendly people, even supper. Lt. Sattler and I feel very comfortable. I am so tired and just wish the people would go to bed, as I am to sleep on the sofa.

Tomorrow is supposed to be my son's special day.

18, March 1945

Norbert's Confirmation (?)

As I awaken, I wonder if they are going to church now at home. I just hope and pray they do not have an acute war situation.

While I wash and shave, and get ready, I concentrate with all my being on them at home. I see my family sitting there in the old church, listening to the pastor. I see my big boy as he stands up, reciting his Psalm, which he learned by heart. I see how he receives the blessing, how my sweetheart, in spite of being brave, cries quietly, because the father of our oldest child, cannot be there. This child who has given us so many worries and concerns with all his illnesses.

How much it hurts me, I cannot even feel it now, maybe at a later point. One has become so tough. If I just knew how he looks in his new suit, how the whole solemn ceremony will affect his young heart. I eat some of the cookies, which were baked especially for his day and drink some of Opa's wine, just as if I was there. I know they will have tried to cook and bake something special this day, even if it was hard and meant a lot of sacrifices. If only I knew, that my mother had a safe trip there.

Maybe the confirmation did not even take place at all. Maybe at this hour there is fighting going on, maybe they are all in the tunnel in fear for their lives, or the precious house with everything in it burnt to the ground? Oh, I must not let myself think these things, but who can give me answers to these questions?

We get some coffee from these friendly people and I enjoy Lt. Sattler's company. Around 10 am, there is an air alert. A formation of Marauder's circles overhead and across the Rhine they drop their terrible bombs on the city. It is a very uncomfortable feeling to be here so close to the bridge. There is no protection. A second and third formation arrives and we beat it out of there.

Shortly before the 3rd formation arrives we hurriedly leave with the truck at top speed and sure enough, there are the bombs falling on the bridge we just crossed yesterday. We make it to Heppenheim, where we take a break for lunch. At the Red Cross we get a good meal, even pudding for dessert. In the evening we stop in Rheinbach, get a slice of lunchmeat, bread, and some red wine. We fill our canteens with red wine and drive in the direction of Fürth, in beautiful sunshine and I don't complain about this afternoon, spent most pleasantly. Around 5 pm we arrive at our destination at Waldmichelbach. I report to Lt. Engelschall and everything is OK.

I find quarters with the Schmitt family, with a wonderful bed, a piano, a clean household, with two kids. I can eat at the table with the family. I play on the piano some of the hymns, they may have sung today on Norbert's confirmation: "Lord, I pledge a new faith in you" and "Let the children come unto me" As I go to bed I ask God, to be with them and to keep them well and safe.

19, to 24, March 1945

We stay for 7 pleasant days in Waldmichelbach. Frau Schmitt is a good cook and every morning I get my coffee with milk. We have given our rations to the civilians and in turn we get to eat our main meal there. How great it is to be able to sit at a table to eat good food and to be able to sleep through the night. I recuperate from day to day.

Up to now the people here have not experienced any war situations, but they are afraid.

In the evening of the 20th we take a trip to Heidelberg. This city is one of the few in the whole country that has hardly any damage from bombing. We are to pick up some meat at a butcher. Getting back it has to be weighed and distributed and that takes most of the day. Every noon I eat one hardboiled egg I still have from home with a glass of beer.

The whole Pfalz is flooded with American troops, only at the Westwall there is still bitter fighting going on. In the clogged Neckar Valley is nothing but retreating divisions. Everything is in a disorderly confusion, the men are unenthusiastic, exhausted and depressed. This is the beginning of the end. What has happened to our proud and victorious Armed Forces?

At the A.V.L. there is terrible crowding. Hundreds of units want to get food at the same time. There is nothing to be done but wait. We spend all night without receiving anything and have to go back the long stretch.

25, March 1945

This should be Palm Sunday. Frau Schmitt with her daily exclamations: "It is terrible"! I help her carry canning jars into the cellar.

We are to move to Darmstadt, which supposedly is still free from the enemy. We make it to Zwingenberg; there are German tanks, which turn us back. The American tanks are expected any minute, so we turn around and head back. We are lucky to get some food in Bensheim, but no bread, instead 13 sacks full of Zwieback and all kinds of canned food. We will not starve. The supplies are passed out hesitantly. In the next few days Mannheim and Weinheim expect to be taken. Near Darmstadt the enemy has pushed up to the Spessard Mountains and will take Hanau. What will become of this? There was no resistance at all along the Rhine River, but **Göbbels sickenly drivels of a German victory.**

In an inn, I get two bottles of good Hessian wine. I leave a letter with the friendly Frau Schmitt for my family, which she will mail later on.

In the evening a special order. I am to secure accommodations in six different villages. The trip was treacherous on mud slick roads without lights. In the little village of Hohenstadt there is a chance to get quarters for our echelon. Everything has been arranged with the friendly mayor of the town. Gerber has gone ahead, I lie down on the sofa and look forward to a quiet night, when orders come to return immediately. We arrive at 3 am and I can sleep some. Why could we not drive directly to the new deployment place? But this is typical for the stupid and impractical orders of the military.

30, March 1945

Good Friday

We have a warm and humid spring morning. The violets are blooming and the birds are singing.

I was a guest for dinner with the nice Lang family in House #12. I want to write to them later. In the afternoon I have to sleep. Woke up at 5 pm. Gerber and I try to follow the convoy, which has gone ahead. In spite of high speed we do not catch up with them until at the new deployment place. Beautiful Bad Mergentheim is still peaceful, but for how long?

Finally around 7 pm we are in Elpersheim, a nice looking town. We get quarters in the House #64 with the Kaiser family. The whole house is filled with people, even refugees. We can get a bed, but nothing to eat.

There is great unrest and fear in the whole village. They have heard horror stories about the Americans. How good, we can sleep through the night.

31, March 1945

Easter Saturday

There is big excitement. Massive retreating convoys; in a big hurry. Are we the last ones? A motorcycle with a sidecar and two officers comes tearing down the road. What is going on? Are we to become a fighting troop and defend the village? But the afternoon passes relatively quiet. Later there is a heavy dive bomber attack behind the village. A bullet fatally hits a 70 year old farmer and in torturous pain the poor man is breathing his last. It is always the innocent people, who have to suffer.

Over there the sky is red as blood from the burning of beautiful Würzburg. All our cities are destroyed. We make it to Rothenburg but passed through a lot of obstacles and clogged roads. We can't believe it, but these bandits have attacked Rothenburg, the pearl of the medieval times with its charming old houses and ancient castle. My heart is bleeding!

In the early morning hours the axle differential on my car broke and I had to be towed up into the woods. The vehicles are camouflaged the men are overtired. I myself have to go with 15 men to the next village.

1, April 1945

Easter

A pitifully poor town with only 11 houses; what dilapidation, dirt, and poverty. I asked a farmer's wife, if she could fix me some eggs. At least it feels a little bit like Easter. What are my children doing at this moment? Will that little sweetheart be looking for Easter Eggs? Oh, I cannot even think of them without the tears welling up in my eyes.

The beds are old fashioned, the kitchen is dirty and smoky, the stables and barns small and dilapidated. In the afternoon I can sleep for a few hours in one of the farmers beds. It is too hot, there is a musty smell, and I awake wringing wet.

In the afternoon an SS troop patrol and this immature "creep" of a Lt. was going to nab us all. That's how low we have come. Poor oppressed people! They are the thugs, these commissioners. We are not far away from being lashed and driven forward by our own superiors.

In the evening we get on the road again, but only make about 15 km. At 10 pm we arrive in Lauterbach and get our quarters immediately. We expect to get a couple of days rest. 6 to 7 men are together in a large room, most of them lying on the floor.

Excerpt From One Of Rösel's Letters:

On March 1st 1945, our little sweetheart has taken her first steps.

2, April 1945

Easter Monday

The whole first day is spent with checking and organizing uniform supplies. That is my new job. Some of the other buddies may have been turned over to the infantry. I hope not. But I am thankful, that God has helped me and spared me so far. The food is excellent. We even had some meat for Easter; three bottles of red wine for 15 Marks each, some chocolate, cocoa, sugar, and canned meat. That is enough to cheer us up. The baggage of the casualties has also been divided up. I was able to get a new shirt and underpants.

In the evening, I go for a walk in order to just cherish my own thoughts and daydream. Oh, if I could just be home. How are you doing? Are you well? Will the Americans have spared you, or are the cruel horror stories, which are reported in the papers and on the radio true? This terrible restlessness of not knowing what is happening!

3, April 1945

We are still in Lauterbach, west of Ansbach. We have excellent meals. We even get eggs and milk. We get large portions of meat and sausage. We have red wine, we get enough butter, and I can sleep nights. Oh, how thankful we are for these luxuries. If I can stay here with this echelon, I will be happy.

Of course there are always dangers. The deterioration and disorganization is increasing. The big shots in the Party are establishing a regiment of fate. The SS wants to snatch up anybody to gather them up to fight on the front lines. What criminals are our people delivered to?

The success and progress of the Americans cannot be stopped anymore. Our Armed Forces are broken and destroyed. And still, we have to keep on fighting. What insanity! The enemy has crossed the Rhine River on all points. They are deep into Westphalia and the Westerwald, Darmstadt and Aschaffenburg have fallen and so has Thüringen.

In my quarters no one sweeps the dirty floor, no one washes their hands and the plates and cups look unappetizing. Oh, dear mother, dear tidy farmhouse in Sembach, oh, wonderful childhood memories!

4, April 1945

There is a drinking party at the Lt.'s. I cannot force myself to be in a good mood. How other people can do this is a puzzle to me. I just want to go home. In the evening I receive orders to leave in the morning.

I have lice!

5, April 1945

I am able to find 45 beds in Engelshausen. The people are friendly, especially the mayor of the town. I get a good meal of waffles with stewed fruit. I am pleased that every man of our echelon will have a bed. There are a lot of evacuated people from the Rhineland, those who have lost everything in the bombings.

6, April 1945

The Anniversary Of My Father's Death

I had slept wonderfully, and then I heard the rumor: the Americans are in Wartenstein. The shooting is increasing and is coming closer. Are those tanks? I cannot get through on the phone, so I just started walking across the field to see the Lt. Why is it, that on this walk our little Sigrid is so very close to me, and her presence is felt so much? I don't know! I can still see her, how she laughs with her little mouth wide open, so that we can see her teeth, my cap on her head. Just the way she looked when I last saw her. I feel like my heart is about to break being homesick and here it is not even four weeks that I last saw them. When will I see them again? Close to nature I wish with a fervent heart to be able to return to my beloved home.

The Lt. thinks the rumor is false. I am being sent back to await further orders. Nonsense! I know what is going to happen. After I get a bite to eat at the Gasthaus Krone, the shooting increases. I play the piano a little and talk to the 9 year old girl; who reminds me so of my Helga. How trustingly she asks and listens, how eager she is to learn and how she loves music. I cannot help myself but to embrace her.

Just then a courier comes by bike and tells me to return immediately and now every minute is precious. I start running through the field. The first shells are hitting. Are they from tanks or artillery? I cannot tell the difference. Explosions detonate all around me, but I am calm. What shall I do? Will I make it? Shall I just stay back and have the Americans capture me?

Maybe that would be the best. And yet, I don't want to be a caught prisoner, I think I may not get home for many years, so I keep on rushing ahead. Over there are clouds of smoke, dust, all around me a hail of bullets. Will I make it? Gasping for breath I keep on running. Every minute is precious and I see the village in front of me. There I see the company leaving in three vehicles, two of them being towed. This is the end. They are leaving me behind.

Desperately I wave. The can, which I carried in my hand, was my salvation, as the Lt. told me later; that's how he recognized me. He stops, yells across the field: "Run, Herzog, Run!"

The street is already being shelled. I feel like my chest is exploding and I can hardly breathe anymore. I can't and still I must. Gasping and stumbling I make the last 200 meters, reach the vehicle, throw myself onto the fender and they keep going. I can rest now and catch my breath. We manage to get across the dangerous road to the next town Wiesenbach.

The people are awaiting the Americans and have white sheets hanging out of their windows. We put the vehicles in a barn awaiting further orders. Half-hour later we continue on to Spielbach. We stop in the woods in pouring rain, we rest and wait. I feel once more having been saved. I ask the Lt. to release me back to the V-Echelon and he writes for me the necessary marching orders, the others move further west. I walk on a dirt road about 5 km to Leutzenbronn and my mind is just boggled.

Never in the history of our people has there been a more shameful crime committed, than the tyranny of the Nazis. It is the subhuman creature that we have been handed over to. We have already heard stories, where the SS have hung decent German soldiers on the next best tree.

I can telephone and find out, that my unit is still there. Thank God! I am a total mess, sweaty, dusty, and dirty, my coat and boots splattered with mud. I have 5 more km to go to Rothenburg and there it is before me in the evening sunshine, the "Gem of the Middle Ages" with its beautiful architecture. And what has become of it? The British Air Force had thrown firebombs and large parts of the city have burned to the ground. I look at the burnt facade of the lovely city hall, walk down the narrow street to the Hotel Eisenhut where I stayed with my sweetheart 12 years ago. What wonderful memories. Oh, I would like to come back here again with her sometime. Later, later!

Then I wait at the post office for the courier of our echelon. According to orders I call the division, get through after an hour of trying to take care of my orders and wait outside for some transportation. After a while a car picks me up. It is cold, wet and I get splattered with mud, but I don't care, I am just glad to get out of here. The last stretch I have to walk, about 3 km long, but it seems like forever in the dark. I get to Lauterbach at 11 pm with a thank God, because I am back with my old unit and I feel safer. The coming days are monotonous and quiet. The continuing advance of the Americans goes on; only at Rothenburg the situation is unchanged.

11, April 1945

Yesterday I went to the Mayor in Schwabsroth, to confiscate horses. No success. All the villages are filled with refugees and evacuated people, everywhere rage and poverty.

The war continues.

Mayors who refuse to defend their village are hung from the nearest tree. I change quarters and move to the Blank family, a well to do farmer, with a modern stable full of a lot of cattle and large fields.

We need to get ready to leave in 1 hour. Again hasty activities with the vehicles and at 1 am we leave with a tractor, a truck, and a car as a scout squad to check things out. At the hillside outside of town we get stuck already. The other tractor has to be used for pulling short stretches at a time with a lot of obstacles and stopovers. Are we headed in the direction of Greilsheim, where the heavy fighting is? What is the sense in that? It's tiring to ride standing on the running board, constantly jumping off and shining the flashlight at the signs, as we drive without lights because of the planes. We got through safely up until now.

12, April 1945

In Bortenberg near Dombühl I have decent quarters here with nice people. In fact, again very poor and backward (how can the people themselves have happy feelings?) but obliging people, their name is Keitel. I can sleep for a few hours in the morning and during the afternoon in a clean bed. On top of that, we had good rations. Had a good night's sleep.

Today at 1 pm, I am so very down and depressed and do not know why. Oh, if only I get through this war alive and safe. Dear God! I want to come home to my family. Oh, bring me back, dear Lord that I can play the organ in Sembach Church again to glorify and praise your Holy name.

The harmony by these friendly people comes across. I exude the music from my heart all the old familiar choral melodies that I learned as a child. The music flows through my fingers and tears come to my eyes.

13, April 1945

Why is today such a difficult and sad day? I cannot help myself, but I walk up to the woods outside of the village. There, where I am alone, I sit down on a rock, pull out the pictures of my loved ones and the bookmark, which Helga has made for me and all the pent up heartache is released in a stream of tears. I feel better after that.

Portrait of Mama, Sigrid, Helga, and Norbert

But why am I so down today? Is there a danger that we may get thrown into the city of Nuremberg, to help defend it? If that happens, we will all be lost. This city will most likely be defended to the last man.

Late in the evening the decision is made. Only a fragmented news unit with Major Seefried is to go on the trip to Nuremberg tomorrow. I feel relieved and go to sleep feeling more comfortable. I have a good bed, decent food, and not too much work.

15, April 1945

Sunday! Four weeks ago was the day of your confirmation, dear boy. What all has happened in these four weeks? I hold my own kind of church service. I walk into the beautiful country, where nature is ablaze with the colors and blossoms of spring. The sky is blue with white puffy clouds and it is warm like in summer.

In the afternoon I sit down at the piano and play the long forgotten folksongs and hymns. I am surprised and pleased to notice how these rough and rugged soldiers sit quietly and listen, some of them even singing along. No one dares to make a frivolous joke about things of eternal value.

I would like to express this vow, when I get home to my family to lead a life more pleasing to God and together with my sweetheart raise our children more godly. Too often I have experienced it myself, how an obvious and visible divine providence has protected and saved me.

16, April 1945

Through the night we experienced heavy artillery attacks, so that the house was trembling and shaking. Is the front moving closer to us? We are still staying, but begin with the usual moving preparations.

We have wonderful spring weather, the birch trees are showing their gentle and fresh young green, the violets and pansies are starting to bloom. We lucked out on our trip to Sengelhof, no artillery, but one hour after we left the guns are shooting at the village. At 1 am we get back. The towns all around Rothenburg are burning.

17, April 1945

In the evening we are leaving. Thank goodness not to Nuremberg. This is a great relief. I hope the buddies there are not doomed!

When I say good-bye to my host family they are so touched, they cry, even the old farmer. I drive the tractor and as long as we can see each other, we wave to each other. I left the 2nd letter with them to my loved ones and hope, that one day they will receive it. It is a trip with obstacles. The tractors are in need of repair and there is a lot of cursing going on, but also many with a lot of patience. Oh, you poor guys. So much competence and efficiency, so much decency and sacrifices and still, everything in vain.

Near Weinberg, the tractor comes to a complete stop. Nothing but aggravation! We finally find part of the echelon in the next town. I have to get back with the mechanic to try and fix the tractor.

The Russians have invaded Berlin in a great offensive move. **Orders of the Führer that every German should die for his Fatherland!**

For him, for his crimes!

18, April 1945

What a beautiful spring morning. It is warm like in summer and the farmers are working in their fields, which is pretty admirable under the circumstances. A day with nothing to do and I am sitting under a linden tree at the gasthaus with a bunch of people evacuated from the Saar.

The Americans are making tremendous progress. The cities Magdeburg, Halle, and Braunschweig have fallen. There is fighting in Leipzig and the Russians are on the offensive.

The SS continues to hang both soldiers and civilians without a trial. These outrageous criminals! No one is safe anymore and every decent German soldier has to fear for his life. The poor people are writhing and moaning in their agony.

We would like to stay here. In the evening we get a good meal of beef broth and liver dumplings and wonderful pancakes with fruit. We are just relaxing sitting with a glass of beer, when the orders come for change of deployment. The division has been changed to our area. So we continue on further south. I drive the tractor and we encounter the usual obstacles. When we get to Feuchtwangen, the people are waiting in the streets for the Americans.

Over in the west there are the giant floodlights in the sky as I had seen them only once before in Bitburg. The night is cold, the ride uncomfortable as the roads are in terrible condition. Everything is rolling south in the bright moonlight. We pass a lot of trucks with baggage and horse drawn carts. A retreating army!

About 4 am we get stuck with the trailer and it takes us a while to get it pulled out. At 5:30 am we get to the town. An old woman has her lights on. I get some hot coffee and can sleep on her couch. I am exhausted and immediately fall asleep.

19, April 1945

I am very tired. I can sleep a little in my quarters at the mayor's house. I wish I could stay here for a little bit. The house is clean and the people are friendly and accommodating. They also give us something to eat. It reminds me of home. Family pictures on the wall, a cozy tile stove, beds with sheep wool blankets, a grassy meadow with wild flowers behind the house, just like in Mehlingen, when I was growing up. The sun is shining and the cherry and apple trees are blooming.

In the evening, a speech is broadcasted by Göbbels with the usual clichés and empty phrases. **Your days are counted! Thank God!**

Tomorrow is supposed to be Hitler's Birthday. Who cares about that!

20, April 1945

I slept so well. What a pleasant place to stay. The lady fixes all my favorites, like pancakes, waffles, hot chocolate, and washes my clothes.

The mayor has his worries. All horses and wagons are to be confiscated. The people are furious.

We have a hot day like in summer. I hope that later on, I will be able to remember this pleasant place in all its details. The lady reminds me so of my aunt in Breunigweiler. If only we could stay here a week or so.

But what is this I hear? Very close artillery fire, even machine guns.

21, April 1945

We were spared once more and I could sleep through the night. I go to the church to play the organ a little. How this fills my heart with joy. My vow is consistent; if I should get back home safely I will begin a new life with innermost redeemer reflection.

Things are getting restless. We hear tank fire in the distance. Shortly after noon we get orders to get moving. Too bad, everyone liked it here. The tanks seem to come closer and the dive bomber's activity increases. The sky is clouding over, that's good, and we finally get going, after saying good-bye to the friendly people. I go up front with the tractor. Then we ride on dirt roads through the next few villages. Helpful civilians show us the way.

There we see SS men with bazookas in the ditches waiting. All tank traps are closed. We ride through the fields at hair-raising speeds. Strangely there are no dive bombers.

Today my little Helga is my patron saint. I cannot get the songs out of my head, which she sang, when I was home the last time.

23, April 1945

The weather is still cold but in the afternoon it clears up. I ride up ahead with the kitchen truck. Dive bombers! We wait at the edge of some woods, until the danger has passed. In Monheim we also have to take cover for an hour or so. We have left the artillery fire behind us, thank God. The trip is smooth now, but slow. At 11 pm we arrive at a little town north of the Danube River.

24, April 1945

This is Bayrisch-Schwaben (the Bavarian-Swabia area of southern Germany). I slept on somebody's sofa. The whole town is full of POWs. It's a picturesque little village nestled in a valley, daisies, dandelions, and blooming apple trees. The day passes quietly, but the enemy is coming closer. Tonight we are to move again. I have eaten the rest of my jam I had brought from home and the last cube of sugar. In the evening the gunfire sounds closer, we move at 8 pm. We cross the Danube.

Dear God! Bring me back across this river again to my beloved home.

We are getting into the area between Augsburg and Munich. We make good time in bright moonlight. We drive through wealthy farming towns with big splendid estates. It is 1 am; by this time we have 40 km behind us. Then we are in an "Oberbayrischem (Upper Bavarian)" village near Aichach.

25, and 26, April 1945

For days now a rumor, which I only hope is true, occupies my mind feverishly. It is too good to be true. Supposedly the Americans are releasing all prisoners over 40 years of age to their homes. Oh, dear God! If this were true, and I would be captured; I could go home. It would totally overwhelm me. The brooding over this possibility almost takes my breath away. The thought does not leave me, I go to sleep with it at night and wake up with it in the morning.

The sound of artillery shelling is coming closer again. The Americans have crossed the Danube, what is going to happen, where will we go? Today a tremendous feeling of homesickness is engulfing my heart. Sometimes I am inconsolable and the nerves and patience are worn.

My beloved "pfälzisches (the Pfalz area of western Germany)" homeland with its splendor, its beauty, and with its fine and happy people. I want to see you again.

27, April 1945

Last night we received surprising orders to move again with the usual slogan: "To defend the city of Augsburg." At the last minute there was a change. We ride through the moonlight about 20 km south. We get lost and notice our error shortly before Augsburg. We finally reach our destination.

In Wollomoos we take a break for some food. Friendly farmers, typical "Oberbayrische (UpperBavarian)" farms with large rooms and a house full of kids. But I can sleep in a bed.

In the afternoon there is a heavy thunderstorm. In the evening a nice get together with some of the buddies and the owners and we play games. I don't feel like it, but don't want to be a spoilsport.

28, April 1945

Attempted Coup In Munich

There is feverish excitement. We do not leave the radio. What is going on? We find out, that the SS has beaten down the revolt. Can anyone imagine how we feel? That would have been the end of the war. And now we keep going. Oh, what a horrible crime is committed on our people.

Around noon we get sudden orders to leave. Again we hear the tanks shooting. Thank God it is raining. We move into the small town of Kreuzholzhausen, where we stay with an old farmer. I do not feel well, weak and tired, I hope I don't get sick now.

The Americans move right along on all roads from the west and the north towards Munich. The Russians have encircled Berlin. Is Hitler going to commit suicide? The front is breaking down everywhere. It can only be a matter of days now. This had to happen and there was no other way. The people just want it to be over with, they want **PEACE** and wait with great expectation, the liberating American troops.

The old farmer at first is not too friendly he has made too many sacrifices. He had three sons and all of them were killed. Later on he warms up some.

29, April 1945

Kreuzholzhausen

Sunday; The Day Of My Capture As Prisoner Of War

We slept innocently and without foreboding premonitions one more time in a comfortable bed with coffee and good food the night before. I had urged the Lt. in vain to leave in the middle of the night. Was it a mistake? Or may be not. In the morning at 9 am we are ready to leave. Too late!

Behind us as well as in front of us violent and severe firing and shelling by the American tanks. In addition to the artillery, machine guns, and dive bombers, it is impossible to get out of the village. My driver refuses to drive. Undecided, I wait. The Lt. is checking the autobahn. Forget it!

The decision is made to break through the rear and approach Munich from the north. In any case I packed a light marching bag in expectation that we do not get out of this encircled area. The Lt. orders the trucks to move. I stay with the tractor, which does not want to start, together with Jäger and Schmitt. 15 minutes later the Lt. comes back on a motorcycle and from a distance waves his arms. He and his driver were shot at and so was our convoy. All vehicles are lost. The people tried to find cover in an open field. There will be casualties. Only two men are running back all out of breath. Now there are only six of us awaiting our fate.

A friendly woman cooks us something to eat and I leave my backpack with her with my home address.

The shooting has subsided, but around 5 pm, violent machine gun firing breaks out. So there will be fighting and that is not good. The civilians are scared and they all run into their cellars. The bullets are whistling around the corners and hit our door with a crashing sound. After a while it quiets down and some of the town's people come and tell us that the Americans are stopped with their trucks by the gasthaus.

Now Our Fate Is Sealed And The Hour Has Come

Confidently, we walk with the Lt., who is still hesitant, down the street. At that moment a small foreign car with an American officer standing on the running board, a rifle in his hand ready to shoot drives up. As he sees us, he immediately aims at us. We raise our hands above our heads and we are lead away. But down by the gasthaus the incredible and unbelievable happens, that I shall never ever forget, as long as I live.

I can repeat what happened in these frightening minutes only in key words. There was a "wild west type" character with the face of a criminal and a sergeant, who was shaking with rage, yelling at me: "You, where is your machine gun?" The sergeant already has his pistol on my chest. I was supposed to have fired a weapon and I did not even have one.

What went on in these terrifying moments inside of me cannot be described. I want to try and forget it. Now in these last minutes of the war I was supposed to have fired a weapon? What a terrible misunderstanding. Everyone watches the scene horrified. Never, ever shall I forget the faces of the women in their windows, who loudly begin to cry.

What about me? I am very calm, I do not shake I am just resigned. In wild flight, thoughts of my loved ones, my happiness at home rush through my being. Only a small reproach stirs inside of me: "So you have forsaken me after all, God, to whom I have prayed so faithfully all my life."

And in this moment, where everything seemed lost, my salvation comes: Lt. Engelschall finally got himself together and talks in fluent English explaining to the American officer the misunderstanding, giving his word of honor as an officer, that I did not have any weapons at all. And what a miracle! The "gangsters" calm themselves down and everyone takes a deep breath of relief.

Can anyone imagine how I feel? Not just overly happy as a matter of fact quite the opposite. I feel physically sick, but very soon I collect myself and I thank my creator, whose love I have doubted. Now everything happens very quickly. We are lined up in a row, checked for weapons and have to turn over our pocketknives. They smash our beautiful Carbine 98 K and break our side arms. The wonderful Walbusch Knife, which has accompanied me through this entire war, is taken from me. Oh, well, who cares! We are just glad that they are not taking our rings and watches, which has happened in many instances.

Now the houses are searched and 6 to 8 more soldiers are found. We are put on a truck and taken away, but where? Another dangerous situation occurs. We are supposed to pull out a truck, which was stuck in a swampy meadow, but without luck. Soon there are a few rounds of German artillery explosions very close by. The Americans throw themselves down flat in the fields for cover. If only we will not suffer for this. But there comes the answer. In a matter of minutes the German guns are silenced by American artillery.

An American vehicle quickly pulled out the truck, which was stuck in the mud. We are just in awe about the abundance of massive material displayed by the Americans. Continually all kinds of vehicles are moving up ahead. Against such a force and might, we were going to make war? What insanity!

The Americans all appear to be well nourished, well equipped, and all young men between 20 and 30. Some of them are friendly, most of them complacent. They come as victors self assured and secure.

In the evening we march for about a half an hour and then wait. An endless wait on a farm with our hands folded on top of our heads. How very tiring and exhausting this is. We are put into a wooden shed, where we cannot sit down or lay down, an endlessly long night.

Lt. Engelschall still believes that we might all be shot. There are many suspicious signs. No one speaks to us. No one speaks German. They are proud and arrogant. There is no relief. Somehow the night passes.

30, April 1945

We are loaded onto trucks and taken to a large farm and herded into a barn, where there are already about 100 men. We eat some of our provisions and sleep in the straw. The Lt. takes a deep breath of relief. There was a Jewish officer who was very decent to us.

1, May 1945

The Weather Is Cold And Rainy

Utilizing approximately 1 dozen trucks, 50 to 60 men are loaded onto each truck, like sardines in a can. We get on the autobahn, but to where? We are heading north crossing the Danube on an excellent pontoon bridge, built by American engineers. Finally we see close to Nördlingen, a huge field with the infamous barbed wire. This is where they take us for the time being. We are herded like sheep through a gate and everybody gets a rough whack across the back with a stick.

Today is the third day with nothing to eat. Our own supplies are used up. I still have as a precious commodity a small piece of bacon. More and more transports are arriving all day long. Soon there are 2,000 to 3,000 men. The night is so cold, that we cannot sleep. Everyone is walking back and forth. Finally the morning comes. Nagging hunger, there is nothing to eat. Grumbling is useless, the guards start firing warning shots. Yes, we have lost the most precious gift, our freedom.

2, May 1945

Hitler is supposed to have been killed fighting to his last breath in the Reich's Chancellery. Göbbels supposedly committed suicide. Is this true, or are they just rumors?

The sanitary conditions are more than primitive. This will mean diseases for sure. Beatings by young punks. The mood is very irritable, no food for 5 days now. It is very cold. No sleep through the nights, because I do not want to lay down on the cold ground with no blanket or anything else. I rather walk back and forth. Some have tried to make a pitiful fire out of cardboard boxes. They fight about a little piece of wood. Continued stealing.

Daily, trucks with new prisoners arrive. It is strangely cold for the month of May. It is amazing, how much a human being can endure, one can indeed live for 5 days without food or sleeping. I sit or walk around.

There are both decent Americans and punks who have a sharp eye for our watches and wedding rings.

The rumors are incredible. One cannot believe anything. Some of these rumors are starting to demoralize us.

4, May 1945

They separate the officers from the enlisted men, so we have to say good-bye to Lt. Engelschall. I owe him my life!

This afternoon I crowd with others onto a transport vehicle. About 10 trucks take 60 to 70 men each. We ride through pouring rain and icy wind to Heilbronn. Here we went from the "frying pan into the fire". There are some 20,000 men. I stand with patience all evening, all through the night, until the following afternoon. How terribly long is such a night!

5, May 1945

Rain and cold

We are in a transit camp in Heilbronn. The city itself has been leveled, a terrible sight. I have lost my five buddies from the V-Echelon.

Provisions: two small cans of American rations. Not even enough to relieve the nagging hunger.

In the afternoon, 10,000 men are to be leaving. There is terrible crowding with no discipline and human beings turn into animals with all the typical instincts. We should be ashamed of our performance before these American soldiers, who watch this spectacle complacently. But there comes the immediate punishment for this disobedience.

The guards push and rush us to a constant hurry. Everyone is running through the pouring rain. We run and stumble through knee high mud, wade through dirty ground water, which is flooding all roads. It is getting dark. The Americans constantly threaten us with their machine guns and sticks. There is no stopping and I am feeling exhausted. I notice much to my dismay that I do not have the physical stamina that I used to have. Our hope, that we would be loaded up, is betrayed. We continue outside of the city at this speed for another 5 km or so. Then we see on a hillside endless rows of lights. No railway station, but a camp.

Now we are totally dejected and despondent. We are herded like cattle through an opening in the barbed wire and left to ourselves in the pitch dark. Nobody can find anybody else; it is pouring buckets. I am completely wet, but also sweating and now start to freeze. Impossible to lie down in the mud, so we stand together shaking. One guy nestles himself close to me, wraps his arms around me to keep warm and this is how we stand and hold on to each other, so we don't fall down with fatigue and weariness. Around midnight I lie down anyway into the mud and fall asleep, but wake up when I begin gurgling, icy cold clay water runs over my face and neck into my collar. I get up and start walking again, until a bitter fight breaks out over a standing space of 4 square meters in a wooden shed, also where the first sick are lying.

Who cares, that he is being stepped upon, or who cares or knows, that someone might be trampled to death? What is life worth anymore? The people are inconsiderate, mean, and nasty. The doctor is screaming and raging, but to no avail. This goes on until early morning. It is still raining and we are wet to the skin. All the sick are now lying on the ground outside.

The first casualties: One man was shot (no one knows why he was shot by a guard) and a civilian, an older man, who in desperation cut his wrist with a razor blade.

As far as the eye can see, there are preparations made for a huge camp. Roads are built, lighting equipment put in as well as more and more barbed wire.

It is Sunday! This past night was the worst of my life.

New fears! One man says that all the villages of the entire Alsenz valley were destroyed.

7, May 1945

As Of Today In The Camp Stalag Böckingen

How long will it be? It is aggravating, that I had to sacrifice my equipment, but I am thankful, that the Americans did not loot my backpack with all my belongings, as it has happened to other buddies.

What I lost: my belt and canteen, my shaving kit, a pair of new socks, soap, aspirin, razor blades, toothbrush, toothpaste, wash rag, a butter dish, a battery, a bag with coffee, salt shaker, etc.

On 7, May 1945 At 23:01, The WAR Is Officially Ended

Senior General Jodl has signed the unconditional capitulation. The Nazi Reich has pitifully broken down. What will happen now for me? I just want to go home.

8, May 1945

Mother's Birthday

I have pain in my joints. I am in a tent with some pleasant as well as unpleasant guys.

9, May 1945

The weather is improving. We are fed with American canned food. It is good, but not enough.

10, May 1945

All day long we line up, count, and walk around. There are a lot of foreigners that are sorted out.

11, May 1945

Hope and hopelessness! Inmates range in ages 14 to 65 and from many different nations.

12, May 1945

Different cages. Daily new ones arrive. Humanity as far as the eye can see; a quarter of a million!

13, May 1945

I share a four-man tent together with buddy Mohr from Alsenz. We are hot, hungry, and thirsty. It's best to be half naked.

14, May 1945

How hunger can hurt and being thirsty tortures! Fights about water. A new water main is built.

15, May 1945

Change over to new rations. Daily in the morning we get a cup of coffee, at noon ¼ liter of water like soup, and at night a slice of bread with margarine. We are glad it finally turned warm.

I have hallucinations of Richard.

16, May 1945

Outbreak Of Dysentery

Daily casualties. Daydreams of food: favorites, all the canned foods in the cellar all at once.

17, May 1945

We longingly look across to the other road to see if trucks are coming. Daily there are new arrivals. Half a million released. Why not us?

18, May 1945

For the first time I feel dizzy and weak. Always tired! I can hardly walk anymore. Want to sit and lie down all the time. Washed and shaved once.

The farmers are picked out.

19, May 1945

I reported to the farmers. I am so weak I can hardly get up. Everything is so hopeless. Dear God! Just let me be healthy. In the night, a heavy thunderstorm, my ditch fills with water. I fall asleep anyway from exhaustion. If only I had a tarp.

20, May 1945

Is today Pfingsten (Pentecost)? I do not know. In the night we have another thunderstorm. I beg someone for some space. I have bizarre and frightening nightmares. My sudden fear for Norbert! Have the Americans taken him?

How hunger hurts. Wounds do not heal.

21, May 1945

Dreary, rainy weather. I have a sore throat. Tired of living. That is a dangerous condition. I have to try and get over this. It rained all night. There are daily deaths. Their bodies just dumped in a mass grave. There are no medications for the sick. They are lying outside even with fever.

22, May 1945

It is still raining. The treatment by the SS Officers. Soon we are one million! No hope for release.

23, May 1945

My warm coat, my good boots! If only I had taken my tarp. How I have learned to lick out cans and spoons.

24, May 1945

Harassment! Last night they made us cover all holes in the ground by picking up dirt with our hands. The people are on the bare cold ground in mud and rain. Today I feel very weak again, have to lie down a lot.

25, May 1945

Last night it was so cold, that I could not sleep more than two hours. Also a terrible restlessness inside of me. Has Hochstätten been shelled by artillery? Is my family still alive? Have they taken Norbert because of his camouflage pants?

The lack of dignity of a German soldier; he traded his Iron Cross for five cigarettes.

I have lost my pencil.

26, May 1945

Theft!
Running the gauntlet!
Beatings!
Bartering!
The hunger!
No water!
Nothing to read!

27, May 1945

Four Weeks Of Imprisonment

A bitter chapter of my life! Defenseless and without honor or rights.

The month of May is unusually cold. Not one single night of sleep because of rain and cold.

New harassment: spot checks, standing in line for hours, checking of bags, no food for the following day, because some papers were found on the ground.

Release in sight? Small hopes.

Again the heat! Washed my shirt. 10,000 pictures from the past and the future, day and night.

29, May 1945

Too weak to wash myself!

I shall never forget this May. Today terribly hot and in the night freezing cold. The imagination and hallucinations of food intensifies to the point of delusion. And still I cannot free myself from it.

30, May 1945

Of course our hopes were betrayed. Other south German camps supposedly have been emptied. Here new harassment: pull out grass; carry sand by hand from point A to point B.

In the evening, we receive the devastating news that all prisoners are to be turned over to the French as a labor unit. I am stunned and dazed with despair. Still there is a small hope that it is just a rumor.

Again tear down tents, put up at a different spot, half hour later tear down again, put up 1 meter next to it, etc.

In the night a thunderstorm with torrential rains, the tent is under water, I am completely wet and shake from the cold. But I don't want to get sick I want to see my loved ones again.

31, May 1945

We are so weak, that we just stagger. New harassment: flatten an area with wooden sticks and drinking cups. What a way to demoralize people. The general mood is disastrous.

1, June 1945

I always want to lie down, always weak and weary. In the evening another thunderstorm, this time the tent holds up without leaking. As of tomorrow a little more soup.

3, June 1945

I am especially homesick today! I take care of myself against illness, heat, hunger, thirst, and colds.

I am too weak to wash my feet!

4, June 1945

SS are picked out and tattooed. No water for the whole day! There is no food until 10 pm.

New terrible fears about my loved ones! Hochstätten indeed was supposed to have had fighting.

5, June 1945

A pleasant day. Not too hot. Was able to get a book, "Kinderschiff" ("Ship of Children"), what a joy to be able to read! I have learned to be content with little.

A year ago was the **Invasion**!

6, June 1945

The mood is dismal again. No water all day long. The soup at 10 pm. In long lines, we are to transport dirt in food cans 100 meters further away. What's the crazy sense in that?

7, June 1945

The brutalized young people. Every morning about 1,000 men in sick bay that is 10%. There is now a camp paper. I read the book "10 Men, 1 Bread".

8, June 1945

No soap to wash clothes. Thieves are punished. What I learn: The patience of an angel.

9, June 1945

I slept in a 10 man tent. Cool and rainy. Scandalous conditions in sick bay.

10, June 1945

Sunday! In the morning Communion, I was able to pick up wonderful strength and hope.

In the afternoon a new disappointment! A new rumor: Camp Heilbronn to become a labor unit in France.

11, June 1945

I have beautiful and ugly dreams of home. Is there a famine at home?

The camp paper brings some hope. Göbbels poisoned himself and his whole family.

12, June 1945

The weather is horrible and it rains all day. I am lying in the tent. There is some movement in the camp. Cattle trains with prisoners arrive. It is raining all through the night and I am freezing cold.

13, June 1945

What a crazy month of June. It is cold like in winter. Rain showers and cloud bursts. Where is the sunshine?

I heard that Hochstätten is supposed to be completely destroyed. What horrible torture I endure! I want to try and remember later on, what I went through in this time of mental agony.

14, June 1945

The provisions have improved some. We get more bread. The first farmers are released. I give 2 letters for my family to a young buddy from the "Alsenztal" (Alsenz Valley), which is close to home.

15, June 1945

Is this the beginning? Farmers from 75 km of the surrounding area come into the D Camp, are passed through, and have to fill out forms.

There are some German speaking officers in groups #1 and #2. What does that mean? New fears about group #2, we will not come into an E Camp. Group #1 is to be released immediately.

New bad rumors! The provisions are better, the coffee is warm, and we get one small piece of bread. Fear and trembling!

16, June 1945

New bad luck! When they came to my group (100 men) they stopped the processing. 1,200 men leave, but where to? What will happen tomorrow?

17, June 1945

Sunday! Cold fruit soup, and we have a raw wind. At noon 1,400 men leave for D Camp. New hopes and new rumors! We get ¼ of a loaf of bread.

18, June 1945

At 5 am, warm food, divided up into 40 men to a group, march through the city of Heilbronn, loaded into 40 freight cars. Where are we going? Not Kelsterbach! But to Bielligheim, Mühlacker, Bretten, and Bruchsal?

Now the decision seems to have been made not to Mannheim, but to Karlsruhe? Still we have a small hope. It now appears that the big decision is not to Wörth, but to France.

A terrible depression fills our hearts!

19, June 1945

The Saddest Birthday Of My Life!

At midnight I cried myself to sleep, filled with rage and disappointment. Strassburg, Luneville, Nancy, Toules. All day long we ride in these cattle cars and cannot see where we are going. Where are we headed? To the South, to the coast? At night we are in Dijon.

I cannot describe what goes on inside of me today. I will never forgive the Americans for turning us over to the French in such an underhanded way. I have lost all trust in the goodness of humanity! I sewed my wedding ring into the seam of my jacket.

In the middle of the night we stop somewhere and don't know where we are. Around noon the next day we continue, nothing to eat or drink. We crisscross the middle of France and arrive in Bourges at midnight. It is raining into the cattle car, no room to sit or lay down.

21, June 1945

The mood is desperate! It is raining. We head south towards Biscaya. Around noon we are arriving at the Loire River. The gold and silver braids and lapels on our uniforms are taken off.

We are indeed to be turned over to the French! Oh, what a day of misery and despair! The hatred of the people is so evident. They throw rocks at us, grimace, threaten, spit at us, and raise their fists against us. The direction is changed. The Americans are trying to lure our rings and watches from us with the reasoning, that the French will take them from us anyway.

We stop in open country for hours. We get only ½ of a ration. At 7:30 pm we arrive at a huge camp enclosed with barbed wire. The tents seem good. At first I am calmed down. At least we are not sent to the coast to clear the minefields. I meet some buddies from Heilbronn. What does all this mean? Have they not been released? I meet much to my great joy Woll and Weber in tent No. 14.

22, June 1945

I have gotten settled in. The camp is clean, the provisions OK. I am weak and tired, but my desperation has abated to a quiet composure. I console myself with many hundreds of thousands.

23, June 1945

I have been detailed as group leader, with a labor command. I will be teaching the French language.

24, June 1945

A day filled with harassment. Constant lineups, counting, double checking everything. In the afternoon the tents are ransacked, as well as people's bags raided and many things stolen. These want to be soldiers?

25, June 1945

To my great joy I met Wilhelm Becker from Hochstätten, a couple other "Pfälzer's" from Langmeil and Höringen. We want to meet each night.

26, June 1945

The ugly and the beautiful dreams of home. What does it mean?

I begin giving the French lessons to my company with the appreciation of my buddies. In the evening I participate in English lessons and make friends with the teacher and minister. I try to get some reading material.

27, June 1945

I try to sew myself a pair of bathing trunks. Sewed all the buttons on and I am pretty proud of myself. I darned my blanket and socks and fill out my day with activities.

The French guards throw rocks into the camp all night long. Punks!

28, June 1945

The weather is cool and rainy. I celebrate the 28th of June with Wilhelm Becker and my triumph 20 years ago in Fischbach. How happy I was then with you, my Sweetheart!

Last night I attended a wonderful lecture, which was titled: "Christian Family Life After Our Return Home", by a minister. I found hope. "O Lord, you cannot spoil me!"

I have put my wedding ring back on and just hope they will not take it away from me.

29, June 1945

Yesterday they picked out the miners. They will be doing slave work in the French coal mines.

Always there is this weakness, faintness, and lack of energy. It's this unbalanced diet with the lack of fat and protein.

30, June 1945

The weather is cooling down again. The camp is supposed to come under French administration. Will this mean a better or a worse change?

I have applied as an interpreter. I still teach the French language every day. As hard as this is for me, I expect to be here for a long time. Daily and hourly I wonder how my loved ones are?

I would like to make this my motto, an inscription on a plaque in front of our tent: "Mach's wie diese Sonnenuhr, zähl die heiteren Stunden nur…." ("Be like a sun clock, only count the happy hours….").

Prison Camp La Fleche

1, July 1945

The road of suffering is just beginning. After 5½ years of uninterrupted participation in the most miserable, most unfortunate of wars, which brought me no gravitating experiences; rather nothing but a chain of disappointments and unfulfilled expectations. It has now also become my fate, to walk the bitter road as a POW.

My wish was to get a chance to see other countries than France; Belgium, Holland and Luxembourg, was not fulfilled. I was not granted the privilege to see Denmark the "Land of Milk and Honey" or Norway the "Land of the Midnight Sun". I have not had the opportunity to study the classical land of "Hellenism" with its rugged ravines or see its pleasant shores of the blue Adriatic Sea or sunny Italy and be able to study the people. What rich inner values would I have received from such experiences? I do not want to be ungrateful though.

Without any doubt my life has been in many different situations visibly and wonderfully saved by an Almighty fate. Such as the Lightning attack (P-38 Lightnings) on our command post in Southern France on 14, August 1944. During a fight with French terrorists while retreating through the Rhone Valley on 21, August 1944. In the heavy bombing attack on Trier on 19, December 1944. In the attack on Trier, Christmas Eve 1944. And at last, but not least, at my capture by the Americans in Kreuzholzhausen on 29, April 1945, where I was threatened with an on the spot execution.

From these experiences I would like to deduce the hope that I may be granted one day to return to my family in good health. **Only when will that be?** With me hundreds of thousands of German men share the same fate, from 15 year old boys to 65 year old men.

But why have we been so shamelessly betrayed, have been abducted, and taken to a foreign country? No one can answer this desperate question to us. Was there a political reason for this? Can no one uncover these mysterious connections?

My diary now shall tell of and report the life of an "army behind barbed wire". Of bitter hunger and thirst, of burning heat and freezing cold, of pouring rain without shelter, of deprivations and humiliations of all kinds, being subjected completely to some people's lack of mercy and raw harassment perpetrated by a "band of soldiers" turned cocky, arrogant, and euphoric in their victory.

I want to tell of magnificent comradeship, kindheartedness, but also of blatant egotism and lowest fundamental attitudes, also of the terrible state of neglect of law and order and the shameful brutalizing of the German people.

In what blackest depth of the human soul have the poor people been plunged into? We are now living through the darkest and most terrible days of German history.

I am content to realize, that I have been able to preserve my human dignity, that my good upbringing by loving and decent parents is bearing fruit and that I can be a good example for others. I am able to give many a lift and watch them gain new strengths through adversities. I myself try with tremendous willpower and strength to keep myself upright physically, emotionally, and spiritually, because I want under any circumstances to be able to go home one day in good health.

I suffer terribly about the uncertainty of my loved ones. Are they still alive? Are they well? If only I knew that! We are not given the opportunity to write one single line home. I feel though, that they are with me at every hour with their thoughts and wishes, as well as their prayers. This way, a deep and profound communion connects us daily.

So I hope, that maybe after months, or maybe even years, the hour will come, when I will be able to step again on German soil, which is sacred to me and maybe happily reunited with those dear ones, who mean everything in this world to me.

Until then I have to arm myself with patience! O Lord, give me your strength and blessings for it!

2, July 1945

There is no change of events in the course of a day. We live in expectation from one meal to the next. How I want to teach my children later the appreciation of food.

The weakness increases. We want to lie down all the time. That feels good. The sweet soups are tasty, just not enough.

3, July 1945

The French guards, wearing English uniforms, throw stones over the fence at us. How childish! They are stirred up to violence and are so full of hatred. Many of them brag that they were in the underground.

4, July 1945

More and more "Pfälzer" from all different counties arrive.

5, July 1945

I participate in the English language lessons and make good progress. I also continue teaching my French lessons. The buddies are grateful. If only I would not feel so weak. There are no seconds with the food. The fights for seconds and every crumb of bread. There are ugly scenes where the food is dispensed. The "animal" in the human being becomes evident. No matter how hungry I am, I control myself and I would never use a curse word or show my impatience.

In the sand on the hillside by our barracks there are some letters placed down made from tin. They read:

"Auch dieser Sand wird einst verwehn
und kein PW wird hier mehr stehn
und nie mehr stündlich fragen dann
Bin ich wohl bald mit Nachschlag dran?"

Translation:

"This sand will not blow here one day
And no POW will stand here anymore
And never ask again by the hour
When will I be getting second helpings?"

I make good use of my time. I read books wherever I can get them. I darn my socks. I wash my laundry and mend my clothes. I am careful not to lose my meager possessions to thieves. I attend an agricultural course, English lessons, and go to church services on Sundays, that renew and uplift me wonderfully. I make friends with people who have values, keep a good comradeship with Woll and Weber, and structure my day as sensibly as possible.

Yesterday much to our great surprise and joy, the Americans made it possible for us to buy different articles. Through skillful trading and with some luck I was able to get some practical things such as, a piece of Lifebuoy soap, which foams well, shaving cream, skin lotion, razor blades, ink, a writing pad, toothbrush, and toothpaste, all the things that are so essential and I did not have.

Every day I saved some of my bread for trading and was able to get a cooking pot. Now the things I lost in my backpack have mostly been replaced.

6, July 1945

The camp is officially turned over to the French. Will it get worse or better? The French officers seem very arrogant. We will wait and see.

They have a parade. What an enormous satisfaction for these people. I can understand, why should they not feel as victors? Over there the Stars & Stripes as well as the blue, white, red Tricolors are raised with the sounds of the "Marseilles", the French National Anthem.

Next week is to bring changes, maybe a work deployment.

7, July 1945

Something new: We are to line up each morning for a counting, that means standing for hours and we are so tired.

Ridiculous rumors: De Gaulle was assassinated. This is hardly true, but interestingly, where do all these thousand's of rumors come from? In the true sense of the word: Latrine promises!

This evening we had some tea, which was very good.

8, July 1945

No church service this morning, because of sudden evacuation of 16 companies with an unknown destination. We are feeling very uncomfortable. The craziest rumors are making the rounds, possible deportation to Morocco or America.

What do we care about such tests of our patience! We sit from 6 am until 5 pm on the ground in the broiling sun and wait. At 2 pm, we are fed some of the famous "water soup" as we call it, water with a few cabbage leaves swimming around in it. Then afterwards, the usual counting with continuous driving and pushing, we are herded through the gate.

There they take away our boxes and cartons with meager belongings. I too have to give up my little box. Well, that should be the least. With clubs and hits of rifle butts we are herded into a railway car, 40 men each in a cattle car. As I look out through a small opening, the most manifold thoughts go through my mind. These moments should be stored for the rest of one's life.

What Are The Lasting Impressions Of La Fleche?

I enjoy the comfortable feeling just before going to sleep, next to my friend Woll, while I munch on my last piece of bread and visualize thousands of dear pictures of home and my favorite meals. The English lessons, getting coffee at 5:30 am, shivering in the cold, the very tiring, shuffling walk down to the exercise square and I slowly drag my feet, putting one foot in front of the other. Oh, what hard work that was.

Dead tired I would arrive and was glad to sit on the little box. Then I get together with my "Pfälzer" comrades, my diligent work, and structured layout of my free time. Now, only 16 days later there is a change. Unfortunately I will be separated from Wilhelm Becker. We say good-bye by the fence and express the hope to see one another in Hochstätten in a better time.

He belongs to the first 8 companies with a different destination. I don't want to forget to mention that I met 2 other comrades, Walmus from Trier and yesterday the fabulous S/Sgt. Winkler, who was my superior in Montpellier. When I think everything over; these many different places in the past were really pretty nice. Why? Because I never was hungry!

How comforting to know, that at home they do not know, how we suffer. Oh, my Lord! Give me hope, so much more hope!

We head back the same way we came, by train, but most likely we are not going home. The night passes and we can even sleep a little, in the hot, sticky night, packed together like sardines in a can. At midnight at some railway station there is some water for us. Thank God! We rush to it like animals.

9, July 1945

Can anyone imagine what it felt like to see people walking with their families, enjoying this Sunday, and their freedom?

What torture to have to ride by peach and apricot trees, bursting with ripe fruit and not to be able to taste it? How would I at this time, enjoy eating the luscious strawberries in our garden in Sembach. How much would I love to eat a single piece of blueberry cake or plum cake!

O God, how poor we are! Lord, give me the opportunity to make up for this! I will gladly wait!

We pass Bourges, Moulins and are most likely headed for Lyon. Our provisions are gone, tomorrow we will be hungry; we still have water.

10, July 1945

We have no idea, whether we get to Lyon today or not. We approach the French Alps in direction of Grenoble. What fate is awaiting us? It's a good thing we don't know. I try to stand unless I am too weak and look out the small opening in the cattle car. This country is often like a wonderful garden, but neglected. The oats have already been harvested.

How ridiculous these people act! Everybody is running as if it meant to view a large exhibit of wild circus cats. With a few exceptions they are all hateful. Whenever they can, they throw rocks at us; the worst are the women. They stick their tongue out, make faces, and yell obscene comments. Even the children raise their fists. Nothing good is awaiting us that we are sure of.

The Americans have shamefully sold us!

It is raining heavily; it is cloudy and dreary. The countryside is charming, but my mood is not cheerful. I am very down and depressed and could just start crying. What will the future have in store for us? We stop for hours in the middle of nowhere and of course nothing to eat. What I would give for a little piece of bread.

At 4 pm, we arrive in Grenoble. The country is beautiful, but what good is that for us? It has stopped raining and the clouds are hanging above the snow covered mountains. At all stations hateful, mocking and sneering comments are yelled at us. Maybe we will arrive tonight.

Annecy, France

In Aix les Bain, half of us, about 1,000 men are taken off the train. The remaining ones of us are to be taken to Annecy. We arrive at 7 pm.

A beautiful, clean city, picturesque with attractive homes and exclusive residential areas, elegant shops and well cared for houses.

There are many officers among our captors; a major has made a good impression. Also, we have a decent guard unit. We march in 4 companies through the streets of the city. Everybody stops and looks, but refrains from any comments. They look at us curiously and almost pityingly. The march is torturous, because we are all so weak. We just shuffle along. Half an hour later we get to a clean looking camp with barracks outside of the city. The first impression is not bad.

On an open square there is a huge pot with soup. It is a good vegetable soup, ¼ black bread, and even some headcheese. Everyone is pleasantly surprised. The black bread is preferred; I myself like the white American bread better.

Then we stay overnight in wooden barracks, which unfortunately are so overcrowded, that we cannot even think of sleep. We sit and lie on top of each other, but somehow the night passes.

11, July 1945

In the morning, there is hot tea. Then the baggage is searched and unfortunately most everything is taken away again without consideration. This plundering I will not understand. I am lucky though. They only take my coat, my belt, my blanket, and my canteen. I hate to have these things taken from me.

I tried to play it smart though, I picked out a Frenchman, who seemed decent to me and showered him with a bunch of questions, got him involved in a conversation, so he did not have any time at all to search me. He frisked me, found no rings, money, watch or soap, not my shaving stuff, the flashlight or the coffee, as I had cleverly hidden everything. By the way, I was able to get another canteen and belt, even a blanket, almost better than the one they took away. I still need a coat.

In the afternoon we had a pleasant surprise, a hot shower, delousing and tomorrow we are to get a medical checkup. Then we will be registered. Personal information then entered into a card file and we receive the infamous prison number.

I am the "Prisonnier de Guerre No. 413727"

The treatment differs, partially friendly, partially hateful. Here in this country, the SS had too shamefully acted with violent rage and the people have not forgotten.

We are divided up into the various barracks and I immediately apply as an interpreter. Now I am in a better environment. I even get a room together with Sgt. Fenzel. I even have an iron bedstead, a table, and a chair. Oh, what it means to have a roof over one's head. In the hallway there is even a sink, so we can wash. Thank God!

Strangely I cannot sleep well, because I am not used to a bed.

12, July 1945

Work starts early. I have a lot of correspondence to take care of, write lists, etc. But it is satisfying. In the afternoon the first 30 men are assigned for work detail. They are not to be envied, because they are sent to the aluminum factory in Chamonix.

Woll and Weber want to apply for the farmers. In the afternoon 500 more men arrive. The food is OK, but it is always the same soup with water, carrots, potatoes, and cabbage. It cannot be nourishing!

I have already made the acquaintance with new comrades and a French adjutant. He might be of help to me in the future. I cannot expect things to get better, even in the dispensing of food. I would possibly have to work hard physically and not necessarily get better food. It is a case of luck.

There are characteristic pictures. In La Fleche, one could see the strangest beards the soldiers grew. Utter nonsense though, are the imaginative caps, which reminded me of carnival, what an undignified bunch. Now all of a sudden they are wearing caps with embroideries all around it. Some of them with names of towns or symbols for it, others put stars or wings or medals on them! How tasteless!

It gets late before I get to bed at night.

13, July 1945

I slept well! Had a strange dream. I saw my sweetheart, we were sitting together happily and there was a sweet child about 2 years old talking and chattering and she let me kiss her. Reminded me of our little Sigrid. Does this dream mean that I will be reunited with my loved ones one day?

A good day! A lot of work! Things are improving for me and I am grateful. I even was able to get seconds on food. The library is available to me. I can get a haircut, wash myself properly, shave, keep my clothes in order, and live again like a human being.

Last night I was able to read two newspapers. The shattering and distressing news about our country.

When will we be able to write home?

14, July 1945

French National Holiday

The tricolor flags are flying everywhere, the church bells are ringing there are gun salutes and fireworks in the evening. Better food for us: In addition to the usual, we get cheese, 1/3 of a bread and ½ liter wine. Everyone in high spirits, oh, yes, the hunger.

A new transport arrives from Andernach on the Rhine River. They inform us the Americans have released all the "Pfälzers". If that is correct news it is enough to drive us crazy.

15, July 1945

The First Letter Home

My best wishes accompany it on its way. May it get there safely and soon give me some good news, that I finally will be able to rest.

"My Dearest;

Finally we are allowed to write! (24 lines) Tell me please just one thing. Are you alive and well? I do not want to know more than that. Great worries about you since 17, March. Did Norbert's confirmation take place on 18, March? Is it true that Hochstätten was fired on and bombarded? Please report! I myself was taken from Camp Heilbronn, near where I was captured by the Americans, to western France. From there we were transported to the High Savoy Mountains south of Lake Geneve. I am content. Rations, accommodations, and treatment are not too bad. Work as an interpreter, therefore some advantages. Have you received letters? Have two buddies of mine from Oberndorf and Obermoschel visited you, they were supposedly released from Heilbronn. Many "Pfälzer's" are here with me. I hope to be released soon. Time is uncertain. I figure at least 6 months to a year. How are living conditions for you? Nutrition? Money? What is happening in Sembach? Mother? Richard? Norbert's school? Little Sigrid? I am allowed to write 4 times a month. If packages are allowed, please send jam, razor blades, cookies, and sugar. Please print address. No more than 24 lines of text. Love Eugen."

I befriended the two splendid pastors, the evangelical and the catholic one. There is a tremendous library and I intend to make good use of it. The first book I read is "Undine" in French and in German. Unfortunately I cannot get any French newspapers. I continue teaching my French lessons.

We do not know what goes on in the world outside. The weekly newspaper in the German language is the usual malicious propaganda. I received a bunch of tasteful recipes from buddies. It is like a sickness, the preoccupation with food, but I hope to present them to Rösel one day.

16, July 1945

Today another 40 men are turned over to the farmers as a work detail, among them, my friends Woll and Weber. Now we have to part after all. They are happy to go.

I got a pair of slippers from a buddy. Today we are supposed to get cookies. Could we possibly have it any better? The work is interesting, the accommodations good. Twice daily we get seconds on food, a structured life. I am content!

17, July 1945

Sometimes I have to think of La Fleche and how I distributed the American white bread, the corned beef, plus the lemon powder, and how exhausted and tired I was. Here I can sleep better and I do not feel so weak.

Slowly I get a hold of various new possessions, yesterday a needle, thread, and a pair of slippers, today a good sweater. The people part with these things because they know eventually they will lose them anyway. Yesterday we received 10 cookies each. What a thrill!

I finally wash my pants, which were in bad shape wearing them for three years. I am hit again with this weakness, because of the long standing and rubbing the clothes while washing. At night I make a discovery, which shocks and concerns me. Am I getting sick?

Could this be a heart or kidney problem? I suddenly notice that my feet and ankles are swelling up and that I can hardly walk, I am so tired. Serious worries get a hold of me and I am getting more and more scared. The night passes, but in the morning my condition is the same.

18, July 1945

Today is my medical checkup. The doctor examines me thoroughly and tells me, this comes from the heart. He prescribes a medication "Sympatol" and orders bed rest. The swelling has subsided some at night, the melancholy thoughts fade away, and I am hopeful again.

Maybe it is a temporary situation. For the first time the thought hits me, that with a serious and potentially life threatening illness, my chances of returning home again could be prevented. How have I, with my excellent health, been so sure thus far, that nothing like that could possibly happen? Now I can only wait and see, if my condition improves or if I have been damaged for life.

19, July 1945

I have read the book "Sorrows And Joys Of A Teacher" by Jeremias Gotthelf and found a lot of passages that let my spirits soar. Reading this book has consoled me and taught me to look to the future with new hope and faith in God.

Oh, if only I could get back to my teaching profession, that fulfills me so. What blessings could come out of it for the people in my town, for my children, what satisfaction I would feel and how happy I would be. And there is a sweet picture rising up in my mind, when I compare the wife of the teacher in the book with my loving wife. And that's when I realize, what a precious gem I have, in you, my marvelous little teacher's wife.

How you are the most wonderful wife, homemaker, and mother of my children. How you so lovingly uplift me, and how you are my best friend in good and bad days. How you share my world, my concerns, and how lovely a home you have created for us all.

May God keep you well and happy for me.

20, July 1945

I have gone back to the doctor. My feet are still swollen. He orders bed rest. When I ask for additional supplementary food, they laugh at me! "Don't you know you are a prisoner?"

In addition, at night I start with terrible diarrhea, which weakens even more. It has become an epidemic in the camp. Everywhere there are crawling and swaying forms of men. We have to get up every night.

As much water as we put into our bodies with the soups lacking nutrition; the body has to eliminate. I used to never have to get up in the middle of the night and now I just put one foot in front of the other, too weak to lift them off the floor. Then I stagger back to my bed. Luckily I can sleep, but that is the exhaustion. The nourishment we get is one sided, no fat, sugar or protein. The vegetables only contain water. If only we would be able to get some noodles or barley instead just potatoes, carrots and cabbage.

21, July 1945

I got up to take care of written reports for the very unpleasant Lt. Fenzel, who also happens to be my roommate. How I suffer under this raw and ignorant person. But I have to be content and stick it out to be able to keep this good position. Some of the other comrades are not doing as well. Many in the work details are mistreated, beaten, don't have better food, and have to work hard. The worst work details are the street construction, the aluminum factory, and the quarries. They are treated very badly, being beaten, and kicked.

That's how far we have come. I just hope I will get my health back.

22, July 1945

In the morning there is a service in the camp church. The ministers are all alike. They miss the most important issues. But my thoughts are at home attending church in my mind with my loved ones, so it still is an hour of celebration for me.

In the afternoon I lie on my bed and read. In the evening there is a soccer game, which the camp commander, a pleasant major, and a few officers attend. We get a daily paper and I fulfill my job as interpreter. There is daily fighting about food. Everyone thinks he does not get enough. People become animals!

At 10 pm it is lights out.

23, July 1945

Very often I dream of home. So for instance today, I had a reunion with my mother and I lovingly embraced her and kissed her on her forehead. I also see father, which is very strange, since he has been gone for two years. Also my sweetheart and I are together in my dreams quite often.

I have noticed something new: In the morning my face is swollen. Is this, another form of edema?

Last night I heard a beautiful ringing of bells from the church tower. I thought my heart would break.

Oh, the precious gift that I do not have anymore is **Freedom!**

I have suffered in 3 months of being a prisoner and more than in 6 years of war. The worst is the uncertainty about our fate. There is talk that we might be kept here from anywhere from 2 to 5 years. This is enough to drive someone mad. All the hope, the wishing, and despair does not help.

In a French newspaper they said, that German prisoners would have to stay for up to 10 years. What insanity! Of course, I would never withstand this physically or mentally. It would destroy me! What all is in store for us? It's a good thing, we do not know.

Yesterday, Sunday, I wrote home for the second time a postcard with 7 lines.

Again and again the beautiful alpine landscape fascinates me. In the evening it is the bizarre, steep limestone quarries of the Swiss Alps turned into soft pink at sunset. Above it, is an incredible blue evening sky and in front of it the green backdrop of hills and meadows with picturesque houses. But all of this is on the other side of the barbed wire.

Over there is **Freedom** over here is **Bondage!** There are people who become crazy over this, but I will master it.

Tomorrow will be a very special day!

24, July 1945

Helga's 10th Birthday

I have made this day in every possible way as special as I could. Awakening in the morning I thought of you, my big girl, with fervent prayers and with good wishes for your being well and happiness. May all these wishes come true for your future and all your dreams become fulfilled. It is bitter enough, that I have missed 6 full years out of your 10 years of life.

My sweetheart knows how I feel and I know it makes her sad. What has been lost can never be retrieved again. How I would have loved to teach you in the first 4 years of your schooling myself. You always loved school and read and write so well. It would have been a source of constant joy for me. Daily and hourly I could have been effective with my educational influence, give you good examples, lead and guide you, share all your joys and sorrows. Open your heart and mind for all the good and beautiful things in life. Rösel is doing the best she can in raising you, but the burden is too heavy for her to bear it alone without a father.

Most painful for me is the destroyed hope, to be able to come home at the end of the war. Now I had to have the misfortune to be abducted and who knows if it won't take years until I get home, if I get home at all alive. If the prayers of my loved ones will not cause a miracle, then a deep hopelessness seizes me.

But today I am cheerful like I have not been for a long time. Is that a good sign? I had saved some of the American cookies. Of those I eat half of one and drink some sweetened tea and imagine, that I would be sitting with you at the festive breakfast table, which I am sure, Mama has lovingly decorated for you. She will have baked a cake for you, will cook your favorite foods, and have a bouquet of flowers from the garden on the table. You will be the center of attraction today. Oma and Opa and your siblings will congratulate you, maybe a little awkward and contrary, with sibling rivalry, but the little "Mouse" I would love to see experience it. Then you will go to school and maybe you will be congratulated there. In the afternoon you will play or be with your friends or go to the garden and maybe Mama has made a pudding for you.

At night you will go to bed surrounded by the love and affection of your family. You will say your evening prayers, promise to be good, not cry so much, and think of your Papa daily. This is how my thoughts are with you and around you all day long.

I still have to keep up the bed rest because of my swollen feet, so I have a lot of time to think.

From a buddy I was able to get a fairy tale book. He was able to order it from a catalog for payment of cigarettes. It has many colorful pictures and you would like it.

I will try to bring it home some day and I hope they won't take it away from me. I read some of the fairy tales and imagine I would be reading them to you.

No sad thoughts today, no discord, a good meal with seconds, even quite by coincidence, some red wine and before going to sleep, the last half of the cookie.

That's how I close this day, your birthday, my sweet girl with a full heart and only one wish, that all wishes may be fulfilled and we can very soon celebrate a happy reunion.

How often do I visualize our children? They have given us some worrisome hours, but at the same time pure joy. Especially Helga, she is so close to my heart. But why is this so? Is it because she has so many traits from me? Or is it because she is a girl and supposedly fathers prefer girls? Oh, no! I love my three children the same and would be ashamed to say I prefer one above the other. But just this child, I have enjoyed the least, because of my absence and her pure and childlike soul, her gentle and sensitive heart, her quick, sharp and responsive spirit, her receptiveness, willingness and sunny nature have made me grow so fond of her and love her so dearly.

She used to misbehave and cry a lot, but then very quickly becomes loving and sweet again and there was no way one could be angry with her. At night I look again at her loving letters with colorful drawings, pull out pictures, and immerse myself in them so intently, that the world around me seems to have vanished.

1939 Picture of Norbert and Helga
(Papa carried during the war)

That's how I go to sleep with renewed hope.

Yesterday I met an architect and asked him about his profession. Often I have worried about Norbert. How much he would need my help right now with school and the sad situation that exists now at home. I could have helped him graduate his school. But then what? The choice of a profession! What highflying plans did we have for him! Would he have made it and why shouldn't he? We had considered anything from teacher, architect, forester, dentist, railroad, banker, and no studies should be too expensive. We would do anything and save, if only he would make something of himself. Of course I would be thrilled if he would choose the teaching profession and would be proud to have started a generation of teachers. He could take over my wonderful library and maybe he would have an aptitude for it.

To be state employed does not pay too well, that's why we thought of dentistry. Well, we shall see. As my mother always said: "Everything is in God's hand."

25, July 1945

The swollen feet have become an epidemic. It is the so-called "Hunger-Edema". I do not believe that it comes from the heart or the kidneys. Some cases are much worse than mine. For hours I feel quite well. The bed rest seems to help. Maybe the body will get used to it. I read a lot and I am content with my workload.

We have new cases of abuse. The buddies who were caught prisoner later have supposedly suffered terribly.

26, July 1945

I try to stop visualizing and imagining the wonderful and magical pictures in my mind about home. How the reunion would take place, what all I would tell them, how I would have to start slowly to eat and drink again normally. Oh, how often have I refreshed myself in my mind of the wonderful strawberries, currants, and gooseberries in our garden, all the favorite foods so that I am salivating.

My recipe collection is growing and I hope my sweetheart will be able to fix some of these wonderful foods for me one day.

There is also an epidemic of severe vomiting, diarrhea, and heart problems. Everything is connected to the lack of nutrition.

27, July 1945

Early in the morning we have a heavy thunderstorm. It is finally cooling down after the heat. I read a lot. I guess it is better to stay here. The food at the different work details is not much better and a lot of abuse happens. I try to get my glasses fixed through a buddy downtown. It needs a new earpiece.

29, July 1945

Sunday

A better meal with a little more bread. Fenzel is impossible, what an ignorant, unpleasant person, I have to stick it out with him as he is my roommate, or I could be transferred to a quarry. The treatment by the farmers varies.

Tonight we have a concert by our buddies from Vienna. A few Serbian officers are waiting to leave. Sitting, walking, and standing is torture, how wonderful to just lie down. Why do I feel like I have 100 lb. weights on my feet? The others don't do any better. I read almost a book daily.

30, July 1945

Yesterday we were allowed the first telegram. Will it be delivered? I fear the answer. What news will it bring me? I also wrote a card to mother with 7 lines.

Many hope to be home by Christmas. I am not such an optimist. Something is broken inside of me ever since the deceit and deception in Heilbronn. It was so decreed by fate and I was obedient, but still cannot understand, what my destiny is planned to be. I just want to be healthy and see my home and family again. But when!

31, July 1945

Oh, how had I visualized in Heilbronn, how I would experience a summer in Hochstätten and Sembach in our beautiful garden at the time of the strawberry harvest, then I had added a couple of months and imagined the time of the plum cakes. Then I imagined how I would fix up my schoolroom and was going to work with so much zest and zeal, in short, a thousand pictures would occupy my mind and then the big disappointment. I have been healed from that, now I am just resigned.

Sometimes my joints feel numb. The cases of edema are increasing.

We still have a lovely, hot summer.

1, August 1945

A new month is starting. What will it bring us? Our wedding anniversary on the 24th and the 6th anniversary of my draft.

What a beautiful dream I had last night. I saw our little Sigrid so content and full after her bottle, playing with my dearest. She loved and held her, and I heard her saying: "Oh, is she not a sweet little thing?" And then she had bought a record player for me, something I had wanted for a long time. Oh, if only these dreams would come true!

Working with Fenzel is getting unbearable, but I want to stick it out and will put up with some unpleasantness, because of my advantages with the meals. Yesterday we had something new, red beet salad, plus 40 cigarettes, which I will trade for bread.

2, August 1945

What all did I want to do at home? I wanted to start Helga with piano lessons, when she turned 10. Norbert needed my help so urgently with school, in order to be successful. Rösel needs me for support and consolation, and not to even speak of my poor mother. Now there is so much precious time lost. Every day and every hour is a loss in my life. It is this torturing uncertainty that gets us down.

If we only had a date! It could be weeks, months or even years. The hateful French talk of 5 to 10 years. Oh, my God, not even thinkable! Who would survive this?

As of yesterday I feel a little less weak. They fed us headcheese again, a change even if it did not look appetizing. In the night everyone is crowding the latrines. All that water! If only we could get some cheese.

3, August 1945

I had envisioned going on a bicycle tour with Norbert. I had planned to get some new things for our apartment; the paper with notes is still in my wallet. Everything in vain and useless. I do not dare to dwell on these "castles in the air" for fear that they will never materialize. Still the hope does not leave me for an instant. Yesterday I heard a Frenchman say: "The Germans will all die!"

Sometimes I remember an episode, when Helga was little and woke up somewhat distraught without her usual happy laugh and Rösel would say lovingly: "Did you have a bad dream?" and then the little "Mouse" without knowing what that meant, faithfully nodded, wrapping her arms around Mama's neck.

Later on I would like to remember, how many times I lay on my bed staring at the boarded ceiling in Barracks #8, always in thoughts of home. Last night I had another sweet dream. I had the first dear letter from Rösel in my hands, recognized her lovely handwriting, and was so very happy. In the letter there were pictures of the children. Oh, may this dream become a reality!

4, August 1945

The disillusionment is setting in. There is news, which depress us all very badly. A mail ban between Germany and Switzerland! That means we cannot write anymore and also cannot expect to receive mail from home. A new blow! Sometimes I could just burst into tears in gloomy desperation. Often I ask myself if my fate will grow ever darker, or if I just need more patience to endure it.

How is my poor sweetheart bearing it, when others come home but not I?

In the Camp Andernach on the Rhine River, the Americans, these hypocrites, have released all "Pfälzer's". And here the crippled, as well as the 50 and 60 year olds are still here, with hard labor and many sick reports. I have to be content and often some good buddies from the kitchen sneak a few raw carrots and onions to me. Oh, the hunger!

If my children could see the humiliating way we lick out the dish with our finger. We can fill up our stomachs with water, but lack the most important nutrients, especially the fat.

How must the burden of responsibility rest heavily on your weak shoulders, my dear precious wife. O God, give me a chance to thank her a thousand times.

5, August 1945

Sunday always was a very special day; because that's the day I wanted to write home. Now that has been taken away. What will I do in this hour? I will go to church and be with you in my thoughts and wish you a happy Sunday.

I am lying all afternoon on my bed and read. There is no one outside, because of the broiling heat. I am reading the German French edition by Storm "Renate" and an adventure story "Flowery Hell at the Jacinto".

My feet are still swollen, also this morning my face was swollen. I need to get some more "Sympathol" pills.

7, August 1945

A refreshing rain which cooled things off and helped the blowing dust. I am thankful to be able to work inside and not like some of the buddies. The miserable wooden shoes they were given are all broken and their feet get sore. There is no way the people can work like this. More and more are coming back from the farmers. By winter the camp will be completely full.

31 years ago today, my father went to war. What kind of a time is this, which our children have been born into? For 30 years almost uninterrupted, there have been wars.

As of a few days ago my joints, especially the fingers and elbows are numb. I wonder if it is due to the malnutrition. Last night a buddy brought me a little bowl with noodles from town; even though they were sour, otherwise he would not have been able to get them. I greedily gobbled them down. It's something different anyway. How will the French feed us this winter? The provisions are insufficient as it is.

In the evening we have a violent thunderstorm. Here in the high mountains it always is a grand spectacle. The thunder is fiercer, the lightning more dazzling, and then followed by a torrential downpour.

8, August 1945

Last night we got 4 tomatoes per person. Finally something different! But I had to get up four times through the night. All these horrendous amounts of water in the body. This can't be good for the kidneys.

It is still coming down in buckets. I feel sorry for the buddies, who have to work outside in those wooden shoes. I cannot complain. I am running out of cigarettes, which I am trading for bread. Still I am hungry all the time and in addition this constant weakness. I was only in the kitchen twice and the second time I did not think I would make it back, that's how heavy my legs were.

This morning it is cool and I put on my sweater. My homesickness is beginning to border on fetishism. So, for example I do not pull on my sweater as I always have, but the way my sweetheart taught the children, put the arms first into the sleeves, and then pull it over the head. And while I do this, such a sweet pain and longing goes through my heart that I think I am going to die. I torture myself this way and build myself up again, to be left again with only a vision and never a reality.

Yesterday somebody claims to have read that the French plan to keep the prisoners of war for 5 years. Dear God!

9, August 1945

Oh, These Useless Wasted Days

Outside it is cool and pouring rain.

I have heard that Russia has declared war on Japan. Maybe a conflict between Russia and America can be avoided. We hope so; otherwise, we will be here forever. No one knows, what goes on in the world. No radio, false and exaggerated news through the newspaper "Weekly Courier" with its malicious propaganda in the German language.

Every morning my face is swollen.

10, August 1945

I am so homesick for our apartment, our beautiful furniture, my expansive library, and my schoolroom.

The three books by Paul Georg Münch carry me back lovingly into the time of my own experiences as a teacher. To my observations of children and again I discover, that I frankly sense a calling, to be a teacher and only a teacher and again, I believe that there could not be a finer profession for our son, to also become a teacher. Maybe in our old days, we can enjoy it and just maybe it will be the right choice of a profession for him. But first of all I would have to come home healthy and happy, as I used to be.

Our boy never was overly exuberant, happy, and full of life. He is serious and sedate, sensible, practical and frugal. This all is inherited from the family of the in-laws. He is not tough rather a little too timid and soft. Sometimes I wish he were a little more aggressive. In some subjects he is having a hard time, but with my help he would make it. That's why I am so inconsolable, that day after day and hour after hour is lost. My Norbert is not a show off or a momma's boy, nor is he precocious or boastful. My Helga is no chatterbox, not a crybaby nor a smart aleck or making up stories. She is much too innocent and loyal, open in character and communicative. Both of them are sunny, wonderful children and the joys of our lives. May they stay that way and keep on developing in that direction.

A few days ago, **Russia has declared war on Japan!** They have moved 3 million men into Manchuria. Now maybe things will happen faster than anticipated. Mysterious Russia!

In addition to this news: A sensational development of the Americans, **the atom bomb.** One single bomb like this has wiped out a Japanese city and destroyed all life in a 100-kilometer radius.

Both of these facts may possibly prevent a war conflict between Russia and America. Therefore we have new hope, that maybe there will not be a war on German soil and here in France no communist revolution, which would get us caught in the middle. Many hope for this case scenario, but I am concerned.

11, August 1945

A second Atom Bomb has leveled the city of **Nagasaki. Japan has capitulated.**

The War Is Over!

This morning I woke up with both legs swollen hugely. The left knee is so big, that I cannot put my both hands around it. In addition stabbing pains in my chest and my face is swollen as well. Dear God! Do not let me get sick. It is the only thing I am asking.

From Münch's book: "To be a teacher means to be a king in a happy land. Is there anything more precious on earth, than to guide young lives and accompany them like young butterflies on their first flight into the world?" I wanted to accompany my own children this way for the years of their childhood. I would like them to have memories of a happy and sunny childhood later on in their lives.

It is 4 pm and from the church tower over there the bells are ringing during the Saturday afternoon. I feel like my heart is going to break

12, August 1945

Even though I have promised myself many times not to visualize lovely pictures of home, I just cannot help myself, especially on a Sunday. That's when the intensity of being homesick seems to consume me totally and I lie on my bed between 7 and 8 and stare at the ceiling of boards above me and let my thoughts wander to Hochstätten and Sembach.

What do I see before my eyes? Our beautiful bedroom with the light green wallpaper, the fluffy snow white curtains, and our attractive furniture; and then, the good morning kiss from my sweetheart next to me. In the room next door we hear the happy voices of Norbert and Helga and in the baby bed standing up our little "Bunny" laughing and cooing. And now she wants to come in our bed and then a happy game begins. Helga slips in too.

Norbert gets up, goes to the kitchen, and builds the fire. Today Mama should get a break. Then she gets up, leaves the two girls to me and makes a good coffee, gets the children and dresses them. After I wash and shave, the breakfast table is set in the bright and cozy kitchen. Norbert has picked flowers in the garden and the Sunday cake tastes twice as good. Oh, what I would give for just one single piece of homemade plum cake.

Now the sun is shining into the kitchen, on the radio, there is nice music, the children are playing outside, and I am working at my desk. Mother comes by for a chat and to enjoy the grandchildren. My sweetheart is cheerful and is happily busy cooking dinner.

Then we enjoy a wonderful meal of rouladen (rolled beef) with potatoes and peas and carrots, but first a markklöschen suppe (marrow ball soup) and I enjoy the comfort and love of my home.

Helga reverently says grace at the table. Then I smoke a good cigar, play the piano and later on we go for a walk to Kaiserstrasse. A good afternoon coffee increases the happy mood and in the evening, after the children have gone to bed there is a time to talk sitting on the bench in the balmy summer night in front of the house.

Dear God! Is it possible, that life could be this beautiful? Am I not worthy of this? What have I done that you punish me so? I want to be humble and modest, if you just give me back my happiness. I will gladly wait months and be patient, just bring me home again.

13, August 1945

My face is swollen again, my urine was tested, and the kidneys are OK. They call it "camp sickness."

Today we got the newspaper with its malicious propaganda. It said in there that France is planning to have 1 million prisoners doing slave labor by 1946.

Oh, dear God! That means no returning home!

14, August 1945

An anniversary! A year ago today the P-38 Lightning attack on our command post "Oedipus". The details of this dreadful day are forever etched in my mind, even here in prison. A miracle had happened!

Last night we get another bad thunderstorm with heavy rain. How strange, that I dream of my father so often. I also saw Richard in my dream. How is he doing? Where might he be? Is he in Russian prison camp? Is he still alive? May be he is even at home.

Yesterday we had ¼ bread and tomatoes. Everyone was excited. With a little onion and salt I made a tomato salad.

The mountaintops are covered with low hanging clouds.

15, August 1945

I guess it is better to have swollen feet than suffering with boils. Half of the buddies have this affliction. There are some whose whole body is covered with these boils. It's also a sign of malnutrition.

Today they gave us some grapes. Hopefully we will get them more often. What we lack is sugar. The "tea" is just colored water. During the night I have to get up 4 times, all that water.

Again my thoughts roam across the distance home. I just cannot prevent it. I need these illusions and wishful thoughts to console myself. The theme: An August Sunday in Hochstätten. We awake happily with the little sweetheart in her baby bed standing up and jumping with glee. Then the good morning hello from the 2 older ones, drinking coffee, and reading the Sunday paper on the veranda. Then we walk to the garden and Opa's beehives and then pick flowers. On the radio there is Sunday music and then we walk to church. In the afternoon a trip to Bad Münster, rowing the boat on the Nahe River and while the kids play at their favorite playground, with the little one in the sandbox, Rösel and I sit on the bench in the shade, watch them, and talk. Later on, a piece of cake for everyone at the Süsse Ecke (Sweet Corner), a happy trip back, supper on the veranda, a good cigar, talking with my love, who works on her needlework. Dear God! Would that be wonderful!

Who can understand me?

17, August 1945

These days I remember Courthezon, the night in the machine gun nest, the freedom fires of the underground all around the mountains, that was the beginning of the end. Who still believed in victory back then was insane. I also remember the very nice French family, Courtil, who were so kind. I only hope, they did not have to suffer for it. That has happened many times.

Yesterday we got some grapes. As always we tear into them like we are starving to death. Oh, how vulgar a human being can become, when he is hungry, like an animal.

Today I feel very run down and listless again. How hard is it to bend down and wash the floor of our room. Also the washing of my shirt and handkerchiefs, plus the darning of my socks.

Now I realize, what tremendous work my sweetheart has been doing, how she quietly and lovingly without a complaint, fulfills the obligations of a housewife. And I have been taking so many things for granted without realizing what a huge measure of work is involved.

18, August 1945

The cases of edema caused by malnutrition are constantly increasing. Many are suffering from boils and heart problems or combinations of these.

We had boiled potatoes in the skin. A buddy had managed to steal some 8 to 10 pieces. We devoured them ravenously. Three guys have killed a dog and eaten it. No, dog meat I would not touch, no matter how hungry I was.

Is the dreary mood today due to the rainy weather? By July 1946, the French will have 1¾ million prisoners. Why do I have to be among the unfortunate ones? Always the same questions, the same accusations.

19, August 1945

Another Sunday Like So Many Others

A week from now would be Kerwe (carnival) in Sembach. Why do I think of this now?

All day long it has been raining. I am very busy since 6 am this morning to process 500 new prisoners, who are transferred from the Camp Chartres. The conditions are worse there. Everyday they have 20 to 30 deaths.

Tonight at 8 pm we have an evening of ballads arranged and organized by Pastor Brach. I envy these people for their zest, liveliness, and energy, with which they are able to accomplish these things. How I loved hearing the old poems, so familiar to me. How I wish my son had had the opportunity to be educated in the beauty of the German language. Also how necessary it would be to have good lessons in history and geography. How I could make teaching come alive for him about the wars of liberation and the war of 1870-1871, just as I have learned as a boy with my old teacher, named Weber. How enthused I was back then, for all this history. Or for instance, science, plant, animal studies, drawings of different leaves of all the trees, and art itself. Will I be able to make up for this one day?

20, August 1945

It is cold and overcast. If only I had a coat. I had bizarre dreams again in the night. I was together with my sweetheart and pretty dreams as well as ugly ones take their turns.

Outside I hear the sound of a threshing machine. Maybe there is one in Hochstätten in front of our door, at the neighbor's. And I cannot have any of the wonderful fresh plum cake they have at that time.

21, August 1945

Another anniversary! Last year we retreated through the Rhone valley and then encountered the attack at Valance-Livron. How close I was to death at that time and miraculously nothing happened to me. I still remember every minute detail and shall never forget it all the days of my life. I also remember the fearful night of the expectation of the terrorist attack in Valence. Too bad I lost all those things, especially my expensive Kodak camera.

Today Fenzel was intolerable again, but I always try to yield and make a go of it.

22, August 1945

Have I contracted boils? The first signs on my left middle finger. I hope I will not get this terrible disease. Some of the guys have their whole body eaten up by these ulcers. They are bedridden and continuously lose their strength. At sickbay today I saw a case of extreme malnutrition that was horrible. The man was only a skeleton.

Half of the barracks is sick. For a few days our city work details bring something back for us such as some bread or a piece of cheese.

We can write again to the French occupied zone, which means home. If only something would get through!

23, August 1945

I traded 3 cigarettes for a new pair of underpants.

24, August 1945

Our Wedding Anniversary

Sixteen years ago you bonded your fate to mine, you, my sweet wonderful wife. In all those years you have given me only joy and delight, you have born three lovely children to me, who are everything to us, you have never saddened me, nor have you been distressed or dejected. You have helped me and loved me and exerted your favorable influence on me without tiring. How, I have to thank you! Will fate give me the opportunity to return to all of you who have suffered innocently? With my most fervent wishes for your well being, plus good health for our children and us. I awake and look forward to the day, whatever it will have in store for me. Let it be a good omen, it is a beautiful summer day with blue skies and bright shining sun, just as it was back then in 1929. I celebrate it in my own way.

I am a guest in your house and you are a guest here by me and there is nothing on this day that will divert me even for a minute from the thoughts of you. How wonderful was our wedding celebration. Our guests, the happy parents on both sides, you so happy and beautiful as a bride and young wife, the church service, the impressive words of Pastor Zinn, the pleasant gathering at your house for the wedding party. After that, our honeymoon in Switzerland and Italy and the moving into our new home, which you, my sweet little homemaker had created so pretty and lovingly. Back then I did not know or appreciate your excellent talents and abilities as a homemaker. Through the years I have learned and found out and thanked you quietly many times.

If we should be able to stay together, I promise to put you on a pedestal and worship the ground you walk on all my life. May God grant us many years of happiness and harmony. May He keep us healthy and give us the joy in watching our children grow and develop. What more could I wish for in these hopeless and dreary days? With great expectation I am waiting for some news from home. May it only be good news!

The day brought a lot of work and restlessness, but nothing could deter me from you, my sweet beloved.

As if fate had planned something special for me on this exceptional day. We were able to enjoy some rare and good food, which some buddies brought from the Americans, spinach with eggs and ham. Fantastic! Also white bread, cheese, and a bottle of beer. I also cooked the rest of my bean coffee. This might be modest for some but for us it was a festive meal.

Now I want to look at your pictures again, after writing a letter to you and in the hour up until midnight I want to be quite alone with you, the love of my life. I will enjoy sipping the coffee and try to forget about my miserable existence. And you, my love, you will be thinking with a torn heart on this, our special day. Maybe you cry hot tears at this hour. Oh, I know your faithful heart, which is bonded in love to mine.

May God bless you and keep you for me and grant, that you and I can celebrate our next wedding anniversary together at home.

25, August 1945

Another Anniversary: 6 Years Of War!

I still remember distinctly how I felt sitting in Kron's kitchen for a pleasant evening and heard of the draft. It had hit me quite badly and if I had only known, what difficult and tragic times were awaiting our people.

What a good thing we did not know this miserable war would last a full 6 years. I do not want to get into the mood of moaning and whining though, or I will go crazy. I have to accept my fate without quarreling and just hope to stay healthy.

The small boil on my finger was lanced by the doctor yesterday and I hope it will heal and there won't be any more. When I feel my pulse it is alarmingly weak and slow. The heart is not able to pump the blood through the tissues, which is so filled with water.

I have read that 9 to 10 million Germans have been exiled by Poland. The Swiss papers write there is a famine in Germany. There is great despair in the whole camp. No hope for a soon release, the sickness increasing.

Today my letters are sent out. When will I get an answer?

26, August 1945

How strange I should think of the Sembacher Kerwe (carnival) so much. The suffering is enough for our children, who hopefully don't have to endure famine and epidemics. We want to be thankful if they have survived the war and our two homes are undamaged.

But what do they know about the joys of a carnival? They know nothing of the fun of an old fashioned carousel, of the stands with the sweets, toys, and a thousand other things. Of the festive preparations a week ahead of time, the baking of cakes and other specialties, the wonderful food and the whole exciting expectation. Especially, Helga does not know any of this.

How many other things do they have to do without, good food, festive highlights, trips, hikes, school outings, and clothes? Where is the sunshine for my children in their growing up years, which can be stored up for their later life to shine in dark days and warm the cold ones? How I would love to take them on smaller and larger walks through forests, fields and meadows, bicycle trips with Norbert, hikes with Helga or a trip by car for the whole family to expand their horizons. I would like to be able to watch my children play, especially Helga at recess in school and to be able to see how Norbert spends his leisure time and what his likes and dislikes are.

Hereditary characteristics: for Norbert, thrift, and quiet uprightness from mother's side, the nervousness and hastiness in eating for instance from me. Helga, the good natured and kind hearted simplicity, the tender soul and pleasantness from her grandmother in Sembach, her talent, love and aptitude for reading, writing and music most likely from me. And what has the little sweetheart inherited from both of us? I do not know. I do not know this child at all.

How vividly is the scene of my last farewell before my eyes, when she wore my cap and kept trying to grab for it and laughing with her mouth wide open so we could see the new little teeth. How I would have liked to get them interested and excited about the stage plays we used to put on in Sembach. Norbert had the opportunity only once, to have a part in a theatre performance. Helga would have been able to use her talent in acting. She is such a little actress!

Physically I feel a little better today, maybe because the sun is shining? Most of all, right now, I hope for some mail from home soon.

27, August 1945

I believe it is one year ago today, when I arrived exhausted, shattered, ragged, unshaven, and unwashed in Sembach and I saw our baby I had not seen in six months. I was so shocked how strange the child seemed and how I did not recognize her because she had changed so much. I remember so well, how she laid in her baby carriage in the kitchen, so tall and looked at me so strangely. But I got used to her so quickly and learned to love her so much in the three days I was there. What wonderful days these were.

At that time the war had not even reached the border of home yet. Nor did I know what all was in store for us.

28, August 1945

We still have beautiful, hot summer weather. Strangely my condition has not improved even though I get seconds on food. I always sleep well and deep. Is that the exhaustion? For instance this morning I feel very dizzy and weak again. Last night two buddies died again. Cause: malnutrition.

What will this be in winter? Last night, today and tomorrow nothing but green salad. Daily I go at 9 am to the doctor with the sick. There is so much misery and pain. What sins have we committed that we should have to suffer like this?

29, August 1945

The boil on my finger has healed well. I only hope, that my blood values continue to be OK. I am still dizzy.

Another thousand men are supposed to arrive. Where will they put them? The more people; the less to eat!

Outside of the camp there are reports of abuse and beatings. Yesterday Sgt. Mann returned beaten black and blue. The French newspapers write hateful articles and the word "German Boche (Pig)" is used continually and they throw us all in one pot. Germany and the German people are at fault with everything.

One of the buddies, who died, is buried today. It was a military funeral with a rifle salute, the officers accompanied the casket, and we were standing in line as guard of honor.

I have noticed with great concern that my short-term memory is not what it used to be. What is the cause? Normally I would say progression of advanced age. But now I say nerves, weakness, or my heart? What do I know? I know in order to stay healthy; I cannot let myself go, not brood so much. If I get mentally sick, I cannot get well physically. I have to try very hard to think of others, who are worse off than I.

I am convinced, that organic suffering is enhanced by mental depressions. This means, more self-control, more strength of life, more will of life.

30, August 1945

One does not have enough sense for the beauty of nature here, which is so awesome especially in the evening. Then the jagged steepness of the pinnacles shines in the red glow of the setting evening sun. That's when I have to remember the beautiful choir in which I sang during my teacher's seminary time with Prof. Faul: "Do you see the clouds in the evening sky, do you see the peaks of the mountains glow…."

If I should have been so fortunate as to have my own children as my pupils there would have been so many benefits. I would have had them start a little garden of their own and I can just see their exuberance in outdoing one another. How important would it be for Norbert to get a good geography education and his reading material would have to be increased.

Since I am a great nature and animal friend; I would have liked to open up the senses of my children for the beauties of nature. I would have talked about events in our daily lives, about school and community, about customs and applications, about getting along with people, about legends and the precious knowledge of music, in short, talk about everything in the fullness of my experience. Dear God! Give me an answer to all these questions!

In surging tremors I feel, that youth, love, and my homeland have given me the best that the world could ever offer me.

31, August 1945

The wound on my finger has healed well. I am not so much afraid of getting the disease of the boils. Also my feet are not swollen so much anymore. But my knees and thighs as well as my stomach are abnormally big and I also have a little trouble breathing because the heart has to pump much harder to push the blood through the tissue.

Often I dream of home and I always wake up happy if one particular dear picture has stayed in my mind. So have I seen my sweetheart last night in a dream in which she told me that she was expecting another baby? Of course when I awoke in the morning it was just another dream. But every dream, that provides me with pleasant pictures, means to me a new assurance, that I will see them again in good health.

That is what I believe in spite of all the doubt.

Newspaper articles report, very soon the German war criminals will be tried and executed.

New rumors: at home famine, epidemics, and confiscation of belongings and furniture. What is the truth?

We now find out, that indeed Germany has been working on the "Atom Bomb" and feverishly has been busy to complete it. But too late! What would have been better? I might not be a prisoner now.

I read in an old calendar how parents can best be influential in raising their children right. By setting a good example. Oh I know, that you, my wonderful wife, even without me, raise my children correctly. You will bring them up to be valuable people until I can come home to help you. I would like to take that burden from you.

Dear God! Shorten the time of waiting and bring me home this year in good health.

1, September 1945

Blue And Sunny The Days

It is not only the memory of the teachers seminary's beautiful choir; which began during my first few days in September at school. Remembering the wonderful hikes we did in fall, the bike tours through the lovely northern part of the Pfalz, in short, the memories of so many happy fall days in my childhood, that makes me sentimental again.

And last but not least the thought, that this is my sweetheart's birthday month. I will make it a special holiday, since it falls on a Sunday.

2, September 1945

A glorious Sunday, with the sun shining brightly. I have a sunflower in my room. Aside from being short of breath, which started a couple of days ago, I actually feel physically better and my feet are not swollen so much anymore. I keep reading good books. The last few days I had some extra food given to me by buddies from American kitchens. How these superior people live!

Such affluence and abundance of foods like all kinds of meats, including ham and bacon, peanut butter, and we heard they are feeding the ducks with some of these or toss them into the garbage. Such injustice and gross unbalance in the world. If only our families at home do not have to suffer from famine.

I make myself a nice day, no work, and what pleases me the most; I am writing you a letter again.

3, September 1945

This morning I feel very weak and exhausted again. I weighed myself and weigh only 120 lbs.

We have such beautiful fall days and I see in my mind Bad Münster, Ebernburg, the Altenbaumburg Castle, our vineyard up on the hill, and all the places that are dear and precious to me.

5, September 1945

My thoughts are roaming again back in time and place. The Farewell Celebration of the men's choir "Germania" 20 years ago in Hochstätten. I had taken mother, as she wanted to be there for this honor of her son. And how happy my sweetheart was. I was so very young then, but enjoyed this special success. The nice speech by Chairman Beck, my thank you reply, the presentation of the picture, which still hangs over our piano, being appointed as choir director of distinction, the presentation of the "Certificate of Honor" and the happy party afterwards.

6, September 1945

Last night the 47 year old POW "XY", from the Ruhr area, died. He had walked around like a living corpse for days now. The cause of his death: malnutrition, he literally starved to death and his terrible suffering from diarrhea could not be stopped. O God, how sad, such a dying. What a blessing, that his family does not know any details.

As far as the French are concerned, there is one "Boche" less.

7, September 1945

This morning I feel physically a little better. There are crazy rumors again. They are much too good to be true. Could it be this has given me more zest? We heard that by December, we would all be released and then the French would employ civilians. Let's just wait and see.

Last night was the memorial service for the comrade, who starved to death. How distressing and shattering. The cheap wooden box decorated with a few sunflowers, the solemn message of the pastor, and the mental pressure on us. We accuse the victors, who have made empty promises and let their prisoners starve to death miserably. We formed a guard of honor at his memorial service. If only his wife and children knew what was happening at this hour.

Woll and Weber have come to this camp. They brought me some bread, sugar, and an egg. Oh, what wonderful pleasures these are. I devour everything in a few minutes behind the wall of the barracks.

We hear that daily, more and more prisoners are released home. Why could I not have been one of the fortunate ones? Dear God! I cannot understand this. And now with all of its force, this built up sorrow breaks out and in a private corner I do not try to stop my tears. When I open my wallet and look at the photos of my loved ones, I think I will go mad.

8, September 1945

Oh, if at least we were still in Heilbronn, at least I had German soil under my feet!

9, September 1945

A Dreary Sunday With Dreary Weather

There is no other way, but for me to escape into painful, sweet memories and let my thoughts drift home.

Sometimes we are grabbed with a frightening force and it feels as if our thoughts are running in our brains back and forth like a captured wild animal. It is a very strange condition and it is described as "Barbed Wire Rage or Prison Madness". Maybe this state of mind is the cause of more and more frequent deaths. Last night another one died, my age.

In addition to the typical malnutrition there is a lack of purpose in life, courage and energy with an increasing hopelessness and despair. I have to fight against this with all of my being.

I will write another letter home.

10, September 1945

I had such a beautiful dream of Helga. She was my pupil in my classroom. I then took her to a large department store and just watched how mature she acted with grownups. I was so pleased and proud of her.

11, September 1945

Last night I dreamed of our little Sigrid, but unfortunately could not remember upon waking up what about. My feet are not swollen anymore, but my knees, thighs, and stomach are. I hope this will not end up affecting my heart.

12, September 1945

Last night I occupied myself with my big boy, Norbert. My favorite idea lately is, to let him think about choosing forestry as a profession. I have talked to a buddy, who is a forester, about his profession and I believe it might be something, he would enjoy.

Such a beautiful autumn day today! It is cool and foggy in the morning, but blue and sunny in the afternoon.

13, September 1945

I long for a fall day in the valley of the Alsenz. Last night in bed I visualized, as I do now, how a morning in Bad Kreuznach would take place. I would go on the same train that Norbert takes to school, enjoy the busy life on the "Mannheimer Strasse (the main business road)", and get a haircut at the barber Steg. Do some shopping, go to the Café Kiefer, look at the window displays, walk to the "Rose Island", and take the tram to Bad Münster. Oh, maybe it is not at all this way and peaceful as I imagine.

There are free people on the other side of the barbed wire. What do we feel? We do not want to see them.

Strangely, last night Oma and Opa were in my dreams.

14, September 1945

A new form of malnutrition, "Tuberculosis of the Eye" is going around. There are five cases in our barracks.

Today another 1,500 men are moved here. Supposedly all people over 40 years of age have been released. This is enough to drive one crazy.

Another worrisome rumor: "All 13 and 14 year olds had been drafted in Germany". I am very concerned about Norbert.

15, September 1945

Tomorrow will be a very special holiday for me, the birthday of my sweet wife.

I found this German Poem:

> I dreamt I was at home
> In Happiness and Peace
> I sat by the light of the lamp
> Together with my Dear ones
> They listened most intently
> To my tales of joy and woe
> The little one I lift him up
> And he whispers in my ear
> Please Dad stay here with us

With Mommy and with me
Tenderly I hold them both
And the world around me stops
Happy and thankful I look up
And see a blinking star
I take the hand that takes me up
Higher and further, so far
A pain and sorrow grabs at me
For way below I see
So far my child and wife down there
And I am so alone
Oh, I only dreamed, that I was home.

16, September 1945

Rösel's Birthday

I greet you from far away, my beloved little wife, and my brave partner in life. May the beginning and ending of this "book", encompass everything that moves my soul.

The fulfillment of my most fervent wishes for your birthday today and finally, a reunion in our homeland, so longingly expected. Can I look at it as a happy omen, that outside, there is a magnificent autumn day? With all the oppression and mental ups and downs, which continually darkens the soul of a prisoner, today though my innermost being is filled with such a quiet joy, cheerfulness, and a confident composure. I am so amazed. Oh, surely tomorrow will come the reaction, but today I will not complain and moan. No! Not today!

I will let myself become beguiled with lovely illusions and dreams. I will let myself imagine how we used to celebrate your birthdays in happier times and how you will celebrate it today. I know you will cry, my dearest, with longing for our harmonious togetherness and because you know, that I suffer and that all of my thoughts today are continuously with you.

The children and your dear parents will try their best to make the day special for you, as is the custom in our family. Norbert and Helga will be presenting bouquets of flowers to you from the garden and maybe a small gift. The little sweetheart will give you kisses, even though she will not know yet, why more today than usual.

What it means to me to be so far from you today, I cannot express it in a thousand words. I escape into a world of memories and try in my own way to give this day a somewhat of a festive touch. I even succeed at it.

I wake up with my first thought of you with a faithful prayer with all the most fervent wishes for your health and well being rises up to Heaven and my soul grows quieter and more hopeful.

Today, because it is Sunday, I will have sweet coffee. I still have some white bread, which some buddies brought me yesterday and I will open the little precious can of American butter, which I have saved for this occasion for a long time. The first butter since my capture!

For our main meal by coincidence, we get something different, some macaroni with meat. I make myself a dessert from melon and a little sugar, which Lisner brought to me. My provisions seem endless. I still can if I want, eat pears, tomatoes, and cookies. We actually have had an improvement in rations during the last few days and I feel physically better and I am not so tired anymore. The edema is still present, but the pressure in the area of my heart is subsiding.

At 10 am I have a chance for a shower and while Norbert Rölle and I scrub each other's backs I have to think of my boy at home. How is he doing? What does he look like?

Shortly before lunch there is a church service. Now I am sitting without my shirt in the warm September sun and read a special book by Eichendorff, which I found in the library. In the afternoon I listen to a concert performed by our camp with a new tenor, very nice and get myself a cup of grape juice.

The fact that I have shaved especially careful today and shined up my boots, is self-understood.

In the evening I fix myself a cup of real bean coffee, write a birthday letter to you, my sweet, smoke a good cigar which Zinsmeister brought to me from Norway, lie on my bed and let my thoughts drift home. At 11 pm I close this day, which was a rare and beautiful one.

Will I dream of you tonight?

Where I celebrated your birthdays in the last few years:

1939--------------------Wiesbaden
1940--------------------Potsdam
1941--------------------Beuville (in Normandy)
1942--------------------Paris (leaving for Corbeil)
1943--------------------Montpellier
1944--------------------Kleinhau (in the Rhineland)
1945--------------------Annecy (in Prison Camp)

17, September 1945

I did not dream of you, but slept well. It will be hot today. In the evening I went for communion in the chapel. This hour of solemn composure and tranquility is meant for yesterday.

19, September 1945

Today I feel very exhausted and listless. I can hardly put one foot in front of the other. In the night it rained and I had nightmares.

Norbert Rölle, the pleasant boy, who is only 4 years older than my son and has become my friend, has applied for work in the woods, cutting down trees, etc.

For 40 cigarettes I was able to trade for an excellent "Dictionaire Francaise - Allemand", from a Frenchman, which will be of great help to me.

20, September 1945

These days I have a lot of hope, but don't know why. Is it just a feeling? Recently I was able to speak to the camp commander, the friendly major. He was very kind and recommended for me to write a petition or application. He could not promise anything, but I work on this every day, to polish and give it just the right form. I have to think of everything and every word is important. Is it worth it? I will see! I will try to be requested by the schools inspector that I am needed at home. If only I would get some mail!

There are these fat, well fed, and smug people from the American commands, who have thrown away into the garbage what we would have dug out of the garbage just to survive. Now they brag and show off. What do these people care about family, wives, and children? They have no relationship or bond.

Frivolous jokes are made about German women and how they sell themselves to the enemy soldiers. They try to tell me that even my wife would be no different and "submit to the dangers of necessity". Oh no! No one can tell me this kind of stuff. I trust in you as I would on a rock. You will be steadfast and true and faithful, that I know.

With a convincing superiority, I reject these stupid insinuations. They are embarrassed and silent after that.

21, September 1945

It is an outrage that the French take things like shoes and boots away from our people and replace them with wooden shoes. These shoes are a catastrophe. The people ruin their feet with them. There are bad problems with feet in sickbay and there is no way these guys can work in those shoes on farms and in quarries.

I enjoy talking with two other interpreters, Klippe and Nietsch, with their good common sense. Actually my health seems to improve from day to day. Is it the little bit of fat that we get sometimes from the city work details?

22, September 1945

When I wash myself in the morning with my bare upper body, I sometimes think of you and how you washed my back at home in Sembach standing in front of the sink or in front of the bathtub. How you had the cold water run over your back, shivering with pleasure. You just could not get enough of it, my little duck. When will I see you like that again with happily smiling eyes? Another dear picture comes into my mind, how you asked Helga, when she was little: "How big is the child?" when taking off her shirt and get her to raise her arms up over her head, which she willingly would do and say: "Soooo big!"

Now pretty soon the little "Bunny" can do this as well.

24, September 1945

In a Swiss newspaper, I read, that only now the mail traffic is functioning again between the individual occupational zones, which means that at home they have not received any mail from me at all.

Today I heard that the Americans have released 75% of all of their prisoners. Only us poor slobs still sit here in France. What a crime!

Today it is pouring rain and an icy wind comes off the mountains.

25, September 1945

A year ago today we left the dangerous area in Kleinhau. I remember the farewell from the friendly family I stayed with. The town was completely destroyed the next day.

Back then the weather was beautiful and today it is pouring rain and in the mountain crevasses, the first snow fell last night.

Today I submitted my request in both German and French. Will it be worthwhile?

27, September 1945

It is still cold. We hope this is not the beginning of winter already. We are glad to have been able to acquire an electric hot plate. This way we can heat up some leftover coffee or toast a piece of bread.

We will freeze during the winter without a stove. The weather is clear and bright, but in our barracks it is cold, we will not receive any stoves.

I have made friends with some gentle, sensitive, and talented people. A musician from the conservatory, a music psychologist, plus a few other artists, who try to preserve their refined culture. They suffer mentally as I do and we often talk and enjoy each other's company.

The broad average of our soldiers regrettably is of a low moral, spiritual, and mental level. No, these people were far from a "Master Race", but rather one of slaves and servants.

28, September 1945

A new disappointment hits me that threw me again into desperate discouragement. Yesterday all academy graduates and teachers were contacted. How revived I felt. Stupid me, how could I be such a simpleton. I just don't learn my lessons from past mistakes. Very quickly I found out that it was nothing else, but we would be approached to give talks in the camp on various subjects throughout the winter. Being angry and disappointed as I was, I had sworn to myself, that I was not going to participate. Abruptly my mood had sunk to its lowest again. There are times such as these, when being homesick is enough to break ones heart. In addition, there is the fear of getting sick. Any foreboding premonitions, which some people have, are not creeping over me yet, but it is the uncertainty, which depresses us so.

Sometimes I find some consolation in talking with fine comrades, such as Wenitsch, the interpreter of B-7, who is so intelligent and knowledgeable and thinks like me, with Klippel, a banker and Michel from Bad Kreuznach; Oh, my beloved Bad Kreuznach!

There is always a sound of home. Our mood is often depending on the weather too. So especially today I feel like just like starting to walk out of here. Not that it would do any good and some of them have tried it but no one has ever made it. They catch them, shave their head, and put them in solitary confinement for 30 days, then they are sent to the punishment drill at the prison Camp Balthasar.

If it is true, that almost all of the German officers were sent to Africa for 5 years, then I have more than enough reason to be thankful, that I did not make officer. Back then I was inconsolable.

Of the 102 people in our barracks, 47 are sick. Most of them with edema and there are worse cases than I. I am concerned though about my heart. I get short of breath often and my stomach is swollen. Many have colds. I am careful and wear my sweater. We covered the top of our room with tarps and old blankets and worked on it all day. It made it much warmer, but we do not have any sun, as we are facing north.

Outside, the trains are passing by to Geneva. Oh, if one could be on such a train!

29, September 1945

For the past few days, I have pains in my back. Does this come from the heart? Sometimes a paralyzing fear grips me, then I escape into prayer as my only support. Most of all I believe in the power of the prayers of my loved ones.

We fear the cold and dreary days of winter, which will surely come and which will also affect our state of mind.

30, September 1945

Sunday

I always look forward to Sunday, because I can write a letter home, even if they do not receive it. When will I get the first answer from home?

In the afternoon there is the usual soccer game. We have not gotten any fruit for several days and we miss it.

Stubbornly, the rumors persist, that all 40 year old men and above would be released soon. I do not believe it, as I have been disappointed too many times. I am getting terribly swollen in my face and my whole body. What is happening?

Now and again a lovely memory comes into my mind, for example, the prayers of my children. Has not Helga always prayed the old touchingly simple child's prayer: "Ich bin klein, mein Herz ist rein, soll niemand drin wohnen als Jesus allein! (I am small, my heart is pure, shall no one live in it but Jesus alone.)" I know, that all of them at home add to their nighttime prayers: "Dear God, bring our Papa home again in good health." Should a child's prayer of a pure and innocent heart be unheard, or be left unanswered?

I do not believe it!

1, October 1945

A new month! Now I am behind barbed wire for 5 months already. The weather is sunny and cold. We are already beginning to freeze in our room. Will we get a stove?

During these days there will be the grape harvest at home. I see you before me, the Alsenz Valley and I remember harvesting the grapes in our vineyard together with mother and Richard, who always came to help and the relatives from Feil. I see the gay and happy life, the joking back and forth, the breakfast sandwich that tasted so good in the fresh air, because as my father told me when I was a child: "the birds had sung over it." Down below in the valley the sounds of the trains, from far away the ancient ruins of the Altenbaumburg Castle can be seen and from our picturesque little village, the blue smoke rises from the chimneys. What a peaceful picture. Then the trip home with the grape mill, the hard job of working with the presses, heavy buckets and barrels, and Opa smilingly figuring his profit.

You will think of me a lot this year, my dearest. Maybe you will take the little sweetheart along with you if the weather is nice? And I am not with you and I spend my days in painful longing.

2, October 1945

It is very cold. The mountains are covered with snow. We are freezing in our room and hung some blankets over the drafty door. We are glad we have the electric hot plate. At least we can heat up some leftover soup.

3, October 1945

We are to go on a trip to Lake Geneva to load and bring back parts for the barracks. It was a quick decision and we leave at 12 noon. It's a beautiful ride through the magnificent snowy mountains. The trip takes 4 hours to arrive in Tonon; a hospital is located there. The lake is incredibly blue and white capping in the wind and thousands of seagulls are in the air. For one hour we ride east along the shore. Then we get to Evian. Here is where we are supposed to pick up the equipment. Over there is Switzerland. Happy people live there in peace. I work hard just to get warm. I talk with a French officer and several civilians. They are all very friendly and give me some newspapers, also try to give me some hope. What do they know?

At 6 pm we leave. It is very cold on the open truck, which is now fully loaded. At 10 pm we get a flat. We arrive back at the Annecy Camp at midnight. I am frozen stiff, but glad to have been able to get out once.

4, October 1945

Because my longing for my choir rehearsals with the mixed choir in the schoolhouse in Sembach is so deep and profound, I decided to join the newly founded choir in the camp. I do not have the strength, determination, and interest to lead the choir myself, but I hope I will learn something.

6, October 1945

The cold weather continues. The wind is howling like in winter at home. I wash with cold water and walk the camp roads back and forth. I want to keep myself fit and healthy. But why am I getting so abnormally big? Others notice it too.

There are alarming articles in the Swiss newspapers about famines and epidemics threatening Germany.

I am surprised about the indifference of many, who just live from day to day. Especially those from the eastern part of the country, who do not know if their families are still alive, if they starved, or froze to death on the long refugee treks. There were 9 million driven away from their houses and farms by the Poles and Russians.

7, October 1945

Thanksgiving Day

Another day I spend with all my heart and soul with my loved ones at home. Here we had a church service with communion. The choir sings two hymns and the French captain participates in the service. The pastor preaches insistent and seriously: "Has God not brought us and kept us by giving us our daily bread? We have not starved, so we shall hope, that He will continue to sustain us, guide and direct us." In deep sincerity I attend communion and think, that at this hour my family at home is also going to the table of the Lord.

I have learned again the meaning and sense of saying grace at the table and I have sworn to myself, that we shall not eat a meal at home, once I get back, without saying a prayer of thanksgiving.

Often I am drawn to the simple chapel. When the morning sun sparkles through the stained glass windows, I think of the church in

Sembach, where I attended all through my childhood and where I was confirmed. I later played the organ there, or directed the children's choir on Palm Sunday, or the adult mixed choir on all of the special festive days, such as Easter and Christmas. I also think of the church in Hochstätten, where we were married, and where I hope, my Norbert was confirmed.

The afternoon is sunny but cold and the usual soccer game takes place. At night there is a successful variety show with the French officers and their ladies attending.

With the help of our electric hotplate we can warm our food, brew some tea or coffee and I have a little more bread through trading my cigarettes.

The sick and 50 year olds are still here. As long as they are not sent home there is no hope for our release. The latest rumor is, at least 2 more years of prison camp. Oh, we are getting so indifferent and dull. We don't believe anything anymore, not anything good or bad.

Some of our men really let themselves go. They walk around like bums. There is a certain category of guys that just pick up cigarette butts and then there are those, who greedily dig through the garbage like a bunch of pigs. No, I would never let myself go like this. I still take pride in myself, I mend my clothes, I polish my shoes, and I wash myself and shave. I owe this to myself.

9, October 1945

Today all teachers in the French occupied zone were reported to Paris. What does that mean? Should I cling again to a piece of straw with hope? No, not this time! I have been disappointed too many times. Maybe it is just for statistical reasons. Besides me, there is Argus, who happens to be the brother of our physician, Dr. Argus back home.

Yesterday there was talk that the French were looting and plundering the homes in the Pfalz. Our beautiful furniture, my library! That too, we would bear.

In the afternoon we roast some apples on our hotplate. I have to think of Oma and how much she loves the warm cozy fragrance and how we used to put apple skins on the hot stove.

We made ourselves a scarf from a cut up blanket.

10, October 1945

Sometimes I let myself be consoled by comrade Michel from Bad Kreuznach, who is stubbornly optimistic and thinks we will get home for Christmas.

This morning there was a little bird by the window. Our children have been raised to care for the suffering creature and to feed the hungry birds in the winter, to be compassionate of the animals.

Oh, and humanity has become like monsters without pity and only seek to destroy each other.

11, October 1945

Is there not even a glimmer of hope for me? My request has been denied. It never even left the camp. This realization affects me so deeply and devastatingly, that I think I could just die.

I am physically worn, I have no appetite, I am restless, cannot work, don't feel like reading, in short, I let myself completely go. The tears well up and I am choking. Is there no place of privacy anywhere here, where I can escape to pull out my family's pictures and cry my eyes out unrestrained? Maybe that would lighten my heart a little. Oh, can't you hear back home, how my heart and soul cries out for you? Can you not help me?

I will try to keep this very bad and devastating day in my mind for later on, if I should ever get home again and in retrospect remember my thoughts and then my mood of this Oct.11, will vividly be before me.

Outside it is beautiful with lovely sunshine, but in my heart it is dark and a dull despair has taken it over. I best not hope at all anymore. In the afternoon I passed out orders and that detracted me some.

Actually I have to be thankful, that I can sleep. A sleepless night filled with thinking and brooding would be awful.

12, October 1945

This morning I awoke almost cheerfully. At least the first few hours of the morning my mental state seems balanced again. Maybe it is because I still live off a lovely dream. I saw my dear ones, most clearly my little sweetheart. Rösel carried her towards me. She seemed smaller and weaker, but laughed happily, but then looked at me strangely.

I have learned in the meantime, not to give in to such revelations, because my hopes are always betrayed, but then I should notice the consequences and effects of ugly dreams, which naturally I do not wish to be fulfilled. So dreams are but shadows. This self-deception leads me to believe in pleasant illusions, which is sufficient though, to push back the wild turmoil of my soul for a few hours.

At night I fall into bed dead tired and thank God, I fall asleep immediately. In the morning I awake refreshed most of the time. This night I slept well. I can hardly feel the pressure in my chest.

We have again an unusually mild day. The variety show evening is repeated and our choir sings again. The French are our guests and they are impressed.

13, October 1945

I finished the book by Eichendorff. As a romanticist he does not quite fit into our times anymore, but his picturesque language and depth of his mind quite grips me and was such balm for my wounded soul.

He writes for example of:

> "The slumbering earth, the silent crevice, the deep shadow, the sparkling morning sun, the golden tree tops, the fresh fragrance of the forest and meadow, of gardens in the moonlight, of the mysterious moaning of the forest, of the brilliant glow of the evening sun and the clear firmament of a starry sky, the cool loneliness of the rushing stream, the sparkling shores, the magnificent castle of gold of the evening, the intoxicating fragrance of the gardenia, of white marble statues and the dreaming emperor's crown, miraculous birds, the sound of the French horn in the distance, the nightingale's song, the gorgeous summer night, the sleepy fountains, the murmuring brook."

14, October 1945

I saw you in my dream, my dear, little Helga in my parent's house. I was standing with you by the window in the front room and told you, how the house used to look when I was your age. I told you of the thin clay walls and the wooden window sills, the view to the yard and looking across over the whole village and how it looked in the summer and in the winter time and you listened to me attentively, eager to learn, as you always were.

Connected with this dream, so many memories of my childhood surface. The snowy front yard in the old house, the activities in the stable and barn, the unloading of sugar beets and potatoes on fall evenings. My hard working father in the stable caring for the animals, my tireless mother busy milking the cows and in between, running upstairs checking on supper, which consisted of roasted potatoes and milk eaten in the cozy light of the lamp. In the wintertime, friends and neighbors would drop by for a bit of chatting about the latest news of the town. Then there was the magic of the Christmas Season, St. Nicolas, Christmas Eve in the sparkling clean living room with the freshly oiled floors, the starched and ironed curtains, the big tree, and all the presents.

There were mother's wonderful Christmas cookies and the books I became engrossed in at a very young age. How I enjoyed helping with the work in fields and meadows. Our plowed fields with the sacred earth, hot summer days, the time of taking the milk to the city by horse and wagon, the festivities of all kinds, the butchering of the pig in fall, the baking of cakes for us and the neighbors, the snitching of currants and gooseberries and so much more. Oh, blissful childhood!

Yesterday in the afternoon there was the opportunity to apply for a command post in the city.

Four men were requested for chopping wood and stacking it at a bakery. I was looking forward to getting out, but it turned out to be a disappointment after all, we were not needed, so back we went. I became newly aware of our misery and a deep despair gripped me. I saw people enjoying freedom, happy men, women, and children.

In nature there are beautiful fall colors now, the leaves of red and gold just like on our picture at home in the dining room. Oh, our beautiful cozy home, with its pretty touches and cared for by you, my sweet, brave wife.

Yesterday one of the buddies, Wagner, a city inspector from Kassel, who likes to come to our room often to talk, said: "Fate affects us old ones much differently than the younger ones. We have much more to give up, so we suffer more physically and mentally. Therefore we run into danger to be defeated and we have to put up all of our willpower, so not to break."

He is right. I heard of a man, age 45, who for weeks now has unbearable headaches day and night, because he eats up all of his anger, heartache, and rage inside. I will never, never get over the fact, that the Americans have shamelessly sold us out to the French with the misfortune to be one of those, who were abducted into a foreign country for an undetermined time.

The soccer game does not interest me; instead my eyes roam over to the mountains, where the leaves of the trees are ablaze in pure red and gold, just as they will be at home right now.

15, October 1945

We have the first morning fog. This morning we were awakened at 6:30. There are two cases of diphtheria in the camp with concerns for an epidemic is expressed. Shortly, a thousand more men are supposed to arrive. We wonder from where?

I still have 1 apple and 2 nuts, which a buddy brought me from outside. The apple I will keep until Norbert's birthday November 6th, and the nuts for Christmas.

The metal heel plates on my boots and the nails, which shoemaker Mai put on last March 12th, are worn down now.

We heard that America won't turn over any more POWs to the French, but what about us?

16, October 1945

Fenzel has another one of his fits, and no one can talk to him then. I myself don't speak to him and just get out of his way. That is best. Three of my letters were censured and they can leave the camp.

The food has turned abominable again, being indefinable green stuff and water. This has to be justified, if there is any justice in this world.

The Swiss Red Cross has sent a note of protest to the American government and stressed the outrage of the malnutrition of German prisoners in French camps. As a result of this protest, the Americans have stopped further deliveries of 300,000 more POWs.

17, October 1945

The first transport with the seriously ill who are leaving for home, including amputees and youths under 18 years of age, as well as some nurses and female helpers. To my great joy, Karl Ziegler from Langmeil is among them. He was all along, in the other camp close by, St. Pierre. I give him 3 letters to take home, one for Rösel, a birthday letter for Norbert and one for mother. He promises to go to Sembach and Hochstätten. Finally my loved ones will have the first news of me. It seems that not one single letter has arrived so far.

With great envy we watch the comrades, who will now definitely go home. Will the hour come for us like this one day and when? Ziegler is with me several times a day and I give him many instructions, what to tell them, and what better not. I want them to only hear good news, no need to worry and upset them.

There is a general feeling of anticipation and excitement in the whole camp and some of them say with great optimism: "This is the beginning!" That can be a premature fallacy, if the French send home the sick; that does not mean they will send home the healthy.

18, October 1945

At 3:30 am, the departure of the returnees takes place. Last night was a church service for them and it took until late at night to complete the formalities. Today they will travel via Lyon to Mühlhausen. My most fervent wishes accompany you, Ziegler, on your trip. If only I knew, what you will find.

In 8 to 10 days the earliest my family will know about my fate and that is consoling to me.

19, October 1945

After I said good-bye to the men going home, I went back to bed, feeling cozy snug and warm. I had to think of the many winter mornings in my schoolroom, when the fire was lit early, the stove was red hot, and the reflections flickered on the walls. There again was the uncontrollable longing for the smell of the air in my schoolroom, like the smell of chalk, stove polish, and oil on the wooden floor. I see my schoolroom before my eyes: The bell has not yet rung.

Downstairs from our kitchen the wonderful smell of coffee wafts up here. The little ones are still asleep, only Norbert sits at the breakfast table, the radio plays morning music, and the field across the road is white with early frost. Now the school bell rings and soon the many feet of the children trampling up the stairs can be heard. Happy laughing voices fill the whole house.

Then I begin teaching my four grades, 5th through 8th, in one schoolroom. About 9 o'clock the door opens up and there is my "Murschel". With an innocent trusting look on her face she says: "May I come in for a little while?" Who could say no to such a question? She "clip-clops" over to the blackboard, climbs on the footstool, turns to me and says: "have chalk?" I give her the chalk and sponge and then she begins her "drawings". As soon as she has made a few circles and lines, they are erased and new ones are made, until she gets tired of this game.

Helga sitting at the school desk next to her brother Norbert

Then she says: "have reading book?" Now she is quiet for a while. She sits in the last bench and "reads" by hastily turning the pages of the book. Then suddenly with a fine ear she hears the sound of the coffee mill downstairs from the kitchen. Now there is no holding her. The book is flung to the side, she runs to the door, turns around to me one more time quickly to shout: "Mama cooking coffee!" and runs out the door much to the roaring and amusement of the kids.

Oh, what happy days were these! Shall they never come back again? Now that my children have grown up, I hope I will be repaid with our little Sigrid. All these memories are so painfully sweet, that they almost hurt physically.

Fenzel's tantrums are over and as of today I can wrap him around my finger again. What a strange bird he is.

I am short of breath again; have aching in my back, and stabbing pains in my chest. Those who are written up with a "C" are possibly seriously ill and might be lucky to get home. But I want to stay healthy and rather be patient and wait, than be sent home a sick man.

20, October 1945

Today there are elections in France. Will that have any kind of an influence on our fate?

We were promised a stove for winter. I personally requested it from the French Lieutenant.

My thoughts these days move around the one and only subject: Has Ziegler made it home yet? It always is a joy for me to write in my diary, because I imagine, it brings me closer to you, my dear ones.

Jakob Neu from Sembach has sent greetings to me. He is with a wood chopping detail high in the mountains. He wants to know when we get to go home. What shall I tell him?

Last night we performed a wonderful Goethe-Beethoven Show with the participation of our choir. The interpretation was perfect and left quite an impression with the French officers and their ladies.

I made a good trade, 5 cigarettes for 100 Francs (camp money) or more like a coupon, for which I could buy some grape juice. Today we got American cookies and better food. The Americans have provided 2 truckloads of additional provisions in response to the protest of the Red Cross. The food situation is supposed to get better.

I myself suffer in the last few days with increased shortness of breath. I will have to go to the doctor tomorrow.

22, October 1945

The political situation in the whole world seems extremely volatile and worrisome. There are extreme tensions between the West and Russia. Could that lead to a 3rd world war? For God's sakes, we hope not!

Humanity has been struck with blindness. Should the West indeed be doomed to devastation? If there should be a civil war breaking out here, we would be in the greatest danger with a possible war with atom bombs? Oh, my God, no! We want peace, finally, finally some peace!

In view of these restless times I cannot understand, how some people can just live from day to day, laughing, playing soccer and making stupid jokes. My thoughts and those of many other worthy people of my age, centers around their home life.

This evening there is a repetition of the "Goethe-Beethoven" evening. I especially liked one part of the presentations: "Closeness of the Beloved." "I am near to you, though yet so far".

23, October 1945

I remember Oma's picture at home: "He, who watches over you, slumbers not, nor sleeps." To be honest, since my capture I have often had my doubts, but maybe I am just too impatient. One hope after the other expires. The expectation to be home for Christmas looks very dim.

I am reading the book "The Last Mohegan" by Cooper. The book does not make the same impression as it did when I read it as a boy the first time.

The 2nd transport is leaving for home: Only the wounded and very sick. One guy from Wörrstadt is taking a letter for me.

24, October 1945

I am not free from superstition. In all kinds of situations and signs, I see clues for the future. Am I childish or are there reasons? Depending on different observations, I expect either a good or a bad omen. One thing is strange though, in all of my hoping, no matter how minute it might be, I have always been betrayed and disappointed the last moment; that's why I continually keep slipping back into this new apathy.

I had thought about asking the doctor to mark me a "C", as my breathing, heart, stomach, etc. is not in the best condition, then I find out, that the next transport of "C" people are not sent home, but were sent to an American camp in Marseille. O God, anything but that.

I have to be resigned to the fact, that I am one of 600,000 slave workers of the French, while the other 6 to 8 million will most likely have been sent home.

I enjoy the relationship with Klippel, Nietsch, and Michels from Bad Kreuznach. They are 3 intelligent people with a decent character. They see things objectively and rationally, which is the only way to get us over these deep and dangerous depressions.

25, October 1945

Last night was stormy and cold with the tops of the mountains white again and it looks like an alpine countryside. More and more, I become convinced, that I have to spend the winter here. I will not complain. I have a roof over my head and eat better than some. I don't have to work too hard physically.

Yesterday, for the first time we received some new American provisions: Noodles and stewed fruit. With the stewed fruit, I had to think of home, how mother or my sweetheart would serve this to me. Oh, what a difference!

I have recuperated from the weakness quite well, but my heart still concerns me.

26, October 1945

This morning I awoke again with a heavy heart. I just cannot help it. In addition, there is a new rumor: All POWs to Africa! How did this rumor start? Most likely in connection with the tensions between America and Russia, which are increasing daily.

It is unthinkable, if this would happen to me. Then it would be irrevocably clear to me, that my entire faith and belief in a higher heavenly power, who listens to prayers, was a mistake. I still identify with the biblical Jacob, who said: "Lord, I do not leave you, you bless me." Therefore I do not give up hope for a change of things, although right now there are less signs for change than ever, in fact it has become very quiet.

I thought of the very successful presentation of my choir on a Christmas morning in the church in Sembach, and again, I am trying to tell myself this is a sign that I might be home for Christmas. A joke, a joke!

Maybe at a later time, if I read this, I might find these instinctive comments naïve. Possibly, but they are typical.

This morning another tune came into my head. It was the song, which I played to my father when he came to see us for the last time in the schoolhouse. Looking at pictures and when playing this song, the tears kept rolling down his face. Did he feel the closeness of his death? The song was the beautiful old Irish song: "Long, Long Ago".

The men go to their jobs in the pouring rain without shoes or coats, slaves with no rights, work animals for the French.

27, October 1945

After lengthy negotiations, we were able to get a stove. We will take care of the burning material. Now we can stand the winter.

The "C" people have thorough check ups. Should we not wish now to be seriously sick? How presumptuous man can become. No, I rather stay healthy and wait patiently. Everything else would be sinful.

I had a talk with the Chief of the Political Bureau Martin. He thinks before too long, many teachers would be released. Should I hope again?

Stilgenbauer is very depressed. He had hoped to be one of the lucky ones, but the doctor didn't consider him sick enough.

28, October 1945

A sunny Sunday, but no sun in my heart! Our room is cozy and warm. I will not complain, thinking of the poor devils working outdoors. Could I have it any better as a prisoner of war?

Still I would rather freeze and be hungry at home than be in relative comfort here. The latest rumors say there is inflation at home. So all our savings will be down the drain.

I ask for nothing more than to stay healthy and that soon, we may be reunited again.

This evening my dizziness is so strong that I have to hold on to stand up, or I would fall over. Also the shortness of breath is really bothering me.

29, October 1945

A New Day Of Bad Luck

Is it not the fact, that today is exactly 6 months since my capture and becoming a POW, no, we are dealing here with an error in justice. I have been sentenced innocently to 5 days in **Solitary Confinement**. I am not calm enough to be able to write everything down logically.

In my inner most being there is an uproar I cannot describe. Such insanity! Now I have proof how totally without rights and protection we are as prisoners. The collision with Mr. M! The behavior and conduct of this man will be forever unbelievable to me. Now I wrestle with the terrible worries about further unpleasant complications even for my family at home.

I cannot eat; I am totally numb. I cannot even cry, which might bring me some relief. I am hardened with so many trials and disappointments and have become so resigned. There is now the very happy experience of the sympathy my buddies have for me. Many pass by my window and try to cheer me up. They try to console me and when it is dark at night many bring me a piece of their bread. I am touched.

I know I am on the right road and my correct behavior towards the people bears fruit. The first impression is the single cell. The guards, who know me, allow me to get my own blankets and my coat. I am glad to be by myself. I would not be able to talk to others about negligible things. I want to be alone with my thoughts. The night is cold and the bunk is hard. What a difference that makes. I have slept in worse situations in this war. Physically I will be able to stand this.

30, October 1945

The 2ⁿᵈ day In Solitary Confinement

By God, this is not a shameful humiliation, rather an honor. If only there was not the fear of possible repercussions for my poor family. How easy would it be for me to prove that I was an opponent of the **Party and the Regime**! But here I am surrendered and abandoned without protection to the whim and mercy of strange people.

What do I think all day long in that tiny cell? I can make just three steps one way then the other. In my soul there is a rage and I cannot calm myself down.

Comrades with some influence; such as the doctors and Pastor Bracht want to speak for me. At night some of the buddies sneak some bread to me again, also a piece of cheese. How thankful I am for everything. For a long time I am lying on my bunk and cannot go to sleep. Oh, if only everything will work out for the best.

31, October 1945

The 3ʳᵈ Day In The Prison Cell

I rack my brain, that I get headaches. There is no point. Spiess and Dame try to calm me down. They do not think there will be any repercussions. Oh, I cling to every little piece of straw. Many come to my window and console me, among them Pastor Brach and the doctors.

I have time to read. I am fascinated with the beautiful book by Pleyer. At one point I read "Our Norbert" and I am touched by it. We always talked that way about our boy. God willing he will be such an upright, solid, sensible, and reasonable human being as the hero in this book. I am thinking of my mother: "You have had so little joy in your life. I know how you are worried about the fate of your two sons."

I am thinking of you, my dearest. How fulfilling motherhood has been for you and how you enjoyed this little baby girl given to us. You were so very happy with this sweet child during my days of furlough and how thrilled I was with you, not knowing that we would not see each other for a long, long time.

1, November 1945

The 4th Day In The Prison Cell

The night was freezing cold, but a human being can withstand a lot. I believe I would perish mentally before I would physically. I have collected myself and become calmer.

In a French newspaper, I read that Dr. Ley hung himself with a towel in his cell.

2, November 1945

The 5th Day In The Prison Cell

I have so much time to brood. I had to think that 30 years ago today a bullet whistled right past my father's head. I remembered that as a boy so vividly. How often have I experienced this myself?

I keep reading the book by Pleyer. I try not to lie down on the bunk in the day, because I will not be able to sleep at night. The French guards treat me well and decent; they all know me. Tomorrow I will be freed.

Fears and hopes alternate. In this mood I am much too sensitive to come to any kind of conclusion. Most likely my secret optimism will be severely punished. I am though and always have been, a pessimist.

3, November 1945

The Hour Of Freedom

5 Days in the solitary confinement, innocent as anyone!

Shortly after 8 am the guards let me out. This was supposed to be the end of it. I am just glad they did not shave my head, as they did with most of them. I lost some weight but otherwise I feel well.

They all congratulate me and I take up my job as interpreter of the barracks immediately.

4, November 1945

Sunday!

I went to church in the morning. Then the devastating news, that there could be repercussions for my family after all. Dear God, what are your plans for me? I give myself up for lost! My insides feel hollow and burnt out. I sit at my table in silence, or walk around the camp aimlessly.

5, November 1945

When the fear and trembling is the greatest, God's help is the closest. Today I experience the truth of this word. I heard from Mr. F. that my anxieties were unfounded. Can I hope again? Oh, it would be too wonderful. Into my despondent heart a new hope moves in. I breathe easier, the tremendous pressure on my tortured body and harassed soul gives way to a pleasant new relaxation.

I look forward to the birthday of my Norbert with calmness and composure. 15 years ago, my dearest anticipated the big event with her bravery, I know so well of her. I remember that we actually ended up going to the hospital twice, how I worried about your precious life and how calm and composed you were, as if you had done this a hundred times.

6, November 1945

Norbert 15 Years Old

One year I was lucky to take a detour on my temporary duty trip and be there for your birthday. I would never have thought back then, how much more unhappy and sad I would be this year. We always consoled one another and said: "Next year we will be together". That's what you said in your Christmas letter 1944, dear boy.

I do not want to complain today, but will turn this, like all birthdays of my loved ones into a holiday. On the wall next to my bed hangs your picture, an identification card picture, and a sketching a buddy did for me, which actually came out quite good. I wake up and my thoughts are with you. It is still pitch dark outside. An unspeakable heartache ties up my chest. If only I could cry.

Never, have more fervent prayers been raised up to Heaven, as I express them on such days, when my complete helplessness is relentlessly before my eyes. While I am in no hurry to get up, my thoughts rush home. Maybe you are still asleep at this hour, my dear wonderful boy.

But you, my sweet loved one, will be awake and stare with burning eyes into the darkness, while your thoughts are with me. You will wish for this child, our firstborn, who has been our child of pain and sorrow, with his many illnesses, the best for his future life.

He has in addition to the worries about his health also given us so much joy. He is not a daredevil or the adventurous type, he does not shoot off his mouth, but rather is a quiet and serious boy of an upright and clean character, frugal, but a little sloppy. His soul is warmhearted, soft and receptive, even though he gives the impression of being somewhat reserved. Learning will not come easy to him. These sad situations that have been created by this miserable war, are at fault here.

At 7 am, having my coffee, I have to think of him again. He will have his breakfast in the kitchen. Having been congratulated by Mama, who surely is the first one, then Oma and Opa. He will grab his backpack and go off to the train station for school. In the afternoon there will be a special table set for him. Maybe he has my letter, which I gave Ziegler. Maybe he will work on his erector set. I remember getting upset with him, when he was not very particular and kept losing the set's screws. When I left in 1939 he was still a child.

Today he is a growing boy, who needs a guiding and strong hand of a father. I will never get over the fact, that I was not granted the privilege to exercise my influence on the most formative years of his life. I know that he is in the best hands with the caring grandparents and my wonderful wife. Only a refining influence is bestowed on him, but it is his learning and education I could have fruitfully enriched for him. I would have liked to awaken his senses and interest for history and geography, so he would have enjoyed these subjects as much as I had. I could have triggered his interest in physics and chemistry; there would have been so many chances during vacation time. I would have been able to help him with his grammar in German, had him do dictations and compositions. I would have worked on his math and opened his heart and senses for all the beauty in nature by pointing out the miracles in the animal and plant world as well as the cosmos. I would have influenced him to pay attention to all of life's continued experiences, which all were a growing one. I would have awakened his interest in a much different way, than some fossilized teacher or a young inexperienced girl teacher was able to.

I had even dreamed in my wildest dreams, to let him learn to play the organ. I know he would have enjoyed that. The conception of tidiness and order; I would have been able to teach him. Just as I was used to, carefully hang my clothes over a chair at night and that everything has its place. Even today I do not have to waste time to look for things and also that you keep everything, which is not always a virtue. I would have liked to teach him good penmanship and give him advice on how to take care of his bike. He would have to do each job with purpose and his inclination to handicrafts would have to be encouraged. Everything is gone, forever, forever!

A dreary, overcast, but mild day. The clouds are hanging low in the mountains. I just remembered how nicely he played the recorder at Christmas 1942. The joy of playing the mouth harmonica he inherited from Opa. I am with you all of this day, my dear, big boy. At 15:28 hours, the precise time of your birth, I steal away from the room where they make stupid jokes. I want to be alone and thank my creator for this hour 15 years ago, when you were born to us. You were such a precious gift!

The doctor, who delivered you, said a few days later, looking at you: "A great baby!" How grateful am I to you, my precious wife, for giving me these wonderful children. I want to celebrate your birthday, but all I have are a few nuts and apples that I saved for this occasion. I enjoy the American cookies and a coffee, which I have saved for special occasions.

A few days ago I had a talk with the dentist Wolf, who told me so many interesting things about his profession, that I am again contemplating the idea of letting him become a dentist. But that is a long way off.

The whole day is to be special, so not only did I shave meticulously and shined my boots, but on the stove there are some apple skins, which create a wonderful fragrance, which Oma always liked. It helps to create an atmosphere of Advent.

While I am still awake from 10 pm to midnight I see you my dear son in a thousand different scenes. I see the worrisome nights during your many childhood illnesses, with your little head so hot from the fever, your first steps on New Years 1932, your effort to talk, "goffeln" instead of kartoffeln (potatoes), your prayer at the table, the school time in Sembach and so many more memories.

The most recent memories are the trip to grandmother's house, where we stayed overnight, walking to Winnweiler over the icy roads at 3 am, then the farewell at the bridge in Ebernburg on March 12, 1945. What I wish for you, my dear boy, I cannot express in words.

May God above, who has so visibly loved and protected us, gives you His gifts, and fulfill all your wishes, which for you, your Mama and I, your grandparents and your little sisters, carry in their hearts today.

Good night, my dear boy.

7, November 1945

Last night I dreamt that Helga had diphtheria, but recovered. I saw how Rösel carried her, clad in her little white nightshirt, walking towards me and she reached out her little arms for me. What does that mean?

I have ringing in the ears, dizziness, and trouble breathing. After a checkup at the doctors I learn, that my heart may have suffered permanent damage.

I want to give Schönfelder and Haffner a letter to take home.

8, November 1945

Today would have been my grandmother's birthday in Mehlingen.

All day my heart is so heavy. Why? Is it the worry of them at home? I have to assume that my loved ones knew nothing of me all summer. We keep hearing, that Group #1 from Heilbronn has not been released yet, which means, that back in June, Rösel did not receive the message, that I was taken prisoner and also that my mail has not arrived. But hopefully Ziegler will have finally given them the news.

There is an additional pressure on us: The unrest and insecurity of the political situation in the world, the striking, the plundering, a new war in China (?), and the atom bomb psychosis. What will be ahead of us? In addition to that, the uncertainty about our fate and the constant worry about the family at home. Maybe, no heat for the coming winter, even famine or plundering!

It is difficult to feel any kind of joy.

9, November 1945

I meet many good buddies, who are sensitive as I am. For instance the musician, a few teachers, my dear friend Michel and they are all equally depressed and hopeless as I am.

Yesterday, Jakob Neu came to see me. He brought me a few pears that were not ripe yet. He has to work hard, the food is only just sufficient, but he does not complain.

I dreamt again of my school last night and that the school education department came and I was not prepared. Oh, if only that had been the case!

On the mountain tops, there is new snow and the landscapes are spectacular.

10, November 1945

I feel good and have recuperated, only that my heart has been permanently damaged according to the doctor.

I do not have to scrub carrots anymore, put onions on my bread, pour water from my canteen onto the food to stretch it, dig the potatoes from the dirt to secretly boil them. I am also not that tired and exhausted anymore.

That's all I really want and hope to keep, pleasant work, a roof over my head, a warm room, enough to eat, and decent treatment.

11, November 1945

A wet dreary November Sunday, rain mixed with snow. I have become so frugal, which Rösel taught me. Not the least little thing is wasted and I take meticulous care of my belongings. I want to be able to bring them home again.

Last night we had a political debate in our room about communism.

Tonight is a variety show in honor of the commander who is leaving. Our choir participates. Almost everyone is growing a beard, except me.

Today we got cookies, 10 pieces per man instead of bread. When I think how we got 6 of these cookies on the way from La Fleche to here for 3 days and how I rationed them. Those were the days!

Today I saw children's tears and smiles. It softens my heart and that of others. Our eyes were riveted to these 5 to 6 year old little girls of a French soldier, who brought them for the performance. One of the guys from Vienna put one of the little girls on his lap and kept stroking her hair, what may his thoughts have been?

12, November 1945

Rain and snow. I am glad I still have my boots and have taken care of them.

Sometimes I think, a miracle will still happen and I will be home for Christmas. There are bittersweet memories arising. The way Helga puts the spoon into her mouth, the way Norbert reads moving his lips like Opa, and also how he likes to put his hands over his ears, when noise bothers him. When Helga, just 2 years old, coming home with Hanna from the bakers, feeling sick, pathetically and miserably cried: " Heia, heia (bed, bed)". She wanted to go to bed, poor thing, feeling the fever. Oh, what worrisome hours we have gone through with these kids and their illnesses.

Your sweater my dearest, the brown one with the gold threads, pretty dilapidated, is my pillow, so this way I am very close to you. Last night I looked very carefully at your bookmark, which you made for me, little Helga, last year at Christmas. What a clever, smart girl you are. Have you inherited Mama's talent in needlework? I hope so.

13, November 1945

We have horrible rainy weather. There was an article in the newspapers that in the Ruhr area, English troops are preparing to beat down a threatening hunger revolt of the people with force. Poor Germany!

On the other hand there was a radio report, that in Mannheim there are soccer and hockey games, that all the sports activities are active again, that daily more and more prisoners are send home, that the Americans have released almost all of their prisoners. What about me? I have to sit here?

One of our people was on duty in town with a French couple for a few days and did not have to do any kind of work, but was just treated with good food, drink, and urged to sleep. There are such people as well and they just felt sorry for the pitiful German soldier.

Our faithful Klemenz! He takes care of us so that we do not do without. I will later, for sure, visit him in Lambdorf.

14, November 1945

The new commander is a good-looking decent man.

I have to be thankful for each day I can open my eyes in good health. Thank you, dear parents, for the good genes I have inherited from you. I find myself with many of father's habits, such as putting my forehead in the palm of my hand, or when I am very tired, be able to sleep at the table with my head on my arms.

15, November 1945

We froze for the first time. Outside it is white, as they say at home.

I have dreamt of home again. I said good-bye as I have so many times after a furlough. I saw all of them and they were very brave and I said to Rösel: "The children by now know, that after a while I have to leave again."

How depressed I am again. When August Wagner speaks of home, his eyes fill with tears.

There was an article in the French paper about the dramatic and cowardly death of Adolf Hitler and Eva Braun. This took place when I was captured and spent the night in the wooden shed in Bavaria.

I go for a walk in the sunshine. It is beautifully warm and I have a magnificent view of the snow-covered mountains.

I feel dizzy again and have stabbing pains in the area of my heart.

16, November 1945

I dream so much of the children, but after awakening, I have forgotten most of the dreams. Only in my sub conscience, the visions are still there like in a fog. So I saw last night very clearly the little sweetheart, because all day long I cannot get her picture out of my mind.

The hour is 7 am, and I am just getting out of bed. The fire is already lit and it is still dark outside. My thoughts drift homeward and I see my loved ones assembled around the breakfast table.

Klippel has received mail, dated October 23rd from Frankfurt. He is happy. I have to be glad in having this good working assignment, which does not stress me physically or mentally. I find diversion in books and in many conversations with buddies, who suffer as I do.

17, November 1945

I saw in my dream the 2 girls, how they were hiding in grandmother's lap with their hair cut short, playing "peek-a-boo". Now at this time Norbert may be on his train to school.

18, November 1945

Last night was the memorial service for two murdered comrades. They were abducted from their place of work in the city by unknown terrorists, taken to a deserted place, shot in the back of the head and thrown into the lake. One of them was a 42 year old man, who was supposed to have been released today.

There is no show today or soccer game commemorating the two.

I have to exist on the rumors, or I will go mad!

453

19, November 1945

An attempt to form a new government in France under De Gaulle was unsuccessful. There is fear that the communists will get into power. What will happen in Europe?

Yesterday I stood by the window for a long time in the late autumn sun and looked north across the snow covered mountains, where in a 700 km distance, I know I have left my happiness behind. Which has left me with a searing pain in my heart.

The increased unfavorable rumors and hopeless expectations have taken its toll on my psyche and I had to lie down for ½ an hour with a pounding and irregular heart beat.

20, November 1945

The Weather Is Damp And Unhealthy.

The latest rumors, soon all people over 35 are to be released. Oh, how we would like to believe this, but tomorrow it will burst just like a soap bubble. I dreamt, I was released and saw myself in a civilian suit in town, but the pictures were very fog like and miles away.

I was able to ask Zimmer from Kirn to go to Hochstätten and tell them, I am well.

The doctor has given me a bunch of new medications.

22, November 1945

Last night some comrades coming from the city showed letters from German women, addressed to Moroccan soldiers. The contents were shameful. An unparalleled lack of dignity!

I have to think of the pure love of my sweetheart and how she would never stoop this low.

23, November 1945

As of immediately, only 1 letter per month may be written. This is an outrage! If only that one would get there.

Hang in there my precious love, so that I will find you again.

24, November 1945

All the hopeful rumors are false. And I clung to them in my desperation. What a fool I am!

According to newspaper articles, 1.3 million prisoners are to be acquired, to help with the reconstruction of the country and we are to be included. What a horrible thought!

I had a terrible night and hardly slept at all.

How can I stand to be in prison from 1, December 1945 until 1, December 1947? If my sweetheart would know this, I think she would cry her heart out. What an incredible fate! Who do I curse?

It is disgusting to have to listen to those stupid, shallow jokes of F. and the commander, which they share on a daily basis. I would just like to disappear. What a superficial mentality, what little character. How dirty they talk about women.

Then I see before me your beauty and pureness of love and I would like to fly to you, hide my tortured head on your shoulder and cry like a child.

Why is there no mail from home?

25, November 1945

Sunday

I am worried sick! In the middle of the night I woke up with terrible pains around my heart. What is this? In the morning I go to the doctor. This morning it's a little better, but when I breathe I still have the pain. Dear God! Just let me stay healthy and bring me back home again.

In the final rehearsal for next Sundays 1st of Advent, I could hardly manage to direct the choir. I am depressed all day.

"F" is in one of his unpredictable moods, but has decorated a small Christmas tree. It means nothing to me. Even on Christmas Eve it will not touch me in any way.

I have no appetite. I cannot continue this way, or I will become self-destructive. I have to stay well.

In the evening we sing at church. I notice I am on the right road with my choir. Only in composing, Dornbusch is so far superior to me. He is a genius. He is now working on a very difficult Advent's cantata.

I would more carefully polish the individual parts. We sing from the military hymnal: "I am only a guest on this earth…"

I remember my grandfather saying this was his favorite song, especially in the last years of his life. I was amazed about the mentality of this ordinary man and he was not even very religious.

The pastor speaks about the 1st Psalm. I remember the three psalms I had to learn for my confirmation:

> Psalm 1: "Blessed is the man that walked…."
> Psalm 23: "The Lord is my shepherd…(my evening prayer…)".
> Psalm 90: "Lord, thou has been our dwelling place for all generations…"

26, November 1945

Good and bad days, happy and sad moods take turns.

Every now and then it bothers me how F. yells at people for every little detail. This is not my style. I have always avoided this kind of confrontation even in a leading kind of a position in the military and have always achieved successful results. This soft, sensitive mind and heart is an inherited trait of my parents. I am glad and thankful for it, because I realize that my conduct has lifted up my reputation in the camp. Everyone seems to respect and think highly of me. There is nothing like good upbringing.

Excerpts from the book I am just reading:

The personification of Sylvia is in so many ways reflecting my sweetheart. That's how a life companion should be. How happy is the man who has such a wife. One example: "Her youthful soul, that constantly was thirsting to travel new roads, her eager desire, to understand life in its truest form, made her an ideal life companion." His courtesy was always the same (towards his wife).

So much to be learned from this!

27, November 1945

What A Day Of Joy! The First Mail From Home

In the afternoon at 2 pm I received 2 letters handed over to me by comrade Zinke with his congratulations. It was a letter from Rösel dated 4, Nov. and one from Norbert, dated 11, Nov. Can anyone imagine what I felt, recognizing the beloved handwriting of Rösel's and Norbert's? With trembling hands I tear open the envelope and scan the 24 lines, they were allowed to write.

Everything is all right. Thank God! A deep inner calm and a feeling of incredible gratitude is following the tremendous agitation and anxiety I had felt. They are alive and well. Oh, how I had worried about them.

Now I have to be alone with my thoughts and feelings, which bombard me. Between the lines, my brave little wife, I read of your suffering and sorrow. I do not want to go into detail and the upbeat happy letter has consoled me so much. Mother is doing well, but not a word about Helga, Sigrid, Oma, and Opa. Hopefully I will hear in the next letter.

Very quickly the news spreads that I have received mail and everyone is happy for me. Norbert wrote: "We had 47 bullet holes through the house and a big hole in the roof from the American tanks." If nothing else has happened, we will not complain.

How happily I will go to sleep tonight.

28, November 1945

Sunshine outside and sunshine in my heart! I have a good enough reason for it. I must have read the letters a dozen times or more. They are under my pillow and I do not get tired studying every word.

The buddies, who were to be released to the Americans, are still here. They are getting impatient. On Sunday, two thousand more men are supposed to come. Where are they supposed to be put? This is getting to be a regular slave market! The care and food is getting worse again and there have been several deaths. Soon our wood for heating will be gone.

Another murder! The old man Goller, was found dead shortly before his return home. No one knows how it happened, but definitely was suspicious.

29, November 1945

I continue to feel upbeat and happy. At the moment, prison is so much easier to endure, than it ever had been before. Surely homesickness and bitterness will set in again and the disappointment, that I cannot be at home, because they need me so much. The letters go to sleep with me and wake up with me. I read them over and over.

How I have feared and yet looked forward to all these months for this first mail. I was so afraid; I would see someone else's handwriting other than that of my sweetheart. It would have devastated me.

30, November 1945

In the morning there was frost everywhere and in the afternoon sunny and warm like a spring day.

The wishful hoping, that we might be replaced, will not be fulfilled. The transport of two thousand men to be turned over to the Americans, will be leaving finally on Tuesday.

I am so glad my mother is still alive and I just pray, that she might be able to live to see the return of both of her boys.

Now I want to close the month of Nov. with many good wishes for the future.

1, December 1945

What will December bring me? At any rate, some days will connect me closely with my loved ones again. Colorful memories will surface, incredibly real, painful, and sweet all at once.

I know these days with my homesickness will create an almost physical pain for me and I will have to use my utmost strength to pull myself out of it.

There is December 6, (Nikolaus Day and the wedding anniversary of my parents), the Christmas holidays, New Years and then several memorable days from the past year.

Will I get some mail again from home this month? I don't want to be ungrateful, if I have the assurance, that they are well, I want to be content. The fact, that I am a prisoner and belong to those, who may not be released home for years, is maybe a punishment from God, but for what?

This evening we have the dress rehearsal for our Advents Cantata. I have tremendous admiration for comrade Dornbusch. I would not be able to do such an excellent composition.

On Monday, they announced 2,400 men are supposed to arrive. That means the provisions will get worse again. I have exchanged some French Francs and can have some bread brought in from the city. The transport of the "C" people to Marseille is finalized for this coming Tuesday.

2, December 1945

The 1ˢᵗ Advents Sunday

As of yesterday, there is an Advents Wreath in our barracks. F. did it and I must admit, that in things like this he is imaginative. I would like to know where he got hold of the pine branches. We found some string to hang it, also candles were whittled from wood and wrapped in foil, some stars from cardboard, also covered with foil, and so the wreath turned out quite nice.

At 4:30 this afternoon the presentation: Advents Cantata by Gerhard Dornbusch. It was a remarkable performance. The message of the pastor was too lengthy. The French were invited as guests, but no one showed up.

What happy memories surfaced: "When I was in charge of the Christmas program, during which I directed the choir, in the festively decorated church. I was proud and pleased in the knowledge, that we have done our best. What an uplifting feeling, to have a disciplined choir at your fingertips and to be assured of the enthusiasm of the audience. I know with great self-satisfaction, that I instinctively rehearse correctly with my people, direct them right and have good musical taste and feelings."

When will I be able to direct my choirs again?

3, December 1945

Again and again I pull out my 2 letters and read them over and over. I study Norbert's printing and try to read between the lines, try to visualize the mood in which the letters were written. I imagine, that they have worries and economical troubles at home, not enough to eat, etc. They should have me home now to be able to help them. I notice that Norbert's script has not improved any and that he is not sure in the punctuation. He tells me of things, he knows I am interested in, like his school, grades, Max, the turtle, etc. My fears, that the Americans may have captured him, since he was just borderline, age wise, in the Hitler Youth, were relieved.

Then the beloved handwriting of my sweetheart. I would also like to have a letter from my Helga and some scribbling of little Sigrid, as well as a letter from my mother. Only then will I have my mental balance again.

4, December 1945

Finally the transport of the returnees to the American camp near Marseille takes place. I say good-bye to many friends and ask them again for the promised favors of contacting my family. My biggest hope is comrade Brecht, who I know he will go out of his way. We wonder if they will make it home for Christmas?

During the night, the 2,400 men came from Chartre. I can see into what nameless misery our people have been plunged. They are all uniquely the same in their dull and gloomy despondency and hopelessness. The first group is a wretched and pitiful one. They are standing there like animals taken to slaughter. They endure everything, herded through the gate with a whack across the back. They just don't care. There are at least 500 youths of 15 and 16. What a crime, they are just children. Some boys are weaker than Norbert, why don't they let them go home. Would that not be the humane thing to do? I have to be quiet about that!

Shortly after unloading the transport, a 45 year old man died, lonely and pitiful. Nobody cared. Just one less "Boche"! Who can be made responsible, that this man, who was sick, was put on this transport, which he could not have survived in first place? The body is stored in the coal shed until a primitive wooden box is ready for his burial. Tonight there is to be a memorial for him.

This morning Zinsmeister came to the camp and stayed with me until 5 pm. He brought me some apples and a little bottle of schnapps. Those are welcome gifts. I gave him some of the wretched leak soup. We talk for hours of our young years we spent together in the little village of Sembach, the school time, the men's choir time, etc. I had to just keep on looking at him, here he is a piece of home, his dialect, his views and many other remembrances, that let the picture of my hometown evolve in front of me.

Suddenly he pulls out a photograph, which I consume with my eyes. It is a picture of my schoolroom, which I myself had taken in 1943 on a furlough and what do I see? At the first desk sits my sweet little "Murschel" next to Willy Rettig. I cannot tear my eyes away from the photograph and I have some trouble to hide my emotions. I look at the picture so intently, that I will most likely forever remember the details. There sits the dear child in a fluffy white summer dress with bare legs, her hair parted in the middle and on each side a pigtail sticking out with ribbons, her mouth slightly open and her eyes big and with a questioning look at the book in front of her. I cannot tear myself away and think my heart will break with the pain. All that is taken away from me. I had wanted to see my children in front of me at a school desk. There still would have been enough time for Helga, had I been sent home this past summer. For Norbert it is too late anyway.

I would love to have the picture, but Zinsmeister is not letting me have it, because his girl is in the picture too. I can understand him. Is it not troubling, that I don't even know, which grade Helga is in now?

When he left me at 5 o'clock by the "Salle de Service" I walk back in the dark by myself, and finally a releasing torrent of tears breaks forth and makes me feel better. No, it is not a disgrace for a man to cry.

All night long I cannot get that picture out of my mind and many memories come up. For instance when Rösel sometimes tenderly calls her "Little Rascal" when she was younger and how heartfelt she used to giggle about that. Or how Rösel said sometimes: "She is a crafty one!" Although being overall a very sweet and considerate child, she could also be quite spiteful and have a temper. I remember how she loved to play games of all kinds during those happy furlough times and was happy as a lark, when she won.

I long for her tender little arms to wrap around my neck when saying good night. How carefully they have learned to brush their teeth and I remember how Helga gargles. How she carefully brings the spoon full of soup to her mouth, so nothing will spill, how with her inborn sense of orderliness and tidiness, it bothered her, that a pair of shoes was not neatly put side by side and she got up to straighten them. How Rösel prepares them for a visit to the doctor, to open wide and say "aaaaah" so no tongue depressor is necessary and the doctor can easily look into their throat. I remember how Helga fearfully cried once: "No spoon, no spoon!"

I should be able to have an influence into her mind and thoughts in her daily life, be able to explain and help her understand. She would be so willing and receptive, that I know.

6, December 1945

This is a double anniversary, the wedding anniversary of my parents in 1902 and "Nikolaus Tag".

Last night we repeated the Advents Cantata for the newly arrived comrades, but it did not make an impression. These people are gloomy and not receptive. The pastor does not give them any consolation either. All he talks about is life eternal and the subordinate meaning of this life, but it is just that, we want to have a life now, where we have been betrayed with so much.

During the performance my thoughts wander home and I wonder if Rösel is telling the little sweetheart something of the magic of "Nikolaus Tag" and I wonder, what she might have understood about it.

I not only think of my youth and the custom of "Nikolaus" on the 6th, which was part of our young years, when someone dressed up somewhat like Santa and came to the house with his back pack, but also a switch, in case you were not well behaved. The children were afraid, but he always had some goodies for them anyway and the parents watched smilingly as he passed them out.

I also think of the magic of Theodore Storm's poem: "Von drauss vom Walde komm ich her...(From out of the woods I come...)". And all the wonderful customs, like singing the song with the children: "Dann stell ich den Teller auf, Niklaus bringt gewiss was drauf...(Then I put a plate out, Niklaus will certainly leave a goodie on it....)". I wake up as always with the thoughts of them at home and try to keep my mental balance.

By 8 am, it starts to snow; soon everything is white, the mountains, and the camp. How beautiful it would be to sit by the window, either in Hochstätten or Sembach and look into the dense swirling of the snowflakes. Soon, the outside light brightly illuminates our room. I am putting some apple skins on the stove to be reminded of the lovely fragrance at this time of year at home.

It is strange, how I always look for an omen of some kind, good or bad. That's why I am so happy, that two good friends came to the camp to see me, Argus and Norbert Rölle. They hit it pretty good with their detail and have a lot of stories to tell. Argus keeps giving me hope and I say good-bye more consoled again. Now my decision, which I am contemplating, for days now, has been made.

With my heart pounding, I enter the lieutenant's room and hand him my request and the newspaper clipping. He will pass it on to the commander and from now on, the restlessness does not leave me. As soon as there is a knock at the door, I jump. When I am informed, that the interpreter of B-8 is to report to the negotiator, I hardly get up enough courage to go in. Most likely my request is denied, I might even get a punishment. Thank God, it was something else; they needed me for the interpretation of a letter. The negotiator still does not know anything, I have only confided in Argus.

So the day passes and I am very torn between feelings and I do not dare hope. With my last thoughts in Hochstätten, I go to sleep with a troubled mind.

7, December 1945

I had a dream. I saw my sweetheart with Helga in the garden in Sembach and two trees with gold colored plums. What does that mean? I am very restless and nervous today.

There is still snow on the ground. In the meantime several buddies have received mail from home. Almost everyone is at home, even officers, only the poor slobs, who were turned over to the French, have to sit here.

The 2,000 men, who arrived here a couple of days ago, are still laying like herrings in a can, on the cold stone floor of the barracks, without straw or coats. They freeze, they are hungry, and they grumble. The food is abominable again. Yesterday they gave us soup made from dry, partially mildewed bread together with some spinach. Today there was no bread, because not enough was brought in. Luckily Argus had given me a piece. We are depraved and going to the dogs, some in rags, evident starvation and dull desperation written in their faces. What a crime!

This is a bad day again. And it does not help to read Theodor Storm's Biography and how much he is like me in his love for his family, his children, how he seeks to influence them in a positive way and refines their characteristics, teaches them, loves them, and is close to nature as I am.

Here are a few excerpts:

"The father occupied himself with his boy as much as time allowed. It was his opinion that it was of a great advantage for the spiritual and moral development of the children to have a few quiet hours together in the afternoon with their parents. Never would the children think of refusing obedience.

Often he could be happy as a child himself with his children. They often would take trips in the spring to the forests and hillsides, they would build a fire and cook breakfast and then they returned tired, but happy, they carried wild flower bouquets for mother and sang folk songs. He would read many books to them, draw animals, and tell them fairytales. He loved walking in the fragrant garden after a refreshing rain.

Every small detail became an experience for him."

The father taught his 11 year old daughter himself. Oh, why can't I do this with my little Helga? Once he said, how wonderful and rewarding it was to have children, and his eyes shone with unspeakable love and kindness.

I have two more good books from the library here, which I can keep over Christmas.

More than anything I would like to get some mail from home.

8, December 1945

Since 10 o'clock this morning, it is snowing again and the blanket of snow looks very Christmassy.

Today 200 more men arrived. Where are they supposed to go? I just feel sorry for all these young kids, mere children, ages 15, 16, and 17. They have become brutalized; they are unkempt, and totally neglected.

I blame first of all the Nazi criminals and secondly, the Americans, for taking innocent children as prisoners. How very fortunate, that this did not happen to my Norbert. I am so thankful for that.

Yesterday I was in the large barracks, which holds 450 men in one single room. There was no room to sit, to lie, or to stand. The straw was rotten and stinking. The people are dirty, full of lice, are hungry and bored, because no one knows, what is to be done with them. They rob each other, beat each other, and curse. That's what has happened to the German man. I have to be so thankful, that I have a roof over my head, a warm room and food, even though it is incredibly bad.

I am thinking of all the buddies, who are suffering up in the snowy mountains with the tree felling details with wooden shoes, or have to work at stingy farmers, who agitate their children against the "Boche". They too have to endure and no one brings them relief.

9, December 1945

The 2ⁿᵈ Advents Sunday

Now we experience the real "High Savoy" winter. As of last night we have a furious snowstorm with an icy wind from the mountains. We are cold even though I have several blankets and have pulled my coat over my face. If only we will have enough wood for heating.

It is a crime what is being done to prisoners here!

I worry about my loved ones, if they have enough wood and coal for heat. Maybe they are hungry and cold? The closer we get to Christmas, the more depressed we get.

The cawing crows remind me of the wintry landscape in Sembach, the fields of my parents and the earth, which was sacred to them. I am deeply rooted with the earth, an inherited trait from my parents and I would have liked to pass this on to my children.

Today I wrote my Christmas letter. Over there in the camp, they are singing "Silent Night" in a jazz rhythm, beat with wooden pieces on the table, and trample with their feet.

That's how low these people have sunk!

10, December 1945

A very **Happy Day!** The second mail from home. A card arrived from Rösel with greetings from Helga. Postmarked 23rd Nov. written 20th Nov.

Everything seems to be fine. One sentence pleases me especially: "In spite of everything I am in good spirits." What does she mean with this?

I am hopeful again. The food gets worse by the day. We seem to get nothing but beet soup, noon and night.

11, December 1945

This morning I saw, how some of the new guys were digging in the garbage for beet and potato skins and I remember when we did the same thing in the American camp right after our capture. The new ones are even trading their coats for a piece of bread. They rather freeze, than go hungry. I made a good trade too, a pair of good soles for my boots for 2 loaves of bread. Now I still have to have the new soles put on the boots. As of today I wear the horrible wooden shoes.

I would like to read good books together with you, my sweet wife. When will we be able to play piano four handed together again? Or have some family music, Norbert the recorder, Rösel the piano and myself the violin?

12, December 1945

We have a constant fight for heating material. More and more we learn to detest these people, who are now our victors, as they are not capable to solve the smallest problems.

The provisions seem to consist of nothing else but sugar beets, the kind that used to be fed to cattle and they have not taken care of obtaining burning material for heating through the winter. The mail problem still exists and absolutely nothing seems to work and there is no organization of any kind.

I would like to just forget these 6 years of misery.

13, December 1945

Another day of rumors. What utter nonsense is circulating. The withdrawal of the French occupational forces, the fairytale of the release of all 40 year olds, and older, etc. All untruths!

Psychologically and extremely interesting, is that these tales continually surface, even though there is no basis to it. They are all believed, although they are mostly made up. They provide comfort, consolation and hope for a couple of days, then just disappear, until replaced by new ones. I myself have become very cautious, although I listen just like every one else eagerly to some positive news.

This morning I don't feel well. My pulse is racing and I go to the doctor, who takes my blood pressure and gives me some more medication. O God! Just don't let me get sick!

In the evening I have some happy news. My 3rd letter from home. It was a card from 25th November with a few sweet comforting words from my sweetheart. They still have not received any mail from me and of course are very worried. They want to mail a package to me for Christmas, but that will be impossible, I am sure. Helga wrote a greeting, but I know nothing of our little Sigrid.

14, December 1945

Oh, Happy, Blissful Day

As long as I live, I shall celebrate this 14th Dec. that brought me my happiness. I will think intensively of this day 21 years ago, when

I arrived as a young teacher in my gray coat and little suitcase in Hochstätten, looked up the teacher Becker and his wife and went to Leonard's for my "room and board".

That evening I fell in love with the little village for all times. I had no way of knowing that within its walls, there lived the dearest human being, the wonderful girl, who was destined to become my life companion and mother of my children. How little did I know back then, what incredible happiness I would find at her side and how much do I ask now, that this happiness would be preserved for me and that the hour of a happy reunion would be in store for us.

It was a day a long time ago, much like today, frosty, and cold with winter fog in the beautiful Alsenz Valley.

Today at noon the sun broke through the clouds, it turned warm with a clear sky and I walked for hours around the soccer field to be alone with my thoughts. In my mind, this day past by me in all its details and I had wanted to tell my children and how much this day has meant to me, just so that the love they have for their mother would just keep on growing and increasing.

In the afternoon I was summoned to the lieutenant and I was afraid my request would be denied and handed back to me. But it was a different matter. He wanted me to report about the mood in the camp. He is very friendly and I keep up the hope for his consideration in my personal request.

How wonderful it would be to be home. **Good night, my dear ones**.

15, December 1945

Today is another day where my mood is at point zero. As to be expected, all the rumors, which gave us some degree of hope, were false.

The conversation I had with colleague Mattes, who is the secretary in the Lt.'s office, is dependable in his judgment and also well informed, has taken all my illusions away. He thinks it will be at least 1947 before we get home. He does have the hope that the question of the teachers needed at home would be brought up again in spring. Should I cling to this piece of straw? All these glum thoughts intensify and double, since it is Christmas time and especially painful, when normally there would be anticipation and a festive mood.

In a Swiss newspaper, I read, where they had children write, which were their favorite toys. The boys wrote of trains, building blocks and erector sets, the girls of course, of dollhouses and dolls. Oh, how I would have liked to get an electric train for Norbert or a steam engine or the third advanced erector set. He is still at an age where he would enjoy these things and not to mention Helga, the little "Doll Mother".

Out of 35 girls, who were 10 years old, 26 opted for dolls. Reality and play is so closely connected with little girls. Helga's favorite dolls are "Hedwig", which had been her Mama's and there is "Oskar" a boy doll and the many other big ones and little ones. The dolls are loved, scolded, punished; have their hair combed, dressed, undressed, taken for walks, bathed, etc.

I physically feel a ton of weight on me and I am helplessly entangled, from which there is no escape. Again I feel like my thoughts are running like imprisoned animals in a cage back and forth.

Today I kept thinking of my first day of teaching in the quaint little schoolhouse 21 years ago. How I loved looking out of the window in the spring of 1925, each morning at 7:15 am, to the bridge across the river Alsenz. Until, at the last minute before the train pulled in, I would spot my future sweetheart, and she was always late, running and wearing her black student cap with a book bag under her arm just to make the train in time. Only then did I resume my classes.

16, December 1945

3rd Advents Sunday

I enjoy a talk with my "Pfälzer" comrades and it picks me up again for a few days. Now is the time when they are baking the Christmas cookies at home. Helga was only 4 years old when I left and she still believed in "Christkind". Now all the magic is gone.

This morning we had frost and it was cold, but no snow. Just almost like that winter day back in 1924.

I like the evenings best, because I know, I will be able to sleep for 8 hours and escape my pain and sorrow. If I awake at night, in a flash the thoughts are there, and with relentless clarity. I am aware, that I cannot get out of this dilemma.

I heat some water and wash thoroughly, because the shower is not working due to the lack of coal.

Will you have during these days a "Dämmerstündchen (Twilight Time)", my sweet love, as you called these evening hours with the flickering light of the fire from the stove with your rich nature and soul? In my memory, we would sit together, the children on our laps, talking and telling them fairytales and you always were against turning on the electric lights, because they destroyed the magic of the moment. If I was home now, the little one would have to take her place in this, I would play "Hoppe Hoppe Reiter (hop hop rider)" with her, bouncing her on my knee and sing all the wonderful Christmas songs with her and so much more. Now in these precious days I would prepare my children to the coming festival of light and joy, do crafts with Helga, cut out and draw, and let her imagination take over. I would read to them fitting stories and fairytales and recite to them on cozy warm evenings in the true Christmas experience. Norbert is not too old yet and the little one could take part in it as well.

We would make special Christmas decorations and the children would secretly work on their Christmas projects, with which they would surprise us.

17, December 1945

I cannot get involved in my thoughts too much, because my work at the "Salle de Service" requires all of my attention. I cannot brood much and this week will pass.

Again and again, I have to be grateful, that my Norbert does not have to share the fate of these poor young people, these 16 year olds, and how they suffer and my heart is bleeding for them. I help as much as I can because I have to think of my boy.

18, December 1945

I have to think of the theatre rehearsals in Leonard's back room, the snowball fights with my high-spirited, happy, and lively sweetheart; oh, how vivacious and full of life she was. May this golden sense of humor stay with you and be passed on to our children. I see you with your ponytail and pink cheeks in your blue sailor dress, absolutely capturing my heart.

I have to stop, or I will go crazy!

19, December 1945

A year ago the miraculous incident happened, that saved my life (It was in Trier, House Esperstedt, on Hosenstrasse). Can I expect that you will continue to protect me, dear God?

All night we had a heavy storm.

20, December 1945

It does not look like we are going to have a white Christmas. Up in the mountains there is snow, but down here we just have rain and dreary weather. F. has managed to get a tree. When I saw it at noon in our room and smelled the wonderful fragrance of the pine needles, I felt a stab in my heart with the memories of home. My only consolation is the rehearsals with comrade Dornbusch: I enjoy his presentation of "Sanctus", "Gloria", "Daughter of Zion" and "Kyrie Eleison" and others. We are planning a Christmas Mass.

Presently, Moroccans guard us. The food is abominable. Nothing but sugar beets, every day!

21, December 1945

The Beautiful Dream

How bitter the awakening, and the rough reality! I saw myself at home in civilian clothes, said hello to all the neighbors, and saw my family around me. It was so incredibly real. Why can such a dream not be fulfilled?

New pictures arise! I would like to see the baby drink her bottle; I want to see her lying in her crib with her little white sleeping cap on, blinking shortly before falling asleep. I want to see the way she turns her head, how she lets herself be pulled up by her hands, I want to see her in her little rust colored coat.

22, December 1945

This would be the day, when the Christmas vacation would start in school. 21 years ago, I went with my class to the "Fallbrücker Wald" and let the magic of the season and the beauty of the wintry forest fill their souls. I told them the story of the "Tannen Grossvater" (Pine Grandfather) and of the little pine tree that longed to shine with Christmas lights. For my Helga, this charming story will not make an impression anymore she is already too grown up. Too bad! Too bad!

Yesterday we received the first newspapers from home. We were satisfied to read, how things are starting to look up at home, how everywhere the people are working hard, trying to get over the difficult times, how they try to make provisions against hunger and cold, with soup kitchens and shelters for the bombing victims. This nation will rise up again from the ashes and devastation and grow healthy again. What about our own individual fates?

In the prison newspaper there was an article, that the military government has requested the people at home to collect food and clothing for the POWs. What an outrage, where they have nothing themselves!

We had a meeting with the Lt. and medical staff, with the result, that the doctor needs to be less narrow minded and give more people the "C" classification.

Finally there is some coal again, so we can have hot water for a shower.

23, December 1945

4th Advents Sunday

I am lying on my bed for a long time and let my thoughts drift homeward.

In the afternoon we have a choir rehearsal. The whole camp is a mess with mud and dirt, as it is raining continuously. I don't care. If only they have a good Christmas at home. I wonder if the children have hung up their Advents Calendar, as is the custom and open up a little window each day? I would like to tell them, how as a little boy, I used to love to stand behind the house in the garden, looking west, where "Christkind was baking gingerbread", as was told to the little ones, when the sky was red with the setting sun.

24, December 1945

Christmas Eve 1945

I could write a whole book about this day and what emotions were triggered in my innermost being. Maybe the impressions will be so lasting after all, that I shall never ever forget this Christmas. **It is the saddest Christmas in my whole life.**

My entire hope, that I might be home on this day, was of course betrayed. How many more Christmases do we have to spend in prison? What a good thing our families have no idea that we may be the last ones to be sent home. But I do not want to dwell on this, not tonight.

Many Christmas Eves flash before my eyes and mind: I remember for instance the 24th of December 1944 in Wittlich, when I came so close of losing my life in the bombing attack. How we cried and begged for our pitiful life. That danger had passed so I do not want to lose hope now either.

We decorate the tree for our barracks and also for the rest of the people. Of course my heart is not in it and I am glad, that the young 17 year old from Mannheim is doing it. With a razor blade he cut small strips of aluminum foil for tinsel. From paper strips he cut out animals and other shapes like a moon, etc. We even got a hold of 3 or 4 candles and put some cotton on the branches for snow.

Our Christmas Eve supper consisted of a piece of headcheese (into which intestines have been cut up) some bread and tea. Shortly before 5 pm, I try to find a little spot to be alone. But there is no place except the chapel. I sit down on a bench, many others are standing quietly, or sitting down, their face buried in their hands. And then I concentrate all of my thoughts on them at home. I see them at this moment assembled around the Christmas tree and I believe that there are tears in your eyes, although you try to be brave and hide them.

Not too long ago I read a beautiful and meaningful paragraph in a monthly magazine: "I promise you on this day there will be no tears. It will be just as if you were here with us, the children should be happy, just as we have promised one another at the farewell. In joyous confidence, I will think of you, because my faith is unwavering." On another page under a picture of three darling children in their beds, were the words: "Six shiny eyes are waiting for the door to open and fulfill their magic of Christmas."

These words are spoken right out of my heart. Two years ago you were pregnant with our little Sigrid happily anticipating her arrival. You were so strong, so brave, and patient. How I thank you from the bottom of my heart. Finally the tension and anxiety is released in a stream of tears. Maybe I will feel better.

I sit there for a long time, remote and isolated, and everything around me has vanished. I visualize, how we used to celebrate Christmas at home, and I think of my own childhood. My parents had a little different custom than the in-laws. They used to put me to bed and later on around 9 pm I was then awakened and carried into the living room, where the Christmas tree was. I remember blinking into the magic of the lit candles and sparklers and immediately looked at the table where the presents were. Christmas at home always was a wonderful experience and those memories last me a lifetime. How fitting the words in the beautiful book by Kowel, "The blissful year".

The fragrance of the pine tree filled the whole house. I waited patiently in my warm bed for the arrival of "Christkind" and to the sound of the silver bell, which announced the coming of the Heavenly Child. While I was still waking up, the arms of my mother picked me up and carried me into the brightly lit up, cozy room. And there was the tree in the corner by the window as every year. Truly a magic tree it was, transfigured to the last little branch to reveal heavenly worlds of fairytales, which even today still enchant me.

So my thoughts have become submerged into the memories of my childhood, when our loving parents always knew, how to make the Christmas Festival extra special for my brother and I, just as it is customary in the house in Hochstätten.

Here a few more details from my parent's house: The big tree on a chair behind the table. The colorful decorations, the sparklers, the manger made from cardboard, the "Glockenspiel", moving by the heat of the candle flames. The many birds and icicles in the tree, my backpack for school with the picture of a horse on it, the phonograph, and another year, the zither. Mother's wonderful cookies, and every year a game to play.

You will be singing all the familiar Christmas songs, then Helga will read the Christmas story and you will be sharing your lovingly wrapped gifts, something for everyone and Mama will say: "I think this one is for Norbert and this one for Helga".

You will then sing "Silent Night, Holy Night" and say the Lord's Prayer together. Then everything will be admired and you will play with your new things.

Maybe for a while the children will forget, that I am not there, but you, my precious wife, will search with your eyes for my picture, which surely is standing by the tree and your heart will ache. But you will be brave and not show your pain for the children's sake.

All this goes through my head from 5 to 5:30 pm. I have found peace and calmness and feel strengthened by a prayer and confidently walk back to the barracks. There, everything is prepared for the Christmas party. It begins at 6 pm.

The tree is standing on a table in room #2. The comrades are sitting on their beds, we light the few candles we have, I say a few words and read the Christmas story, then we sing "Silent Night" and comrade Dornbusch speaks to us, a dear and fine human being.

The day before, he had said to me: "Wounds have to bleed, before they can heal." He was able to impress the rough and hardened group of men in such a way, that they did not hide their emotions and many had tears in their eyes. He said among other things: "Our families see us today in a transfigured light."

Comrade Wolf recites a fitting poem, then we sing "Oh, Tannenbaum" and F. takes care of the gift sharing. What can we give each other, maybe an apple? But not even a few nuts, cookies, cigarettes or a beverage. Well, we did not expect anything, but everyone is content, although the anger grows from day to day. Now we are amiably together for the rest of the evening.

At 7 pm, is the first church service. There are two Christmas trees, one on each side of the primitive altar. The choir sings 3 songs and the celebration is very moving. At 8 pm, the service is repeated for the other buddies and we are getting tired from standing so long.

Then comes the **BIG SURPRISE. My most beautiful Christmas present: Two letters from home.**

The first one is from 30, Oct. and from its contents I have to gather, that they knew nothing of my fate until 15, Oct. My sweetheart, practical as always, had immediately put in a special request, but in vain.

The second letter was a Christmas letter, it contained 6 pages, and in addition there were letters from Norbert and Helga. The little one scribbled some too.

Since I have read these letters, I am overjoyed. A deep peace enters my heart. Now I know that at home everything is all right and I can go to sleep comforted and relaxed. I am happy my dearest is so brave.

She writes such darling things about our baby. She can walk and talks a lot too. Every night she includes me in her prayers. Such a prayer should help in its innocence and purity. Too bad I cannot capture everything, but this letter I will surely keep. How touching, just to mention one episode, when Sigrid misbehaved, she quickly says: I will not do it again (in her cute baby talk). Oh, if only I could hold you and love you, our precious little baby.

Norbert and Helga too, wrote dear letters. Now Christmas again has its true meaning for me. I keep reading my letters over and over, again and again.

Happily I sing in the 2nd church service with a fervor as never before. At 9 pm, Feldhausen, the catholic priest, gives us some watered down schnapps and we wonder, where he got it. Then the evening belongs to me. May the others do what they want!

I fasten Helga's bookmark from 1944 on the wall next to my bed, in addition to the pretty clippings.

I had put some green pine branches by the window and the head of my bed and by the little tree. We had saved some wood for the fire, I brew good strong coffee with some left over beans, and with that I have some toasted bread. Even a couple of nuts, which I have saved for a long time, I will enjoy tonight as well as some chocolate, which Dietrich brought to me.

At midnight we have the candlelight service with the presentation of Dornbusch's composition. The Mass lasted much too long. At 1:30 am, I go to sleep. The weather is not really Christmassy it is raining and mild. It should be, as I read in a book: "The night was beautifully clear and frosty, the bells were ringing for the midnight mass, the meadows covered deeply in snow laid like a coat, that was spread in great soft folds. They carried in its shadows a pure blue color, but the white spread of tiny diamonds and threw out their colorful fire."

The children will have had fun, playing and eating cookies, just as always, but you, my precious love, will have been awake for a long time, with the homesickness and longing and with my eyes closed, I can see you crying quietly. Between your eyelids, the tears well up, your lips are trembling and no one should see, how your trusting heart is hurting. Do you see these tears, O God? Will you hear these prayers, they send up to Heaven this night? I lie down with my last thoughts of those I love at home. Let them slumber sweetly, dear Lord.

25, December 1945

1st Christmas Day

I awake with my first look at the wall, where I see my two "rascals". My first greeting goes to you.

Today is a special holiday for me. I do not do any work. I stay in bed until 8 o'clock. At 10:15 am, there is an evangelical church service with communion, which I attend. At 1 pm, later than usual, our special "festive" dinner. A piece of tough old beef and a spoon full of hard peas.

In the afternoon I read a small book from the library "Without Christmas Joy". At 4 o'clock in the afternoon, we invited Dornbusch, Paul, Wolf, and the commander for a cup of coffee. It is very pleasant and cozy and we are proud to be able to have some guests. At 5 pm, the choir sings in the sick bay, which is appreciated and enjoyed so much. In the evening at 8 pm, a chamber music performance at Barrack No. 37 with the following program:

Serenade by Haydn.
Two poems by Eichendorff.
The choir: Hymn of the night.
"Brothers" a Lithuanian folksong.
Two poems by Möricke.
And in closing: Mozart's "Kleine Nachtmusik".

There are special words by Dornbusch. The concert was a full success.

26, December 1945

2nd Christmas Day

It is pouring rain and very mild.

What will you be doing at home? Surely you will celebrate and play games. I want to try and remember back one year to the 2nd Christmas Day 1944. How I was on the train in the freezing cold, fearing dive bomber attacks, and deciding to get off in Rheinböllen, which was my good fortune. Otherwise, I would have gotten into the bombing raid in Bad Münster. The 3 hour walk over Stromberg followed. My fear that something could have happened to you and the memory of my hurried walk home filled with anxiety and then the happy reunion. So I still celebrate Christmas with a thankful heart.

This evening for supper we had something different, 2 green herrings, which a buddy brought for us from the American Barracks. That was a nice change of pace. Later I play a game of chess with young Benno, thinking they will probably be playing games at home as well.

27, December 1945

Christmas is gone. The anxious question arises; will we celebrate next Christmas still in prison?

What are my children doing at home? Norbert will be building things with his erector set and Helga will be playing with her dolls, the little "Doll Mommy", maybe do crafts or draw. She is so good in drawing and has so much imagination. Or play with her baby sister? What did the little "Mouse" get from "Christkind"?

It is raining day and night and I have caught a cold, a cough and stuffed up nose.

28, December 1945

Yesterday I wrote to Rösel: "Oh, just once to be able to ruffle Norbert's thick hair, to kiss Helga on her snub nose and hold the little sweetheart's well formed head in both of my hands. During these evenings, they will be sitting in the living room at the table with the beige embroidered tablecloth and play all the many games we have. Maybe they will pull out the zither and play Christmas songs and folksongs.

29, December 1945

It is pouring day and night, but I am thankful for a cozy warm room. Tonight I am playing 4 different games of "Mühle" with Benno. I won 2 and he won 2. I kept thinking that Helga should be my partner, knowing how she loves to play games and again a heartbreaking homesickness got a hold of me. Can you hear how I call out for you, my sweet little "Murschel"? Will your prayers have the strength to bring me back home again? And you, our little baby and your innocent prayer: "Dear God, bring Papa home soon." and you, Norbert, my serious, big boy and even more so, you, my precious love?

Actually my faith should be like a rock, but sometimes it is not. Will our wives know that there is also a sexual need for prisoners? That too should be mentioned.

30, December 1945

Sunday

For the 2nd time some prisoners have escaped. They have not caught them yet but they probably will. I am glad for everyone who makes it, without getting caught.

We have miserable weather; rain mixed with snow.

I am glad we get some food smuggled in by a comrade from town. The daily beet soup is enough to make us throw up. In the near future the bread rations are supposed to be shortened again.

I think back a lot of this past year, also of my growing up years and many pictures come alive. I believe that my parents in their simplicity, knowingly or unknowingly have passed on more riches of the soul, than I could ever imagine. The same is the case with my sweet loving wife and I can only hope, that this depth of sentiment has been passed on to our children.

They have lost so much, but this was the fault of this miserable war and I am still inconsolable, that I have not been able after these bitter 6 years to finally come home. I do not want to complain. If they release me during the year of 1946, maybe it won't be too late yet.

I am thinking of the games of my youth, which we played at recess around the schoolyard, like "catch, hide and go seek, etc". The games on warm summer nights after a refreshing rain, playing marbles with the neighborhood boys, the wonderful winters sledding down the hill behind the house, my first skates, the homemade shoes, which father insisted I had to have made according to measurement. The fairytale books mother ordered from a catalog, the threshing machine, which came in fall and was such an impression for a young boy. How I devoured the books of "Karl May" about the cowboys and Indians in far away America. During my young years, going out with my father to the fields, the forests, and meadows. The village festivals, the carnivals, the smell of burnt milk that had boiled over on the stove on winter mornings, because mother had to run down to the stable to care for the animals. The memories of petroleum lanterns, feeding cows in the stable, and father chopping wood in the shed are so vivid. The cozy evenings after sunset and the day's work was done, the neighbors would come over just to sit and chat, the men smoking their pipes, the first rubber eraser father bought for me, and so much more.

The memory of a year ago, when I rode on the open truck in the freezing cold all through the night and arrived in Wittlich on New Years Day. The dreadful sight of smoking, burning ruins everywhere and the caskets, hundreds of them. Many people were still buried under the rubble.

31, December 1945

New Years Eve

I cannot get the tune out of my head: "Des Jahres letzte Stunde" ("The Year's Last Hour"), which I had learned in teacher's seminary, also the song "New Year, I greet you", which is in a book at home.

I look over the past year solemnly, pensive, and thoughtfully. What did it bring me in good and bad?

In the beginning, a few short, but precious furloughs with my loved ones, it brought me March 17th, the retreat across the Rhine River and finally through Southern Germany, with the Americans in hot pursuit. Defeated armed forces without resistance or hope, crushed and broken, mindless and desperate. It brought us the pitiful collapse of the "Third Reich", Hitler's death and lets us feel for the first time the superiority of the victors.

It brought me April 29ᵗʰ, the day of my dramatic capture by the Americans and subsequent imprisonment at the camp in Heilbronn. The camp was a huge field surrounded with barbwire, with no shelter for several weeks. Our daily hopes to be sent home, the handing out a piece of paper, which no one could read, and let us believe it was a "release" paper. Then the unbelievable betrayal by the Americans happened, who turned us over to the French for the injustice of an imprisonment, which surely could not have been in agreement with the Geneva Convention.

That's why all the existing liking for the Americans has been wiped out and left is hatred and disgust. We should have been treated decently, as would be common among civilized people. **What impressions I have accumulated since that time and to this day, I will not and cannot talk about it, but forever keep it hidden away in my heart**. What I have to ask myself is this: "Was I too self assured, possibly not humble enough, and is this my punishment?"

But who can blame us, myself and thousands of my fellow soldiers who only did their job. To visualize in our fantasies, going home, once this wretched war was over. What is the reason you have sought me out O God, to punish me like this? I cannot fathom this just yet.

Oh, how I had visualized this homecoming in all its brilliant colors, when and how I would arrive, by train, on foot, from north or south, how I would greet them, what I would tell them and how I would spend my time. I had hoped to be able to celebrate my 42ⁿᵈ birthday at home. What an idiot I was.

I wanted to eat cherries and strawberries from our garden, sit on the bench on summer evenings in front of the schoolhouse in Sembach. I was going to move our furniture back in the apartment, go on field trips with the children, listen to the radio, give Helga piano lessons, go to a movie with them, go shop for new things, visit relatives and friends; in short, live, as if war had never happened. I even went as far as imagining teaching school in Hochstätten, because colleague Mai might not be available.

I was going to teach my children the love of their homeland, our beloved country in spite of all the disgrace, humiliation, ruins, and deprivation. I wanted to take them on outings into nature to teach them and open their hearts and minds for the beauty all around them.

I brood about all these questions and cannot find an answer. Why do we have to suffer, my loved ones at home and me here. How much longer? Will the year 1946, answer these questions?

At 11 pm, an evangelical church service began, which I left at 5 minutes before midnight, because as always in these years, I had to be by myself at the turn of the New Year. I stood in the shadows of the chapel and directed my thoughts to wander north to the quiet village, where I know my happiness is at home. I tried to cross over time and space with such intensity, that I almost had a hallucination seeing them all before me.

When our brass band started playing exactly at midnight the beautiful song: "Ich bete an die Macht der Liebe (I Pray for the Power of Love)"; my heart melted in immense loneliness and I looked up at the clear starry sky, seeking help there and praying for the fulfillment of my most fervent wishes. I could see you my dearest, your head on your pillow with burning eyes and you cried with an aching heart. Maybe the bells ringing in the New Year woke you and you woke the children and folded your hands to pray. The little sweetheart surely slept into the New Year with her pure and innocent prayer: "Dear God, let Papa come home soon". Maybe the older ones stayed up and you had made, as was our custom, glühwein (hot, spiced wine) and had Christmas cookies, played music and games until midnight. I do not know.

Here, a lot of good wishes were passed around: "May the year 1946, bring us home" was heard most of all. But at midnight, there were no fireworks or ringing of the bells, as it is customary in Germany. These people see in a festival no more than eating and drinking.

We light the candles on our tree one more time and let them burn out, symbolic for ending the year that is now in the past. I stayed, until the last one had burned out. The fragrance of the candles and pine needles lingered in the room. I then left to go to the 2nd part of the celebration, a variety show, which lasted until 3 am.

I went to bed with a last look at the bookmark made by Helga on my wall.

<u>1946</u>

1, January 1946

New Years Day

Quietly and confidently I wake up. No assurance, but a very strong hope fills me and a fervent prayer rises up to heaven: "My beginning and my end, I commit into your hands, my Lord." With this devoted attitude I attend the New Years Day church service. Pastor Brecht's message was heartwarming and not as abstract as usual. Other than that the whole day brought us nothing but unpleasantness. Do they intend to humiliate us even more?

There were constant roll calls and they had us running around the camp under the supervision of the guards with loaded guns, announcing various punishments, closing the coffee shop, the sounding of taps for the whole month of January at 9 pm and other harassment. Oh, all those humiliations leave us cold. We just laugh about it. How small they are!

In the afternoon one of the buddies, an artist and painter, painted a portrait of me. I had to sit for 2 hours, but it did not turn out very good. Do I really look this emaciated? Later I brew myself some coffee and for supper we had green herring again. At 9 pm, the lights were ordered out. This hour from 9 to 10 belongs to me. I am lying awake thinking. How happy would I be, if I knew they received some mail from me lately.

Will this year bring me my freedom?

2, January 1946

Today Jakob Neu came to see me. He has to work hard, but shows the French farmer some of his ingenuity and efficiency. He is tough and sticks it out, also does not seem to suffer from being homesick as I do. He brought me a canteen filled with milk, some apples, some cheese, and meat. What wonderful welcomed gifts! I was able to get him a jacket to work in, for which he was very happy. I gave him some of our "wonderful" beet soup and we talked all afternoon together. He showed me pictures of Sembach. I want to ask mother in my next letter to talk to his family.

Today we took down the Christmas tree. It is probably still standing in Hochstätten, as was always our custom, until the "Holy Three King's Day".

3, January 1946

As of yesterday, it has turned very cold and we have ice flowers (frost) on the inside of our windows. What would we do if we did not have our dear Klemenz who steals coal with his bare hands every morning in the darkness behind the kitchen?

4, January 1946

The French people have been put back on bread rationing and are infuriated. According to the papers there is unrest in Paris and other big cities. **"Let us go home, if you cannot feed us"**. We know that for the next few months we will get for both noon and night only sugar beet soup. I just feel so sorry, for these young boys and I am reminded of Norbert.

5, January 1946

We have decided after the 6:30 am roll call, to go back to bed for a couple of hours in order to save our heating fuel. Why not? They should give us coal!

A year ago I made the trip to Wiesbaden to the General Command and the adventurous march to Moselkern.

Tomorrow is a special day!

6, January 1946

Little Sigrid, Darling Child

You are 2 years old today. A Sunday child, a sunny child! I think of you, my little darling in the same manner as I do of you, my precious love, because so many new joys are given to you by this baby each day.

You wanted to have this child and looked forward to it from the first day on. You were so brave 2 years ago and it is so evident, that you took on all the trials and tribulations mostly for me. How I want to thank you for as long as I live. You believed this child would compensate me for all I had lost in those years of war with the other two. In Sembach, I would wish, that I could have lived through all the steps of our children's development. But in order to be able to do this, I would have to come home soon, or once again, it will be too late. But what have I had of this child so far?

I saw her briefly 2 years ago from, Jan 10th until the 28th and I was able, happily, to be there when she was brought home from the Sister Petschel Clinic to Hochstätten and I could also be there for her Christening. I did not see her again until August, and then for the brief furlough between Christmas and New Years in 1944/45, and in the spring days of the year before.

Last time on March 12th, giggling with my hat on her head, since then the hat became my good luck charm.

I am so thankful, that we have you! I delight in all the sweet things Mama wrote to me about you, how you can walk and talk, and how you pray for me. I even saw you very briefly in a dream last night, with short blond hair on your little baldhead. On the wall next to my bed I have your picture, which I hung up today and the calendar with the "Three Kings Day" which is also a Sunday today.

For this day I saved the last 2 apples from Jakob Neu, the last of the bean coffee and a couple of cookies.

In spite of the cold there is beautiful sunshine outside and I finish reading the book "Light in the Darkness" and I am at home with my thoughts. That's how I celebrate your birthday.

How will you be celebrating at home? What do I wish for you, my darling baby? I cannot put it into words, but may all my wishes be fulfilled. Keep praying for me, my beloved child.

Norbert, Sigrid and Helga, Summer 1946

<u>7, January 1946</u>

I am still completely under the influence of yesterday. On such days my innermost being is in a complete turmoil. Late, this child was given to us. She is a good baby, a wonderful, sunny child, as you write, my dearest. Can you just imagine how heavy the burden of this separation is weighing on me? I do not know what the baby looks like; cannot hear her little voice, cannot play with her. I can only keep on looking at the picture taken at age one and try to imagine her saying now: "I will be a good girl!" Oh, if only I could cry again!

My head hurts from the constant brooding, I feel sick to my stomach, and it does not get any easier, only harder every day.

How many of these diary books have I written? I guess this is No. 20, and I have secretly always hoped that a miracle could have happened at the end of my writing.

I drag myself through these days secretly always carrying the small glimmer of hope but most often it is completely shattered. With a definite legitimacy, good and bad days take their turns.

The cold continues, but we do not have snow.

8, January 1946

The misery of the young people is pathetic. Pushed by hunger they break in, steal and rob in the kitchen and the clothes supply room. The three in our barracks are 1 year younger than my Norbert!

How thankful we have to be, that our son was spared this fate. When I see this, I am a little more content and seek to endure my situation. There is a good kid from Neuss, whom I give my "seconds" of beet soup every day. He is so grateful! I do not believe my Norbert would steal, no matter how hungry he was. How rotten some of these young people have become; by being associated with so many inferior people with a lack of principles.

9, January 1946

I went back to the doctor because of my shortness of breath. It is not enough to be classified as an "R". What hope is left for me?

The stubborn rumor is going around; that in spring something is going to happen. But what could it be? Maybe they are putting together a work battalion to be sent to Normandy?

Yesterday we were threatened and it was partially carried out, to take the stoves away from us. That would hit us hard. Fortunately, they dropped that idea. But the food is getting worse by the day. We get nothing but this horrible beet soup, made with sugar beets, which at home is used to feed the cattle. The 2,000 people who came from Chartre are still hanging around. What an incredible lack of organization. They still like to talk about the thick soup they got, so thick, the spoon would stand up in it.

10, January 1946

Two years ago today I received the happy telegram that our Sigrid had arrived. That same night I left to go home. Oh, what wonderful memories.

11, January 1946

On days like this, I again gain my mental balance. The evening two years ago, when I arrived in Hochstätten, is before my eyes. How happy and excited the whole family was about this joyous event. I myself on such a high, that I remember telling jokes with the in-laws all night. Oma and Opa, as well as Norbert and Helga, could not stop laughing. I had telephoned my sweetheart at the clinic, and promised her, I would visit the next morning. Oh, how happy I was in spite of the war.

Outside there is a rainstorm. The Austrians and the sick are still here. I have six letters to give to some people, who are going home. I myself am anxious for some mail.

Recently a Swiss minister came, but he was not able to give us much comfort, which we needed.

12, January 1946

Two years ago I saw our little baby for the first time. What a darling child and my sweetheart, so pretty, healthy, and happy. Oh, how motherhood has made you glow. I felt like a king! Could there be a more beautiful picture in your inherent human quality, to be a mother?

I should not let this beautiful day be spoiled by the completely pessimistic comments of both pastors, also not by the dreary rain outside and the darkness in our room.

How much we are depending though of such exterior influences. I would rather think of the happy hours two years ago. I still had plenty of fruitcake and Christmas cookies from my dear ones when I stopped for a short visit in Hochstätten. I remember the treacherous trip over the rubble of the destroyed railway station in Bad Münster, how I walked through slick, icy roads and high snow, to wake them in the middle of the night. Oh, how happy we were to greet each other, no matter what time of night it was. And how thankful we were for the few hours we had together.

13, January 1946

Another Sunday, that again plunges me into deep hopelessness. I heard from comrade Mattes in the office, that no way are the French intending to let the older and married ones go home. He also was completely devastated. What good is it, that even a dear buddy, like the railroad inspector Maasen who desperately clings to all favorable rumors and still keeps hoping, as does the librarian and buddy Michel, who get carried away in their optimism. I myself have become more realistic, one man has supposedly heard, that we have to stay until 1948. What a horrible thought!

I just cannot be happy today; can't even concentrate to read the excellent book by Ina Seidel, "Lennacker". Also Paul, an attorney from Wuppertal, who clings to every piece of straw, is very depressed. In spring they are all going to beat it out of here. What a joke!

Only one thing can calm down the uproar in my soul, that's when I see the starving adolescents in their thin, torn uniforms outside in the freezing cold and I know my Norbert is safe, cared for, and warm. I will gladly endure, if I can spare you, my dear boy, from this.

Still, my faith in justice and balancing rules is greatly shattered. Why do others, some who are even responsible for this misery, sit at home and the innocent ones have to suffer? Who can answer me this question?

14, January 1946

Opa is 71 years old today. May God, in whom we all do believe so strongly, keep you well and healthy for many more years. You are such a good father and grandfather, with your soft heart and kindness, your honesty and decent fundamental attitude. May you share in the happiness of your child and your grandchildren for a long time to come. This I wish for you with all my heart.

We wish so, from year to year, the fulfillment of ones dreams and one waits and waits. Shall there not be any happy times for our generation anymore?

Yesterday I was so depressed that I could hardly participate in the awarding of prizes for the best entry in drawing, poetry, etc. There were excellent creations submitted in the fine arts and it is pretty remarkable, what talent can be found in this camp. We have several artists, writers, and actors.

Today is the coldest day this winter and an icy wind blows down from the Alps. I remember indeed, that I was home a year ago today and in the morning, it was still dark when I left, wished Opa a happy birthday. Then I walked the treacherous road in slick ice to Bad Kreuznach and from there I left on a late train to Gaulsheim, where I stumbled in a tremendous hurry over the ruins of the railway station. Then I walked to the Rheinstein Castle, was picked up by a car to Boppard, from there by truck to Koblenz, and arrived in Urbar that night. I remember looking up and seeing the streams of silvery glittering bombers, thousands of them heading east. That was the beginning of the end!

To close this day, I want to recite a portion of a memorable book: "… many a night I almost perished with grief and worry, and that I begged God, to surround him with my intense love, and that all my worries should be like an umbrella over him, that he might get through this unspeakable danger well and whole, and that he might come back to me, then I can protect him with the wonder of my love…!"

"I hope and wish, that I will be able to bring back home with me these diaries. I had always hoped, that my superiors and later on my captors would not find them and confiscate them."

"They should be for later on, a true and honest mirror image of my years, months, days and hours in this miserable war, my subsequent imprisonment and all its consequences. It should be a memory for me and in my old days, God willing, reflect the state of my mind, and for my children and grandchildren as well be a lasting legacy of a very sad time!"

My buddy Glaser found a music box, which he let me have and like a child I get lost in the simple tune. I think of my childhood and of my loved ones, and in this way, close the day.

15, January 1946

Something is going on, but what? We cannot see through the whole thing. All "C", "L" and "D" people, who are not working in the camp, in addition all youths under 17 years of age are to be packed up and ready to leave. But where nobody knows. Acquaintances of mine are among them, also Wolf, Maasen and Heinz from Andernach. Of course they are all hopeful. Oh you poor fools! There is no question in my mind that this again is an absolute deception with their hopes all in vain.

It is bitterly cold again. Two days ago two buddies from outside work details have died. The reason: They would not let them go to a doctor. Dear God! Just keep me healthy!

How glad I have to be, that with Klemenz's help we have some more fuel, I have enough blankets for covering and my coat. I have not caught a cold yet.

While I read the book of a Swiss Theologian Barth, who writes very realistically about Hitler and Germany, I am reminded of our good friends, the two pastors Degen and Zinn.

16, January 1946

How they pick out the ice cold dirty beets from the garbage with their hands blue from the cold. How they stand with hungry eyes, maybe without socks or underpants, in the front room, staring at the beet pot. How they actually beat each other up over a ladle full and how they unfortunately crave cigarettes more than food, these pitiful and pathetic youngsters. Last night there was the drama of the two liars, which neither one admitted to, and ended up beating each other bloody. It is terrible, that we don't even care anymore to witness such things!

It will be a cold night again. At 5 pm, there are already ice crystals on our window.

The transportation of the "C", "L", and "D" people has been postponed; of course, as to be expected.

Supposedly 21 sacks of packages have arrived. Will there be one for me?

17, January 1946

A man, who contracted the terrible sexually transmitted disease syphilis two years ago and still suffers with it, does not want to go home. How can anyone express such a terrible wish? Well, I can understand the fact, that he is marked for life.

How comforted I feel, that I can come back to you, my dearest with a good conscience. I come to you pure and clean, as you so well deserve and I cannot wait for the hour, which brings me back into your arms.

I have noticed quite often, that most of the buddies, who work outside on farms, actually have a very good relationship with their patrons. Even though they cannot converse, our people have captured the respect of the French everywhere, with their diligence, their skillfulness, and their decent behavior. There were exceptions of course.

On the other hand, our people make a lot of observations, how backward the French are in many ways, often dirty, unpractical, incompetent and not at all efficient, especially the women. We are always amazed to hear these individual reports. No, our people will not perish. The good seed is there, even if it is hidden away.

I did not sleep well, my stomach bothered me, and also I awake from the cold in these stone barracks with the thin walls.

19, January 1946

Another bad clash with F. I do not tolerate his insults and will not deviate from my character, manners, or attitude. I know I am right and this man has much to learn. Never have I known anyone who, in his 14 years of being a military superior, has become so brittle, aloof, and austere. Here, the good inheritance from my parents helps me: Give in, even if it is hard sometimes, giving in just to keep the peace. The commander came and helped straighten things out, so everything is back to normal. I would not want to give up my position here, because surely I could make a worse trade and that I want to avoid. All the favorable rumors have been marked as "Nonsense".

Klippel has made it and is classified as "R". Soon the "R" transport is to leave.

A very happy day! My Christmas package came. I signed for it at the post office unpacked it under supervision; it had to be checked by the French.

How soft my heart gets when I see the careful way you packed it, sweet wife. You have in your clever and practical ways kept exactly to the rules. There was a jar of honey from Opa's beloved bees, a package of sugar cubes, 20 razorblades and Christmas cookies. With how much love you have packed everything. How dear and precious is every piece to me, because it went through your hands and your thoughts of me, when you packed it. Maybe the little sweetheart was allowed to help. Helga for sure and Norbert had written in his letter from December 6th, that you were baking gingerbread cookies. Oh, I recognize your cookies, my dearest, definitely the best! If only something was in the package from mother. If only Richard will come home safely.

Tomorrow, Sunday, I will make myself coffee, eat a piece of bread with honey, and eat one cookie every night.

How I thank you!

20, January 1946

The cold has broken. Outside it is blindingly white with snow. This afternoon I will continue reading the book "Lenacker", while the others play soccer.

I slept very well last night, maybe because of the package. I just broke my small blue pocket mirror. They say broken pieces bring you luck, but I am not superstitious though, it is just nonsense.

Quite often I catch myself, anytime during the day, visualizing my homecoming in the smallest details. I try to push these thoughts from my mind, but they keep coming back. So what! I seem to have these illusions to escape for a few hours from the reality. Even if it is a farce, fantasies can be beautiful!

This afternoon the theatre performance, "The Night Watchman" was repeated. In the final scene, where some young boys are the actors, it became painfully clear to me, that my children Norbert and Helga were cheated out of the fun of being on stage in a laymen's performance, which I would have organized as I used to back then.

Gone forever!

21, January 1946

The argument with F. has resulted in our working relationship being severely breached. In fact I was advised, to take over the position as interpreter with the new French physician. I do not give in though, even if it means disadvantages for me. Some think it could be an advantage for me for later on.

Why do I dream so often of my dead father?

22, January 1946

I have my first interview with the French doctor. He makes a very good impression and also seems to be pleased with me. I can keep my old position and work for him only when he needs me.

The commander straightens things out again, of course I do not speak with F. for the next few days, I have my pride, too.

24, January 1946

The "R" examinations by the new doctor are very strict. He is too exact. There are many betrayed hopes. Of 60 selected people only 23 get the "R".

25, January 1946

This afternoon I work for the first time for my new boss. He is very nice, gives me a cigarette, and talks with me.

26, January 1946

I had an almost sleepless night, with my stomach bothering me again. I tossed and turned all night. What is wrong?

Today 150 hospital personal came back again. They had made a bad trade. Again we have proof, that our situation definitely could be worse. So let's be satisfied.

27, January 1946

I have slept so well and woke up so happy, but why? Am I nurturing false hopes again? At 8 am, the disillusionment is here already. From the area of the Saar and Pfalz, a lot of mail came, but nothing for me.

We hear that the Poles, Hungarians, and Rumanians have still not been released yet, but sent to different camps.

It is 4 pm, and Klemenz and I make some coffee and I share a piece of bread with honey with him and smoke the last cigarette for this month.

From day to day the mood among the prisoners gets worse. They all will try to escape in spring. What utter nonsense! In a court martial in Lyon, one guy has been sentenced to lifelong hard labor in Morocco. Horrible!

28, January 1946

Was that a year ago today, when I asked Lt. Storz for a few days leave time and he so readily granted it? When I walked with wet feet through ice and snow to Montabaur, by train to Wiesbaden where there was a bombing attack in progress, and I spent the day in a cellar near the "Ring Church", leaving the next morning at 4 am. Caught a train to Ebernburg, then walked to Hochstätten and shortly before the village took cover under a tree from low flying "jabos". My loved ones were in the cellar, Opa in the school cellar with the little sweetheart, as they did not make it home.

Oh, what wonderful 3 to 4 days those were!

29, January 1946

Was that really a year ago, when we had so much fun with that little one? When she was standing one night on the sofa in her white nightshirt, clutching her teddy bear in her left arm and waving wildly with her right hand, squealing so excitedly and loudly, that her little face turned bright red and her voice almost cracked. What joy we had then!

Today was another day, which I would rather not talk about. One thing is certain, there are no sympathies created with such treatments. And all that, because the orderlies refused to work under abominable conditions. These are only little needle pricks and we just laugh about them. But the passive resistance is growing more and more.

30, January 1946

Because of the not so ordinary circumstances today (how narrow minded and vicious, this revenge) we are all very tired and I slept well.

We have bad weather today with heavy rain showers and thunderstorms. We need to be more appreciative, that we can be indoors and dry.

When my homesickness gets too bad, I pull out the little music box, which I will bring home for my little Sigrid and play it some. I get calmer after that (human beings are strange creatures). Will there be a time later on, when I will laugh about these things? Maybe! But only those who have ever been a prisoner-of-war can possibly understand our psychosis.

We experienced a small earth tremor here yesterday. Some houses downtown received cracks, some people were injured, we had only a slight shaking of our barracks, and the light began to swing back and forth.

31, January 1946

Its father's birthday! He would have been 69 years old today. It was not meant for him to live to see the end of the war and see his two boys coming home. Both of them are still not home!

Today is another day of reflection. I recall in all the details the events of last year, when I was on the trip with Norbert in the freezing cold train without windows in the dark, and how handsome he was; my big boy in his gray coat and blue hat. In the fresh morning breeze his cheeks were pink and he looked so healthy. I remember how we tried to buy some vitamin drops for the little one at the Winnweiler Pharmacy, but it was still closed. How we marched through ice and snow and then had the reunion with my good mother. She had not expected us and hardly recognized us, but when she did, she joyously clapped her hands as was her habit and rushed toward us.

Now she had her son and grandson, and was happy to wait on us and feed us. She cooked us our favorite dinner, then we went to the schoolhouse. Norbert picked out a few books from the library. Later Norbert visited his friend Jakob. Then we went to sleep in the cozy room as guests of grandmother in father's bed, and I felt comforted, as I used to be as a child.

In the early morning at 3 am, we said good-bye, trying to catch a real early train because of the danger of air attacks and went back to Hochstätten. That was the last time I saw my mother.

Here every day is one like the other. It has snowed again, but is mild.

Among the choir members, is one fellow, who looks a lot like Richard. Oh, if the poor guy will only be able to come back home safely. That, I wish for him today, on our father's birthday. Suddenly, as we rehearse "Brahms Lullaby" with the choir, I have the fervent wish, to sit by Sigrid's crib at bedtime and play on my violin this lovely tune. Then wait until she has closed her eyes and in the morning quietly sit by her bed again, to wait for the moment, when the sparkling blue eyes will open and happily greet the new day.

It is now exactly a year that I am separated from my family.

1, February 1946

Farewell from them at home in 1945. I can still see mother sitting in her bed, composed as always, as she has had to say good-bye so many times in these seven years, but always hoped for a reunion. God willing, all of us will have a happy reunion some day.

While I make out my morning report, I am thinking how I walked with Norbert through the icy patches and snow puddles, the long way to Winnweiler, how sincere and attentive he listened to all I had to say. He bravely carried his backpack and is not at all soft, as I thought. He is not a child anymore, but becoming a young man. I kept asking him if he was not cold. It is so hard to accept, when one's children grow up!

We arrived safely in Hochstätten at 9 am, and I had to get packed up again. I remember leaving in the afternoon by truck and Norbert riding along with some of his friends for a little while. He is used to saying good-bye.

I remember the crazy ride with the truck with snow chains, full of drunken soldiers to Bad Kreuznach, where there was an air raid in progress. Quickly on to Münster-Sarnsheim, from where I walked in the afternoon sunshine to Bingen. I still remember today, how happy and joyful, and full of life I felt, because spring was coming and a fragrant tang was in the air, reminding me of Easter time.

It is 2 pm; I put my book down to let my thoughts drift back. For a year now, I am carrying around father's handkerchief, which you, beloved mother, gave to me. I keep it in his honor. Is it a sin to hang with one's heart on such things? Maybe later on I might smile about these things, but right now, let no one dare to ridicule my emotions.

2, February 1946

I wait with great anxiety for some mail. If only mother would write that Richard is at home. Outside it is stormy and rainy. It is so dark in the afternoon that we have to have the lights on. I have lost more weight and feel dizzy.

I found a few passages in the book "Lenacker", which I could so identify with: "…are my children not planted in me, like roots, and what I have, they have also? But my restless spirit and sadness are like mildew on their souls. I hope not! This rationality was the drawback of a lonely existence, but seeking contact and companionship of a yearning mind. I believe I was an easily guided, incredibly good natured, for kindness and friendliness, deeply receptive child, whose soul was open quite like the sunflower to the light and the warmth, ready for love."

I believe my Helga would fit this!

3, February 1946

Sunday! I have slept well. Outside, spring seems to be announcing itself and starting at noon we have bright sunshine. My thoughts are drifting to the little room above the bakery, where I had my room and board in Hochstätten as a young teacher. That was in 1925, the spring of our new young love. Do you remember, what a sweet, wild, young thing you were back then and how you had completely captured my young heart? How homey a feeling it was, when at 10 pm, the last train came in, the doors were slammed, the conductor yelled: "Hochstätten", and then the engine started up again puffing and snorting.

Oh, my Alsenz Valley, my unforgettable homeland!

6, February 1946

Hahn had killed and slaughtered a dog and ate it with his buddies. They are strange people. No, no, no matter how big the hunger is. I have lost more weight. Daily at noon and at night we get this horrid beet soup with soy meal. The monotony of every day. Still I am calmer than months ago.

The Austrians and the "R" people have been waiting since October for transport.

7, February 1946

The winter days are dreary and I have memories of such mornings in Sembach at my parent's house or in the schoolroom. Oh, blissful childhood! Our living room with the view of the snowy yard, impressions of country living, the hard working parents, happy years, they are gone forever. And not to mention, the schoolrooms. There was the "little" one, for the lower classes, with a cozy fire in the pot belly stove, the special schoolroom smell of chalk and waxed floors, the view down the road, the happy group of kids. The "big" one for the upper classes 5 through 8, which I was teaching. Oh, how enthused I was and with so much joy and initiative I would teach "my" kids. I felt so much at home in this schoolroom, where I myself had been a pupil for 4 years with "old teacher" Weber.

There were the dark winter mornings of conferences in Alsenz. How the charming countryside of this little valley grew close to my heart back then. As if I had known, someday, I would put down my roots here. And for that I am thankful.

8, February 1946

What luxury! Last night we got a cup of cocoa.

Tonight after waiting in vain for some mail, I wrote my February letter.

9, February 1946

It is raining day and night. That means the game for the soccer players will be postponed. This morning I ate the last bit of my honey. Now I only have the sugar left. Surely my sweetheart would send me some spread for my bread if she could. How worried she must be, not to get any mail from me.

This beet soup, we can hardly stomach anymore. With disgust we choke it down. In the afternoon we roast some bread and drink the rest of the warmed up tea. By 3 pm, the rain had turned to watery snow. It is terribly boring. I don't even feel like reading. At home precious hours are lost for me. Nothing makes sense!

For hours the POWs have to march around the camp like a herd of sheep.

10, February 1946

Sunday! It snowed through the night. Around noon the sun comes through. I saw you in my dreams again, my dearest.

I write some sheet music for my friend Gerhard Dornbusch for our choir. Within the next few weeks we want to do an evening of folk music. For tonight, there is another "variety" evening. I could care less about that. I just go to pass the time.

11, February 1946

Today is a very difficult day. One of those days, which takes away every bit of joy in life.

It did not start very good. I did not sleep well, had bad dreams and nightmares. Last night after a successful show there was the narrow minded harassment of a row call by a German hater at 11 pm. This morning the usual rumors and negative newspaper articles; in addition, no mail, feeling sick with a cold, beet soup, a constant pressure of unpleasant events, searching of the barracks, etc. etc. These people don't realize, that they just don't do anything but spread seeds of hatred. There is no way this world can come to any kind of peace and understanding this way.

I have a lot of work to do.

I am so tired, so tired! I go to bed with a terrible headache.

12, February 1946

At least I had a good night sleep. This morning, hundreds are forced to march around the camp from 9 to 12 and from 2 to 5. What is the point of that?

We cannot make a fire because we have no fuel. I sit here in my coat and write.

What unbearable monotony of days, what unnecessarily wasted time.

13, February 1946

Our night's rest was disturbed. At 2 am and at 5 am, the barracks chiefs were summoned. The usual narrow minded harassment. We are angry and I cannot get back to sleep until 6 am. In addition I don't feel well with a bad cold.

Another strange dream: I saw our little Sigrid. I was at home and Rösel brought her to our bed. She did not know me, was afraid of me, and started crying. Her face was covered with freckles.

14, February 1946

It is very cold again today. I do not feel any better, rather worse. My head hurts and I have the chills. We have no fuel to make a fire. I can hardly breathe; I am so stuffed up. If only spring would come.

17, February 1946

Another dreary miserable Sunday. When it rains, it pours. I did not sleep well, my nose is stuffed up, I have a headache, it is cold, and we have nothing to burn for heat. Outside, it is cold, windy, and rainy. The general mood of everyone is rotten and I feel so tired and weak.

18, February 1946

"R" (Repatriation)?

This day brought me most likely a change of the most enormous dimensions, so immense, that I cannot comprehend it yet, nor do I dare to believe it. Is it right to decisively grab the spokes of the wheel of fate? The future will tell me.

Briefly, I spoke with the French physician Dr. Janco. This conversation was so monumental, that I was completely dazed. On his part, a momentary pause, as if to think or consider, a questioning look at me, then the walk over to Lt. Peters and his comment: "J'ai des bons information! Vous etes bien vue (I have good news! It looks good!)"

I have a medical checkup by him and three German doctors. This experience has so moved me that I could not sleep all night. Can anyone imagine, what a possible success could mean for me?

It would mean going home!

20, February 1946

There is nothing to report, other than I still have my cold. I am swallowing all kinds of pills, but no improvement I have no taste and no smell.

But all that is trivial and of no importance, compared with the fearful uncertainty, will it all work out?

21, February 1946

"R" (?)

Today is the 2nd most important day. Is it supposed to bring to me a decision? Everything is prepared. At 1:30 pm I walk to town to see a specialist, Dr. Giorgie. I cannot possibly write down, how I feel, when I have to wait two more hours for my turn. In my subconscious, there is the paralyzing fear, something could go wrong, but still there is a small spark of hope, in spite of an all consuming impatience. I am aware, that my whole body is shaking.

I remember saying a quick prayer as I enter the room. I spoke French with the doctor and after checking me out he wrote something down and I walked out as if I was anesthetized. I went back to the camp in a driving blizzard.

Will this day have brought the decision?

23, February 1946

Our men are to be pitied more and more. Many of them bravely keep to themselves in spite of the difficult circumstances. Others walk around in rags. Soon they will not have a shirt, underpants, or shoes anymore.

In the meantime, some escapees have been brought back. Their heads get shaved; they are put in solitary confinement for 30 days, then a punishment detail after that.

25, February 1946

Today I had hoped for a decision. I spoke with Dr. Meiner and he wants to stand up for me.

I received a request from Pfarrer Degen. They gave it to me together with the French translation. How can I ever thank him? I know that my sweet little wife has arranged the necessary steps.

27, February 1946

The weather is improving. Yesterday there was tremendous activity in the "Salle de Service". A lot of trading and swapping things is going on. Many men were sent home as farmers.

There are so many injuries, burns, and accidents of all kinds. One guy died. No one cares. But at home they are getting information about us.

28, February 1946

I compare my dear, sensible, and serious boy with some of these kids, not much older than him. Oh, you would not be so immature. One 18 year old, who did not want his "R", but rather "works" for a French farmer, lies and steals there, was brought back by the police, filthy dirty and depraved. He got his head shaved and put in solitary confinement for 30 days.

1, March 1946

What Will March Bring Me?

The work in the "Salle de Service" is finished for the time being. I am sorry, although the work was hard, but I always had a heated room.

An article in the Saarbrücken newspaper writes about the teachers, who are to be sent home from French prison camps. Shall I be hopeful again? I have become so complacent and tired. All my hopes since June 18, 1945 have been betrayed.

I am going back to church again, to have some of my faith restored, but must admit, that I was not uplifted in any way. However, everything left me quite unmoved and that is not good.

I cannot get rid of this stuffed up head.

4, March 1946

I am in a terrible state of unrest. I still have not been introduced to the French doctor. The last and hardest hurdle is still to overcome. Continually escaped prisoners are brought back. There is no point in even trying.

5, March 1946

Six years ago today I was in Gensingen and Rösel, Oma, Norbert and Helga came to visit me. Helga, my little "Murschel", had become tired and slept on my bed. Then we said good-bye by the bridge.

What beautiful weeks those were. What a good thing I did not know back then, that I would have to wear this hated uniform six more years.

How often in later furlough days, Helga would beg me at bedtime: "Tell me about Michel." He was the shaggy dog in the camp there.

6, March 1946

As I have heard, the list of the "R" people has been completed and closed. But what about me? Surely one way or the other I did not make it.

One part of a book comes to my mind: "For some unfathomable reason, some do blatantly well, in spite of their meanness and selfishness, and others for the same unfathomable reason do incredibly bad in spite of their genuine efforts to live an honest and upright life."

7, March 1946

Today is another day of humiliations and harassment. At 5:30 am, everyone is lining up outside fully packed. What is that supposed to be?

It was nothing, absolutely nothing at all. After standing for 3 hours in the freezing cold, back into the barracks. These eccentric screwballs cannot shake us up anymore.

One of the adolescents has embroidered on his hat: "HOME TO MOMMY". This expresses the entire unspeakable misery of a betrayed youth. How homesick those poor kids must be.

8, March 1946

There is the constant struggle to get fuel to heat. Klemenz picks up anything and everything that burns. Burnt out coal from the kitchen, that is still hot, old toothbrushes, cardboard, rubber and leather pieces from the garbage dump, etc.

How glad am I that my blood is healthy and I don't have any boils like so many people. There are some real serious cases, where people's whole bodies are covered with these boils.

10, March 1946

Richard

There is only one thing I want to wish for your birthday today. That you may be alive, that you are well and that you can return home soon to your poor old mother, and to your wife and child. And also to me. The war has strengthened our love for each other and we will forget everything that has at times separated us, yes, I want to make up for wherever I may have failed you, dear brother.

11, March 1946

This morning the first "R" transport left. I gave one guy a letter with 10 lines. When will I be able to walk through this gate?

With great joy I finally received mail again. Also there was the receipt of the telegram, which I had sent in November, but was not received by Rösel until December 28, 1945. Everything is OK. Thank you God!

12, March 1946

A year ago, I had my last furlough in Hochstätten. All the details are vividly in my mind, including the farewell, Helga's tears and saying good-bye to Norbert in Ebernburg. I remember my advice to him for his confirmation. A whole year has gone by and it seems like an eternity to me. This is the longest time ever I have been separated from my loved ones.

The fearful question hangs over my head will this be the day of decision? I make it a day of happy anticipation and the fact, that this is the first warm sunny spring day adds to my positive feeling.

Now it will not be days, but maybe hours that matter. I am tossed between doubt and excitement. Later I will try to remember what I went through between 3 pm and 5 pm. I cannot concentrate. I am restless, I pace in my room, and I go to the soccer field to walk around aimlessly and deep in thought. Shall I pray, shall I beg for the unspeakable gift, shall I just calmly wait?

Oh, a human being can withstand a lot, except the ruination of our health. We have suffered for our entire future life. Everything is depending on the decision I await today.

5 pm! The decision was not made. But F. received his "R". A new blow! Shall I despair? No! Tomorrow is another day with a small glimmer of hope.

In the evening I bump into Dr. Janko, my patron, who came to the prison camp. I speak to him and he says: "Il le fera (It will be done)" (He meant by his successor).

With renewed hope of tomorrow, I go to sleep.

13, March 1946

I have renewed, but only a small hope. Today Dr. Meiner is on duty for the last time, I have to be introduced today and yet I am reluctant to be pushy, that just goes against my grain.

Again I go through torture from 3 pm until 5 pm. At 5 pm, when I was next to be introduced, the French doctor quit and left. Left me in the dullest of hopelessness. What is this? What is this with me?

14, March 1946

Today? That is the fearful question. Impossible, for today the French officers have a party celebrating their farewell, among them Dr. Weiss. The chief of staff surely thinks only of his farewell and has forgotten about me. Shall I curse, shall I sit and brood impassively, or shall I still hope?

Resigned I think back over my whole life and how often it has happened, that my hearts desire was destroyed last minute, how I always had to fight for everything and nothing ever fell into my lap.

Today the 2nd transport of "R" people left. Among them was Heinrich Kuhn from Bretzenheim. I gave him five old letters, also the Christmas letters for the children. He promised to deliver them and bring them greetings.

15, March 1946

The "R"

March 15th, finally, finally brought me the "R". The decision was made at 3:58 pm. The excitement of this day was so tremendous, that I will never forget the details.

The days between Feb 18th and March 15th, have stressed my nervous system very badly, but now I feel like a huge weight has been lifted from my heart.

In brief, at 3 pm, I was summoned to the doctor, No.14, as the last one. There were reports by two doctors, who left yesterday. Dr. Meiner's comments to me, when saying good-bye: "I have spoken about you to the chief of staff, Dr. Von Droste". I am very calm. I know that now the decision has been made. They all help me and keep their fingers crossed.

Then at 3:55 pm comes the fearful moment. The physician Dr. Von Droste presents my case well and at the moment, when everything was on knife's edge, the report by Dr. Giorgie made the difference and was the decisive factor. Numb with happiness, I leave the room and accept the congratulations of my comrades outside. Oh, if I could only tell you back home right now, that there is a good chance, that I will see you soon.

After the incredible stress of nerves, there follows now a reaction of complete relaxation and comforting tiredness. The tremendous pressure has left me. My heart is filled with an overwhelming gratitude to my creator and guide of all of our destinies.

Late was the dice tossed, but tossed in my favor. I cannot express my emotions in words. Incredibly happy, with teary eyes, I look at the picture of my children and Helga's bookmark on the wall and my thoughts fly across space and time to you and tell you of my joy and overwhelmed I sink onto my knees by my bed.

16, March 1946

How well I slept and how happily I awoke. No wonder! The world is beautiful for me again. The weather is cold but sunny. How many buddies envy me, but most of them are real happy for me.

18, March 1946

I had believed a year ago, that Norbert was confirmed on this day.

Again a sunny day and some very happy news: Richard is alive and in a Russian prison. He wrote a card on Christmas 1945, which arrived on Feb. 6th. He may be in Siberia. If only he is well, he will endure everything and come home safely.

I am especially happy for my mother. She has suffered so much these last few years. She writes: "I am waiting for my two boys". This sentence contains all the riches of her motherly love. May she be with us for a long time to come. Her letter was here rather quickly. It was written March 5th, and I received it on March. 18th.

The schoolhouse is empty and waits for you. Yes, I am coming! I am coming soon!

19, March 1946

One part from the beautiful book "Bread": "The many empty days had taken its toll and had worn him down, and broke him. How many times he was surrounded by the night during these last, long months." Yes, all this fits us so well.

Our food: Cattle turnips and soy meal.

20, March 1946

Another happy day! I received a package from home, packed with so much love. Everything is in the best condition. A cake, cookies, sugar cubes, dried plums, and a can of homemade liver sausage. How can I thank you for your love. Right away, I will make some coffee; we still have a little left.

Later in the afternoon, I get a card postmarked January 4th; everything is all right. On such days I fall asleep immediately and sleep well all through the night.

21, March 1946

Beginning Of Spring

A beautiful sunny day! Soon we will not need a fire anymore.

In the evening a dear letter came from my sweetheart. Everything is OK. That's all I want to know. They had left the Christmas tree standing until March 3rd, hoping, and still waiting for me.

Sgt. Fritsch is already back in Bretzenheim. Now my family have the letters he carried for me. Maybe Kuhn has been in Hochstätten in the meantime and has also given them my letters. The trip had taken from Thursday until Sunday. Oh, if only it was our time!

22, March 1946

One part from the book "Don Juan": "...do you know, what I have gained? The realization, that there can be only one woman you love with all your soul, blindly, unconditionally, without thinking what was and what will be, because she is past, presence, and future, your whole being…."

23, March 1946

An observation I have been able to make: After the shock and trauma, which each and everyone of us experienced as a result of the collapse, the lost war, the devastation of our country and utter chaos afterwards, that has often brought out the animal in the human being, a calming effect is occurring. Slowly, very slowly our soldiers are becoming decent again in their whole mannerism and behavior and the hateful expressions and rudeness are disappearing.

24, March 1946

We read that at home in the English zone the food rationing has been reduced by half roughly 1,000 calories per day. That is not enough! I hope it will be better in the "Pfalz".

26, March 1946

Am I getting sick? I have a headache and my joints ache. I have flu like symptoms and a horrible case of diarrhea. I take an aspirin and go to bed. I also have a temperature.

27, March 1946

I had a bad night, thought I would burn up with the fever. In the morning I am a little better but I stay in bed.

28, March 1946

I feel a little better today, but still I feel like I have been beaten up. Today and yesterday there were extensive medical checkups of all "C" and "CLD" people. Of 300 people only 45 were approved to see the French doctor.

Our poor Klemenz, in spite of all our efforts and reports by a French nose throat and ear specialist about his poor hearing, did not make it. I am so sorry! Tears were in his eyes when he told us. This means he might still sit here 2 or 3 more years. Again I am reminded to be so very thankful.

30, March 1946

This morning I am getting up again, but still don't feel quite right.

A year ago was Good Friday and Norbert's confirmation. I heard about it much later though. Details he can soon tell me in person.

I do not believe this was the flu, but maybe a slight sunstroke. I was in the strong March sun too long. The French know this and warn us. They say being in the sun can lead to tuberculosis. There are enough fanatics, who don't care and just want to get a tan.

Today I am with my big boy with all my thoughts.

31, March 1946

Nature turns more beautiful from day to day and spring is coming in force.

Yesterday we were able to take a shower again, and afterwards I felt much better. Please don't let me get sick now!

Poor Klemenz is desperately trying to get the "R". He is beginning to not eat at all, so he will be skinny enough to be put into sickbay.

Experiences of POWs outside the camp: We hear of insults and beatings. In a village some drunken civilians had a German prisoner kneel down, had him raise his hand and yell "Heil Hitler", then stabbed him to death.

Oh, my Germany, beloved homeland, land of sad misfortune. Land of so many contradictions, we love you even more in your wretched misery.

What I have learned being in prison camp: to become harder, more suspicious, more reserved, do not believe in rumors, do not believe in the good of people, nor the bad, and only act upon your good common sense.

What did March bring me? It brought me the "R". What more could I expect? What will April bring to me?

1, April 1946

Will April bring me my "Homecoming"? We have all become extremely cautious and mistrusting. Life does not seem to have a cheerful side again. We have all become branded and the faith in the good of people has seriously become shaken long ago. The multitudes suffering in a prison camp, which only can be comprehended by those, who have been prisoners themselves, have reformed and matured us. That is why neither joy, nor sorrow can particularly surprise us, because our senses have been dulled. Promises, which obviously are made to be broken, are not believed anymore. For disappointments of all kinds we are constantly prepared. That's why we believe in the fulfillment of our longing to be sent home only when we are outside of the barbed wire fence.

How wonderful, if I could be home Easter. Little Sigrid! Little "Mouse"!

The sun is shining warmly and the trees begin to bud and bloom.

2, April 1946

Today I received a dear letter from Rösel. She now has her hopes up. May it not be betrayed!

3, April 1946

Comrade Argus always thinks of us. He sent us a bottle of red wine. That is a rare treat. Everyone is feverishly excited. Will the last "R" people leave for Lyon, or somewhere else? When will we be going? I can wait!

6, April 1946

Today is the anniversary of my father's death. Also, it's a Sunday, as always with a soccer game. It has turned cold again, we have to build a fire, and soon we will have a cozy warm room.

Klemenz is very unhappy about missing out on his "R".

8, April 1946

Excerpts from Ernst Wiechert's book "The Major":

"….but he who comes back, does not come back from the war, but from hell and this hell is the creation of human beings. To torture an animal for 1 hour is vicious and cruel. But to torture a human being, thousands of human beings not for 1 hour, but for years, a whole life, yes even several lives is not only vicious and cruel, but heinous and devilish, so diabolical, that no God could understand this."

"He knows this sleep from the camps behind the barbed wire, a sleep filled with dreams of which one knows nothing, but that they are laying heavily on ones numb and dazed soul. And he knows the awakening from this sleep. Waking up blind and disturbed in the early morning with no memory but a horrible pain in the totally hollowed out chest. It's the waking up to an empty totally hopeless day to a chain of days, months, and years. The awakening of a damned without judgment."

9, April 1946

Today, Zinsmeister came after a pause of almost 4 months to the camp to see me. He brought me some schnapps and a couple of eggs. He had heard that I got the "R" and was not able to hide his disappointment and envy. He as well as Neu, have been very depressed. They have to work hard and don't think they will be able to go home for a long time. I help them as much as I can. I am able to get them some shoes and from F. a pair of pants. Then we talk about Sembach. I promise him to look up his family. When leaving he was choking back the tears.

10, April 1946

We are inoculated against typhus. Today we get the second injection. Those shots always hurt very badly.

The different types in the camp: the butt collectors, those who wet the beds, the food scroungers, the "rumor heinies", the ragged ones, that don't wash or shave anymore, or mend their uniforms, and have no socks anymore.

11, April 1946

We hear that the men working outside the camp are beaten, kicked, slapped, and insulted, even by children. These mistreatments on the outside are on the increase. A wave of hatred is directed towards the Germans. But the French people have to admit, that the German workers are invaluable, because of their quality work. With envy they are recognizing this and therefore they approach them with fury and anger.

It's a good thing they don't know at home, what the lot of a prisoner is in reality. An incident, where for trivial reasons, a German man was shot and killed by a guard. Was the guard punished? Oh, no!

13, April 1946

We had the small hope to be home on this day. Nothing!

Last night, a wonderful and successful evening for Dornbusch. That man is so very talented and is to be admired. With borrowed records, he introduced us to the "Matthäus Passion" by Johann Sebastian Bach. What a tremendous experience.

15, April 1946

I got to go to the city as the interpreter for Diltzter, accompanied by a Moroccan guard. A wonderful walk through the beautiful city. What an experience just to get out.

I see people, activities in the streets, stores, window displays; I feel like a kid on Christmas. I can buy and bargain, talk with people and am treated everywhere very well. I have always tried to be correct and therefore was treated decently. We go into a few drugstores; I buy newspapers and postcards, etc. Oh, it is just like old times, before we were behind barbed wire. Satisfied, we return to the camp.

In the evening we had a thunderstorm with a beautiful rainbow. Over against the mountains is the splendor of the spring blossoms.

How is it at home?

17, April 1946

There is the desperate struggle by everyone for the "R". Right now there is no expectation of anything happening. No one knows if and when there will be any action. On Saturday 600 new ones are supposed to come. There is no way we will leave before Easter.

18, April 1946

Today we get the 3rd injection for typhus. We are glad that this is over. We are hungry again, because no supplies are delivered from the city.

19, April 1946

Good Friday

In France, Good Friday is not celebrated; it is a day like any other. Beet soup as any other day, noon and at night.

I read the newspapers that we get once in a while from home.

20, April 1946

I wonder if they color Easter Eggs for the little "Mouse" today! The silent hope to be home for Easter was not fulfilled! Now they all believe, it will take a long time!

21, April 1946

Easter Sunday

We have beautiful Easter weather. There is a bouquet of lilacs on our table and its fragrance reminds me of our custom at home to walk with the whole family to the Altenbaumburg Castle on Easter Day, where all the many lilac bushes were in full bloom and their fragrance was absolutely intoxicating. We would sit outside under the sun umbrellas and enjoy coffee and cake. What happy memories.

I awoke feeling good and remembering a nice dream. I was home and saw all of them. We were in church all morning for both the Catholic and Evangelical services singing with the choir ("Sanctus" and "Benedictus").

Ours was a communion service, which I partake in. All through the service I am thinking how the little sweetheart might right now at this moment be Easter Egg hunting in the garden just like my "Murschel" used to do.

Oma, Opa, Norbert, and Helga (Murschel)
(Easter 1938)

Maybe they will go to the Altenbaumburg Castle this afternoon.

We had a fantastic dinner, but only because we were able to buy an ox on the black market using the surplus from the cafeteria account. We had noodles with a very fat goulash. We will probably all get sick because our stomach cannot tolerate the fat anymore. We even got a boiled egg.

In the afternoon at 3 pm, there was the soccer championship between barracks #10 and #11. There even was some betting going on. The players got a piece of bread with jam and a bottle of beer. The score was 2:0 for barrack #10.

At night we get some cheese and margarine. A truly festive meal and we are pleased.

About 5 pm, we had a tremendous thunder and lightning storm, with a lovely refreshing rain.

I wonder if they had a nice festival at home?

22, April 1946

Easter Monday

It is cloudy and the weather is getting worse. A Swiss Pastor conducted the Easter Service. He brings us greetings from the bishop and the Pastor Dr. Niemöller, who is well-known. Those greetings are nice enough, but do not help us.

I will finish reading my book and think of them at home. I am somewhat connected through the lilac fragrance, in church, in the theatre barracks and our room.

The food was really what made it extra special. Surely the French would not have bought the ox for us for 70,000 francs.

I am sure they were disappointed at home that I could not be home with them.

23, April 1946

What poor organization. Months ago 600 people were to arrive here. Saturday for sure they were supposed to come. Of course they did not come. It is the same with the transport of the "R" people. Who knows how long we still have to wait here?

They don't know how to celebrate a festive occasion, what do they know of Easter.

Klemenz keeps on by desperately eating nothing but "flour soup". We think he is ruining his health.

24, April 1946

I read in a paper about all the divorces in Germany. This subject is not even a question for us, my dearest. What other man is this fortunate to know such a treasure at home, as I do.

25, April 1946

There is a bunch of lilies of the valley on our table. Delightful!

This evening Dr. Karus came by with the comment: "You can get your farewell present ready for me. Next week things are moving." No one wants to believe it. Through the whole camp it is like a new deep breath of air; like the breeze of spring. The "R" people are on a high with happy faces. I would like to get home in time for mother's birthday.

We experience the needling because of the escape of one of our guys. Getting up earlier, confiscating the light bulbs, no water, threats of sharp shooting, no choir practice, curfew, etc. We don't care!

26, April 1946

There are wild rumors going around about the upcoming transport. Some people say next week, some pessimistic ones say June or July. Now all has to go well. I cannot get sick, nor anything else can happen.

30, April 1946

Thursday, May 12th, the train is supposed to leave. What Karus says is as a rule dependable.

The preparations are beginning.

1, May 1946

Now begins the calling out and all the tediousness of the technical preparations.

Yesterday, 600 new ones came from America. They have been shamefully deceived just the same. They were promised the release home to their families, but were "sold" to the French. The poor guys have angry, spiteful, and hopeless expressions. They know they will have to stay here for years.

Our joy is so immense, that we can hardly compose ourselves. We get envious looks everywhere. Oh, we can understand and we would like to help, but can't. There was a hateful outburst from a 52 year old. Hopefully the old ones can go home soon.

Now comes the farewell preparations. Everything is packed for a long time already. The choir brings us a farewell serenade in the cafeteria. At the last choir rehearsal, Gerhard Dornbusch had the nice idea that every one of the 6 returnees from the choir could request a favorite song. The choir sang it for each one. Pastor Bracht was present, too. There was a toast with water, but it tasted as good as champagne to us. There were speeches and in the afternoon the many good-byes began from the many comrades, who had become close to every individual. The indifferent ones, the strangers, the blatant and impertinent ones, the brats and rude ones, we leave out of consideration.

Once more I go to see Klemenz and wish him well. I hope he will make it soon. He was one of the best.

I have at least a dozen letters to bring back and visits to make.

2, May 1946

What A Day! Freedom!

Our successors, Sgt. Höhn and his interpreter, plus the pharmacist, Spahmer, have already moved into my room.

I cannot describe the feeling I had this morning, to wake up for the last time here in this room with the view out of the window to the barracks next door. Gratitude, nothing but overflowing joy and gratitude fills my heart.

I have to think again of the wonderful sermon of Pastor Bracht yesterday: "not forgetting to be thankful, not forgetting the prayer of supplication, not forgetting our divine task..."

This time there were tears in his eyes, he, who has had farewell sermons of this kind before, but still has to stay, to continue to serve his fellow prisoners. I had a good friendship with him and he honored me especially by letting me sign his memory book. I wrote the beginning of the 91st psalm: "He that dwelleth in the secret place of the most high shall abide under the shadow of the Almighty. I will say to the Lord: He is my refuge and my fortress, my God, in him will I trust."

And now we wait, until Sepp will blow his whistle for the last time and we hear his tremendous voice: "Repatriates of the American, British and French zone, line up on the camp road!"

One more look at our room, a hasty handshaking of the buddies, then we are called up individually according to occupation zone. The last one to say good-bye to me is Stilgenbauer.

Then we stand by the gate, are called up again, get our papers, each one of us a small loaf of bread, a clump of headcheese. The latter I give to someone right away, because the disgusting stuff starts melting right away and already stinks. Besides, I have for some time taken care of things and planned ahead. For some time I have saved some cheese, a can of sardines and the 5 eggs from Zinsmeister, which I have boiled and also traded some bread. I will survive the trip this way.

A Moroccan searches us and I am lucky. He does not take anything away from me. In front of us is Sepp, our transport guide. On all the faces there is a joy, which is difficult to repress.

We marched through the gate for the last time not in step.

It Is 9:30 AM, The Hour Of Freedom

We look back a few times see the sad faces and wave to the comrades. Oh, you poor guys! Then slowly we walk to the train station. The baggage gets heavy. I have on my belt my canteen and a bread sack, my carry bag, the leather briefcase and the cardboard box. The walk takes a ½ hour, and then we get into the four cattle cars for 180 of us. In my car there are 45 men, way too many.

At 10:30 am, the train leaves in the direction of Lyon. In the evening we stop on the tracks near Amberieu. We are to stay here through the night. We try to get comfortable, if that was possible and try to sleep, not very well, but happily.

3, May 1946

During the night we notice, that we are moving again and indeed in the morning we find ourselves at the station in Lyon.

Then we ride all day in the northern direction. Sometimes we pass prison camps with the French flag and working POWs. We quickly avert our eyes, because the emotions are too great. We ride all through the night. We are very uncomfortable, but no one complains. Each mile brings us closer to home.

What an incredible feeling. That was May 3rd.

4, May 1946

We arrive in Strassburg in the morning. Gone is the dream of this being a German city, maybe this time forever. Now we cross over the Rhine and on the other side the entire German misery grabs at our hearts. Oh, you poor German Homeland! Bleeding from a thousand wounds!

Something else is filling our hearts with incredible joy, the quiet happiness of all the people. Everywhere they wave at us, sometimes from their windows or doors, sometimes from the fields, where they work, but everywhere people greet us with sympathy and compassion. Many women have tears in their eyes.

Yes, This Is My Homeland Again!

In Hasslach we make a short stop. Here I can send my telegram with the negotiation of a friendly lady and a railroad employee. I know what to say: "I am coming! I'm on German soil already!" What happiness this telegram will bring them.

Now the train climbs through the beautiful Black Forest Mountains past Triberg, then back to flat country until we reach the French reparation camp near Tuttlingen, at 4 o'clock in the afternoon. A hateful Polish Sergeant inspected us in an open field.

Quickly we are separated according to occupational zones and have already lost one another. It is evening before it is our turn. In a big hall some comrades are feverishly working on the papers. Then we are searched one more time and they took my nice mess hall kit. In the dark, close to midnight, we climb up the embankment and find a cattle car with straw and enough room to stretch out.

Now we are really free! Date of the release on the "Liberation Provisoire", 4, May 1946.

I have to keep these papers; maybe I will need them one day. We continue on to Villingen. Here I am able to get a Red Cross Package with a few things I would like to take home for them. Among which there is some chocolate for the children. I almost lost my leather briefcase in the straw of the railroad car with important things, such as the letters of the comrades, the fairytale album for Helga, the music box for Sigrid, and the scarf for Norbert. I want to have something for the children.

A comrade found the briefcase. Now we are stopping for hours. In the morning we continue until Offenburg, there we change trains to Karlsruhe.

5, May 1946

From here we cannot get to Landau, because the Rhine Bridge is bombarded. So we continue on to Mannheim. From the train we can see the misery of our people, undernourished and depressed. From Mannheim we have to walk across the temporary bridge. On the other side there is a French Control of our papers and the first very bad impression: German girls in gaudy make up, arm in arm with strange soldiers. A people without dignity! They deserve their fate.

Ludwigshafen is badly destroyed and the railway station in a dreary state. We get a cup of coffee at a Red Cross Station. It is well-known not too many are remaining. In the pouring rain, the train goes as far as Neustadt, where I cannot get a connecting train. I get something to eat in a "gasthaus", wash and shave and walk tired and exhausted through the streets of the charming well-known city. People look at me, full of pity, some ask me, where I come from.

In the evening a friendly Neustadter invites me for no reason at all for a glass of wine. I can stay overnight with these nice people without charge. I can hardly wait until morning.

6, May 1946

The Homecoming

I take a train to Kaiserslautern in the morning. I try to telephone from there. Impossible! I take the noon train in a freight car down the Alsenz Valley. How calm I am. How can I be so composed? Is it suppressed anxiety or the assurance that everything is all right?

Before the last curve I have to look out of the right side of the train and see the first houses of my beloved little village of Hochstätten and the train station. Maybe, just maybe someone will meet me? There! In a split second I see my Helga standing by the gate. What do I care, that the whole train witnesses the reunion with my child? She flies into my arms and hangs around my neck and won't let me go. I cannot find any words, but then I look into her eyes and find, she is still my "Murschel". She has changed little and hasn't even grown much taller. I quickly ask about the others, Mama, Norbert, Sigrid, Oma, and Opa. They are all healthy, what more do I want? My heart is overwhelmed with gratitude. I have every reason to be thankful.

Now the two of us walk through the village slowly and without haste, but I want to tell Helga to go on ahead and tell them, that I did not come. I turn into the little lane. There it is the dear old house. How my heart fills with joy. I do not stand in front of the door very long. In the hallway my sweetheart takes one look at me and throws herself into my arms, young, beautiful and desirable as always, my pretty blossom of a woman. We embrace each other in silent bliss. We cannot talk and don't need to. We only look in one another's eyes and read our love for one another.

What is there to write about? Nothing that can be expressed in words. The emotions of this moment will be forever kept in our hearts. Then I greet the grandparents. Opa does not look well, has gotten very thin and old looking. Oma stayed the same. And then Norbert, my big boy, a strong good-looking boy. How favorably he has changed. Frank, open and carefree, he hugs me and I like that. What about my little baby? She is still sleeping. Rösel shows me the picture, which they had done for me. I look at the child for a long time and cannot even find a resemblance from last year. I am almost a little apprehensive to see her. This child most likely will have changed the most.

Now I walk through all the rooms, so precious to me. Everything is in its place. Thank God! Even though the house was fired upon, when the American tanks invaded Hochstätten and turned the corner by the church, with the house sitting there almost like a target. There were actually 47 bullet holes throughout the house and a large hole in the roof, which Opa had fixed. This happened on March 16, 1945. But other than that, they are alive and we have a roof over our heads.

There was actually quite a bit of fighting going on, because some German troops were still hiding in the hillsides. At that time, the family was in the shelter until it was all over and they were ordered to get out by the Americans. That's when my 10 year old Helga saw her first American, a tall, black soldier. The first black man she had ever seen. She told me how frightened she was because he pointed his machine gun at her and that she asked Oma, who was urging her on: "Isn't he going to shoot us?" However, he was quite "nice" and let Oma take the baby carriage, which he was standing directly next to it outside the bunker. A firebomb had hit Laubenstein's stable, who are our next door neighbors, and all their cattle were burnt. There are still many stories to be told in the days to come, but we are most thankful, that no one was hurt.

And then came the big moment, where I witnessed the waking of our little one. Rösel is asking her: "Is this Papa?" and the incredibly blue eyes look at me surprised and questioningly. What went on in your little head at that moment, you sweet thing? I pick her up and she does not object. Then I hear her little voice and am amazed at how fluent she speaks and chatters. Especially how she croons: "Papa, Papa!" how precious from her mouth to hear this word. Her hair has turned all curly and she walks like a little wound up toy doll. I am so very happy!

Now to just get rid of this hated uniform for all times! I want to be a human being again!

Epilogue

<u>Back At Home</u>

<u>12, August 1946</u>

I went by bike with my violin and books to Sembach. Mother is happy. Oh, my good, wonderful mother!

<u>13, thru 25, August 1946</u>

<u>Starting My Teaching At The School In Altenbamberg</u>

One evening Rösel, Norbert and Helga went with me by train to Sembach. Played the organ for the first time and Norbert still has no school yet.

<u>27, August 1946</u>

What a difficult Monday with the letter from Richard's comrade containing the details about his death. My mother's crying is heart breaking.

<u>4, September 1946</u>

I still teach school in Altenbamberg. I do not want to stay here. It's the beginning of the fall vacation.

The decision will have to happen within these few days. I would like to go to Sembach. The children do too. Rösel, sensible as always, is flexible and does not care.

<u>6, September 1946</u>

Slowly we plan for our move and begin with the packing. We plan to leave the baby with the grandparents for the time being. She is such a precious darling.

<u>7, September 1946</u>

Today is Gudrun's birthday. Was her father still alive then?

9, September 1946

My brother Richard is **dead**? No one knows for sure or the exact date.

21, September 1946

Richard died in Russia, in a coal mine in Siberia. And we did not know it.

You poor dear boy! What have you suffered?

29, September 1946

Following the fall vacation, I am back to teaching school in Altenbamberg. I have the upper grades. I go there by bike. The school itself is OK. The schoolroom, the library, the teaching aids and materials as well as the level of education leaves something to be desired. The people are not very friendly.

Should I request to be transferred there? The children seem to like me, but I have looked at the apartment and I do not think I want my family there, more than primitive.

On Sunday I went with Norbert to church and communion. Had I known, what happened a week ago, I would not have gone. In the afternoon the whole family went for a nice walk to the Fallbrückerwald Forest, then back again through Rotengraben.

Schäfer, the other teacher, puts little effort into his teaching!

6, October 1946

Sigrid wakes up from her afternoon nap with a fever. Her little head is suspiciously lively, a sure sign for me of a temperature. Is it diphtheria? She got the serum and does not act sick. But why do all of our children have to have all these horrible diseases?

We work hard moving into the apartment in Sembach. Much will not be as it used to be. Everything has been abused. Rösel and grandmother work very hard.

10, October 1946

I went to Freisbach last night and was welcomed very cordially. I stayed overnight with my aunt. Was able to bring back 100 kilos (200 pounds) of onions. Arrived late at night back in Hochstätten.

19, October 1946

The unfortunate clash with Norbert. I have hit the boy and have severely hurt his pride. I am so very sorry. I believe he quietly cries into his pillow. He won't eat and does not speak to me. Why did I do this? I am so unhappy! "Come home again soon, my dearest, and help me raise these children (this was a quote from Rösel's letter)".

He begins his middle school. I watch how he tries to do his homework and will not ask for my help. I offer to help him, but he refuses and struggles on alone. I would like to take his dear defiant head in my hands and kiss him.

24, October 1946

As of today Norbert speaks with me again. He has forgiven me and is glad, that our good relationship has been restored again.

26, October 1946

The constant struggle for food! There is no more rationing; there is just nothing to be had. We are lucky to be able to get about 400 lbs. of potatoes. We don't have to worry about milk either. We get some from the farmers every day.

In the morning Rösel and Norbert went to collect "Bucheln" (beechnuts) for oil. There is a struggle for oil.

6, November 1946

Norbert's Birthday

Our big boy learns a lot in school and there is a lot expected of them. Today I gave him a book from the library, "Atom Weight 500". He has wanted to read it for a long time.

Aunt Helene donates a rabbit. That is a more than festive dinner. Such poor terrible times, when you do not get enough to eat. Most people survive on what they grow in the garden or eat sugar beets. Sugar beets cooked into a syrup as a spread for bread, sugar beets with potatoes for lunch, sugar beets with carrots for supper. I feel sorry for the women, not knowing what to put on the table for their families. We are just happy and thankful, that we are able to get milk from a different farmer each night. That was not possible in Hochstätten.

9, November 1946

Today I make the trip to the relatives in Einselthum, which I had planned for some time. Disappointingly, the train only runs as far as Marnheim. It is freezing cold and there are no window panes in the train. No one can give any information either. I borrow a bicycle and peddle the rest of the way, about 20 miles. I am able to get about 30 pounds of poppy seeds for oil and eat some bread with homemade sausage.

I travel back sweating from dragging the heavy sack in the freezing cold train. Only if we had had some oil.

10, November 1946

A cozy beautiful Sunday. We have a fire lit in the stove. Rösel has baked a modest cake and we are happy together.

13. November 1946

Helga worries us. She is precocious, impertinent, slow to do her work, tends to talk back. Other than that she is a sweet child.

14, November 1946

The library can be reopened again. More than half of the books have to be burned. Anything that is in any way patriotic, our "Lords" will not tolerate.

Starting at 5 pm, my time belongs to Norbert. I need to help him with his French.

23, November 1946

There are a lot of repairs to be done in the schoolhouse. Locks, bookshelves, water pipes, stoves, everything is damaged and in a state of disrepair. One cannot get anyone to come and work. The windows are a struggle. We would like to have the storm windows put up again, but there is no wood or glass. The carpenter cannot repair them.

We do not dare to build a fire in the living room, because we have to save fuel. Norbert fixed up his little room in the attic nicely. There we sit together and study. He has built a practical electrical bell all by himself. I am proud of him.

5, December 1946

Helga is sweet and a good pupil. A smart child, but lazy and does not want to help her mother with the housekeeping. Has to be asked three times for everything, keeps reading books all day long, but she is clever and talented for working, especially for crafts.

6, December 1946

Helga worries us. She is thirsty all the time but does not eat, except sweets. She is skinny and weak, reads books all day, is very talented, especially musically, but does not mature physically.

13, December 1946

We are looking forward to the reunion with our little sweetheart. We want to spend the vacation in Hochstätten. I have to be glad that I have two suits to wear for school. There is nothing to be had any more.

14, December 1946

It is very cold and the schoolroom just does not get warm. It is not clean either, because there are no cleaning agents. Norbert has "winter vacation" because there is no fuel to heat the schoolrooms.

He is busy chopping wood, collecting dry brush in the forests and studies his French lessons.

16, December 1946

Official Notification

Never can I forget this day. Richard dead! Oh, my poor mother!

How can we comprehend this unspeakable injustice! Oh, you poor, dear boy. You were so young and healthy, so strong, so handsome, how could this have happened? This horrible awakening! Why can it not be just a very bad nightmare?

How can I believe, that this poor human being, my one and only brother will never come home again? I know this event will leave a deep, painful scar on my soul, which will never heal again.

His wife Helene is more composed than mother, who just wants to die. When I see his poor child, who now has to grow up without a father, it breaks my heart. I am having a hard time teaching school, everything has become so senseless.

We have very cold and frosty nights. Mother cries out: "Richard does not have to freeze anymore!"

20, December 1946

Now we are to make preparations for Christmas. We have to think of our children, who have a right to live. Why did this tragic news have to reach us just before Christmas? There will be no joy!

The cold weather is increasing. We will probably have a white Christmas, just as the children had wished for. Norbert is ice skating every day. We watch him and he is very good at it. Helga is sledding down the hill with her friends.

21, December 1946

We bake cookies to take to Hochstätten with us. We collect milk, save our meat and begin to pack. How happy the little "Mouse" will be to see us. It is planned that mother goes to visit her sister and family and then come to see us over the holidays.

24, December 1946

In the evening there is a Christmas pageant, performed by the school kids with their teacher. Nothing interests me, but I stare hatefully at Karl Schäfer, who safely came back from Russian prison camp.

The preparations take place, as always, but there is no joy in it not for Rösel or myself. I know how much my poor mother will be crying tonight.

At 7 pm after supper we have our Christmas celebration and modest gift sharing. The little one is very happy.

25, December 1946

Traditionally, I go to church. I sit there dull and full of rage and feel nothing else. The children are happy and enjoy the Christmas tree. A little better dinner makes us realize that there is a holiday. We had saved our meat ration and even have some cookies. We go for a walk and read and play games. The little "Mouse" is able to sing most Christmas songs without mistakes. Only carrying a tune is pretty gruesome, so that I say, the child is totally unmusical. But she wants to sing all day long and wants me to play the piano.

The gifts are less than modest. There is nothing for the grownups. For Norbert there are old games and some of my old books. Helga gets an apron, a monogram, and more books. Sigrid receives a wooden train and a windmill.

29, December 1946

We had expected my mother today, but she could not come, because there were no trains (lack of coal).

She comes the next day and I meet her at the train in the darkness. Trembling with the cold and her sorrow she cuddles into my arm and allows us to fuss over her and spoil her. She has some news of Richard from someone who came home and is from Imsbach.

31, December 1946

The last day of the old year! It brought me the homecoming, but death for Richard.

In the evening we play games and have some hot, spiced wine. At midnight, mother's crying is heartbreaking.

1, January 1947

New Year's Day

I continue to be dull and depressed. When I look at mother, it tears me apart. She cries on and off all through the day.

When I hear the zither, I want to burst out crying!

2, January 1947

I went to Bad Kreuznach by foot in snow and ice in order to have Norbert's skates sharpened. It looks like the bombed bridge in Ebernburg will never get repaired. I am able to get a bowl of soup in a restaurant. But everywhere there is hopelessness, poverty, misery, and despondency.

Mother is knitting all day long for the children and for us. Her busy hands never rest. She helps with the housework as well. How very much I would like to ease her burden, but I am not able to cheer her up. She cries day and night: "My life has no sense or value, I just want to die!"

Oh, I can understand you! How can a loving heart of a mother be so cruelly crushed?

5, January 1947

Mother goes back home with the 8:30 am train. I walk her to the station and will never forget the way she looked at me saying good-bye.

6, January 1947

Sigrid's Birthday

She is 3 years old today. No gifts, but a lot of love and a little cake, that's all. For dinner, waffles and applesauce. The child has made tremendous progress. She laughs all day long and plays quietly by herself.

I help Norbert with his French and shorthand. Helga reads a lot. Unfortunately the two fight a lot.

11, January 1947

I went to Alsenz to try and get some meat. There are long lines everywhere. Often, by the time you get there, nothing is left. We have to be very frugal with our burning material and lights. It is a catastrophe.

13, January 1947

The beginning of school! I am back teaching in Sembach. Impassive and without joy I start my teaching. Mother cooks for me. This will help getting her mind off things a little. I wanted to rehearse a play with the children for spring, but I just don't feel like it.

15, January 1947

After a few mild days, winter sets in again, with full force and terrible cold. We have unending problems with the water pipes freezing and bursting. During our vacation our cellar was flooded due to burst pipes.

I went by bike to Rockenhausen to pick up the "ZSK" decision. It reads:" Employment granted, advancement is frozen for 4 years.

20, January 1947

I start playing the organ in church again. The pastor preaches before empty pews.

We have no chalk, no blackboards, no paper, and no ink. The people become poorer all the time. Norbert still has school vacation because of the cold.

The mood is one of despair. The French requisition everything: Food, supplies, furniture, etc. We had to give up our beautiful living room curtains as well.

27, January 1947

Our village has invited 200 children, those who had been bombed out, from the city for the second time for a meal. The people are so grateful.

Often it is 10 o'clock in the morning before the schoolroom is warm enough and the frost has disappeared on the windowpanes. The children are freezing and don't want to study. At recess I have to leave them upstairs.

30, January 1947

I feel so sorry for my mother who just cannot get over her sorrow, pain, and mourning for Richard. At night she seeks a little diversion in our house and knits continuously.

1, February 1947

Yesterday my father would have been 70 years old. What a blessing, that he did not live to see this tragedy!

Either the trains don't run at all or they are 3 to 4 hours late.

2, February 1947

Memorial Service For My Brother

I play the organ for him and no one can take that away from me.

3, February 1947

There is an outbreak of measles in town and school is closed because of it. I build a fire in Norbert's room and try to get caught up with correspondence, filing, and curriculum.

5, February 1947

To witness mother's pain is heartbreaking. She does not want to live anymore, cries and sighs continuously, but happy, that she can find love and understanding in our home. Tonight it poured out of her: "He, who has beaten my son, his hand should fall off!"

7, February 1947

I take the bus to Kaiserslautern, to do some errands. The city gives a dreary and hopeless impression. Bombed out ruins, poverty, hunger, despair, cold, and a mortally wounded people! But the guilty ones still are not punished.

The extreme cold continues. What a horrible winter!

9, February 1947

Finally we built a fire in the living room. We enjoyed the coziness of it. In the evening Richard's wife Helene came and stayed until midnight. She too is wounded deeply in her soul. "He was so good!"

11, February 1947

Helga gives us cause to worry: She does not eat. No threats, spankings, or pleading helps. No vegetables, no soups, no meat, only noodles and sweets. In addition she is ill mannered, is talking back, is stubborn and unruly. At the same time she is musically talented as well as in art and reads a lot.

She is high spirited and basically a sweet child.

13, February 1947

Grandmother takes care of us. Her mother's love has no limits.

There are no light bulbs and we struggle every day for food and heating material. We will not forget this bitter winter with ice and snow and with temperatures of minus 10 degrees Celsius.

17, February 1947

Rösel did not arrive yesterday as planned, but she arrived this morning. Norbert picked her up at 8 am.

I went to the woods near Baalborn to order some wood. I stomped around in the snow and an icy northern wind with freezing cold feet.

I went back in the afternoon with Norbert to stack up the wood and later had Fritz Hack bring it home with his horse and wagon.

20, February 1947

Today I spend the day with Norbert cutting the wood and stacking it. Surely the French will not allow us any coal. What will it be like next year with wood?

22, February 1947

Helene and Gudrun still have the measles. I cannot separate myself from the grief about Richard. In the evening Pastor Degen stops by.

I work on the index tables for the Public Library and I have announced that school will begin on Thursday.

Helene suffers emotionally more than we realize. That's why she is so sick.

10, March 1947

It is Richard's Birthday!

15, March 1947

Sunday Service

Mother went to church for the first time.

16, March 1947

Rösel went to Hochstätten with Helga for 2 days. Tomorrow they will come back. They will bring 4 chickens, which were hidden in a sack in the attic, when the French Control came.

17, March 1947

This was the result of Helga's checkup at the pediatrician's Dr. Gralka: No cause for concern, however, she is underdeveloped and only weighs 53 pounds at 12 years of age.

18, March 1947

Mother brought the first lilies of the valley from our garden to place in front of Richard's picture on my desk. How her heart must be bleeding! She harbors the strange hope, that he may still be alive. Oh, if only that was true!

On my desk I have his pictures surrounded by flowers. How very handsome he is on his wedding portrait.

23, March 1947

We have a rainy spring and not much sunshine, just as we feel in our hearts. Norbert is turning out to be very social and plays music with his friends in his room.

Sigrid wrote in one of Oma's letters: "Dear Mama; I hope you will bake goodies for me. Thank you for everything. Tonight, Oma made meatballs, which were very good. As long as it is cold like this I will not come to Sembach. We have a nice warm room. I am well and healthy. If the weather is nice, I will go sledding.

Greetings and kisses;

Your little Sigrid."

Memories of Richard

"Beginner!" something he picked up in Karl Seebode's classroom. He had often recurring expressions of past experiences: "conceivably good or bad". His characteristic quality as a young cavalier. His trip to Switzerland. The theft of his motorcycle. His comment when he saw the motorcycle in the store, which he wanted: "I would have no objection to it!" It was his pure joy.

His expression: "With God's luck," when he drove the milk delivery wagon to the city.

9, April 1947

On father's 4th anniversary of his death we received the news from a comrade, that Richard died one night peacefully in his arms.

Gudrun, his only child, was here with us during the afternoon. She was quiet and shy, as if she was dejected for her whole life. I feel the incredible loneliness of the poor child.

If only you knew, my dear, poor guy, how much we honor your memory, how much I love your child and how I think of you day and night.

<u>End of Epilog.</u>

Papa's last diary entries were written on April 9, 1947.

CPSIA information can be obtained at www.ICGtesting.com
Printed in the USA
BVOW05*0205080615

403623BV00001B/10/P